WELLINGTON
INVADES FRANCE

Greenhill Books

IN MEMORIAM
MARGARET HEWSON
1947–2002

WELLINGTON
INVADES FRANCE
The Final Phase of the Peninsular War, 1813–1814

Ian C. Robertson

GREENHILL BOOKS • LONDON
STACKPOLE BOOKS • PENNSYLVANIA

Greenhill Books

Wellington Invades France

Published 2003 by Greenhill Books, Lionel Leventhal Limited, Park House,
1 Russell Gardens, London NW11 9NN
and
Stackpole Books, 5067 Ritter Road, Mechanicsburg, PA 17055, USA

British Library Cataloguing in Publication Data:
Robertson, Ian C., 1928–
Wellington invades France:
The Final Phase of the Peninsular War, 1813–1814

1. Wellington, Arthur Wellesley, Duke of, 1769–1852 – Military leadership
2. Peninsular War, 1807–1814 – Campaigns – France
3. France – History, Military – 19th century
4. Great Britain – History, Military, 19th century
I. Title
940.2'74

ISBN 1-85367-534-2

Library of Congress Cataloging-in-Publication Data available

Edited, designed and typeset by Roger Chesneau
Printed and bound in Great Britain

CONTENTS

ILLUSTRATIONS

31. Commissariat mules descending towards the Bidasoa.
32. The Guards wading into France, 7 October 1813.
33. The monument on Cadoux's bridge, Bera.
34. La Rhune—a view from the summit towards the ridge of La Petite Rhune.
35. Pack-mules being unloaded at Irun.
36. Urrugne—a former French hutted encampment, looking west.
37. The quay and House of the Infanta at St-Jean-de-Luz.
38. The Château de Larraldia, St-Pierre, as it is today.
39. Wellington's residence—2 rue Mazarin, St-Jean-de-Luz.
40. The bridge of boats over the Adour.
41. Bayonne, seen from the wooded sandhills to the west.
42. A mid-nineteenth-century view of the Capitole at Toulouse.
43. The citadel at Bayonne, seen from the south.
44. The Coldstream Guards' cemetery, Bayonne.
45. French wounded leaving Spain.

MAPS

PREFACE

It had long been my intention to have a closer look at the concluding phase of the Peninsular War, between the battles of Vitoria (21 June 1813) and Toulouse (10 April 1814), terminating the long-drawn-out contest. Too often, the several actions fought during that period in the region of the Pyrenean frontier—among them Sorauren, Nivelle, Nive and Orthez, and the siege of San Sebastián—are assumed to have been of less importance than the more obviously spectacular encounters during the war, notably (apart from Vitoria itself) Salamanca, not to mention those of Corunna, Talavera, and La Albuera, whose names may be more familiar. One book published on the war in recent decades—compiled, admittedly, around the subtitle 'His Peninsular Dispatches'—comes to an abrupt end on reaching the French border, as though whatever happened later was of scant consequence, which was very far from being the case. In the first volume of her popular biography of Wellington, *The Years of the Sword*, Elizabeth Longford dedicated barely thirty page to these critical months, although it is of interest to note that when Sir William Napier wrote *English Battles and Sieges in the Peninsula*, the condensed version of his great history of the war, two-fifths of it was devoted to the post-Vitoria period.

Sir Charles Oman covered these final ten months in the latter part of volume 6 and in volume 7 of his *History of the Peninsular War*, first published in 1922 and 1930 respectively, and reprinted by Greenhill Books in 1996 and 1997. In the Preface to the first of these post-First World War volumes, Oman admits to having never tramped over Soult's route from Roncesvalles to the gates of Pamplona, or from Sorauren to Etxalar, and regretted that as far as the greater part of the ten days' Campaign of the Pyrenees was concerned, he had been dependent for topography on the observations of others. He stated also that his understanding of the topography of Maya and Roncesvalles owed much to the sketch maps in General Beatson's *With Wellington in the Pyrenees* (1914). However, for his final volume, Oman was able to visit and survey the complicated battlefields between the Bidasoa and the Adour, and the wide area extending east to Toulouse. Meanwhile, Beatson's study describing Wellington's crossing of the Gaves and the Battle of Orthez had appeared in 1925, while that dealing with the passage of the Bidasoa and the Battle of the Nivelle followed in 1931, after the seventh volume of Oman's magisterial *History* had been published.

Although in recent decades several reprints have been issued, among the more important being Frazer's *Letters during the Peninsular and Waterloo Campaigns*, together with contemporary narratives describing the latter part of the war – notably *The Wheatley Diary, An Ensign in the Peninsular War* (the letters of John Aitchison), *A Gentleman Volunteer: The Letters of George Hennell* and *The Napoleonic War Journal of Captain Thomas Henry Browne* – there has been no general study concentrating on the strongly contested engagements taking place during those critical last months. In the present work, while I have endeavoured to maintain continuity, the flow of the narrative is inevitably erratic, but I have tried to provide a balanced history of the many major actions taking place in that 'seat of war', describing them intelligibly while at the same time referring only briefly to the political developments which affected Wellington's strategic decisions. The complexities of these developments have been admirably explained in Rory Muir's *Britain and the Defeat of Napoleon*.

The complement of maps and plans, together with a number of both contemporary illustrations and recent photographs, will, I trust, provide the reader with a good idea of the contours and landscape of the battlefields covered. I have chosen not to include any plates of Pyrenean heights obscured by those low clouds which enveloped and so disconcerted Sir Lowry Cole (and which I have experienced also), of flooded valleys under drenching rain, or of snowbound passes. No entirely misleading imaginary scenes, too frequently embellishing what are professed to be historical studies, are reproduced.

My interest in the Peninsular War was motivated by my marriage to a Basque, whose parents now lie in the cemetery of Sare, a village through which part the Battle of the Nivelle was fought. Forty years ago, there was little of any consequence in print concerning Britain's struggle against the forces of Napoleonic France which had taken place in Spain and Portugal, and I was in a position to both commission and edit Jac Weller's *Wellington in the Peninsula*, first published in 1962, which, together with his *Wellington at Waterloo* and *Wellington in India*, has been reprinted by Greenhill Books. Since writing *Wellington at War in the Peninsula* – a very general 'overview' and guide – I have contributed introductions to reprints of both Gleig's *The Subaltern* and Larpent's *Journal*.

In the following pages, among many other of his contemporaries at the seat of war, Larpent has been quoted frequently. His record is of additional interest and value because it was written by a civilian at Headquarters together with the most intelligent and best-informed staff officers, and in regular direct contact with Wellington himself. Yet it is bracingly free of any military rhetoric, for what he wrote were private letters, without future publication in view, and his pages abound with incidents which public history passes as beneath her notice. Such first-hand narratives and notes jotted down shortly after the events they describe, even if their authors are not in full possession of all the facts, can provide valuable—albeit perhaps subjective—evidence of an encounter taking place, although their authors were not always able to appreciate the importance or otherwise of such actions in the context of a battle or the campaign as a whole.

As Rory Muir has reiterated in his masterly study *Salamanca 1812*, even when concentrating on a single major engagement it is rarely possible to be sure of the exact position of every unit at every moment during its progress, many of them being conjectural, or even of the precise time at which a specific action occurred: there will almost always be incon-

sistencies and imponderables. It should be emphasised also that, in attempting to describe the flow of military events over a longer period, some minor episodes cannot receive
such detailed coverage as others: nevertheless, I hope this survey of the critical final
campaigns of the Peninsular War has made them more comprehensible.

Fighting battles is only part of a much wider scene: the struggle against the elements in the winter months was such that few encounters took place during that period, as
Antony Brett-James was well aware when he compiled his fascinating *Life in Wellington's
Army*, covering several subjects I have hardly touched on (among them the deplorable
conditions under which the medical department operated*). Other subjects that deserve
more detailed study include the complex problems of logistics and communication with
which Wellington was faced, the transportation and custody of prisoners and the control
of muleteers and camp-followers; but to deal adequately with these matters would greatly
overextend the length of this book.

Although avoiding actual blizzards, but not fog, in the Western Pyrenees, I have
long experience of the extremes and vagaries of the climate of the Peninsula, and a good
idea of the very severe physical conditions that the contesting armies had to endure—and
which should never be underestimated. By the summer of 1813 a high proportion of
Wellington's officers and men, whether British, members of the King's German Legion or
the troops of their Portuguese allies, had been exposed to several years of marching and
fighting under a blistering sun, or in driving rain and freezing winds, when not in snug
winter cantonments. The imagination must be well stretched in this enervated twenty-
first century to appreciate properly the stamina and fortitude required to survive the
strenuous course of a campaign: one had to be very tough, both physically and morally.

It may be helpful to add here a practical note on cartography, for those requiring
more detail than can be reproduced on the maps provided. At the time, only the grossly
inadequate provincial maps of Spain by Tomás Lopéz, Cassini's maps of France and those
of the État-Major were available and to hand. Few of them gave little more than a very
rough representation of the terrain, as with Arrowsmith's map of 1809, based on Roussel
and La Blottière's of the Pyrenees (1730), with additions from López and Topino de San
Miguel's work (unfortunately, the latter's chart of the coast stopped at the French frontier, and failed to cover either St-Jean-de-Luz or Bayonne). Even Cassini's extensive
series of maps, many updated between 1798 and 1812, could not be relied upon; nor could
that of the Peninsula by Jasper Nantiat, published by Faden on 1 January 1810 (it 'de-
serves to be burned by the pubic hangman', in the opinion of General Graham). Although
Sir George Murray, Wellington's very competent QMG, had accumulated much first-
hand topographical information and had maps drawn at a scale of four miles to the inch
for most of central and north-eastern Portugal before the start of the Vitoria campaign, he
could not, of course, send his specialist staff to compile topographical information much

---

* Unfortunately, a copy of Dr Martin Howard's *Wellington's Doctors: The British Army Medical Services in the Napoleonic Wars* reached me just
too late for me to take advantage of the impressive amount of significant information it contains—information not easy to
find elsewhere.

further afield. (Among them, Captain Thomas Mitchell later returned to the Peninsula and was responsible for compiling what became known as *Wyld's Atlas* of the Peninsular War battlefields, published by James Wyld in 1841.)

As far as the areas of fighting described in this book are concerned, good general coverage—for the motorist—is provided by Michelin maps 442 (Northern Spain) at 1:400,000; 234, and 235 (Aquitaine, and Midi-Pyrénées) at 1:200,000; or, alternatively, the IGN.(Institut Géographique National) R02 (Aquitaine) at 1:280,000. For more detail, IGN produce 113 (Pyrénées Occidental) at 1:250,000; and, at 1:100,000, nos 69 (Pau/Bayonne), 62 (Bayonne/Mont-de-Marsan), 63 (Tarbes/Auch) and 64 (Toulouse/Albi).

I have found several of the IGN *Série Bleue* at 1:25,000 particularly helpful, notably 1245 OT (Hendaye/St Jean-de-Luz), 1344 OT (Bayonne/Biarritz), 1345 OT (Cambo), 1346 OT (St Jean-Pied-de-Port), 1445 O (St Palais), 1444 E (Orthez), 1643 O (Aire), 1745 O (Tarbes) and 2143 O (Toulouse). IGN issue a *Carte de randonnées* for the Pays Basque Ouest at 1:50,000; and also a town plan of the Bayonne/Biarritz area, but unfortunately the latter does not indicate contours.

The Spanish Instituto Geográfico Nacional publish topographical maps at 1:50,000 (nos 41,65,66,90, and 115) and also at 1:25,000, which, when in San Sebastián, may by acquired conveniently from their office at Plaza Lasala 2, 5°. In 1995 the Servicio Geográfico del Exército published a map at 1:250,000 in their series 5L, entitled 'Pamplona', which covers much of the area, as do their earlier maps at 1:100,000, series C, nos 12–2/3 (San Sebastián), 13–2/3 (Irun), and 13–4 (Pamplona). Editorial Alpina produce ramblers' maps—Bidasoa/Belate and Alduides/Baztan.

Numerous improvements in communications have been made in recent decades, which must be taken into consideration when attempting to follow by car certain routes taken by Wellington's or Soult's troops. Among them is the modern highway (N 121A) between Pamplona and Irun, which tunnels below the Puerto de Velate, and then turns down the narrow and tortuous Bidasoa valley, where (at the time of writing) widening and tunnelling is still taking place north of Sumbilla, cutting through several acute meanders, and bypassing Bera. In France, while both the A 63 and A 64 *autoroutes* may provide a very smooth ride, only by turning off on to minor roads will one get some slight idea of the difficulties of traversing the convoluted foothills of the western Pyrenees, where, apart from the few paved *chaussées*, the countryside was threaded by muddy tracks only, often virtually impassable in wet weather.

Most topographical names are spelt in the form printed on the most recent IGN maps, both Spanish and French—Bera, rather than Vera, for example—except when placenames occur in quotations. Some inconsistencies may still be found, although I have tried to standardise them. As Oman wrote seventy years ago, 'Certain names of Basque villages are never written with the same letters by any two persons who have occasion to mention them', and they have proliferated in recent decades, with many reverting to what are claimed to be earlier placenames. San Sebastián, Pamplona, and Vitoria are referred to thus throughout, not as Donostia, Iruñea and Gasteiz. In some cases, variant forms are included in the index.

I trust I will not be castigated for not substantiating every statement or quotation by a footnote. All errors of fact, among other infelicities and misinterpretations the volume will inevitably retain, are my own. It would be much appreciated if any such lapses were brought to my attention.

I must gratefully acknowledge the encouragement received from a number of friends, notably Andrew Hewson, Rory Muir and Arthur Boyars. Among others who, in a variety of ways, have provided advice, information, and assistance, practical or otherwise, or given permission to reproduce material, have been Monique Beaufils at Biarritz, Gilbert Casagrande at Toulouse, Paddy Griffith, Francesco Grubas, Felipe Guruchaga at San Sebastián, Eileen Hathaway, Andoni Esparza Leibar at Lesaka, Nathalie Marthe-Bismuth, Glenn Mitchell, Mark Nichols, John Tomes, Andrew Uffindell and Jamie Wilson; and the Scottish National Portrait Gallery, Edinburgh.

Most of the illustrations have been accumulated over many years, and although the sources are indicated after their captions in several instances, I have not been able to establish these in every case. While every effort has been made to obtain permission to use what may be copyright material, the author and publisher apologise for any errors or omissions, and would be grateful to be notified of any corrections that should be incorporated in future editions.

My wife has continued to tolerate my incursions into the past with exemplary patience, perhaps the more so as so much of the fighting described took place among her native hills, through which and elsewhere she has indefatigably driven me once again.

Ian C. Robertson

The Area between Vitoria, Pamplona and Bayonne, reproduced to indicate contours.

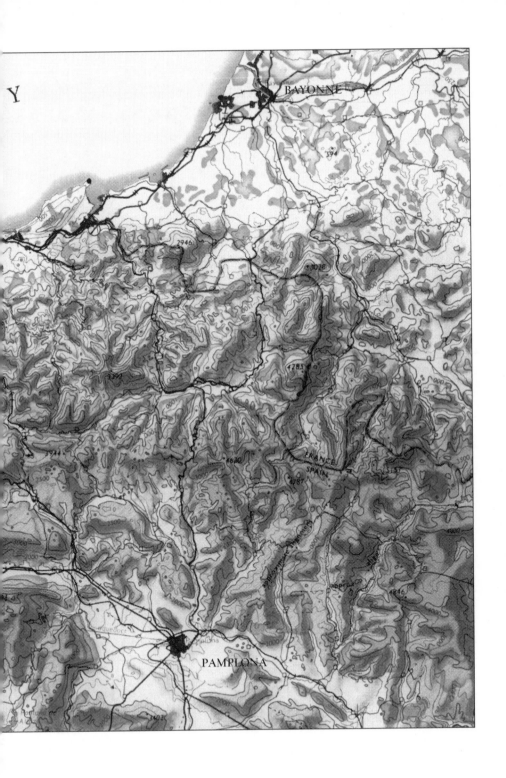

1

FROM MONDEGO BAY TO VITORIA

THIS preliminary chapter attempts to summarise the main actions of the Peninsular War in which the Allied armies under Wellington's command took part, and is intended to put into context, for those readers less familiar with them, the events leading up to the crucial last ten months of that struggle—which this volume sets out to amplify.

It is not generally known or appreciated that virtually all the fighting on land between the British and French during the Napoleonic era took place in the Iberian peninsula. Spain had found herself committed to France, whose Revolutionary armies were already masters of much of mainland Europe. Any French pretensions to controlling the seas were dashed by Nelson's victory at Trafalgar in October 1805, when the Spanish fleet was also largely destroyed.

After the peace treaty with Russia, signed at Tilsit in June 1807, Napoleon felt able to turn his attention to Portugal, Britain's remaining continental ally other than Sweden, and force her to sever that connection. On 19 July the Portuguese minister in Paris was informed that Portugal must closed its ports to British shipping and seize all British goods in the country or they would risk Napoleon's ire. The threat was followed up on 12 August by French and Spanish ambassadors in Lisbon, insisting that if Portugal failed to submit to such demands and actively ally itself with France, this was likely to precipitate hostilities (although war was not declared specifically). The British government learnt of Napoleon's threat in late August, and immediately agreed to send military aid to her 'oldest ally' as soon as possible. However, this would take time: eleven months passed before the main expeditionary force disembarked in Portugal, where there might be a better chance of establishing a firm foothold on mainland Europe than anywhere else. General Brent Spencer, with some 5,000 men, had embarked in mid-January, 1808, but, reckoning Lisbon to be too strongly held by Junot to attack, he had sailed on to Gibraltar, where he had been overtaken by events in Spain.

Units assembling at Bayonne in late July were reinforced during the ensuing weeks, and on 18 October troops under General Junot marched into Spain, ascended through the western foothills of the Pyrenean range, moved south-west across the high-lying Castilian *meseta* and gratuitously proceeded to invade Portugal. Virtually unopposed, their vanguard limped into Lisbon on 30 November. The Portuguese royal family, court and ad-

17

ministrative hierarchy had embarked aboard a scratch fleet and sailed to Brazil just in time to avoid capture, leaving the country at Junot's mercy.

Naïvely, Spain, when allowing his troops to traverse the highway to Portugal, was unaware that Napoleon had designs on itself. With the door to the Peninsula wide open, additional French units entered, those commanded by Marshal Murat occupying Madrid on 23 March 1808. The Spanish royal family were decoyed to Bayonne and taken prisoner, and remained in captivity for the duration of the war then imminent, for on 2 May ('El Dos de Mayo') the population of the capital rose in a briefly energetic revolt, ruthlessly suppressed by Murat. Within weeks the whole country was up in arms, but their ill-equipped, badly-organised and worse-led armies suffered severely whenever they did put up a fight, as at Medina de Rioseco, Tudela, and Ocaña. Fortuitously, they were successful at Bailén (north-east of Córdoba) on 22 July, when an entire French corps of 20,000 men commanded by General Dupont capitulated to General Castaños's Spaniards. It should be emphasised that, although Napoleon chose to refer to the French troops as 'picked men', the majority of those engaged in the battle were un-drilled conscripts, municipal guards and Swiss mercenaries in the Spanish service compelled to transfer their allegiance: only one battalion consisted of veterans. After Bailén, the French concentrated north of the River Ebro.

The presence of Spanish 'armies', other than that of Castaños's, pinned down large numbers of French troops, which continued to pour into the Peninsula, but they were soon to find that their lengthening lines of communication with France were continually harried by resourceful guerrilla bands: strong escorts were essential if supplies or messengers were to get through. There is little doubt that the constant war of attrition practised by these partisans bled the French white, and their importance in contributing to the eventually successful outcome of the war should not be underestimated, although their merciless depredations made them as unwelcome to the population under duress as the French, whose protection some sought as being the lesser of two evils. Lord Londonderry, when referring to these guerrillas in his *Narrative*, came close to the truth in remarking that 'all who have served in the Peninsula can attest that a less efficient and more mischievous body of marauders never infested any country'.

Meanwhile, in June, Spanish patriots had sought British armed intervention on their behalf. This was an additional invitation, supported by assurances that Spanish armies and supplies would be available with which to prosecute the war, promising to make the Peninsula as a whole the base of an attack on Napoleonic Europe. Portugal had already been promised aid, and the Tagus estuary would provide a secure harbour, but as Lisbon and its vicinity were strongly garrisoned by the enemy, it would be sensible to land the British expeditionary force further up the coast.

On 1 August 1808, this small army of 14,000 men, commanded by a 39-year-old lieutenant-general, Sir Arthur Wellesley, disembarked from its transports at Mondego Bay, near Figueira da Foz, on the Portuguese coast west of Coimbra. But this was only the advance guard: reinforcements were *en route*, including Moore's troops, expected back from Sweden. Wellesley—not until after the Battle of Talavera known as Wellington*— led his troops south past Obidos, and at Roliça forced the French to retire behind a ridge of hills to evade the pincer movement which was intended to, but did not, encircle them. In the more critical battle fought at Vimeiro three days later, on 21 August, when Junot's columns, marching north from Lisbon, precipitately attacked Wellington's lines, the French suffered a serious reverse, and capitulated.

Under the terms of the subsequent Convention of Cintra, their troops were repatriated in British ships rather than taken prisoner. Although much criticised in England, the Convention did enable Portuguese territory to be cleared of the enemy for several months without further bloodshed. Wellington was called back to London to face an enquiry into the more disgraceful terms of the Convention, for which he was not responsible, and was entirely exonerated.

During this period, the command of the expeditionary force devolved on Sir John Moore, who had landed belatedly with reinforcements. Later, he led the army into Spain, on which the French were tightening their grip, having been assured that Spanish armies would be fully cooperating with him, only to be let down by the duplicity and time-serving propensities of Spanish generals and *juntas*, repeatedly displaying their incapac-ity to provide either the units or the supplies promised. Meanwhile, Napoleon himself had reached Madrid, where he had his brother Joseph installed as king. Learning of Moore's whereabouts, Napoleon led an army north-west across the Guadarrama range in a snowstorm, hoping to isolate and crush him. Moore, although escaping the net, was forced to make a winter retreat through Galicia, hard-pressed by Soult, who had been left in command of the pursuit by Napoleon, impatient to get back to Paris. Moore was mortally wounded in the battle at Corunna (16 January, 1809), in which Soult was kept at bay until Moore's troops had embarked on the naval transports sent to retrieve them in what has been well described as 'the Dunkirk of its day'.

Wellington, now formally nominated Commander-in-Chief, sailed back to Lisbon, where he landed on 22 April. By 12 May he had ousted Soult from Oporto in a lightning attack which took the French entirely off their guard, and sent them scurrying back into Galicia, leaving virtually all their equipment and *matériel* behind. As further pursuit would have been impractical, Wellington turned south to Abrantes, before leading his army east across the frontier to cooperate with Spanish forces commanded by General Cuesta, who was planning to attack the French under Marshal Victor in the vicinity of Talavera, in the Tagus valley. Here, under a blistering sun on 20 July—three weeks after Napoleon's defeat of the Austrians at Wagram—the French were worsted in a Pyrrhic victory. It was a 'murderous battle' in which British losses were severe: the total casualties recorded were 5,365 men, a quarter of their entire force. French losses were heavier—7,268—but were a lower proportion of the numbers involved. The Spanish proved that they could not be

---

* Under which surname he is referred to throughout this book.

relied upon either to fight or to provide their allies with any of the essential supplies promised, and Wellington had little alternative but to lead his famished and sadly depleted troops back across country into Portugal to lick their wounds and recuperate. Nevertheless, the French had been put in their place smartly, and on 16 September Wellesley first signed his new name, Viscount Wellington, having been granted that title when the news of his victory had reached London.

Fourteen months passed between Talavera and the next major battle of the war It was time well spent by Wellington and Marshal Beresford: the latter was busily occupied in superintending the training of Portuguese troops, while the former supervised the con-struction of a series of forts in depth across the hills north of Lisbon, later known as the 'Lines of Torres Vedras'. Wellington was convinced that, as long as he retained a foothold in Portugal, the British army could continue to keep up the struggle against the French, and more advantageously in Spain than elsewhere on the Continent. Inevitably, a second French invasion of Portugal would occur. While Napoleon was selecting units to 'finish the business', Wellington was putting into practice a 'scorched earth policy' beyond the Lisbon defences, from which wide tract the civilian population, together with its live-stock, would be evacuated. The whole area behind the Lines was to become virtually an entrenched camp, largely manned by the Portuguese militia, leaving the British troops free to support them wherever needed.

Although Napoleon had planned to lead his 'Army of Portugal' himself in a spring offensive 'to drive the [English] leopard into the sea', in the event—partly because of his impending divorce from Josephine and the protracted negotiations leading up to his marriage to Marie Louise of Austria—the command of these 138,000 men devolved on Marshal Masséna.

It was not until late June 1810 that Masséna pushed west from Salamanca via Ciudad Rodrigo and Almeida, the latter being forced to capitulate prematurely after a chance shot had blown up its main magazine. He was then obliged to follow one of the worst possible roads in Portugal, for all others had been destroyed deliberately by Wellington. This one led via Viseu directly towards the eminently defensible ridge of the Serra de Busaco, not far north-east of Coimbra. Here, behind its crest, Wellington lay in wait with his entire Anglo-Portuguese army, over 51,000 strong. Masséna, undissuaded by the saner counsel of those of his subordinates aware of the hazards of making a frontal attack on Wellington when in such a position, insisted on sending his massed columns up the steep slope. However, he found them repeatedly repulsed by the punishing reception they were not expecting to receive. The rate and accuracy of fire of the well-disciplined Portuguese troops, now brigaded with the British, was such that, in the words of Commis-sary Schaumann, 'the French believed them to be Englishmen disguised in Portuguese uniforms'. By midday, although Masséna had still 20,000 fresh infantry with him, the battle was over. French casualties had by then risen to 4,600, including 300 officers—a higher percentage of officers to men than was to occur in any other action during the war.

Those of the Allies, 33,000 of whom had not even come up into the fighting line, were a mere 1,250, of which only 200 were killed. Eventually, French cavalry found their way round the northern extremity of the long ridge, leaving the Allies to retire across the River Mondego at their leisure.

While, as a matter of course, Coimbra itself was sacked by Masséna *en passant*, the 4,500 French left there, including the inadequately guarded sick and wounded, were captured by militia commanded by Colonel Nicholas Trant, an enterprising Englishman in the Portuguese service, referred to by Wellington after his death as 'a very good officer, but as drunken a dog as ever lived'. Masséna drove his opponents south 'in full retreat' after what chauvinistic pens had written up as his 'great victory', only to be brought up short by the unexpected sight of the Lines of Torres Vedras: the Allies forces, entering them on 8 October, had been placed by Wellington in an impregnable position, and Masséna, smarting from his recent experience, knew it.

To Wellington's surprise, the French, isolated from receiving reinforcements or supplies of any sort (not a single dispatch got through to them), were able to subsist in their front for another five weeks before retiring to a more defensible position near Santarém, where they remained until 5 March. Already in late December, impressed by their resilience, Wellington had reported to London that he was astonished that the French had survived so long, for they had brought no provisions with them, adding that 'With all our money, and having in our favour all the good inclination of the country . . . I could not maintain one division in the district in which they have maintained not less than 60,000 men and 20,000 animals for more than two months.'

Masséna's emaciated and shrunken 'Army of Portugal' eventually tramped north towards the Mondego valley with the Allies hard on their heels, and, after a number of rearguard actions, notably at Sabugal, re-entered Spain. Here, rapidly re-equipped and receiving reinforcements, Masséna returned to the fray intent on redeeming his reputation. During the first week of May he attacked the Allies at the frontier village of Fuentes de Oñoro, but was unable to shift them from the stubbornly defended site. This was to be Masséna's last battle: his recall had been announced already, and his place taken by the redoubtable Marshal Marmont.

On the 16th of that same month there took place an equally hard-fought but even more bloody encounter between Beresford and Soult at La Albuera, south-east of Badajoz, in which both contestants suffered severe casualties. Those of the Allies amounted to almost 6,000, of which a disproportionate number—4,039—were among the 8,738 British taking part, while it has been estimated that the French losses were between 7,000 and 8,000.

Several comparatively minor actions took place near the frontier during the remaining months of 1811, among them those at El Bodón and Arroyomolinos, while in January 1812 Ciudad Rodrigo fell to Wellington after a short siege, surrendering before the French could relieve it. Badajoz was a far tougher nut to crack, its breaches being stormed on 6 April with much bloodshed. The fortress was then sacked: some officers, when trying to restrain them from the worst excesses of rape and murder, were shot by their own men, inflamed by drink, for the violence was indiscriminate, forty-eight hours elapsing before any semblance of discipline could be restored among the rampaging survivors of the storm.

On 24 June Napoleon commenced his invasion of Russia. The time was ripe for Wellington to resume the offensive, and on 22 July Marmont's forces were defeated and scattered at Salamanca in one of the more brilliant of Wellington's offensive battles.* The Allies entered Madrid on 12 August, but their stay there was short-lived. Wellington attempted to revitalise the local politicians and military, having been able to distribute large amounts of captured equipment to the Spaniards, but it was a thankless task. He remarked at the time how extraordinary it was that the revolution in Spain 'should *not have produced one man* with any knowledge of the real situation; it really appears as if they were all drunk thinking and *talking* of any object but Spain: how it will end, God knows!' The next day he expressed the view that the only way 'to get them to do anything on any subject is to *frighten* them'.

Soult evacuated Seville later in August and, joining forces with Joseph Bonaparte, marched on Madrid, reoccupying the capital in early November. Meanwhile Wellington had struck north and laid siege to Burgos, a costly failure on his part, partly due to not having any siege train to hand. The French opposing him having been reinforced, Wellington's dispirited troops, their rearguard continually harassed, had little option but to retire south-west. Torrential autumn rains turned the roads into quagmires, rations were short and discipline deteriorated. A stand was made near Salamanca, where they had thrashed the French only three months earlier, which only aggravated the chagrin of having to retreat in the face of the enemy. By 19 November the Allies were back to their former cantonments in Portugal, while the French, suffering equally from the appalling weather, likewise dispersed to find food, forage and what shelter they could in the way of winter quarters. The December 'morning states' record that thirteen Allied regiments had more 'sick' than 'effectives': no fewer than 18,000 men were in hospital, and, in British battalions, there were only some 30,400 men present with the colours.

Looking back on the year, Wellington had several reasons to congratulate himself and his army, in spite of their present sorry state, for very extensive areas of the Peninsula, including the whole of Andalusia, had been liberated; almost 20,000 prisoners had been shipped back to England; huge quantities of enemy *matériel* had been captured; and the enemy's prestige had been shattered and his confidence severely undermined.

It did not take long for the Allied army to recuperate after the fatigue and exposure it had experienced. It was well fed, re-clothed and re-shod; morale was restored and reinforcements had been received. It was drilled rigorously throughout the winter and underwent extensive training in readiness for the spring offensive, plans for which Wellington kept close to his chest. Among several improvements effected during those months were the replacement of heavy cast-iron kettles by those of sheet-metal, light

---

* Admirably described in Rory Muir's study of the battle. See Bibliography.

enough for the men to carry themselves. The men were supplied with blankets, more portable than the heavy greatcoats with which they had been encumbered formerly, and in March 1813 the infantry were issued with Trotter's bell tents, in which twenty-five men could shelter, providing drier cover than if bivouacking. A corps of military police was formed to deal with delinquents; hospitals were set up; and, in general, the Allied troops were in a more disciplined and healthier state than ever before.

Although there had been rumours that Napoleon's Russian campaign had met with disaster, it was not until 18 January 1813 that any formal confirmation reached Wellington's headquarters. It was to influence his future strategy. Newspapers were soon arriving, containing awesome details, the reading of which gave a further boost to morale. Such disheartening news could not be kept from the French troops for long, which, throughout the winter, had remained the object of unremitting guerrilla activity carried out by the now more confident and better-armed Spanish partisans. The latter also supplied Wellington with information concerning enemy dispositions in addition to that received from his own intelligence officers. He was almost as well aware of the situation behind their front as the French were themselves.

Already, on 10 February, Wellington had written to Henry Bathurst in London, requesting him to order the embarkation on transports of the ordnance and stores listed in his dispatch, ready to sail to Corunna, to be at his disposal when needed as it was likely that the campaign he was preparing would require *matériel* to undertake a siege or two in the north of Spain. He did not wish to be caught unprepared, as had been the case at Burgos the previous autumn. *Twice the quantity of each article listed* should be in readiness to sail from England at what date and to what destination he would later specify. In the middle of 1812 Bathurst had accepted the position of Secretary of War in Lord Liverpool's administration. Both men supported Wellington to the best of their ability, even if, during the Vitoria campaign, he had received some extraordinary inept projects from them, 'thrown out for consideration'. One of these, suggested by Colonel Bunbury, under-secretary at the War Department, was that once the French had been evicted from Spain, the bulk of the army should be moved to either Italy or northern Germany—a hair-brained scheme rejected out of hand by Wellington in July 1813. Before long, after Vitoria, he was given virtually complete discretion in the conduct of military operations, and his advice on a variety of other pertinent problems was sought and accepted.

Wellington had calculated that there were then still over 200,000 French troops south of the Pyrenees, and that well over half this number comprised three armies within a week's march of Salamanca. Although it was likely that Napoleon would be withdrawing a proportion of veterans from them to strengthen the remains of his 'Grande Armée', doubtless he would be replacing them with other contingents.

To prevent any concentration against him, Wellington had planned a diversion to keep Marshal Suchet occupied, for the latter still commanded some 60–70,000 men—the largest single French army in Spain, even if a high proportion of it was penned up garrisoning captured fortresses. There had been several changes of commanders during recent months, and although Wellington may not have chosen General Sir John Murray to lead the units available, he acquiesced in the appointment: as Oman has remarked, 'perhaps he thought that here at least was a general who would take no risks, and have no dangerous inspirations of initiative.' Murray duly landed his heterogeneous force on the Mediterranean shore. After a creditable action at Castalla (north-west of Alicante) on 13 April, his 15,000 Anglo-Sicilians were transported up the coast in early June to Tarragona, which he intended to besiege, but the whole operation was a fiasco, for which Murray was later court-martialled. Nevertheless, it had the effect of engaging Suchet's attention to the extent that he sent not a single man to support Joseph Bonaparte and Marshal Jourdan.

By now, even if Wellington had serious reservations concerning their reliability, he had been given (nominal) command of both regular and irregular Spanish forces, despite some indignant opposition. This gave him additional troops of varying quality to dispose whenever expedient, as long as they scrupulously avoided confronting French armies by themselves, which had been the fatal penchant of too many Spanish generals. However, there were one or two of them—Pedro Girón, for example—who might be trusted when the time came to make his long-planned advance towards the Pyrenees.

The Anglo-Portuguese field army now totalled some 70,000 effectives, with the addition of some 12,000 Spanish regulars. Of this combined strength, the British contributed almost 41,000, including General Sir Stapleton Cotton's 6,500 cavalry, while 106 pieces of field artillery were also in readiness. With remarkable circumspection and secrecy, Wellington had ordered his pontoons on the Tagus near Vila Velha de Ródão to be carried north across country to the Douro on horse-drawn carriages, using axles and wheels borrowed from the artillery rather than relying on lumbering ox-transport, and this enabled him to complete within four weeks the complex exercise he had planned. On reaching the Douro near Barco de Alva, north of Almeida, these pontoons formed two bridges. Towards them, from mid-May, 70 per cent of the Allied army—some 60,000 men, together with part of the cavalry, which had wintered near the mouth of the Mondego— converged from their cantonments. Commanded by General Sir Thomas Graham, these columns, forming the left wing of the army, crossed the Douro by means of ferries and these pontoon bridges and reached positions of assembly in the vicinity of Miranda do Douro, in the rugged, high-lying, north-eastern province of Trás-os-Montes, to await further orders.

Already, on 12 May, Judge Advocate-General Larpent, who had recently joined Wellington's staff, noted that there were indications of an impending move at Headquarters, then in the village of Freineda, 'such as the packing of Lord Wellington's claret, etc.' Eight days later, after a delay caused by heavy rain, the Light Division, three cavalry brigades and a contingent of Spanish troops set out from Ciudad Rodrigo in the direction of Salamanca. After a running fight with a French division and two cavalry brigades defending it, the city was captured, together with a quantity of *matériel*, accumulated supplies and baggage. By the evening of the 26th, reinforced by General Sir Rowland

Hill's Corps, marching from Béjar further south, these Allied troops were deployed east of Salamanca. Wellington deliberately flaunted his presence, hoping that the enemy would get the impression that the entire British field army stood opposite him, although in fact it was only 30 per cent of the total. In the face of Hill's approach to Salamanca, General Villatte had withdrawn a detachment from Ledesma, to the north-west; but, by retiring to a new defensive position not far east of Salamanca, he no longer had any direct communication with General Daricau at Zamora on the Duero.*

Now took place one of the more spectacular movements of the entire war. At dawn on 28 May, Wellington, with a few aides, rode out of Salamanca, by dusk reaching the Duero 50 miles to the north-west, opposite Miranda. Here, he and his party were slung across the swirling river in 'a kind of hammock' suspended by ropes and worked by a windlass. Next day he joined Graham at Carbajales, north-west of Zamora, to inspect the army and supervise the crossing of the Esla, a tributary of the Duero, both then swollen by melting snow. At daybreak on the 30th the troops waded into the icy river, an infantryman hanging to the downstream stirrup of each trooper, taking the French picquets by surprise. Although Daricau's cavalry, stationed at Zamora, had made a sweep to the west only a few days before, seeing no sign of movement they had reported that there was no reason to suspect any attack from that quarter.

    Outflanked, the French lining the Duero had no alternative but to retreat precipitately east from Zamora and through Toro, already approached by the vanguard of Hill's Corps. Ordered forward on 2 June, by means of forced marches they reached and crossed the Duero by fords and a makeshift structure replacing the damaged arch of the bridge at Toro, and by noon on the 4th virtually the entire Allied army was established north of the river, leaving only Julián Sánchez's cavalry to mop up along its south bank towards Tordesillas and a Spanish division to garrison Salamanca. Wellington had almost 79,000 men, 8,300 cavalry, and 90 guns at hand.

    Although several sharp rearguard actions took place, Joseph Bonaparte and Marshal Jourdan—who had been outmanoeuvred by Wellington's advance, which they were powerless to stop, and who had attempted to concentrate at Valladolid—retreated towards Burgos. They were followed by General Gazan, withdrawing from Arévalo, and General Leval from Madrid. Leval had received orders to evacuate the capital only on 26 May, as it had seemed likely that Wellington would thrust due east from Salamanca, in which case he might find himself isolated. By 2 June no French troops of consequence remained south of the Duero: they were streaming north-east along the highway, their progress hampered by a vast train of baggage and plunder, together with the carriages of numerous *Afrancesados*.† Wellington, with the central of three columns, together with Hill's Corps to his right, pressed hard on their heels, having no intention of allowing them time

---

* As the Douro is spelt in Spain.
† Collaborating Spaniards.

to unite with Clausel's army, reported to be in the upper Ebro valley or further north in Navarre, for he would then be outnumbered.

From Melgar de Fernamental, west of Burgos, Wellington sent a dispatch to Colonel Bourke, stationed at Corunna, instructing him to order all transports carrying heavy artillery, ammunition, biscuit and flour, which had arrived there, to set sail for Santander, off which, protected by naval vessels, they were to wait until that port had been evacuated by the French. Meanwhile Graham's column, with Girón's Galicians, marched parallel to Wellington's left flank across the *meseta*, later entering the convoluted Cantabrian ranges. On 13 June, alarmed by what was only an Allied reconnaissance, the French retired from Burgos after blowing up its fortifications. Wellington now swung north into more mountainous country, but continued to outflank the French.

Apparently Clausel was in the vicinity of Pamplona on the 16th, although not yet showing any sign of joining Joseph and Jourdan: it was imperative to bring about a general action before he did so. This took place in the wide valley of the Zadorra, west of Vitoria, on 21 June. As not being an essential part of this particular study, the ensuing battle is described in outline only. Joseph and Jourdan commanded 66,000 men, 11,300 cavalry, and 138 guns. Outnumbering the Allies in cavalry and guns, the French, however, had 13,000 fewer infantry. Their first line of defence consisted of four and a half divisions under Gazan, deployed on rising ground facing west at no great distance east of the Zadorra river, which wound across the valley here from north-east to south-west. Some of General D'Erlon's troops were positioned near the Pass of Salinas, not far north-east of Vitoria itself. Neither General Foy nor General Maucune were at hand. Foy, who had been collecting isolated garrisons along the coast to reinforce his division, when *en route* to Vitoria, had turned east towards France to avoid interception by Graham; and Maucune's division had set off that morning to escort a convoy along the main *chaussée*, the highway to France. While this disencumbered the future battlefield to a certain extent, it also reduced Joseph's strength at a crucial moment; and there was still no sign of Clausel.

The engagement started with Hill's Corps ascending the Heights of Puebla from the south-west corner of the Zadorra valley. Wellington, with two columns, entered it from the west, but held back until firing was heard from the north-east. It was from that unexpected direction that Graham's wing, together with General Longa's Spaniards, after threading their way through the mountains, would be falling on the French. Wellington's columns then unleashed their attack.

By 10.00 Longa had cut the great road to France; by noon, or shortly thereafter, two bridges over the Zadorra, unaccountably left intact, were in Allied hands, and troops were pouring across. Under relentless pressure, Gazan was unable to consolidate his defensive line, and the French centre broke. By about 5.00 in the afternoon, Joseph, who only just escaped capture, ordered a general retreat. His army, now entirely demoralised, had decomposed into milling groups. Encumbering packs and even muskets were flung away in an endeavour to hasten their flight, and then panic ensued once it was realised that the main route of retreat had been cut. Virtually disintegrating, the army fled east, abandoning

all but two of its guns. Four hundred and fifteen caissons and vast quantities of equipment were left on the field, congested also by an immense park of vehicles and carriages
of every type waiting to be plundered. The Allies found this irresistible: no wonder only
2,000 French were taken prisoner, for here was far more valuable loot to be picked up.

Rain now descended in torrents, making roads impassable, and the cavalry, which
should have carried on the pursuit, after skirmishing with a slender rearguard, were called
off. Any idea of capturing Joseph's army *en masse* was given up; nor, for several days, was the
Allied army in any condition, exhausted as it was by a pitched battle after advancing 300
miles in less than thirty days, to follow up—after the orgy of celebration—what was,
materially, their most profitable victory. Politically, it was one which resounded throughout Europe, causing the coalition against Napoleon to harden; in Vienna, Beethoven
composed a martial piece in its honour, replete with rolling cannon-fire and musketry.

Wellington himself, although well pleased with the outcome of the battle, had every
reason to be critical of the ensuing indiscipline, which made serious inroads in the
number of his effectives. Writing to Bathurst eleven days later, he made the notorious
observation (frequently quoted out of context), 'We have in the service the very scum of
the earth as common soldiers', which referred more specifically to those few who had
chosen to ignore the wounded they had been instructed to attend, preferring to join in the
indiscriminate pillage. He continued: 'The loss of British rank and file in the battle was
3164 . . . from irregularities, straggling, &c., since, for plunder, 2733. The loss of Portuguese rank and file in the battle was 1022 . . . and their diminution from the same causes
is 1423'. Total Allied casualties, including Spaniards,* have been estimated at 5,150, of
which 840 were killed.† French losses must have far exceeded 8,000. Some 55,000 made
their escape, the majority filtering back to France through the mountain passes of northern Navarre during the next two or three weeks, although numbers of them would not have
survived the pitiless attacks of partisans.

---

* In fact there were comparatively few: Girón's Galicians, arriving in the wake of Graham's column, were never engaged.
† Oman, whose casting up of figures was not always too accurate, calculates differently, for naturally some of the wounded
died, some stragglers returned to the ranks, and there are always several imponderables to be taken in consideration
when scrutinising such 'official' returns.

The Pyrenees: A Contemporary French Map

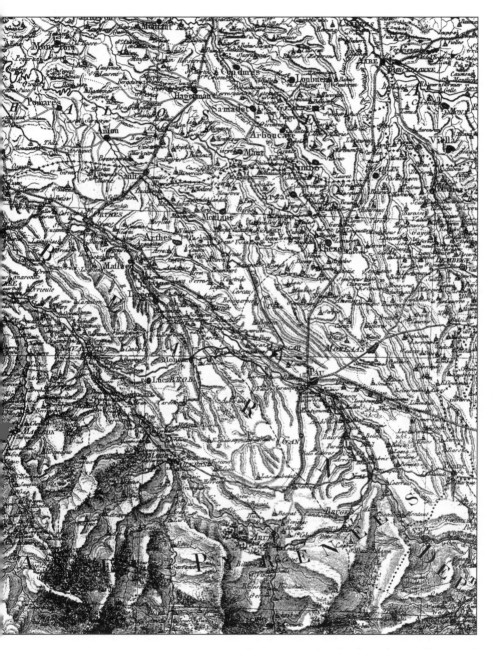

Note: This map is a greatly reduced reproduction of the original.

2

FROM VITORIA TO THE BIDASOA

ALTHOUGH the rain had washed away the blood and settled the dust, it was some time before anything like normality returned to Vitoria. One of the first essentials was to bury the dead and establish a hospital base there for the severely wounded. Some of them, during their recuperation, may have been among those frequenting the local booksellers, for Captain Joseph Moyle Sherer, author of *Recollections of the Peninsula*, records that he was assured by one—but perhaps merely to ingratiate himself—that he had sold more books to the British in the fortnight after the battle than he had disposed of in two years to the French, who were constantly passing through the place.

Units of the British cavalry—notably the 10th and 18th Hussars—in pursuit of the French retreating due east along the road to Salvatierra, had lost touch with Reille's rearguard during the night. Joseph (who had not even a change of clothes with him) and Jourdan, after a brief halt at Salvatierra, had ridden on through the rain to Pamplona, with a shattered army in their wake. Wellington had issued orders to his commanders to keep up the pressure on the enemy, assuming their men were capable of marching; too many of them were not.

Before following the French, it would be as well to describe the topography of the area in which the ensuing campaigns took place, because, to a large extent, the terrain was different from that fought over by Wellington and his troops in the past. Since he had struggled through the broken hills of northern Portugal in pursuit of Soult's demoralised units four years earlier, Wellington had had few encounters in such tortuous, rugged, country: no longer would his divisions and their camp-followers be moving comparatively rapidly across the bleak, high-lying, calcined, treeless, keen-aired, wide-horizoned plateaux of Castile, León, and Extremadura. Admittedly, on approaching Vitoria from the west and south-west, the Allied columns had threaded a number of valleys intersecting the Cantabrian sierras, a westward extension of the Pyrenees, cutting off Vitoria from the Biscay coast; but now they would be entering a far more intricate and far greener area, extremely hilly and thickly wooded when not mountainous, and with an abundant rainfall. North of Pamplona rose the main chain of the Pyrenees, dissected by valleys running north and south from the higher ridges, rising more abruptly from the French side than on the Spanish flank. Communications within the convoluted massif were poor, often only possible by rough and stony mule-track: lateral communication over intervening ridges and spurs entailed steep climbs. The higher passes were frequently mist- or fogbound, and invariably snowbound during the winter months. Its few rivers, rarely spanned by bridges, became impassable torrents after a downpour, isolating one bank from another for days on end. The injunction to 'attend to the provend' had to be taken seriously by the commissariat: little food or fodder would be found in its impoverished valleys and uplands, and the columns of bullock-drawn wagons would find the going very slow up those rutted roads. The Basque-speaking villages—often the refuge of guerrilla bands in recent years—were few and far between. It was also impracticable to use cavalry to advantage in the mountains, except to carry dispatches or reconnoitre, for as yet these remote regions were unmapped by Wellington's scouts. To traverse the convoluted foothills of the western Pyrenees was never easy: to deploy divisions and manoeuvre armies within its ranges would be a hazardous operation at the best of times.

Not until 10.00 on the morning of 22 June was the bulk of the Allied army ready to march east, and then in three columns: Wellington rode with the centre, flanked by Hill's Corps to the south and Graham's to his left. Wellington was aware that Clausel's by no means negligible force (some 12,500 men) was still in the vicinity, near Logroño (over the hills to the south), and could not be ignored; but there was also a chance of cutting it off. However, should Clausel decide to attack, the 5th Division was left to defend Vitoria, together with a cavalry brigade, shortly to be reinforced by the 6th Division, which, far in the rear, had taken no part in the battle.* The 5th then followed the tail of Graham's column as it proceeded towards the coast.†

Clausel was on the road from La Guardia, which traversed the Sierra de Cantábria to approach Vitoria from the south, but on hearing belatedly of Joseph's defeat and that Mina's guerrillas were threatening, he decided to turn on his tracks, collect the Logroño garrison, and make his way as rapidly as possible towards Pamplona, where, he assumed, the French would now be concentrating. Girón's and Longa's Spaniards were to press north-east along the *chaussée* to France in pursuit of Maucune, and to cut off, if possible, the Bilbao garrison together with any troops being hustled back towards the frontier by Foy. To make more certain that this could be done, Wellington approved quartermaster-general Sir George Murray's suggestion, made during the afternoon, that it would be better to reinforce them by sending Graham's column by an ancient track—now abandoned—which, climbing north-east from Salvatierra to the Puerto de San Adrián in the Sierra de Urquilla, descended to Segura in the valley of the river Oria. It then led through Villafranca (de Ordizia) and Tolosa to San Sebastián. Owing to poor staff-work, Graham himself, who in spite of driving rain was well ahead on the road to Pamplona, did not receive the dispatch notifying him of this change of plan until next morning. Meanwhile, the light brigade of the K.G.L. at the rear of his column, together with the rest of the

---

* General Sir Henry Clinton, its usual commander, had only just ridden up Lisbon, and taken over from Pakenham on the night of the 22nd.

† See below, pp. 36-9.

1st Division and Bradford's Portuguese, were soon countermarching to Salvatierra to follow the new route decided upon.

This sudden change in orders caused some confusion, in which Captain Norman Ramsay, whose battery was attached to Anson's cavalry brigade (then part of Graham's force), was later to take the brunt, being arrested briefly for what Wellington had assumed to be flagrant disobedience. The blame should have fallen on one of Wellington's staff-officers for not clearly defining the original instruction, which was to follow Anson's brigade. He had neglected to tell Ramsay, who supposed it was still trooping east, that Anson had been ordered to turn back. Thus slighted, Ramsay, a brilliant artillery officer who had gained his laurels at Fuentes de Oñoro, was never promoted. Wellington, criticised by some for rarely giving his artillery its due, would never admit that Ramsay had been treated unjustly. The latter would die at Waterloo.

Being less than vigorously pursued, Joseph had assumed, wrongly, that the bulk of the Allied army had followed the highway from Vitoria to the frontier, with only Foy's detachments anywhere near it to impede its immediate invasion of France; but, if Foy was reinforced by Reille, this might be arrested. For this reason, when passing through Irurtzun on approaching Pamplona, Reille's two divisions and a cavalry brigade were ordered to diverge from the main line of retreat and make their way north-east as fast as possible along mountain tracks to Sanestéban (Doneztebe); from there, they could thread the Bidasoa valley back to the frontier.

On approaching Irurtzun on the afternoon of the 24th, the British vanguard became engaged in skirmishing with D'Erlon's troops, now forming the rearguard of the main body of Joseph's army, which, having followed the road towards Pamplona, skirted the fortress and veered away. The enemy had only about 100 casualties in these minor actions. Gazan then led his troops north-east up the Arga valley to Zubiri before ascending through the mountains towards Roncesvalles on the frontier and climbing down to St-Jean-Pied-de-Port.

At dawn on the 25th the bulk of D'Erlon's force set out to tramp due north up the Ulzama valley—passing by the village of Sorauren—to the Puerto de Velate and into the Baztan valley, where they halted. By the evening, George Hennell, with the 43rd, had entered Villava, no great distance north-east of Pamplona, where his company, on taking possession of one of the better houses, found it rifled already by the French in retreat:

> Every chest & drawers was broken open & the clothes they did not choose to take away strewed knee-deep on the floor. They demanded of the richest man in the town (a priest) all his shirts, and they even stripped him of his boots. He gave them some excellent wine & because he neither would nor could give them more they cut out his tongue & stabbed him. Some of our officers saw him dead.

THE PURSUIT OF CLAUSEL

Earlier that day, Victor Alten's light cavalry had circled round to the south of Pamplona, leaving picquets on the roads leading from Logroño and Tafalla (due south), by either of which Clausel might be approaching in an attempt to escape by the same route as had his compatriots. During the afternoon, Wellington received intelligence from Mina that Clausel was still making for Pamplona: if this was correct, there was every chance that he might be intercepted, and appropriate orders were issued. In the event, Clausel, finding his most direct route via Estella (now Lizarra Estella) and Puente la Reina cut by Mina's guerrillas, veered south to cross the Ebro at Lodosa on the following day. He was now well on the way to evading Wellington's pursuit, having destroyed the bridges behind him at Lodosa and reached Tudela on the afternoon of the 27th.

Meanwhile, on the 26th, General Sir Lowry Cole, with the 4th and Light Divisions, had marched south towards Tafalla, his cavalry entering Olite to find that Clausel was already 35 miles further south, on the far bank of the Ebro at Tudela. Having collected its garrison and destroyed the bridge, Clausel pushed ahead to Zaragoza, which he entered three days later to find General Paris, the governor, still entirely ignorant of the disaster which had overwhelmed Joseph at Vitoria on the 21st!

Hill's Corps was sent forward to relieve the 3rd and 7th Divisions following Cole, which it did at dawn next day. The 6th Division, still at Vitoria, was ordered to make forced marches across the hills to the south-east to enter the Ebro valley and fall on Clausel's rear, but on reaching Logroño on the 27th, it found that 'the bird had flown' two days earlier. There was no chance of catching up with him and, on approaching Tafalla from the west, Clinton called a halt.*

Before dawn on the 28th Wellington received another report, which made him conclude that Clausel might attempt to reach France by bearing north-east across the desolate region of the Bárdenas Reales to Jaca and over the Somport Pass. This caused him to make the snap decision to re-route the Light and 4th Divisions, together with the 3rd and 7th—some 30,000 men. He turned them abruptly east over the hills towards Sangüesa in the hope of cutting off Clausel's march on Jaca, only to cancel the order next day, by which time only the 3rd Division had entered Sangüesa. The four divisions were then marched back directly towards Pamplona—on which the 6th Division also converged—blockaded by Hill's Corps, together with Silveira's Portuguese and Morillo's Spanish troops.

Wellington's reasons for this *volte-face* were that Clausel had got too long a start; and if he had succeeded in cutting his line of escape via Jaca, Clausel might well join Suchet, which was undesirable. Moreover, as he confided to Bathurst, he was displeased by the disgruntled state of the army: both officers and men regarded the last few days' unprofitable manoeuvring as a wild goose chase, although it might have met with success.

In the event, Clausel did set off for Jaca, which he reached on 6 July. Here he waited for a few days, should Suchet decided to march on Zaragoza, in which case he would return there; but on the 11th he learned that General Paris, by now surrounded by a tightening cordon of guerrillas, had chosen to evacuate the city the previous day before his position there became more hazardous. Clausel, leaving some 1,500 stragglers or sick

* The 5th Division had also started out from Vitoria, but was re-routed soon afterwards to join Graham's forces on the road to San Sebastián.

to the mercy of Mina, led his 11,000 infantry, 500 horse and six mountain guns north across the Somport Pass (1,632m) into France; by the 15th they had entered St-Jean-Pied-de-Port.

On 1 July Hill was ordered to march north up the Ulzama valley and to eject D'Erlon from the Baztan valley. Silveira and Morillo would take over the investment of Pamplona, where they would be reinforced within hours by the 7th Division, and then by the 3rd. Andrew Leith Hay describes the fortress as being encircled by a ring of nine redoubts—the completion of which was being superintended by Major Goldfinch of the engineers—sited between 1,200 and 1,500 yards from the walls and armed with some of the field artillery captured at Vitoria.

Two days earlier, Francis Larpent, writing up his *Journal* at Cáseda—on the river Aragón south-west of Sangüesa, the furthest east reached by Headquarters—noted that the army, in their pursuit of Clausel, was 'already terribly harassed and out of sorts', and went on to comment that

> In marching, our men have no chance at all with the French. The latter beat them hollow; principally, I believe, owing to their being a more intelligent set of beings, seeing consequences more, and feeling them. This makes them sober and orderly whenever it becomes material, and on a pinch their exertions and individual activity are astonishing. Our men get sulky and desperate, drink excessively, and become daily more weak and unable to proceed, principally from their own conduct. They eat voraciously when opportunity offers, after having had short fare. This brings on fluxes, etc. In every respect, except courage, they are very inferior soldiers to the French and Germans. When the two divisions, the fourth and light, passed through Taffalla the day before yesterday, the more soldierlike appearance and conduct of the foreigners, though in person naturally inferior, was very mortifying. Lord Wellington feels it much, and is much hurt.
>
> The 23rd and 11th Portuguese regiments, who behaved on the field on the 23rd as well as any British did or could do, are on the march, though smaller animals, most superior. They were cheerful, orderly, and steady. The English troops were fagged, half tipsy, weak, disorderly, and unsoldierlike; and yet the Portuguese suffer greater hardships, for they have no tents, and only bivouac, and have a worse commissariat.

Although Sir George Larpent interpolated a footnote when editing his half-brother's *Journal* to excuse his reflections on the moral deficiencies of the British soldiers, suggesting that his position as Judge Advocate-General had brought him in contact with the *delinquents* rather than the real, steady soldiers of the army, it should be emphasised here that these words were written within a few days of Wellington's *Dispatch* to Bathurst, in which he excoriated the rank and file of his army as being composed of 'the very scum of the earth', a stricture reiterated in conversation with Stanhope in November 1831, for which he was later criticised speciously. As Richard Glover observed in his *Peninsular Preparation*, these drunken reprobates 'were tough with a ruggedness unknown and scarcely conceivable in the decorous modern England of today' [1963; *sic*]. These brutes could only be brought to heel by flogging, the commonest form of punishment, which was some deterrent to other than the incorrigible and thick-skinned; and while 'nothing is easier than to denounce so barbarous a punishment as this, yet it baffled the wit of the authorities to devise a punishment that could control the appalling thugs of whom the rank and file of the British Army was largely composed.' As Wellington had retorted, when questioned concerning some of the more flagrant incidents which had occurred during the sacking of Badajoz:

> People talk of their enlisting from their fine military feeling—all stuff—no such thing. Some of our men enlist from having got bastard children—some for minor offences - —many more for drink; but you can hardly conceive such a set brought together, and it is really wonderful that we should have made them the fine fellows they are. I have never known officers raised from the rank turn out well, nor the system answer; they cannot stand drink.

Should it be imagined that Wellington's scathing comments were excessively reactionary, unprejudiced evidence is found in the pages of *Recollections of an Eventful Life of a Soldier* by Sergeant Joseph Donaldson (94th Foot), with whom one can well sympathise when he recounts that

> . . . there were few . . . with whom I could associate that had any idea beyond the situation they were in; those who had were afraid to show that they possessed any more knowledge than their comrades for fear of being laughed at by fellows that in other circumstances they would have despised. . . . If [a man] did not join with his neighbours in their ribald obscenity and nonsense, he was a Methodist—if he did not curse and swear, he was a Quaker—and if he did not drink the most of his pay, he was a miser, a d—d mean scrub and the generality of his comrades would join in execrating him. In such a society it was a hard matter for a man of any superior knowledge to keep his ground, for he had no one to converse with. . . . Thus many men of ability and information were, I may say, forced from their intellectual height which they had attained down to the level of those with whom they had to associate; and everything conspired to sink them to that point where they became best fitted for *tractable beasts of burden*. Blackguardism held sway and gave tone to the whole. Even the youngest were led to scenes of drunkenness and debauchery by men advanced in years. All, therefore, with few exceptions were drawn into this overwhelming vortex of abject slavishness and dissipation.

According to Larpent, Wellington himself 'seemed knocked up yesterday'—the 28th; 'he ate little or nothing, looking anxious, and slept nearly all the time of sitting after dinner'.

On that same day, August Schaumann, Commissary for the 18th Hussars of the K.G.L., describes them bivouacking at Cáseda, where a jumble sale of plunder from Vitoria was held. They had already rifled the royal kitchen-wagon of delicacies after the battle, when every officer 'got a hermetically sealed tin which when opened disclosed a wonderful roast joint or fowl in aspic, perfectly fresh and delicious to the taste. Some of these tins contained preserved fruit or jam', all of which were thoroughly enjoyed while they lasted. Schaumann had seen some officers with priceless sporting guns inlaid with gold, which had belonged to King Joseph; others had acquired royal underclothing, superfine shirts and silk stockings, with a 'J' embroidered on them in red silk. Schaumann himself 'purchased a whole sackful of candlesticks, teapots, silver ingots bearing the treasury mark, plates, knives and forks for half their value', but what astonished him was the quantity of military and court uniforms belonging to the king, his staff and entourage, covered with gold lace, which were then cut up to serve as jackets and forage caps: 'Nearly every officer in our brigade had one of them. Watches, crosses of the Legion of Honour and gold stripes were to be had by the score. The crosses . . . were bought up at any price by our vindictive Spanish muleteers, and slung on their mules' tails with a view of casting scorn and mockery on the French'.

The Hussars were then quartered at Olite for a month to keep an eye on Pamplona, where apparently a good time was had by all; Schaumann had 'plenty of affairs', one with an organist's wife, 'who always availed herself of her husband's duties in the church' to visit him. On 7 July Henry Somerset, Marquess of Worcester, a lieutenant in the 10th Hussars, gave his second ball, for which he had engaged the band of the 18th to play. As they did not turn up, Worcester sent an NCO in search of them, and the latter eventually 'found the whole in a room [elsewhere] dancing, completely naked, except having their pelices across their shoulders'. Lieutenant George Woodberry, also in the 18th, had understood that there had been some women present, but he had not heard whether 'they were stripp'd or not'. The cavalry had a reputation for organising such local hops: Schaumann had previously described what he referred to as 'barbarously brilliant' balls being held at Covilhã in Portugal, when Sir Stapleton Cotton's headquarters, to enliven the long winter evenings.

GRAHAM'S ADVANCE ON TOLOSA AND SAN SEBASTIÁN

Before following in Hill's track, Graham's operations further west must be outlined. Foy had met Maucune's division entering Mondragon on the evening of 21 June. Although Maucune had heard heavy gunfire behind him, neither he nor Foy were aware until next morning of the result of the battle which had been taking place at Vitoria, when fugitives arrived with news not only of the disaster but also that the commandants of the forts guarding the Salinas passes, having spiked their guns, were falling back on Bergara, assuming that the Allies were in full pursuit.

Longa's Cantabrians had set out to force these passes at dawn on the 22nd, followed after some delay by Girón's three Galician divisions, for they had turned back briefly on hearing that Clausel threatened, which proved to be a false alarm. The Spaniards now totalled some 12,000 infantry; being weak in artillery, they had been lent two batteries from Wellington's reserve. Longa's division had pushed far ahead, but, after bickering all afternoon with units Foy had ordered forward again to defend the defile of Salinas, at nightfall had only reached a point about two miles beyond Mondragon. Foy received reinforcements during the evening, and made another stand the next morning, hoping to keep the Spaniards at bay long enough for the Bilbao garrison, among other detachments, to pass behind him to safety. Longa, aware that Foy had been reinforced, but not knowing to what extent, cautiously waited for Girón's exhausted and rain-soaked troops to arrive, which they did by noon.

Although Girón planned a concerted attack on Bergara the following day, this did not take place, as Foy, having by then picked up his missing brigades, had started to retreat east to Villareal (on the Río Urola opposite Zumarraga) well before dawn. Foy had guessed that Longa had deliberately remained inactive in the hope that he might linger where he was and find his retreat cut off: and he was right, for on the 22nd the vanguard of

Graham's columns had been re-routed, and was already crossing the Sierra de Urquilla and descending into the Oria valley intent on intercepting him at Villafranca. With great prescience, Foy ordered Maucune, who was a march ahead of him, to leave his convoy at Tolosa and countermarch to Villafranca without delay, as it was very likely that an Allied column might cut the vital crossroads there before his 8,000 men reached it.

This Maucune did on the 24th, blocking the valley south of the junction—and just in time, for Graham's vanguard had entered the valley already, and it was at dawn that very morning that Anson's dragoons and Pack's Portuguese, bringing up the rear of the column, reached the front. Graham immediately set his troops in motion, hoping to drive in Maucune before Foy's could get past. In this he was unsuccessful, but, by thrusting ahead both his wings, he was able to force Maucune back on to higher ground, where he continued to resist for a time. Longa's Cantabrians, unaware of Foy's early start, were unable to catch up with his rearguard until they attempted to thread the defile of the Puerto de Descarga. Longa turned their defensive position here, but it was not until mid-afternoon that he was able to join up with Graham, who had by then outflanked Maucune's line. Maucune slipped north to follow Foy down the road to Tolosa. Meanwhile, Girón's troops had caught up with Graham's column, comprising some 10,000 Anglo-Portuguese and 16,000 Spaniards, which inopportunely had out-marched its supplies and was massed along the highway. Foy's troops awaiting them at Tolosa now amounted to 16,000. Although Wellington's plan to trap Foy had failed, through no fault of Graham's, it was now up to Graham to push the French across the Bidasoa, which formed the frontier not far east of the fortress of San Sebastián.

Foy had resolved to put up a stand at Tolosa, still under the misapprehension that Joseph's armies, having fled east from Vitoria—and he was still ignorant of the extent of their defeat—would be marching towards Tolosa, to regain the main *chaussée* to the frontier and Bayonne. Little did he realise that it was only Reille's two divisions that had turned off the Pamplona road at Irurtzun but had then veered north-east through the mountains to enter the Bidasoa valley near Sanestéban—not in his direction at all.

Tolosa stood in a narrow valley threaded by both the highway from Vitoria to France and the River Oria. It was encircled by high but ancient walls, additionally strengthened by blockhouses and palisades, where guns had been mounted. Troops had been redeployed at strategic points in and around the town, some units being placed on one of the surrounding heights which commanded the Pamplona road, entering from the south-east. Maucune's division was held in reserve to the north. The ponderous convoy cluttering up the place was sent trundling off towards France, escorted by four battalions commanded by General Berlier.

However well-prepared to resist a frontal attack, Tolosa could be circumvented, as was evident to both contestants, although this would involve time-consuming detours. Graham ordered Longa's Cantabrians and Porlier's Asturians to circle east and cut the Pamplona road near the village of Lizartza in the Araxes valley, and then turn north to take Tolosa in the rear. A closer circuit to the east was made by Bradford's Portuguese, supported by units of the K.G.L. A battalion of Pack's brigade and part of Girón's division made a corresponding movement to the west, only to find a precipice impeding their approach to a hill dominating Tolosa, which they had hoped to occupy. The rest of Graham's column marched directly towards the town, but halted some distance from its gates. Advised that irregulars under Mendizábal were near Azpeitia (further west), Graham sent off an aide begging them to make their way rapidly across the hills to block, or at least demonstrate against, the highway at some point north of Tolosa.

Desultory fighting took place during the morning, in which Portuguese units captured a ridge, but it was not until the late afternoon that firing to the north confirmed that both Longa's and Mendizábal's men were in action. Graham then ordered a general advance, in which the leading K.G.L. battalion sustained heavy casualties in attacking the fortification facing them (the strength of which had been underestimated), being caught in a cross-fire and finding little cover. Graham then brought up his guns, which cleared the adjacent walls and destroyed the Vitoria Gate, now rushed by the K.G.L. battalions checked there earlier. There was confused fighting in the streets, but Foy, realising he was now in danger of encirclement if he lingered much longer, extricated his men without many casualties (although some 200 were taken prisoner) and set off north at speed, reaching Andoain that night. Here he was joined by some of Berlier's men, together with a few detached units converging on the highway. Altogether, despite recent losses, Foy still had 16,000 infantry, 400 sabres and ten guns at his disposal. Longa's indefatigable Cantabrians soon appeared in the front of his positions, but allowed Foy's forces to retire unmolested to Hernani.

Still unaware of Joseph's situation and intentions, Foy detached Berlier's brigade the next day as a search party. Setting out along the Bidasoa valley, it discovered Reille at Bera, but, as his troops were in no condition to fight, Reille ordered Foy to evacuate Hernani and, after leaving units at intermediate Oiartzun with which they might keep in touch with San Sebastián, to join him along the lower reaches of the Bisasoa.

Joseph Bonaparte had nominated General Emmanuel Rey as Governor of San Sebastián two days before the Battle of Vitoria, where he had commanded a brigade. The fortress had been disgracefully neglected and was certainly in no state to withstand a siege, which seemed imminent. Its garrison—if it could be called such—consisted of about 500 *gendarmes*, some raw recruits and a number of pioneers and sappers, some 1,200 men in all. The town had been left insufficiently provisioned with food, among other essentials, and was crammed with several thousand French and *afrancesado* refugees, which Foy ordered to be escorted to Bayonne by the outgoing garrison. This he replaced by Deconchy's brigade—2,000 or so infantry—together with as many gunners as he could spare. Two days later, the garrison of Getaria (Guetaria) arrived by sea, followed by numbers of military stragglers, which increased the total to about 3,000 by the time the place was invested. Meanwhile, Rey set about clearing the glacis of the sheds and other lumber with which it had become obstructed.

On 29 June Reille ordered Foy to evacuated Oiartzun, and within hours 3,000 of Mendizábal's irregulars were swarming around San Sebastián, isolating it by land. On the following day, Foy's and Maucune's divisions crossed the Bidasoa by the bridge at Béhobie and were distributed among neighbouring villages. General Lamartinière's division remained at Bera; that of General Fririon* occupied the fortified village of Hendaye, at the mouth of the Bidasoa, here marking the frontier.

The 1st Division and Graham's Portuguese units were halted near San Sebastián and most of the Galicians between Hernani and Renteria (Errenteria), close to the small landlocked port of Pasajes (Pasaia), the garrison of which, too late in leaving for the Béhobie bridge, were captured by Longa's Cantabrians, the vanguard of Graham's army and the first to reach the Bidasoa late that afternoon. Almost the last to cross were four battalions of the Bayonne reserves, which had been posted on the neighbouring ridge of San Marcial to guard the troops filing over the exposed wooden bridge. A detachment remained in the palisaded stone blockhouse at Irun, a target for Graham's guns next day; but, as there was no point in trying to hold the insignificant bridgehead, this detachment was withdrawn, losing 68 men before gaining the French bank, after which the four nearest arches of the bridge were fired.

It was not until 1 July—nine days after the battle—that news of the rout of his armies at Vitoria had reached Napoleon at Dresden. Characteristically, and deaf to all argument, he had within hours ordered that a counter-offensive be set in motion. Marshal Nicolas Soult, Duc de Dalmatie, who had attended the Imperial headquarters for several weeks prior to the death on 1 May of Marshal Bessières (killed by a chance bullet when reconnoitring the future battlefield of Lützen), was to take entire charge of all French forces in the south-west of France without delay. In Napoleon's opinion, Soult had 'the only military brain in the Peninsula', and he had sufficient confidence in Soult's abilities to entrust him with the immense task of reorganising and revitalising Joseph's devastated army: he should never have left it in his brother's incapable hands.† Within hours, Soult was *en route* from Dresden to Paris to consult with Clarke, the Minister of War, before proceeding to Bayonne.‡

On that same day—1 July—Graham's and Girón's units took possession of the left bank of the Bidasoa. They had 25,000 men between them, which would be more than enough to keep Reille, Foy and the Bayonne Reserve in check. In any case, reinforcements, in the

---

* Replacing Sarrut, killed at Vitoria.

† Wellington may well have agreed with Napoleon's opinion of Soult's capacity in this respect. When the subject came up in conversation with Stanhope many years later, he remarked that Soult, while he 'knew very well how to bring his troops on to the field, but not so well how to use them when he had brought them up', he 'did not quite understand a field of battle', and therefore Wellington did not consider Soult to be the equal of Masséna.

‡ Soult's experience of having Wellington as his immediate adversary had been slight. Since his ejection from Oporto in May 1809, the only time they had been in close proximity had been on the 17th and 18th of the previous November, when Wellington had offered battle on the River Huebra, which Soult declined, allowing the Allies to continue their retreat unmolested to the Portuguese frontier.

shape of Mendizábal's Biscayans and the 5th Division, were expected to reach the front shortly. Simultaneously, the main Anglo-Portuguese army started to move into the western Pyrenees, the foothills of which rose immediately north of Pamplona. If Wellington regretted having wasted several days attempting to intercept Clausel rather than overtaking Joseph's troops and destroying them in detail, he kept his misgivings to himself. His cavalry could have caused further chaos among the fleeing enemy, for it was very doubtful whether the French could have rallied. Too many had escaped, admittedly, but those who did were thoroughly demoralised. They had lost virtually all their guns and most of their *matériel*, let alone most of their plunder: they were a spent force.

Apart from several practical problems which he had to resolve, Wellington was preoccupied by the very unstable political situation. On 2 June, after Britain's Northern Allies had been defeated by Napoleon at Bautzen on 21 May, hostilities were suspended, and the Armistice of Pläswitz, signed two days later, extended the truce until 20 July. However, the British representatives at Allied headquarters had not even been consulted about the armistice, causing justifiable alarm in London, for any separate negotiations thus entered into would only undermine the strength of the Coalition. If the Northern Allies made a premature peace, Britain would be left to carry on the war virtually alone.

Britain was able to sign a treaty with Prussia on 14 June, and another with Russia on the following day, formally committing them *not* to make a separate peace, even if treaties of this nature would be unenforceable. When advised of the state of affairs, Wellington naturally remained very cautious. It is fruitless speculating whether it would have been better had Wellington chosen to detach only a light force to harass Joseph's demoralised troops, and make a determined dash directly for the French frontier on 22 June with the bulk of the Allied army, although it has been suggested that if he had done so, and invaded France and captured the important military base of Bayonne, this would have had an invigorating effect on what otherwise might appear to the Northern Allies to be a lack of enterprise on Britain's part. It is interesting that Larpent, close to Wellington, had noted in his *Journal* on 2 July that 'If the armistice produces a Russian and Prussian peace, and we are left here to Bonaparte's sole attention and undivided care, I fear we may again see the neighbourhood of Portugal before six months have passed . . .'

Partly because of the delay in dispatches reaching him from London, caused by frequent bad weather in the Bay of Biscay, Wellington was still ignorant of the result of discussions between the Northern Allies concerning possible peace proposals, which would affect his decision whether or not to invade. Until the diplomats had come to a decision, it would be wiser to confine himself to securing what he had gained and wait on events, as he had remarked to Lord William Bentinck.* If Napoleon was able to reinforce his troops in the south-west, Wellington would be left in the invidious position of having to pull back his own troops, if they had crossed the frontier. If the war continued, he might

---

* Wellington had ordered Bentinck, who had superseded Sir John Murray, to keep Suchet occupied at all costs.

be able to establish himself in this region, although it was unlikely that he would be 'at Paris in a month', as some sanguine souls in London seemed to expect.

As the intentions of Austria regarding a re-entry into the conflict were still unknown, Wellington chose to remain on the Spanish side of the Pyrenees, confident he could hold that line, although he could never defend it in the same way as had the Lines of Torres Vedras, north of Lisbon: the front was too long; there were far too many passes by means of which the enemy could infiltrate; and the French had the advantage as far as communications were concerned. Time was spent explaining the topography of the area to Lord Liverpool, the Prime Minister, who seemed to assume that it was merely a matter of 'plugging' a few passes in a wall of precipices, not appreciating that any line of fortifications could be turned by an enemy scrambling up any accessible intermediate slope. When Lord Liverpool had naïvely suggested that Spanish troops might be left to man the Pyrenees, Wellington was able to reiterate that the Spanish government had consistently shown its incapacity to feed, pay, clothe or transport its own troops, and it would invite disaster to entrust it with any such task. As it was, he was at that moment in acrimonious correspondence with O'Donoju, the Spanish Minister of War, over the removal of Castaños and Girón from the scene.

It had been on 28 June, when near Sangüesa, that Wellington had received the disturbing news from Cádiz that Castaños and Girón had been deposed by the Spanish Regency, which he rightly concluded must have been a political machination on the part of the so-called 'Liberal' party, by which they were hoping to secure their domination of the government. They had made entirely unconvincing excuses for having evicted the few people upon whom Wellington had come to rely. He wrote forthwith to his brother Henry Wellesley, the ambassador at Cádiz, to bring pressure on the less politically unscrupulous members of the *Cortes*, intimating that he would have no compunction in resigning from the position of *Generalissimo*, with which they had invested him six months earlier— when it had been agreed that they would not make or revoke any military appointments without notice or without his approval—unless they used their voting power to reverse these decisions. The Minister of War at Cádiz was informed that Wellington considered himself to have been 'most unworthily treated'.*

By now Wellington had acquired such an ascendancy over Liverpool and his ministers that, for the most part, they were content to accept his decisions and demands. As he had explained to them, he had more urgent problems closer to hand with which to contend. Allied troops were at present living off the country. This was a practice he deplored, but he had little alternative, having out-marched his transports, now ordered to sail to Santander and other ports nearer to San Sebastián (among them Deba), which he had every hope would fall to Graham before long. His troops needed time to recuperate after the battle, and the exertions and excesses of the last few days. He was, moreover, starting to run short

---

* Girón, in particular, could be relied on: many years later, when Marques de las Amarillas, he was referred to by Richard Ford, who had known him at Seville, as being unusually well-bred, and honest, and a true friend to England.

of ammunition. His immediate preoccupation, while awaiting news of the latest diplomatic manoeuvring, was to neutralise both San Sebastián and Pamplona: until both fortresses were in his hands, any idea of advancing into France could be shelved. As it was,
he did not receive belated confirmation that the Armistice had ended and that Austria
had re-entered the war, declared by them on 11 August, until 7 September.

General Cassan commanded a garrison of 3,600 men at Pamplona, and had over 80
guns mounted on its walls. The job of blockading the place was to be undertaken by the
Spanish 'Army of Reserve of Andalusia', some 11,000 men under Enrique O'Donnell,
Conde d'Abispal. He was now free to do this, for by 30 June the last of the small forts
guarding the defile of Pancorbo, outflanked by the Allies when advancing on Vitoria,
had fallen to him, and their garrisons taken prisoner.

HILL'S ADVANCE

On 2 July, Hill, with the 2nd Division and Silveira's Portuguese, started to march north
from bivouacs near Pamplona, followed by the 7th, and the Light, with orders to evict
D'Erlon's troops from the Baztan valley, from where they would then establish contact with
Graham's troops along the lower reaches of the Bidasoa. Meanwhile John Byng's brigade
of the 2nd Division was detached towards the Roncesvalles Pass, through which French
units had only recently descended to St-Jean-Pied-de-Port (leaving Nicolas Conroux's
division to hold the pass behind them), plundering the French Basque peasantry, fleeing
at their approach, and taking all their corn and cattle as if they were still in Spain.*

Hill (with Alexander Cameron's and Robert O'Callaghan's brigades, and Charles
Ashworth's Portuguese) discovered that D'Erlon's troops were still in the process of being
relieved by Gazan's divisions, the latter hardly in any better condition to put up a fight;
and it was at noon on 4 July, while this exchange of units was taking place, that Hill's
vanguard started skirmishing with them near the Puerto de Velate. The French rearguard
was pushed back towards Irurita, but as Hill, with only 8,000 men, would have been outnumbered should Gazan decide to counter-attack before the 7th and Light Divisions
come up, he waited until Wellington arrived from Lanz at noon the next day. Then,
although with only Da Costa's Portuguese in reserve, Hill took the initiative.

On the 6th, Larpent entered the small fortified village of Berroeta—on a rough track
between Almándoz and Irurita—from which a much superior force had been ejected by
units of the 2nd Division the previous day, some twenty only being wounded in the skirmish. The local peasantry—'a fine, stout, tall, well-made race of mountaineers'—had
behaved with spirit, and 'with their own fire-arms, mingling with our light troops, brought

---

* Larpent, writing on 2 July, had stated that it was expected that Allied troops would be moving towards Roncesvalles
the following day, although this was not yet settled. It had been his opinion that this 'should have done this immediately,
without going after Clausel; but no doubt Lord Wellington knew best what to do.' He went on to remark that they were
in 'great distress for horseshoes', and that a mountain march was expected. However, within a few days, when at Lanz,
Larpent bribed a farrier to re-shoe his mount, even if the heads of the nails were 'half an inch square, upon six of which
heads in each shoe the horses walk, as the shoe never touches a stone; these skaits are, however, much better than
nothing.'

in two prisoners'. Some insisted upon joining a mounted picquet, and when Major Brotherton warned them that they were acting foolishly, as he could offer neither protection nor support if enemy cavalry turned on them, they replied that 'they could run as fast as those French horses' and would not be caught. Not surprisingly, there were difficulties in communication: Larpent was not alone in finding the Basque language incomprehensible, indeed 'very barbarous'. The little Spanish he had managed to pick up was of no use, and he was almost reduced to 'the state of the deaf and dumb, to have to recourse to signs and acting.'

On that same day (6 July), once the 7th Division, temporarily commanded by Edward Barnes,* had crossed one of the Donamaria passes and entered Sanestéban, Wellington could count on having 14,000 men in the vicinity. The Light Division under Charles Alten would be there by the following evening, and at the front by the morning of the 8th. Barnes was then sent north-east across mountainous country, which would bring him behind Gazan's right flank, while Archibald Campbell's Portuguese brigade was approaching the valley of the Aldudes, having been ordered along a more easterly route, via Zubiri and the Col de Urquiaga.

Gazan assumed that not only Conroux might be threatened (by what was merely a reconnaissance on the part of General Morillo), but that his own troops were likely to be cut off from General Leval's units near Sanestéban by forces of unknown strength—and he suddenly panicked. Without realising that he would be retreating before a force little more than half his strength, Gazan ordered Leval to proceed north down the Bidasoa valley towards Etxalar, and both Villatte (near Irurita) and Maransin were directed to retire up the Baztan valley to the Puerto de Otxondo (570m), often referred to as the Pass of Maya.

The French were certainly in a quandary as to where Wellington might strike, for Byng was approaching the pass at Roncesvalles and Conroux was fearful that he had a much larger force now opposing him. Archibald Campbell's men, having entered the Aldudes, were seen as an additional threat to cut Conroux off entirely. Joseph and Jourdan, acting on the hypothesis that their left was about to be turned, sent the majority of their available troops east by means of forced marches towards St-Jean-Pied-de-Port, leaving only Reille's units to face Graham near the estuary of the Bidasoa. Gazan remained with Maransin's division and Gruardet's brigade near the Puerto de Otxondo, with Villatte's division down in the valley behind him at Urdax (Urdazubi).

On the 7th, Wellington sent O'Callaghan's brigade to turn the French left and Cameron's brigade to seize the Altzola (a spur of the Alkurruntz) to their right, but Villatte's men reached it first, and they were able to hold it. Then, in the early afternoon, a dense sea mist blew inland to envelop the front: the 7th Division was unable to approach the area, where all action ground to a halt. At dawn the next morning, Gazan retreated, leaving Hill to occupy his positions.

---

* Dalhousie had remained behind to conduct the blockade of Pamplona.

That same evening, 'from the dressing of Lord Wellington's dinner', the chimney of the house in which he was quartered at Irurita took fire, and was only put out 'when the fire-bell had collected all the town buckets full of water, and a wet blanket had been pushed down', while Larpent described Wellington as standing hat-less in the rain giving directions, and with a silk handkerchief over his head. Too often, when it was not pouring with rain, the coastal ranges of the Pyrenees were subject to the *sirri-mirri*, a fine, saturating, Scotch mist, in which it was difficult to keep one's powder dry.

Wellington wanted to see for himself how Graham was progressing at San Sebastián. One worry was the fact that Graham had been complaining for some time about his deteriorating vision, and might have to return home. This would be a serious loss, for Graham would not be easy to replace, even if it had been hinted in some quarters that he was tiring and that he no longer displayed the same initiative and resolution as he had shown at Barrosa on 5 March 1811 (he was now almost 65 years of age).

On the 11th, leaving Hill in charge of the Baztan front, Wellington and his party rode west through Sanestéban to Zurbieta, from there ascending through the mountains via Goizueta to approach San Sebastián. It was a hazardous trek, during which two of General Murray's mules rolled into a river, and two of Dr McGrigor's slipped on the rocks and were killed. By the 18th—preceded by Wellington himself on the 14th—Headquarters had been established at Lesaka, over the hills some four miles south-west of Bera (Vera) in the Bidasoa valley.

The troops which Wellington had brought close to the frontier were distributed as follows. The Light Division was at Sanestéban; the 7th moved back south-east to Elizondo; Hill's two British brigades held the Otxondo Pass above Maya; and Ashworth's and Da Costa's Portuguese guarded the Col de Izpéguy (dominating the Aldudes valley and St-Etienne-de-Baïgorry) to the east, while keeping in touch with their compatriots under Archibald Campbell near the southern end of the Aldudes. The latter were in contact likewise with Byng's units, and with Morillo's Spaniards on the right wing beyond Roncesvalles. The 3rd, 4th and 6th Divisions were still in the vicinity of Pamplona, for O'Donnell's Spaniards did not start arriving until the 16th, although due to relieve them on the 12th.

Wellington considered it most unlikely that the French would be able to mount a counter-offensive for some time, although he may not have been fully aware that, although Gazan had retired, six and a half divisions had by now accumulated in France north of the Puerto de Otxondo. Nevertheless, on 25 July Wellington took the precaution of occupying the villages of Bera (with a bridge on an elbow of the lower Bidasoa) and Etxalar, to its south-east, by which he was able to shorten his line of indirect communication between his left wing on the coast and units further east in the Pyrenees. The 7th and Light Divisions, and some Spanish units from both Longa's and Girón's commands, would hold this central sector. Under pressure, General Lamartinière's division of Reille's army retired into the hills rising further north, leaving the Light Division in possession of Bera, while the 7th extended east towards Hill's units at Maya.

John Cooke, with the 43rd Regiment, describes the Light Division, after having cut down two or three fields of Indian corn and stored it up as provender for the animals, as being encamped on the stubble close to the Bidasoa, where during the night 'the rain descended in torrents. For two days, it continued to fall so heavily as to swamp the ground on which our tents were pitched. It was with the utmost exertion that we kept them upright, owing to the frequent gusts of wind tearing the pegs out of the liquid mud.' Several days later, when the weather improved, he 'was reclining on the parched and sunburnt turf at the tent door', a milch goat nibbling particles of hard biscuit out of his hand . . .

The Basque peasantry, among whom the army were to dwell during the next few months, dressed entirely differently from those of other provinces. They were frequently employed as guides, and paid a dollar a day, for they 'were well acquainted with every inch of ground or by-paths for leagues around their habitations. They knew the various fords across rivers and tributary streams', etc. The females, as portrayed by Cooke, possessed

> . . . very fair complexions and are extremely beautiful. . . . Their hair is combed back without any curls, and plaited into a long tail, which hangs down below the hips. Their jackets are of blue or brown cloth, and pinned exceedingly tight across the breast. . . . The woollen and only petticoat . . . is of a light or mixed colour, reaching to the middle of the calf. . . . They are remarkably nimble of foot, and always carry their little merchandise on the top of the head. They seldom wear shoes or stockings, except on Sundays and saints' days.
>
> The men go bare-necked and wear a blue cap or bonnet, similar to those worn in the highlands of Scotland, with bushy hair hanging in ringlets on their shoulders. They are gaunt, sinewy, and remarkably alive race of men, of sallow complexion. Their limbs are admirably proportioned, and they are as upright as a dart. With long and rapid strides, or at times breaking into a short run, they traverse the steep acclivities with their shoes and stockings frequently slung on a long pole, which they carry sloped over their shoulders, or grasped in the middle like a javelin. They use it to assist them in scaling or descending the crags, or frightful precipices. Their waistcoats are double-breasted, without a collar. The breeches are of brown cloth or velveteen, fitting tight over the hips, without braces, and reaching to the cap of the knee. . . . A red sash is twisted round the loins. In hot weather they usually carry the short blue or brown jacket slung over the left shoulder.

While Cooke and his colleagues may have been musing on what female company they might get to know better, storm-clouds were ominously gathering, for on the afternoon of 11 July, Marshal Soult's carriage had rattled into Bayonne.

Joseph Bonaparte had been forewarned of Soult's imminent arrival. It was humiliation enough, for there was no love lost between the two, but he chose not to resist his supersession, and thus there was no need for Soult to arrest him, as he had been given permission to do, if necessary. Soult had denounced Joseph to his brother eleven months previously, insinuating that the king had entered into treacherous negotiations with the Spanish government in Cádiz to relinquish the south of the country if they would let him retain the north.*

---

* This compromising letter had been sent to France by sea from Malaga rather than overland; the ship, to avoid capture by a British vessel, had sought safety in French-occupied port on the Mediterranean coast and the document handed to Suchet, who maliciously passed it on to Joseph himself. By 18 October it was being read by Napoleon in Moscow, delivered in person by Colonel François Desprez, with a covering note demanding Soult's dismissal. It had arrived at an inopportune

Thus, on the day after Soult's arrival at Bayonne, Joseph moved discreetly to a house in the neighbourhood, from which he escaped surveillance shortly after. Apprehended, he was confined at the Château de Poyanne (east of Dax) until a dispatch arrived from Napoleon, then at Dresden. This permitted him to retire to his estate at Mortefontaine on condition that he avoided all intrigue against him: should he be found doing so, or ever set foot in Paris, he would be imprisoned forthwith. Joseph was pardoned later, as was Marshal Jourdan, but neither need be mentioned again on these pages.

---

moment: the Emperor had more urgent problems to resolve; and Joseph was ordered to put up with Soult for the time being. In the event, Soult was recalled by Napoleon, but not until the following March, and certainly not in disgrace: the Emperor intended to employ him more advantageously in reconstituting the *Grande Armée*.

3

THE FIRST ASSAULT ON SAN SEBASTIÁN

ON 12 July—the day after Soult had entered Bayonne—Wellington had ridden over to San Sebastián. It was his first visit to that front, and it was soon evident to him that operations there were not going as well as he had hoped. This was partly because of its position on a narrow isthmus, strongly defended by walls and Vaubanesque outworks, which made it difficult to approach with ease. It was essential to take the fortress before carrying the war into France, as had been agreed in principle with Liverpool and Bathurst: he had undertaken to do this once the French had been driven from Spanish soil, if not in Catalonia, at least from the Basque provinces and Pamplona in Navarre.

San Sebastián crouched behind its formidable fortifications, dominated by a steeply rising, sea-girt rock, its bald summit surmounted by the fortress of La Mota. It stood between the tidal River Urumea and a sandy, land-locked bay, in which lay the small island of Santa Clara. South of the isthmus was the hill of Ayete, on which stood the Convent of San Bartolomé, fortified by the French. Some distance to the east, beyond an expanse of sand hills known as the Chofres, rose the ridge of Monte Ulia, extending as far as the narrow inlet of Pasajes (then usually referred to as 'Passages'), beyond which was another long ridge, that of Jaizkibel, which descended towards the frontier fortress of Fuenterrabia (now also Hondarribia), guarding the estuary of the Bidasoa; Pasajes would provide a very convenient port of supply for the Allied troops. To the west of the bay of San Sebastián rose Monte Igueldo, of slight importance during the ensuing siege.

On either side of the central bastion and horn-work projecting from the high curtain wall of the narrow land-front of San Sebastián were the demi-bastions of Santiago, dominating a small harbour, and of San Juan, overlooking the Urumea. On its west bank, here spanned by the remains of a bridge destroyed by the French, were some burnt-out houses (the suburb of Santa Catalina), which would provide some cover; another similar group of houses (those of San Martín) stood between the glacis of the central bastion and San Bartolomé.*

---

* While the distinctive physical feature of San Sebastián—Monte Urgull, with the citadel (the Castillo de la Mota) disfigured by a statue dominating the rebuilt old town, the *parte vieja* at its foot, and dividing the bay from the River Urumea—is still obvious, the urban sprawl that has developed over the decades is distinctly chastening. A path behind the church of Santa María, looking down the Calle Mayor, ascends the hill past the shamefully desecrated relics of the former English military cemetery. One of the better panoramic views may be obtained from the summit of Monte Ulia, rising to the east. As will be apparent when perusing the contemporary town plan, the Alameda (between the Puente

San Sebastián in 1813

Preparations for the siege were being conducted by Sir Richard Fletcher, on whom Wellington had long relied as Chief Engineer, and whose plan for placing guns facing north along the isthmus and on the sand hills to the east he approved. Major Charles Smith, the senior engineer with Graham's column, on first surveying the fortress, had suggested that the obvious side to attack would be exactly where Marshal Berwick had so successfully battered and breached the walls when besieging the place in 1719, which was also from the east bank of the river. Wellington had raised no objection on the 12th when discussing operations with Fletcher and Colonel Alexander Dickson, commanding the artillery. When the tide was high, the Urumea washed the foot of this eastern wall, but at low tide it was left exposed, and it could be reached by foot over shingle, rocks and mud flats.

It was essential to take the fortified convent of San Bartolomé first, for this would enable troops to advance along the isthmus to support this attack, even if the eastern wall, once breached, might also be approached without too much difficulty by troops wading across the river at low tide. On 28 June an unsuccessful attempt to storm the convent had been made by Mendizábal's Spaniards, and a few days later their camp was surprised when two columns sallied out from the fortress and a number of prisoners were taken. Graham, visiting the Spanish lines on the 6th, was so astonished by their lack of any proper idea of how to defend themselves that he replaced them the following day by the 5th Division and Bradford's Portuguese brigade. Mendizábal's men trooped off to join the perfunctory blockade of Santoña, along the coast towards Santander. Bradford's units established themselves on the Chofres, where they started digging parallels, while the 5th Division, temporarily commanded by General John Oswald,† faced the Ayete hill and convent of San Bartolomé.

In response to Wellington's appeal to the Admiralty, Captain Sir George Collier, with the frigate *Surveillante*, a corvette and two brigs, supplemented by local pinnaces and fishing boats manned by Girón's Galicians, attempted—but without much success—to stop the garrison receiving supplies and reinforcements from St-Jean-de-Luz. Eluding their vigilance, small vessels continued to run the blockade at night, bringing in additional gunners and later evacuating the wounded. Lord Melville at the Admiralty, when taxed by Wellington for not providing him with sufficient support, replied with a feeble broadside of excuses, among them that the Biscay coast was notoriously one 'where ships

---

del Kursaal and the *Ayuntamiento*) was laid out on the site of the former curtain wall, although the horn-work extended south, on the apex of which rises the *Diputación*. The position of the main breach was approximately where stands the market-place—the Mercado de la Brecha—at the junction of the Alameda and the Calle San Juan, which extends north and just west of where rose the main defensive wall, formerly lapped by the Urumea, to gardens fronting the Museo de San Telmo (a former convent). Above and just north of the latter are the remains of the Mirador battery, commanding the site of the minor breach. The Chofres sand hills, on which the modern Kursaal rises, are largely built over, as are both sides of the now embanked river further south. This is spanned by the Puente de Santa Catalina, on the emplacement of the former ruined bridge, to reach the Avenida de la Libertad, passing over the site of the former suburb of that name, while that of San Martín is recorded by the Calle San Martín, further south. The convent of San Bartolomé stood on the hill rising not far west of the 19th century cathedral of El Buen Pastor.

† General Sir James Leith, who had been wounded at Salamanca, had not yet returned to the front, although expected.

cannot anchor without extreme risk', at the same time remarking on the impropriety of Wellington having made complaints to Collier behind his back about naval incompetence, which were 'injurious to the public interest', etc. In reply, while resenting the offensive tone of Melville's dispatch, Wellington merely made the sardonic comment that 'If the navy of Great Britain cannot afford more than one frigate and a few brigs and cutters . . . to co-operate in the siege of a maritime place, I must be satisfied, and do the best I can without its assistance.'* At least, a naval convoy had been able to transport the battering train and stores accumulating at Corunna to Santander, off which they hove-to on 29 June. This coincided with the arrival there of Major Augustus Frazer, who, having ridden across country from Vitoria, had orders for it to sail on to Deba, closer to San Sebastián. At the same time, every little harbour along the coast was swept of any vessels likely to be of use. Another dispatch ordered the guns and *matériel* being landed at Deba to be re-embarked and sent further east to Pasajes, which was far more convenient. By 6 July Frazer had reached the front at Hernani, where Graham was determining what might be the most effective method of reducing San Sebastián without undue delay. Frazer was 'convinced of the necessity of an immediate attack on the convent', although some of his seniors differed in their opinion. However, Colonel Dickson, who was expected hourly, was 'a sure card for decision'.

Transports anchored in the creek of Pasajes on 7 July, and working parties were detailed to unload the ordnance, ammunition and stores. However, the parties were inadequately supplemented with sixty only of Collier's sailors. Graham had to rely on harbour boats rowed by brawny local women to help them. On 16 July, Frazer was at his

> . . . wit's end, or nearly so, with the ladies here: . . . they do every thing . . . row, unload vessels, bring shot on shore, yet I have been a week begging, praying, and urging in vain, that they should receive rations, and some remuneration. Lord Wellington has ordered it, and a commissary is said to be coming, but he does not come, and I have to make all manner of excuses to them.

On the previous day Frazer had reported that General William Spry's brigade had been placed at his disposal and was 'amusing itself with dragging [six] 24-pounders up a slippery mountain [Ulia]', and that howitzers had been positioned 'to take the advanced redoubt of the enemy near the convent in reverse.' A previous bombardment by 8-pounders had made little impression, but the howitzers had been effective, and the convent, successfully stormed on a second attempt, was evacuated by the enemy on the 17th, by then having received '2,500 18-pounder shot (most of them red hot) and 450 shells' (after which a thousand of the shot were recovered from its smoking ruins). Allied casualties in clearing the loopholed convent and barricaded houses amounted to 207: those of the French, who had put up a spirited resistance, were 240. Two batteries were now moved on to the isthmus to enfilade the sea wall facing the Chofres.

By this time Graham had 40 pieces of artillery with him: specifically twenty 24-pounders, six 18-pounders, four 68-pound carronades, six 8-inch howitzers and four 10-

---

* By mid-September, when Admiral Byam Martin disembarked to pour oil on the troubled waters, Collier's flotilla had been increased to three frigates, and fifteen sloops and brigs.

inch mortars. In addition to the 28 guns landed at Pasajes, six had been lent by Collier from the main deck of the *Surveillant*, while another six pieces from the heavy battery which had followed the army from distant Ciudad Rodrigo had also belatedly arrived.

Torrential rain during the night of the 20th/21st delayed the digging of parallels on the isthmus, when only about one-third of their length had been completed. Near a redoubt on the western side, the entrance to a large drain—in fact, the aqueduct supplying the town with fresh water—was discovered. It was dry, as Spanish troops had already cut off the source. Lieutenant Reid of the Engineers volunteered to crawl along it. After 230 yards he found it blocked at a point he estimated would be below the counterscarp of the hornwork. Here was a ready-made site for a mine. Sandbags were piled at its far end, then thirty barrels of powder and more sandbags, and a train was laid to the mouth of the channel. When exploded, this should bring down the counterscarp and the débris would fill the ditch, across which the horn-work might be stormed: it would be worth putting to the test.

At dawn on the 20th, by which time 32 guns were in position to the east of the fortress and eight to the south, Allied batteries opened fire: by midday on the 22nd (the anniversary of the Battle of Salamanca) a breach 100 ft long had been made in the curtain wall, assumed to be practical, for it had been entirely levelled. Counter-fire had been accurate: by evening only six of the eleven guns on the Chofres were firing, one having been split by a ball striking its muzzle. Frazer was now ordered to turn his guns obliquely on to another piece of wall, further to the right (north). This stretch, if carried, would turn the flank of those defending the main breach, but it was more difficult to approach as there was less space exposed at low tide between the foot of the wall and the river, and those attacking it would have to skirt the wall for a distance of some 300 yards. Meanwhile, the interior of the horn-work and main bastion, together with several streets, had been severely damaged also, largely by the high-trajectory fire from the distant batteries on Monte Ulia.

Jones, in his *Journals of Sieges*, states that, on the 22nd, the fire had been notably vigorous: 'expenditure from the breaching battery alone amounted to 3500 rounds; . . . which, for ten guns in action, averaged 350 rounds a gun, expended in 15½ hours of daylight. Such a rate of firing probably was never equalled at any siege, great accuracy of range being at the same time observed.'

By the 23rd the parallels excavated in the Chofres, approaching the river bank from the east, were ready. But, as Frazer reported, it might take another two days to make a second breach. Meanwhile the first would have been entrenched by the French, and he would have 'to begin again the work of destruction'. He was correct in his assumption that Rey would not waste those two days, during which his troops were busily preparing additional defences behind the main breach, for the wall had fallen outwards here, leaving a 15–20-foot drop from the rampart wall facing the street, to reach which would require ladders. Houses, already damaged, which had their backs to the wall were demolished, as were any steps or stairs providing access to it. The backs of any surviving buildings facing the breach were loopholed, and stone barricades were constructed in the intervening alleys. The rampart-walk on each side of the main breach was blocked, so that any troops getting that far would be forced to advance parallel to the eastern flank of the horn-work, lined by picked marksmen, who had live shells to hand which they could roll down on to the adjacent strand and on to the massed units detailed to make the assault.

By the evening of the 23rd most of the visible enemy guns had been silenced, and arrangements were made to storm the breaches the next morning. However, enfilading fire from the battery on the isthmus had set alight several houses in streets near the main breach, and at dawn the following day these were still blazing fiercely, making it impossible to enter the town. Graham therefore countermanded his orders: they would have to delay the assault for several hours. It was not until late on the 24th that the French could move in to reoccupy the smouldering ruins, after which Rey calmly awaited the inevitable storm, having already refused a premature summons to surrender. During the night his few remaining guns, which had been withdrawn and kept under cover, were placed in positions from which they were trained on the main breach.

The assault was timed for 5.00 in the morning of 25 July, although daybreak was at not until about 5.20, while the extreme of low tide was at 6.00. It was agreed that the signal for the advance from the parallels would be the blowing up of the mine in the culvert, mentioned above. Portuguese units waiting in the trenches were ready to make a dash at the west flank of the horn-work, while the head of the right-hand column, composed of the 3/1st, a ladder party from regiments of Hay's brigade and the 1/38th, was to pass between the leading units and run the gauntlet along the exposed river bank towards the lesser breach. The 1/9th brought up the rear in support of whichever units would most need it, while the 8th *Caçadores*, in sheltered positions scraped in the sand just in advance of the parallels during the night, were to fire on the enemy defending the eastern flank of the horn-work.

In the event, immediately after the explosion of the mine (apparently before 5.00), the Portuguese, although able to cross the covered way and into the ditch, failed to get any further and withdrew after suffering several casualties. This was due largely to the fact that no proper preparation had been made to take full advantage of the damage to the fortifications likely to occur, for, apart from causing considerable alarm among the defenders here, the explosion blew down the west flank of the counterscarp and filled the ditch with earth. At the same time, it was found that the opening made in the parallel to the east was too narrow for more than a few at a time to clamber out abreast. The troops soon found themselves not crossing a sandy strand as expected, but slithering on seaweed-covered rocks and stumbling into pools as they made for the main breach in the darkness. Lieutenant Harry Jones of the Engineers and Major Thomas Fraser (commanding a wing of the 3/1st), on reaching the lip of the breach, found themselves faced with a 20-foot drop on the far side, while brisk musketry fire converged on them from the barricaded rampart-walk and the loopholed walls of the ruins. Grape-shot from the guns flanking the breach, placed in these positions only hours earlier, ploughed into them, Both officers were wounded—Fraser mortally—as was every man reaching the summit. Any of them still able to fire back threw themselves down wherever there was any protection, but the impetus of the assault was lost. The survivors crawled back down the slope of the breach, left strewn with dead and wounded.

A number of the Royal Scots, led by Lieutenant Colin Campbell (1/9th), on reaching the opening of the ditch between the horn-work and the front of the demi-bastion behind it, had turned into it in the dark and were met by enemy fire from an entrenchment which had been thrown up between the two. The tail of the column now found its way blocked by this accumulation of troops, on to which shells were being rolled down. Several attempts were made by their officers to rally and lead back the storming parties towards the breach, but they were never able to form a sufficiently compact body, and each time they reached the crest they were shot down. Such carnage could not be allowed to continue, and the senior captain surviving gave the order to retire. The mass of men nearer the demi-bastion, which had also suffered heavily, likewise gave way, pressing back on the 1/38th: so slow had been the process of emerging from the trenches, that they had only just come up. Colonel Greville halted them briefly, but within minutes the whole was one confused mass falling back along the slippery river bank, straddled with both canister and musketry. Several men of the 1/9th, still filing out of the parallel, although ordered back, were among the numerous casualties of the costly failure. A flag of truce was hoisted, and for an hour all firing ceased while the French chivalrously removed the wounded from the foot of the breach and adjacent strand, where otherwise many would have been drowned by the rising tide.

General Oswald was later blamed for positioning the storming units too far from the breaches, to approach which they were obliged to defile past the still intact and well-garrisoned horn-work, which should have been made untenable beforehand. In the circumstances, it was virtually impossible for the troops to have broken into the town: the whole undertaking had been badly managed, largely because it had been carried out in far too much of a hurry, although there might have been a chance of success had the attack taken place in broad daylight.

Allied casualties of all ranks amounted to 571, of whom 330 were among the 3/1st, while six officers and 118 other ranks, mostly wounded, were taken prisoner. French losses were eighteen killed and 49 wounded. Among the prisoners, and one who left an account of his experiences, was Harry Jones, who recorded that some of the French had behaved despicably. When wounded and lying helpless, a soldier next to him had exclaimed 'Oh, they are murdering us all!' On looking up, Jones

> . . . perceived a number of French grenadiers, under a heavy fire of grape, sword in hand, stepping over the dead, and stabbing the wounded; my companion was treated in the same manner: the sword withdrawn from his body, and reeking with blood, was raised to give me the *coup de grâce*, when fortunately the uplifted arm was arrested by a smart little man, a serjeant, who cried out, 'Oh mon Colonel, êtes-vous blessé!' (the serjeant must have mistaken my rank, from seeing a large gold bullion epaulette on my right shoulder, and the blue uniform, rendering it more conspicuous) and immediately ordered some of his men to remove me into the town.

Jones later confirmed that, as far as the practicability of the breach was concerned, he was 'carried up to the terreplein of the rampart by four French grenadiers without the slight-est difficulty.'

Wellington had remained at his headquarters at Lesaka on the 24th. He was pre-occupied with intelligence being received concerning enemy troop movements, but be-fore he could make any counter-dispositions it was essential to know the result of the siege. Dispatches were sent to Graham during the morning, confirming that Wellington was aware that Soult had been moving troops away from the coast, but this was probably 'only because he entertained serious designs to draw away out attention from the side of Irun, and then to attempt to pass the river.' Girón was warned likewise by a dispatch sent at 11.00, with the additional comment that, as the guns at San Sebastián could no longer be heard, he was 'hoping that its business has been settled', not then being aware that the conflagration had caused Graham postpone the storm and that he had ordered the firing to cease to save ammunition for that event.

Larpent had observed that on the 24th Wellington had been

> . . . very figetty [sic] . . . when I went to him about two poor fellows who are to be hung [sic] for robbing Lord Aylmer's tent; and today he came out to the churchyard [the terrace of San Martín], where we were listening, about eight o'clock, to judge from the noise of the guns whether our batteries had ceased, and what the firing was. He was been once over [to San Sebastián] himself, but appeared to wish to leave it to Graham, and not directly to interfere. At eleven this morning, however, Colonel [de] Burgh came over with an account of our attempt having failed. . . . Lord Wellington has ordered his horse, and is going over immediately.

In fact, as on the previous day, the rumble of distant gunfire had unaccountably ceased after a short time, on this occasion at 6.00, while the wounded were being recovered.

In a letter dated the 26th, Frazer confirmed that Wellington, in making this flying visit, had reached San Sebastián at about noon the previous day to inspect the scene of the disaster, and remained until 4.00 that afternoon. Either Larpent or Frazer must be wrong, for if Wellington rode off soon after 11.00 he could not possibly have reached San Sebastián only one hour later: as the crow flies, the distance between it and Lesaka was about fifteen miles (24km), and across very hilly country.

Orders were given that the siege must continue, even if it took time before another storming took place. It was essential to batter down the horn-work and San Juan bastion first. More guns and ammunition—the latter already running short—were due, together with reinforcements.

While returning to Headquarters, reached at about 8.00 that evening, Wellington was met by an officer sent by Q.M.G. George Murray to report that heavy gunfire had been audible throughout the afternoon from the direction of the Puerto de Otxondo, above Maya, although no explanatory dispatch had yet been received either from Gen-eral Sir William Stewart, stationed at Maya, or from Hill, in charge of the defence of the Baztan. An hour later a messenger from Lowry Cole galloped into Lesaka to report that he had been attacked in strength at 1.00 at the Pass of Roncesvalles, but that his line still held.

At 6.00 Murray had received intelligence from Dalhousie that, although fighting was taking place at Maya, D'Erlon may have been repulsed. This was inaccurate. However, as a precaution, Murray had already directed Dalhousie to mass the 7th Division at Etxalar and had advised Alten, at Bera, to have the Light Division in readiness to march at dawn if necessary. It was not until 10.00 at night that a verbal message eventually arrived from Stewart, who had been engaged with the enemy since 11.00 that morning that he had been forced to retire from the Puerto de Otxondo but would try to hold a position further south in the Baztan valley.* Wellington was still in ignorance of Cole's predicament.

Late as it was, Wellington did not delay for a moment in dispatching his aides with provisional orders, choosing not to wait for further messages to come in. O'Donnell, blockading Pamplona, was directed to send one of his two divisions to join Picton and Cole and to replace it with Carlos de España's division, due to arrive on the 26th. He also directed O'Donnell to instruct Mina to move his men north-west from Zaragoza forthwith; at the same time, he was informed that the British heavy cavalry, cantoned in the neighbourhood of Olite, had been ordered to ride north without delay to a position immediately north of Pamplona.

Graham was advised that, although this movement by Soult might still be a feint, should that not be so and the relief of San Sebastián be his intention, he—Graham—had better re-embark his artillery at Pasajes immediately, with the exception of two guns from the breaching battery and two howitzers, which were to maintain a desultory fire against the fortress. The blockade must be continued, even if with a minimum of his units; the remainder were to concentrate along the south bank of the Bidasoa to await events.

Although the heavy guns were dragged away during the following night, Rey was not so easily deceived. He had already observed that batteries were being disarmed during the 26th, and had noticed unexplained troop movements. That night, partly to satisfy himself what the Allies were up to, he sent five companies on a sortie from the horn-work. Taking by surprise a detachment of Spry's Portuguese brigade guarding the parallels, they swept along them, taking prisoner three officers and 108 men. For the Allies, it was a mortifying incident which further compounded the last few days' reverses.

---

* The message was confirmed by Hill in a dispatch reaching Wellington at 4.00 the next morning (26th).

4

THE BATTLE OF THE PYRENEES: MAYA

WE must now follow developments taking place behind Wellington's back during the previous fortnight. He had been kept regularly informed of Soult's activities and was well aware that troops were accumulating at St-Jean-Pied-de-Port, and that additional units were marching towards it. Soult was being informed likewise of events at San Sebastián, which was likely to fall unless relieved. Pamplona, although blockaded, was neither hard-pressed nor in any immediate danger, and should be able to hold out for some time yet. Therefore, although Soult might be moving troops away from the most obvious crossing-points along the lower reaches of the Bidasoa, this could well be no more than an attempt to mislead Wellington, already alerted to the fact that Villatte was constructing pontoons or flying bridges at Urugne, no distance north of the river. However, should Soult's real intention be to penetrate the Pyrenees far inland, on 23 July Wellington had taken the precaution of instructing Cole at Roncesvalles to support Byng in the defence of the passes as effectually as he could,

> . . . without committing his troops and the 4th Division against a force so superior that the advantage of the ground would not compensate it. You will be good enough to make arrangements further back also, for stopping the enemy's progress towards Pampeluna [sic], in the event of your being compelled to give up the passes which General Byng now occupies. . . . A sure communication should exist with General Sir Thomas Picton, and Sir Thomas should be apprised of any movement of troops, either by the Roncesvalles road, or upon that of Eugui and the Alduides, in order that he may make arrangements as circumstances may dictate for giving support, should such events occur. . . . It is desirable that you should transmit a daily report for the present to Head Quarters.

On the following day, Murray sent more specific orders to Cole:

> Lord Wellington has desired that I should express still more strongly how essential he considers it that the passes in front of Roncesvalles should be maintained to the utmost. And I am to direct you to be so good as to make every necessary arrangement for repelling any direct attack that the enemy may make in that quarter. . . . Lord Wellington attaches very little importance to any wider turning movement which the enemy might make upon our right. The difficulties and delays of any wider movement are considerable obstacles, and would retard him sufficiently to give time to make other arrangements to stop his progress.

On arrival at Bayonne in the afternoon of 11 July, Soult did not waste a moment putting Napoleon's commands into effect, invested as he now was with full powers to reorganise and revitalise the recently defeated and disoriented French armies and to take the offensive within as short a period of time as possible. What is extraordinary, considering the demoralised state in which the majority of the French troops had staggered back over the Pyrenees, was that Soult was able to do this within less than a fortnight of reaching his base of operations.

On the 15th, having just received more specific instructions from the Emperor at Dresden, Soult issued his orders. The former armies of the North, the South and the Centre, and of Portugal, would forthwith cease to exist: together, they would now form a cohesive whole, to be known as the 'Army of Spain' (Suchet's troops in Catalonia remained entirely independent). Under Soult's Chief-of-Staff, General Gazan (who had served with him in that capacity previously), the army would be divided into three main groups or 'Lieutenancies' of the Right, Left and Centre, rather than 'corps' (a term now prohibited by Napoleon, even if they remained so in all but name), even if—as would inevitably be the case—their positions on a front would not necessarily remain in that order.

To command these 'corps',* Soult named Reille, D'Erlon and Clausel respectively: in addition, was a large General Reserve under Villatte. Each 'corps' was composed of three divisions. Reille's contained the 1st (Foy), 7th (Maucune) and 9th (Lamartinière), with 17,235 men present; D'Erlon's comprised the 2nd (Darmagnac), 3rd (Abbé) and 6th (Maransin), with 20,957 men; and Clausel commanded the 4th (Conroux), 5th (van der Maessen) and 8th (Taupin), together numbering 17,218. Thus there were 55,410 men in all.

With Villatte were several units from former divisions and garrisons, including the old Bayonne Reserve—seventeen battalions in all, amounting to 9,102 men. In addition he had at his disposal 6,602 foreign troops (Germans, Italians and Spaniards; not entirely to be relied on), together with 1,550 *Gendarmes* and National Guards, making another 8,152 and hence 17,254 in all. Thus Soult's available infantry totalled 72,664 men; but see below. It may be remarked that very many of Joseph's senior officers, after the retreat to and the débâcle at Vitoria, and having made the best of their way through the Pyrenees to Bayonne, had applied for service in the 'Army of Germany', but in almost all cases this had been refused.

Soult had two cavalry divisions to hand, one commanded by his brother Pierre and the other by Anne-François Treillard (3,981 and 2,358 men, respectively), while another 808 acted with the field army, which was sufficient for scouting purposes. Amounting to 7,147, together with the infantry, they brought the total number of his 'bayonets and sabres' to 79,811. The artillery, together with sappers and miners, numbered another 4,000 men.

Napoleon had intended that each infantry division be supported by two field batteries, and each cavalry division by one of horse artillery. He advised Soult to create a reserve of two horse artillery batteries together with batteries of guns of position. In the event, Soult was unable to follow these instructions to the letter: only one battery apiece could be supplied to each division, leaving a reserve of two batteries of horse and two of field

* These units will continued to be referred to as 'corps' in these pages, to avoid possible confusion.

artillery. All 140 guns were horsed—72 with his infantry divisions, 32 with Villatte, twelve with the cavalry and 24 in reserve. In addition, there were three mountain batteries of 2- or 3-pounders, which were carried on mule-back. Soult was responsible also for over 4,500 non-combatants—transport train, ambulance services, etc.—apart from 2,110 detached troops and 5,595 half-trained conscripts of the Bayonne Reserve. At the same time, he was encumbered by 16,184 sick and wounded, all of whom had to be fed. These figures do not include the garrisons of San Sebastián, Pamplona and Santoña, nor General Paris's units, isolated at Jaca, which were under his overall command.*

Soult, by playing very astutely on the sense of honour of these Peninsula veterans, and harping on the bad generalship of his predecessor—the gross incapacity of Joseph and Jourdan (how much must he have enjoyed this opportunity of taking a swipe at them!)—was able to impress upon his troops that under his experienced leadership the disaster of the recent campaign would be blotted from their memories and that very shortly they would be advancing triumphantly again: the 'motley levies' of Wellington could not possibly resist them. Whether or not he felt as confident himself, he was able enough to instil some optimism among his dejected subordinates: to Clarke, impatiently awaiting news in Paris, he reported that, with the distribution of regular rations, marauding had ceased, discipline was restored and that he was entirely satisfied by his army's state of morale.

The Commissariat had done wonders finding food for everyone while in the neighbourhood of Bayonne; but, having lost virtually all its wheeled transport on the recent retreat, together with very many of its beasts of burden, the army faced a grave problem when it came to providing for and keeping up with any advance into the Pyrenees which might be in Soult's mind, especially an advance into the deserted foothills on the far side of that deep range. Soult scanned—doubtless superciliously—Jourdan's 'memoranda' of three alternative operations formulated prior to his dismissal, which had been passed on to him for what they were worth and might possibly have turned the tide. With his latest maps (none of them too reliable) laid out before him (he had scant personal knowledge of the intervening ranges), Soult decided that the most viable operation would be the immediate relief of Pamplona. As late as 23 July Soult was still under the impression that there were only three British divisions blockading that fortress: it should not be too difficult to destroy them.

The lack of proper transport could not be remedied to any great extent, even if all possible vehicles in the vicinity of Bayonne were to be commandeered. There was also the question of how to provide enough ammunition for both the infantry and artillery, should the campaign last more than a few days. If a thrust could be made rapidly enough, and if wet or misty weather did not prevent the arrival at the front of as many successive convoys

---

* It may be remarked here that in his *History*, vol. 6, p. 768, Oman mentions that Soult had stated that his field army numbered 69,543 only, including the Reserve. It is possible that Soult was referring to his three infantry corps only, plus the National Guards and *Gendarmes*, and foreign troops *less* Casapalacio's unreliable Spanish brigade, but *not* including the bulk of Villatte's reserves, for, together with the cavalry, they amount to virtually that figure.

as possible, all well and good. However, if progress were slow, or if ammunition were expended in indecisive actions, then the army would be at serious risk. Soult calculated that, by supplying his columns with four days' rations, he would have every chance of traversing the mountains and, within five days of setting off, would defeat Wellington decisively: it was a risk he felt justified in taking.

The plan of campaign was simple: D'Erlon would lead his 'corps' of 20,000 men up from Ainhoa and Urdax to force the Puerto de Otxondo, descend the Baztan valley, cross the Puerto de Velate and proceed down the valleys of the Lanz and Ulzama directly to Pamplona. In doing this, D'Erlon would also defend the main thrust against any flank attack. This would be made simultaneously further east across the Roncesvalles Pass (the Puerto de Ibañeta) by Reille's and Clausel's 'corps' combined—together 35,000 bayonets—which Soult would lead in person from St-Jean-Pied-de-Port to converge on Pamplona from the north-east. Villatte's reserves would remain on the coastal front, in a sufficiently strong posture of offence to convince Wellington that it was San Sebastián which was his objective. Once he had received intelligence that D'Erlon was well south in the Baztan and threatening Wellington's flank, then he might confidently cross the Bidasoa. Graham would be obliged to raise the siege if Wellington's centre in the Baztan were broken and pushed west. Alternatively, Wellington might be forced to make the wider detour over the Donamaria passes, west of the Puerto de Velate, before being able to deploy enough troops between the French and Pamplona—by which time it would be too late.

Soult had made several miscalculations regarding the positions of the Allied units. He had assumed that there was only possibly one division, that of 'General Bird' [sic] near Roncesvalles, together with Archibald Campbell's Portuguese brigade in the Aldudes valley, and only Stewart's division and Silveira's Portuguese unit holding the passes of Izpegui (Ispéguy), between the Aldudes and the Baztan, and Otxondo, above Maya (Amaiur) and further to the north-west. He was unaware that Pack (provisionally commanding Henry Clinton's 6th Division) was in reserve at Sanestéban; that Cole's 4th Division was not far down the Pamplona road from Roncesvalles while Morillo's Spaniards were up in line with Byng; or that Picton's 3rd Division was at Olague (Anue), not far south of the Puerto de Velate. Soult reported to Clarke in Paris that, having examined the whole Allied line, he had come to the conclusion that their right wing was their weak point, and it was precisely here that he would attack by a flank movement which, as he thrust southwest to relieve Pamplona, would have the effect of threatening their rear.

On 19 July Clausel's 'corps' was cantoned in the neighbourhood of the small frontier fortress of St-Jean-Pied-de-Port, and only a long march from the pass at Roncesvalles; D'Erlon's troops waited between Espelette and Urdax; and Reille's units were still lining the lower Bidasoa. The last had to be moved unobtrusively towards St-Jean-Pied-de-Port to cooperate with Clausel in making the main thrust. East of Cambo was a good road they could enter, which, via Helette, led directly to St-Jean. With good reason, Oman wondered why it was that Soult did not get Reille's men to replace D'Erlon's in making the advance towards Maya and order D'Erlon's to join up with Clausel's, which would save him two-thirds of a long march. Those who had personal knowledge of the condition of the roads in the area had advised Soult that, if he wanted to carry out this movement, Reille should follow the longer though better route via Bayonne, but this was ignored, although in fact Lamartinière's 9th Division (together with some guns) was obliged to make this detour, as the bridge over the Nive at Cambo had been carried away by the river in spate after torrential rain on the 20th.

Reille's outposts had been replaced by four brigades of Villatte's reserve during the previous night, and his three divisions, concentrated near St-Jean-de-Luz, trudged east towards Cambo along by-roads churned into quagmires, but the majority were able to cross the bridge before it broke. Nevertheless, the weather was causing enough delay: Reille's vanguard did not reach its destination until the night of the 22nd, although Soult had been awaiting it since the 21st, and the 9th Division did not come up until the 24th. His great stroke through the Roncesvalles gap could now be put into operation, with 34,000 men (followed by two cavalry divisions) making the slow ascent, ready to fall on the Allies first thing the next morning.

D'Erlon had received his orders on the 23rd: 'to make his dispositions on the 24th to attack the enemy at dawn on the 25th, to make himself master of the Puerto of Maya [Otxondo], and to pursue the enemy when he shall begin his retreat . . .' Soult presumed that Allied units between there and Roncesvalles would withdraw the moment they were aware of the latter thrust, which was the time for D'Erlon to push south to Elizondo and the Puerto de Velate; or, if they veered further east in their retreat, to follow them over the Col de Berdaritz and Collado de Urquiaga (Urkiaga). D'Erlon was to get into communication with Reille, but at the same time 'he must send strong detachments in pursuit of any hostile columns that may try to get off to their left [i.e. westwards], to discover their routes, worry them, and pick up prisoners.' In the event—as will be described in the next chapter—D'Erlon did not hear of the pass at Roncesvalles falling to Soult, nor did the Allies retire as it was assumed they would, and thus, in the words of Oman, he found himself 'let in for one of the bloodiest battles on a small scale that were fought during the whole war.'

Hill was in charge of the sector from the Maya Pass as far south-east as the head of the Aldudes valley, with the 2nd Division (less John Byng's brigade, which had been detached to Roncesvalles) and Silveira's Portuguese. To his left was William Stewart, with the brigades of John Cameron, William Pringle and Charles Ashworth. Pringle knew neither his troops nor the ground, having only just arrived from England to take over from Robert O'Callaghan, and Ashworth was at Erazu, a hamlet no distance south-east of the village of Maya, defending the Puerto de Izpegui (Col d'Ispéguy) leading into the Val de Baïgorry. Silveira was with Hippolito Da Costa's Brigade, holding the line south towards the Col de Berdaritz among other minor passes: this was extended by Archibald Campbell's brigade near the head of the Aldudes valley and already in close touch with Ross's units near the Lindus and Puerto de Ibañeta at Roncesvalles. Some distance to the west of the left flank of the 2nd Division, on the Puerto de Otxondo above Maya and near Orizqui and

Etxalar, was Lord Dalhousie's 7th Division, north-west of which, at Bera (Vera) in the Bidasoa valley, was Charles Alten's Light Division.

The first distant sounds of action were heard very early in the morning of 25 July, when a detachment of National Guards, which had been ordered by Soult to distract the attention of Archibald Campbell's brigade in the Aldudes or Val de Baïgorry by assembling on a wooded mountain called Hauzey (Hausa), not far north of the Lindus and opposite the Portuguese camp, and light fires as if bivouacking in force. This incited Campbell to lead his men towards them, and drive them precipitately down the valley. It was a very minor action, but the noise of firing had the unfortunate consequence of drawing Hill's attention in that direction. He rode south-east from his base at Elizondo to investigate, and it was while he was there, at the extreme southern end of his sector, that D'Erlon's columns were converging on the Puerto de Otxondo, the real point of danger. This was coincidental, not a deliberate ploy on D'Erlon's part to distract Hill. William Stewart, well aware that D'Erlon's troops were not far distant—Abbé's camp near Ainhoa was visible from the pass, and his advance units were at Urdax, only about four miles as the crow flies below his position—instead of supervising the redeployment of his own inadequately dispersed units at Maya, officiously rode over to join Hill (together, as Surgeon Walter Henry has reported,with all his aides and leaving Henry as the only commissioned officer at his headquarters). For this there was no excuse.

In Stewart's absence, command of the 2nd Division fell on Pringle, only a brigadier and with no authority to make new dispositions, for his commanding officer was still technically present, even if he had neglected to advise Pringle of his whereabouts. Pringle—described by William Gomm, one of his former staff officers, as 'a man who is liked by all the world in private life, and respected by no man in public'—was left to make the best of the situation in which he now found himself.

The area to be defended may be best described as a broad, grassy saddle between the peak of Alcurrunz (934m) and that of Anchastegui or Aretesque (804m), also referred to as the Pic du Gorospil. The main road from Urdax curves up towards the middle of the saddle and then bears west for about a mile to reach the watershed, where it turns south to descend into the Baztan valley. South of the saddle rose a wooded height known as the Goizamendi (677m).

Across this saddle, from east to west, ran a track at that time known as the 'Gorospil Path', which led up from near Espelette, crossed the frontier at the Gorospil and, after skirting the Anchastegui, briefly joined the main road before branching off to the right at the crest. It then passed north of the Alcurrunz and wound in a south-westerly direction over the hills before descending to the Bidasoa valley not far east of Sanestéban. From a point west of the Alcurrunz, a path diverged from it towards Etxalar. Much work was done to put this lateral communication in a better state of repair during the ensuing weeks, and it has been known ever since as the Chemin des Anglais.

Cameron's brigade (1/50th, 1/71st and 1/92nd, the Gordon Highlanders) was encamped by battalions just behind the crest and on each side of the main road, which could be swept by the four guns of Major Da Cunha's battery, mounted on an adjacent knoll. The eastern sector of the saddle had been inadequately protected, with only a picquet of 80 men of the 34th from Pringle's brigade guarding a point where the Chemin des Anglais reached the watershed, and from where a path led steeply down to the village of Maya (two and a half miles to the south, but entailing an hour's stiff climb), where the rest of the brigade were camped, with the exception of four light companies placed on the rear slope of the main ridge as a support for the picquet.

The Maya position contained a certain amount of dead ground, noticeably to the north-east, where intervening ridges and valleys obstructed any clear view, but Stewart had neglected to reconnoitre regularly, and certainly no Portuguese vedettes had been sent out at dawn on the 25th to investigate beyond a low hill directly in front of the picquets. If they had done so, they would have noticed the van of D'Erlon's column and Darmagnac's division from Espelette snaking up the track, followed by Abbé's division from Ainhoa. No sign was seen of Maransin's division, which, unobtrusively advancing up the main road from Urdax, had been ordered to keep massed but under cover until the main body had occupied the eastern end of the saddle, by which time Cameron's brigades would be moving towards them: Maransin could then make a surprise attack on Cameron's flank.

Although at about 10.00 an outpost of the 71st had noticed distant movements far down in the valley towards Urdax, these and other troops fleetingly seen beyond Ainhoa did not appear to present any obvious threat. Nevertheless, when his picquet reported back, Pringle took the precaution of sending up the light companies to support them, so it was by chance that 400 men rather than 80 were suddenly confronted by 7,000 French. Among them was Captain Joseph Moyle Sherer, who soon found himself heavily engaged, for by 10.30 D'Erlon had reached a point little over half a mile from the most advanced British sentry. Eight light companies were collected together and their knapsacks stacked, and 700 were sent ahead as a swarm of *tirailleurs* to surprise the detachment, which they did. The 16th Léger followed them in column, while the skirmishers divided to outflank the position. Sherer described the enemy's numbers as increasing 'every moment; they covered the country immediately in front of us, and around us. The sinuosities of the mountains, the ravines, the water-courses, were filled with their advancing and overwhelming force.'

Realising their predicament, Major Joseph Bradbey of the 28th ordered his units to group themselves around the upper slope of the Gorospil knoll, surmounted by rocky outcrops, where they were able to hold their own for some 40 minutes, repulsing several attacks and inflicting heavy casualties. By then they were surrounded, with Darmagnac's eight battalions fanning out on the saddle behind them. Six unwounded officers (among them Sherer) and 140 men were taken prisoner; the other 260 were almost all killed or wounded. Sherer records that he was conducted to D'Erlon, 'who was on horseback, on a commanding height near, surrounded by a large group of staff officers', but on being introduced to him as an English captain, the general

. . . took off his hat instantly, and spoke to me in a manner the most delicate, and the most flat-tering, asking no questions, but complimenting highly the brave resistance which had been offered to him.

It was a strange scene—French faces and uniforms all around me; and two columns of his reserve halted just behind him. . . . Their clothing was nearly new, their appointments excellent, and their whole appearance clean, steady, and soldier-like.

Belatedly, having sent his three battalions (the 2/34th, 1/39th and 1/28th) one after the other uphill in a piecemeal fashion to join in the combat then raging, Pringle himself set off up the main road to order the 1/50th (Colonel George Walker) of Cameron's brigade east along the saddle to cooperate with his own battalions. Colonel William Fenwick, leading the 34th, was shot from his horse and severely wounded; he lost a leg. The Portuguese guns had now opened fire, not against the enemy (for Maransin had not yet come into view), in order to signal a warning to Ashworth and others, including the 7th Division, that serious fighting was taking place. This must have been soon after 11.00, for no sound of gunfire had been reported by the time Wellington set off from Lesaka to San Sebastián that same morning.

The 2/34th and 1/39th approached the crest but were unable to contain the French advance and were pushed back downhill. The 1/28th, having entered the fray slightly further west (nearer the Goizamendi), were reinforced by the 1/50th approaching Darmagnac's line from the west, but were driven back likewise by the superior numbers opposing them and took little further part the action. Pringle now sent half a battalion of the 92nd in a two-deep line against the advancing swarm. The 34th retired behind the Highlanders, who, by extending their wings over both sides of the Chemin des Anglais, were able to keep firing directly into the massed enemy for the next twenty minutes. This fire could not be returned effectively, nor at first could the French put their numerical superiority to advantage in such a constricted area until, inexorably, the Scots were forced back as additional divisions reached the front. It was only when 60 per cent of the 92nd had fallen that the senior of their two surviving officers ordered the rest to fall back on the 1/50th, who had re-formed in their rear.

Between 1.00 and 2.00 William Stewart, drawn north by the sound of gunfire, belat-edly reached the scene and reassumed command. He realised that there was little chance of holding the pass, but he might be able to detain the French on the saddle for a little longer, for Pringle had already sent urgent demands for help to the 7th Division, units of which might arrive at any moment. Meanwhile, the two intact half-battalions on the crest were pulled back. Although Pringle had ordered back the four guns, the order was coun-termanded by Stewart, with the result that after firing a round or two of canister at ap-proaching skirmishers, their gunners, in trying to extricate them from positions into which they had been manhandled with difficulty, jettisoned two into a ravine. The other two weapons were captured—the only field guns lost to the French by Wellington during the whole war, which rankled.

There was now a break in the action, as D'Erlon re-formed Darmagnac's troops, which had suffered severely. Maransin's division, by now deployed on the saddle, supported by

Abbé's units, moved against Stewart's new position just east of the Alcurrunz at about 3.00. Here the left wings of the 71st and 92nd, together with survivors of right wing of the 71st and the 50th in a second line, were drawn up on either side of the main road. The first line, after delivering a volley, retired behind the second, which repeated this manoeuvre. They were forced thus to retire through their former camps, which were overrun, the tents being cut down and their contents pillaged.

By 4.30 the 1/82nd from Grant's brigade of the 7th Division had come up to reinforce the second line, but they continued to lose ground and, having used up all their cartridges, started pelting the enemy with stones, of which there were plenty to hand. Although wounded in the leg, Stewart continued to command. It was at this point—at about 6.00—that two battalions of the 2nd Brigade of the 7th Division (the 1/6th and Brunswick Oels), 1,500 men led by Edward Barnes in person, reached the scene of action hot-foot from their positions some nine miles further along the westward extension of the Chemin des Anglais. Coming in diagonally from this direction, and hardly taking breath, they surprised, charged from the flank and trampled down the leading French battalion, which lost fifteen officers within minutes. The remnants of the right wing of the 92nd, headed by their remaining piper, followed Barnes, and the counter-attack forced back not only Maransin's leading brigade but also its supports, rolling the mass back uphill towards the head of the pass.

D'Erlon, assuming that the entire 7th Division had now come up, ordered a brigade of Abbé's division across the crest, behind which Maransin's shattered units sheltered, and recalled Darmagnac's brigade, which had descended towards Maya in pursuit of Pringle, and where they were about to be engaged by Ashworth's units retiring from the Ispéguy Pass. Sensibly, Stewart halted on the summit: to press on with six battalions (three of which had suffered severely enough) to attack eighteen would have been foolhardy. Although firing continued for a time, it died down at dusk. D'Erlon, unnerved and on the defensive, made no further move.

By then Hill, riding up from Elizondo, after intercepting and reading Cole's dispatch to Headquarters at Lesaka, and aware that Cole was giving up the pass at Roncesvalles in the face of 35,000 men, had come to the understandable decision that Stewart and Barnes must also retreat; there was little alternative. Leaving many badly wounded men on the pass, and exhausted by ten hours of fighting, during the night they staggered down the Baztan valley through Elizondo into that of the upper Bidasoa. It was not until the following morning that D'Erlon was aware that the Otxondo Pass had been abandoned. Cameron's casualties alone had been 800 out of 1,900 present (343 of which were among the 1/92nd); of 2,000, Pringle had lost 530 (including the 140 unwounded prisoners); but those among Barnes's men, engaged at the eleventh hour, amounted to only 140.* D'Erlon reported

---

* It may be mentioned here that companies of the 5/60th were attached to the brigades of Cameron and Pringle. These were armed with rifles, which, although they had a slower rate of fire than the Brown Bess musket, had a longer range and were extremely accurate up to 150 yards (and still dangerous at a distance of 200 or 300), allowing riflemen to pick off officers and colour bearers. The French infantry were at a distinct disadvantage in that they could make no similar reply, and this had a considerable effect on their morale: Napoleon, in his wisdom, had ordered the weapon to be withdrawn from the Republican army as early as 1802.

casualties of 2,100, not a high proportion of his 20,000 effectives. Although he had overrun the Allied position, he admitted to Soult that the affair had been one of the most desperate that he had ever witnessed.

During the night, a verbal message from Stewart reached Wellington at Lesaka explaining what had occurred on the pass, from which he had ordered his men to fall back: this was corroborated by Hill's dispatch, which arrived at Headquarters at 4.00, well before dawn on the 26th, confirming that he would try to hold a position at Elizondo. Oman is a little unfair in remarking that it was owing 'to absolutely criminal negligence on the part of his subordinates' that Wellington was only informed of details of an action occurring twenty miles away eleven hours after its commencement, although a line of communication had been established along the Baztan to Lesaka. It was some of the most difficult and intricate country in which to fight and to keep any form of direct contact with Headquarters, as is evident when scanning a good modern contour map. Even in the heat of such a battle, fought by troops left in the lurch by their commander, some message should have been sent back; Dalhousie had been contacted, at least. But certainly Stewart, however personally brave, behaved irresponsibly on this occasion, and deserved to be blamed.

Before dawn on 26 July Wellington, after a disturbed night, prepared to set off for the Baztan, having first sent fresh orders to both Dalhousie and Alten. The former was directed to march up the Bidasoa valley to Sumbilla, while the Light Division were to retire from Bera and move either towards Yanci (south of Lesaka) or towards Sanestéban if necessary, while Longa's Cantabrians were to block the rough hill road between Lesaka and Oiartzun. Graham was urged to hurry the embarkation of his siege-train. The third brigade of Pack's 6th Division was to remain at Sanestéban, in touch with Dalhousie at Sumbilla; the other two were to move east and join Hill near Irurita, in the lower Baztan. Wellington, with his remaining aides, rode up the Bidasoa valley to meet Hill, holding the position at Irurita, just taken up. Hill had about 9,000 men with him—the survivors of the British brigades from Maya, including the battalions from the 7th Division which had reinforced them, together with Ashworth's and Da Costa's Portuguese. Hill had estimated that D'Erlon had 14,000 at the Puerto de Otxondo, when in fact, even after the losses he had suffered, they still amounted to 18,000. No obvious offensive movement could be observed from that quarter.

Indeed, D'Erlon was being prudent, still under the impression that Stewart had made a strategic retreat and was likely to be receiving further reinforcements from the west, which would threaten his flank if he descended further into the Baztan: it would be wise to make reconnaissances before pushing south towards the Puerto de Velate. D'Erlon advised Soult that he would leave Abbé and Maransin at the Puerto de Otxondo, where they were expecting half-rations sent up from Ainhoa. Darmagnac was sent ahead to check on the situation in the south-east corner of the Baztan, as Hill appeared to be in strength not far south-west of Elizondo. That evening, on learning that Soult had forced the pass at Roncesvalles, D'Erlon felt himself justified in ordering a general advance next morning. This had left Hill unmolested all day on the 26th—wasted on D'Erlon's part—which made any simultaneous convergence on Pamplona virtually impossible to carry out.

Wellington, knowing that Pack and Dalhousie were at hand, did not reckon that Hill was in any danger, and so rode on south with the intention of finding out exactly what the situation might be in the vicinity of Pamplona, being still in the dark concerning the precise position of Cole's and Picton's forces. Headquarters on the night of the 26th was at Almándoz, deep in a valley north of the Puerto de Velate.

5

THE BATTLE OF THE PYRENEES: RONCESVALLES

W E must put the clock back to dawn on 25 July, with Soult's main thrust from St-Jean-Pied-de-Port developing north of the Puerto de Ibañeta towards Roncesvalles. He had chosen two parallel routes. The more easterly, formerly a Roman road, to be ascended by Clausel's three divisions, led past the ancient fort of Château Pignon and over the Col de Bentarte, dominated by the Pic de Leizar Atheca (1,409m.), from which Roncesvalles could be approached from the north-east. Sappers had been busy making it more practicable for artillery and wheeled vehicles. Before reaching the watershed, the Puerto de Ibañeta (1,057m), it skirted a ridge near the peak of Mendi Chipi and past the Alto Biscar, with the higher peak of Orzanzurieta (1,570m) rising further to the south-east. From near the Col de Bentarte, a track led south-east, later descending past the Fábrica (foundry) de Orbaiceta into the valley of the Irati.*

The route followed by Reille's divisions was little more than a mountain track further to the west, which climbed out of the Val Carlos below a ridge near Arnéguy and then circled to the south along what is the narrow-frontier Argaray–Laurigna–Aristory ridge (referred to by Oman as the ridge of Airola, with the French Aldudes valley of the Hayra below its western flank), which undulated towards the Col de Lindus (Linduz; 1,166m), not far north-west of the Puerto de Ibañeta. This would enable his troops to advance downhill rather than be faced with a stiff climb at the end of their progress towards Roncesvalles.

Just south of the Lindus were cross-tracks: the one ahead descended steeply past the Mendichuri height towards the village of Espinal, while to the west extended a very rough track along the crest above the Aldudes, known as the 'Atalosti Path'. Immediately west of the Lindus stood a ruined redoubt, a relic of the war of 1793–94, guarding this ganglion of ridges; to the east, between the Lindus and the Alto Biscar, was a broad, three-mile-long saddle of slippery grass, its sides not providing easy footholds for infantry carrying 70lb (30kg) of kit and a heavy knapsack. The lower slopes of the hills were shaded with beech, oak and chestnut woods (although many trees had been wantonly cut down by

---

* The present main road, the D 933, was completed in 1821 and winds up the deep Val Carlos from St-Jean via Arnéguy to the Puerto de Ibañeta. It follows approximately the same course as that depicted on Roussel and La Blottière's map of the Pyrenees, issued by Arrowsmith in 1809. Soult chose not to use this valley road, as the final climb to the watershed was particularly steep.

Republican troops in 1793), as was the westerly ridge, while the saddle was covered with fern, brushwood and thickets, likewise providing cover. The old abbey and hamlet of Roncesvalles stood a short distance due south of the watershed.

John Byng's Brigade of the 2nd Division had been stationed at the pass for three weeks, together with General Pablo Morillo's Regiment of León, further to the east at Orbaiceta. To reinforce them, the 4th Division, commanded by Lowry Cole, had marched up from Pamplona eight days earlier and had bivouacked below the southern slope. On 23 July Cole had received the dispatch from Wellington warning him to expect to be attacked; the second instruction appears not to have reached him until he was already heavily engaged in defending the pass on the 25th.

It was correctly assumed that the main enemy thrust would be up the old road, but perhaps also up the Val Carlos, which was being watched by a battalion of the 1/57th, while Morillo's left-hand brigade was posted well down in the Val Carlos, although only a picquet of one company of his men was stationed at the old redoubt on the Lindus. Behind Byng's picquets waited his first line of defence, placed on either side of the road near the Leizar Atheca hill, the rocky upper face of which provided good cover. This was held by three light companies of his brigade, the attached company of the 5/60th and one battalion and three light companies of Morillo's brigade. It was supported by two more of Morillo's battalions, together with the 2/31st and 2/66th, the 1/3rd and the 57th (the Buffs). Byng and Morillo commanded 2,000 and 3,800 men, respectively, on this right flank.

During the night of the 24th, on receiving a report from Byng that his picquets had been bickering, Cole ordered up his brigades from Viscarret, the first of which, that of Robert Ross (1/7th, 20th, 1/23rd and a company of Brunswick Oels), started at 2.00 the next morning from Espinal to make the steep ascent up the Mendichuri Path to the Lindus. The vanguard (the 20th), after a four-hour climb largely in the dark, reached the summit to hear Byng's troops being engaged to the east. However, as all seemed quiet in their own front—the Spanish picquet was found half-asleep—they piled arms, had break-fast and relaxed, although Ross took the precaution of sending off the Brunswickers to reconnoitre the spur of the Aristory ridge beyond them. In the distance to the north-west, they could discern the camp of Campbell's Portuguese, on the far side of the Aldudes valley.

It was on the Aristory ridge, filing along hardly more than two abreast, that the whole of Reille's column (the divisions of Foy, followed by those of Maucune and Lamartinière, and totalling 17,000 men), were laboriously picking their way, but it was not until about 11.00 that the Brunswickers noticed some dust rising above the copses in the distance and subsequently caught intermittent glimpses of troops. Reille had with him eight moun-tain guns carried on mule-back, plus a train of pack-animals laden with ammunition. All his wheeled vehicles and the remainder of his artillery were being dragged up the road in the wake of Clausel's divisions—van der Maessen was in the van, followed by Taupin and Conroux—together with all their impedimenta, making yet another interminably long procession, slowing ascending towards the Leizar Atheca positions. Reille's cavalry was also with this column.

Local National Guards, strengthened by a battalion from the 59th Line under Colonel Loverdo, had peeled off from Clausel's column, making their way across the hills towards the foundry at Orbaiceta, where they skirmished for hours with Morillo's units, who were able to hold their ground. Nevertheless, the constant firing from that direction made both Morillo and Byng nervous that their right flank might be being turned by a far stronger force.

Although Byng's picquets had been molested earlier, it was at 6.00 that his main forward position was attacked frontally by a swarm of *tirailleurs* from van der Maessen's leading brigade, led by General Barbot, which was soon brought to a halt. Profitless bickering continued for three hours, with the French suffering disproportionately high casualties. Clausel, infuriated by the delay, and with battalions accumulating behind him, sent his aide-de-camp Lemonnier-Delafosse to Barbot, threatening to cashier him unless he got a move on. Thus menaced, Barbot twice attempted to push Byng off the Leizar Atheca position, but failed. It was not until van der Maessen led his other three battalions on a detour to the east—which turned the hill (now being shelled by his guns, brought up from the rear)—that Byng eventually retired towards the Alto Biscar, by which time it was past 3.00. It was soon apparent to Clausel that the new position taken up by Byng would be even more formidable to attack frontally, and he therefore sent Conroux's division to circumvent it by a long detour south of the higher Ozanzurieta peak.

At 5.00 a dense low cloud, reducing visibility to twenty yards and bringing fighting to a standstill, enveloped the whole area: all the opposing troops could do was to bivouac, which they did within sound of each other.* Casualties had been absurdly few on that flank—Byng and Morillo had only 120 between them—considering that 6,000 men had successfully held up 17,000 for eleven hours.

THE ACTION ON THE LINDUS

Further to the west, after listening to firing between Byng and Clausel for three or four hours, Ross was visited by Cole and advised that both Anson's and Stubbs's brigades were on their way up from Burguete to reinforce the Spaniards at Orbaiceta and Byng on the Puerto de Ibañeta, respectively. At about noon Ross sent the Brunswickers ahead to verify whether the crowd of stragglers they had noticed earlier were Morillo's units retiring from the Val Carlos or the enemy. Meanwhile he would bring forward the left wing of the 20th to support them, leaving the rest of the brigade standing to arms on the small Lindus plateau.

The sixty Brunswickers went forward half a mile to find themselves suddenly confronted by Foy's leading battalion emerging from the trees and bushes, and fell back on

---

* These sea-mist or fog clouds can appear quite suddenly. Jac Weller records having been on the Lindus one bright afternoon when a cloud blew in from the coast, and he could only find his way back to his car at the Roncesvalles Pass by using his compass. The author has had a similar experience in the vicinity.

their supports, at the same time firing on their pursuers. Ross ordered Captain Tovey's company (the leading company of the 20th) to charge in what was a comparatively rare hand-to-hand confrontation—fencing with bayonets—but, on seeing the French closing in, Tovey ordered his men to retire behind the four companies coming up, which opened fire by platoons at a distance of 100 yards on the astonished enemy. The fighting became more confused, but the 20th, 1/7th and 1/23rd kept firing down the constricted glade along which Foy's defiling units were approaching—and with devastating effect. Foy's troops had also to traverse a cutting across this spur, which had formed an outer defence to the old redoubt, to reach the Lindus plateau. No attempt was made by Foy to turn Ross's line by the upper slope of the Val Carlos. It was not until 3.30 that Maucune's first battalion reached the battlefield, and 5.00 by the time his rear stumbled up, but by then the area had become enveloped by the same dense cloud.

Meanwhile Cole had ordered Anson and Stubbs to return to the main pass, where they would form part of a continuous line of 11,000 men between the Alto Biscar and the Lindus. Campbell, of his own accord, having scattered the National Guards in the Aldudes, had led his men east along the Atalosti Path, and was now in a position to take in flank Reille's slowly advancing units. Soult's thrust—or, rather, the interminable files of his two columns—had been brought to a virtual halt.

The total casualties at Roncesvalles among the adversaries had been very moderate: those among the Allies was about 350, while French losses cannot have been fewer than 530. Although the struggle could not be continued in the fog, Byng was convinced that, during the night, Clausel—while still facing him—would be sending his other divisions to outflank Morillo at Orbaiceta, who could not have stopped them, and that from the Irati valley they would swing round and attack Roncesvalles from the rear. Cole, isolated as he was on the far right flank, but not usually pessimistic, took counsel of his fears and agreed that it would be wisest to retire by the Pamplona road before being forced to retreat across difficult terrain by the Mendichuri or Atalosti tracks. He took this decision in spite of having received Wellington's orders (sent at a time when unaware of the full facts of Cole's situation) by 10.00 that morning, when already heavily engaged. These had reiterating that Cole should 'maintain the passes in front of Roncesvalles to the utmost' and disregard any wide turning movement to the east which Soult might make.

Wellington, when reporting to Lord Liverpool in London ten days later, stated that it was Cole's evacuation of the pass which had 'occasioned the retreat of the whole' and that Cole had retired 'not because he could not hold his position, but because his right flank was turned. It is a great disadvantage when the officer commanding in chief is absent. For this reason there is nothing I dislike so much as these extended operations, which I cannot direct myself.'

While it is certain that Cole could have remained on the pass for another day, if the fog had lifted during the night—which it did not—Soult might well have sent two divisions on a night march to outflank him, and Cole would then certainly have found himself in a very precarious spot. Amateurs of 'alternative history' may ponder on what might have taken place had Cole obeyed his orders to the letter.*

Soult was entirely unaware that during the early hours of the night both the Alto Biscar and Lindus positions were being discreetly evacuated, which enabled Cole to steal a march on him and retire unmolested along the Pamplona road. Soult had also lost a day, in which he had gained hardly a foothold on the pass, and his adversary had escaped. It was not until about 3.00 the following afternoon that a party of his *chasseurs* came across Cole's rearguard.

Ross's units had descended by the Mendichurri track to the main road, down which Byng's exhausted troops had marched, to Burguete (Auritz), where Morillo's units met them. Anson's brigade—which had not seen action—formed the rearguard. Campbell's men had returned west along the Atalosti Path for some distance and then veered south-west on cross-country tracks towards Eugi (in the upper Arga valley, just north of Zubiri).

Inexplicably, although Clausel's divisions followed Cole's down the Pamplona road, Reille's column was sent along the Atalosti Path—as this appeared to lead directly west towards the Puerto de Velate—with the intention of dividing the two parts of Wellington's army. The plan, which entailed threading a mountainous mule track, was as impracticable as that which Soult had decided on for the previous day's advance. The fog did not lift until noon. After a mile or two, Foy's vanguard, probably guided (or deliberately misguided) by a Basque smuggler, found itself lost in the woods, not knowing which of a maze of paths to follow. Reille, acting on his own responsibility, sensibly ordered his column to descend south, where they later took their place in the rear of Clausel's divisions.

Wellington was at Almándoz when, at about 8.00 in the evening of the 26th, he received belated and disquieting news from Cole, then at Lintzoain (in the Erro valley), confirming that, in the face of the advance of 35,000 or more of the enemy, he had retired from the Roncesvalles Pass with the intention of joining up with Picton's 3rd Division, which he expected to do at Zubiri in the next valley to the west, that of the Arga. It was by chance that this dispatch reached Wellington as early as it did, for Cole's aide, while making for the last-heard-of headquarters at Lesaka, had at Lanz (south of the Puerto de Velate) run into General Robert Ballard Long, whose cavalry were keeping up tenuous communications between the two halves of the Allied army. Long, apprised of the importance of its content, had taken the precaution of making a copy, which was sent to Hill at Berroeta and immediately passed on to Wellington at Almándoz.

Orders were sent immediately to Picton, instructing him to detain Soult at Zubiri at all costs. Picton would be reinforced by one of O'Donnell's divisions within hours, and

---

* Cole, although generally considered a competent divisional commander, has been referred to by Alexander Gordon as having 'very moderate talents', while Arthur Kennedy, when writing to his mother (who was related to Cole), has commented, '. . . our cousin Lowry did not shine in defending the Roncesvalles Pass. It is said that he was surprised. His talents are not thought very much of with the army *entre nous*.' On another occasion Kennedy remarked that he thought Cole 'as great a humbug as I ever saw' and that 'He is I hear hated most cordially by the army in general.' However, it seems that he later revised his opinion, which was probably influenced by some jealousy or ill-feeling in the family.

soon after by the 6th Division from the Baztan. Meanwhile, he should report back on the situation on his front every few hours.

At about 3.00 that afternoon, Taupin's division found itself faced by Cole in order of battle on an easily defended height near the village of Lintzoain.* Picton—wearing his tall civilian hat and blue undress frock-coat, and flourishing his furled umbrella, as was his wont—was by now only three miles behind Cole. Although in a bellicose mood, Picton was aware that his position could be turned on both flanks once Soult's troops had accumulated, but he reported to Wellington that, with almost 19,000 men at his disposition— some 6,000 of Cole's and 5,000 of his own, Byng's 1,700 and Campbell's 2,500, together with Morillo's Spaniards (almost 4,000)—he could delay Clausel's column for several hours yet (Reille's was still far to the rear) but would retire under cover of night. Although there was a succession of ridges in that hilly country on which he might keep Soult in check, with the excuse that they could all be outflanked, Picton proposed taking up a position much closer to Pamplona.

After a minor action later that afternoon between Anson's and Taupin's units, Cole retired through Picton's fresh division, which now took over the duty as rearguard. Joined by Campbell's units from Eugi, by 11.00 that night the whole corps were *en route* southwest, marching down the Arga valley from Zubiri, where they were overtaken by Wellington's aide. The sun was well up on the early morning of the 27th by the time the head of Cole's division entered the village of Zabaldika.

Although Clausel's vanguard was close on Picton's heels, Soult, in an attempt to relieve the congested state of the road and speed up his advance, had ordered Reille to veer left into the hills near Erro, south of Lintzoain, where he briefly followed a track partly obliterated by recent rain, but, finding it extremely wearying to thread, he had directed his divisions to make their way down on to lower ground. Lamartinière's units descended west to enter the Arga valley opposite Larrasoana; Maucune's emerged further south, near Iroz; while Foy's troops dropped down from the hills near the village of Alzuza, south-west of Iroz. The detour through the hills had sufficiently delayed Reille's column from participating in any concerted attack on Picton and Cole on the 27th—which might otherwise have been possible—and accounts for Soult's apparent lack of enterprise when so near his goal.

Meanwhile the Allied forces had been deployed in a far more formidable position than that which Picton had at first thought of taking up. This was along the crest of a range of low hills in the open country east of the village of Huarte, within a meander of the Arga and at no great distance north-east of Pamplona. Between Huarte and the village of Villava, to its west, the line of hills was extended by the Cerro de San Miguel and, beyond the confluence of the Ulzama, by the ridge of San Cristóbal, due north of, and less than two miles from, the blockaded fortress. Cole soon realised that Pamplona's guns commanded the only road of communication behind these hills and persuaded Picton, his

* The present main road—N 135—circles to the south of the village, while the older road bears right, to re-cross the former at the Puerto de Erro before entering the Arga valley.

superior, to let him place his units, which would form the left wing of their position, further north on the much higher hill of Oricain, which rose abruptly between the converging valleys of the Ulzama and Arga and entirely dominated the latter.

Parallel to and north of the Oricain hill, but with a lower saddle joining the eastern flanks of both, rose another ridge (always referred to as 'Clausel's Ridge'). The Oricain—that on which Cole now deployed his troops—was more easily ascended from the hamlet of Sorauren (to its north-west) than from the south-west, up which food and ammunition would have to be brought. On the north-western summit stood the pilgrimage chapel of San Salvador. Below the Oricain's south-eastern slope was a spur, already occupied by two battalions of O'Donnell's Spaniards, the majority of whom lined the ridge of San Cristóbal, having been relieved from their blockading duty by the belated arrival of Carlos de España's troops.

Cole's divisional battery, commanded by Captain Frederick Sympher, was now placed on this spur, its barrels facing directly up the Arga valley and the road from Roncesvalles. Two battalions of Morillo's men were in position on a steeper spur, further north, overlooking the village of Zabaldika, while his remaining units lined the Cerro de San Miguel behind Sympher. Having approved Cole's deployment of the 4th Division along the summit of the Oricain, Picton aligned the 3rd Division east of Huarte, facing Alzuza, his right flank covered by cavalry (Robert Hill's, William Ponsonby's, the Hussar brigade and D'Urban's Portuguese) previously ordered up from the south.

Cole's line was composed, from right to left, of Anson's brigade, stationed above Morillo's spur (the 'Spanish Hill'), and Campbell's Portuguese (except one battalion sent to support Morillo), behind which Stubbs's Portuguese were placed, with Ross's brigade on the left flank, overlooking Sorauren. Byng's brigade was posted behind the summit of the Oricain hill. Light companies and *Caçadores* were placed some distance down the slope and his main battalions were withdrawn behind the crest and out of view, in the approved Wellingtonian style.

Clausel, on approaching Zabaldika, and discovering the Oricain heights already held in strength by Cole, halted Conroux's division in the valley facing the 'Spanish Hill' without awaiting further orders from Soult, and, having sent a cavalry detachment ahead, directed Taupin's and van der Maessen's to ascend the slope to their right and occupy the length of the northern ridge parallel to Cole's, which commanded from the east the village of Sorauren, down below in the Ulzama valley.

Clausel, after surveying his adversary's position, sent an aide to Soult stating that from the summit behind his line he could discern a baggage train in motion away from Pamplona, seen beyond a gap in the hills to the south-west. Perhaps the siege was being raised: would this not be the moment to attack? Disbelieving, but pressed by repeated messages, Soult rode up to the summit in person, though remaining cautious. Reille's column had still not come up, and it was tempting Providence to advance across the Allied front. The time was now 11.00 on 27 July.

6

THE BATTLE OF THE PYRENEES: SORAUREN

A T dawn on 27 July Wellington, together with Q.M.G. George Murray, Fitzroy Somerset (his Military Secretary) and three or four aides, ascended south from Almándoz, crossing the Puerto de Velate to Lanz. On hearing rumours of Picton's continuing retreat, Wellington advised Hill that it might be necessary to swing back the right (southern) wing of the army to the west, and that his two divisions, together with those of Pack and Dalhousie (the 6th and 7th), after traversing the Puerto de Velate, should veer south-west down the Ultzama valley towards Lizaso; in which case the Light Division was to retire to Zubieta (west of Sanestéban) but keep in communication with Graham. Meanwhile, until receiving further orders, the previous ones should stand: the 6th Division was still expected to reach Olague (Anue), while, as there was a reasonable road between Lanz and Olague, this should be the route followed by Silveira's guns and those of the Light Division.

Briefly halting at Olague, Wellington sent back additional instructions: on arrival, the 6th Division should keep a sharp eye open for any movement of enemy troops from Eugi, due east, which must be blocked at all costs. Once over the Velate, Pack was to turn off all wheeled vehicles down the Ultzama valley, where they should wait at Lizaso. Pack's troops, having rested at Olague, must be ready to march again at a moment's notice.

Wellington found General Long awaiting him at Ostiz, three miles south of Olague. Long confirmed that Picton had abandoned Zubiri during the night and was taking up a position along the San Cristóbal Heights, just north of Pamplona: as the French were approaching in force, it was likely that serious action was imminent, although as yet no firing had been heard.

Leaving Murray at Ostiz to pass on whatever orders he would be sending back, Wellington and Somerset, out-racing the other aides, galloped on south down the narrow valley, which after three miles opened out slightly on approaching the village of Sorauren. Ahead rose the mass of the Oricain heights, along which, extending east from the hill-top chapel of San Salvador, Cole's deploying troops were visible, while Taupin's and van der Maessen's units could be seen thrusting west along the nearer, parallel ridge (usually referred to as Clausel's) overlooking the village itself, with their cavalry vedettes descending towards it. They were a mile away at most. It was now about 11.00. The events of the next few minutes are most graphically described in Wellington's own words:

Why, at one time it was rather alarming, certainly, and it was a close run thing. When I came to the bridge at Sorauren, I saw French on the hills, on one side, and it was clear that we could make a stand on the other hills in our position of the 28th; but I found that we could not keep Sorauren, as it was exposed to their fire and not to ours. I determined to take the position, but was obliged to write my orders accordingly at Sorauren, to be sent back instantly, for had they not been dispatched back directly by the way I had come, I must have sent four leagues round in a quarter of an hour later. I stopped therefore, to write accordingly, people saying to me all the time, 'The French are coming !' 'The French are coming !' I looked pretty sharp after them, however, every now and then, until I had completed my orders, and then set off, and I saw them just near one end of the village as I went out at the other end: and then we took our ground.*

Somerset, with the thirteen-line orders in his sabretache, spurred north up the valley, unseen by the French. Within half an hour, amplified by Murray, the orders had been distributed, making Lizaso the point of concentration for all the central divisions. The 6th was thus able to reach that village by dark, and rest.

Wellington rode alone up the steep track from Sorauren towards the hill-top chapel, and his familiar silhouette—wearing his 'grey frock coat, buttoned close to up to the chin, with his little cocked hat covered with oilskin'—was immediately recognised by O'Toole's line of skirmishers, whose welcoming cry of 'Douro! Douro!' was within moments taken up by the swelling cheers of the 4th Division. As John Bainbrigge recorded,

I can never forget the joy that beamed in every countenance when his Lordship's presence became known. It diffused a feeling of confidence throughout all ranks. No more dispiriting murmurs on the awkwardness of our situation: now we began to talk of driving the French over the frontier as a matter of course.

Wellington reined up in front of Ross's brigade and turned to survey the French positions through his telescope. Soult and his senior officers formed a conspicuous group. Ross remarked that 'this time Soult certainly meditates an attack', to which Wellington, still intent on observing the deploying enemy, answered: 'It is just probable that *I* shall attack *him*.'

Although Clausel's three divisions were up, Reille's, still descending the Arga valley to the east, were several miles away

Whether or not Soult was aware before the early afternoon of Wellington's arrival is unknown. What is certain is that he opposed Clausel's demands for an immediate assault on the Allied lines. Having spread out his maps and taken lunch, he chose to have a nap, leaving Clausel to beat his forehead against an oak, and—as recorded by Lemonnier-Delafosse—muttering 'Who could go to sleep at such a moment?'

---

* This was jotted down by Larpent a month later, when Wellington was explaining the situation in which he had found himself. He had also remarked confidentially—albeit with hindsight—that if only Cole had kept sending sufficient regular information on the 26th and 27th, the French might have been stopped sooner. But, as he was to admit, 'In truth, I suspected that all Soult's plan was merely by manoeuvres to get me out of the hills, and to relieve one or both of the besieged places . . . and I expected him to turn short round towards St Sebastian accordingly. I had then no notion that with an army so lately beaten he had serious thoughts, as I am now sure he had, of driving us beyond the Ebro.'

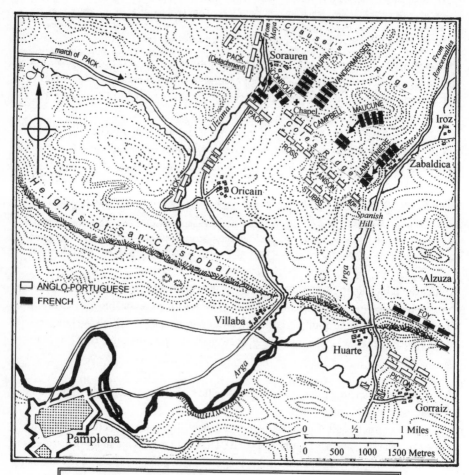

THE AREA BETWEEN PAMPLONA AND SORAUREN

Before taking the offensive, it was essential to demonstrate against Allied positions to determine in what strength they were held. Conroux, ordered to try to occupy a spur south-west of Zabaldika, found himself repulsed by a charge in line of O'Donnell's Spaniards, and never reached the summit: it was obvious that this spur formed part of the main Allied position. Conroux's casualties were estimated at about 200. Later in the afternoon, Foy, whose units had reached Alzuza by then, was directed to probe the heights further south. Two columns forded a stream to approach Picton, who, after his divisional battery had fired a warning round, displayed his whole line. At the same time heavy cavalry showed themselves to his right in front of the hamlet of Gorraiz. Foy ordered his men back: it was evident that the Allied right wing was held in strength, and by all arms.

Soult was preoccupied with the fact that both his cavalry and artillery were still blocked in the Arga valley, while the latest news from D'Erlon was that he had only just occupied Elizondo; indeed, it seemed likely that Hill's troops, which D'Erlon had been ordered to keep occupied, would reach Sorauren before him. Of four days' rations, only one day's remained. It was vital to crush Wellington without delay. After conferring with his generals, Soult decided in favour of a concentric attack on the Oricain position by five of his six divisions, leaving Foy to contain the Allied right wing. Taupin's and van der Maessen's divisions would move against Cole's line between Sorauren and the lower col to the east of the parallel ridges, along which Maucune's would drive. Two of Reille's divisions—those of Lamartinière's, marching from Iroz—would cooperate by assailing the col and the 'Spanish Hill' in their front. Foy would be lent some cavalry to cover his flank. These movements would take place first thing next morning (the 28th), for it was foolish to transfer them during the night over steep and unknown ground.

Wellington made very few changes in Cole's dispositions. On the 'Spanish Hill', the 40th, from Anson's brigade, replaced O'Donnell's men, sent round to the west towards the village of Ollacarizqueta* to guard against any possible turning movement, for Wellington had intended that his reserves would approach from this direction. At 4.00 that afternoon he sent another dispatch to Murray: Pack's 6th Division was to march south from Lizaso directly to Ollacarizqueta, followed by its artillery and reserves of infantry ammunition, unless faced by serious opposition. Dalhousie's and Hill's divisions, having left small rearguards at defensible passes to delay D'Erlon, were to follow Pack's, and all wounded and other impedimenta were ordered west to Irurtzun.

The future field of battle started to cloud over, and both armies were soon drenched by a violent thunderstorm; many remembered a similar downpour on the eve of Salamanca, a year and a week earlier. Although this delayed the march of Dalhousie and Hill, Pack was able to reach Ollacarizqueta before 10.00 the next day.

The storm cleared the air, however, and the morning of the 28th was fine and bright. Visibility was good, allowing Wellington, from the summit of the Oricain, to see what was going on behind the French positions. Conroux's division, abandoning Zabaldika, was ascending the hills behind Clausel's line, then dropped down and deployed south of

---

* On a by-road between Lizaso and Pamplona. Napier refers to that of Marcalain, a short distance further north.

Sorauren, from where Taupin's units moved slightly east, closer to those of van der Maessen's. Part of Lamartinière's division replaced Conroux's, stationed opposite the 'Spanish Hill'; the rest remained beside the Arga. Maucune's division climbed to its designated position opposite the col or saddle between van der Maessen and Lamartinière, on the slope behind which stood Montfort's brigade as a reserve. Pierre Soult's cavalry moved south to take up a position guarding Foy's left flank. Four howitzers were brought forward to fire on both the 'Spanish Hill' and the col: with the exception of some mountain-guns near Sorauren, they were the only French artillery employed in the ensuing battle.

In comparision, very little movement took place among the Allies. Once the 6th Division had reached Ollacarizqueta, Wellington ordered Pack to thread a track leading south-east down a little valley and entering that of the Ultzama opposite the hamlet of Oricain, one mile south-west of Sorauren, leaving George Madden's Portuguese brigade on the far bank. His two British brigades, having crossed the Ultzama, should turn north along its east bank towards Sorauren to cover Cole's left flank. Madden's troops began to appear at about noon.

In view of Pack's approach, Clausel, forewarned by one of his scouts that additional troops were *en route*, decided to make a pre-emptive attack by ordering Conroux's 7,000 bayonets to deploy across the valley and advance in two lines of brigades against Pack's approaching column. At the same time, he instructed his other divisions to move forward the moment they were ready, which brought on the first clash half an hour before the time appointed by Soult.

Conroux imprudently pressed ahead, only to find himself between two fires, that of Madden's men on the west bank and that of Ross's skirmishers on the lower slope of the Oricain, below the chapel, while at the same time facing both Stirling's brigade in line together with John Lambert's in column. Their concentric fire was too fierce for Conroux, who disengaged as best he could—having Brigadier Schwitter disabled—and retired on Sorauren. There was a lull in the action here, Pack having been ordered to cover Cole's flank but not to attack.

Meanwhile, Clausel's other divisions had descended in echelon from the right at the commencement of Soult's concerted frontal attack on Cole's ridge, with Taupin's brigades slightly ahead of van de Maessen's. Maucune's then started towards the col, but it was almost 1.00 by the time Lamartinière's division assaulted the 'Spanish Hill'.

Several comparisons have been made between Soult's attack on the Oricain hill and Masséna's on the much longer ridge at Busaco almost three years earlier. However, Cole's ridge was neither as steep nor as high as that at Busaco. There, Reynier's Corps of 13,000 had ascended towards Picton's 6,800 (including units moving to support him); at Sorauren, Clausel, with 20,000, was ascending towards Cole, with 11,000. The proportional difference was very similar. But, as at Busaco, the attack was made by a series of brigade columns up a steep slope defended by troops in line: the assailants had every disadvantage except a preponderance in numbers. Whether Soult condescended to listen to any words of warning that Clausel, Foy or Maucune may have been prompted to make—all three had been present at Busaco—is doubtful; but he should have done so.

Taupin's right-hand brigade was the first to cross the intervening hollow and start the climb towards Ross, while his left-hand brigade approached Cole's line, where the units of Ross and Archibald Campbell met. Campbell's centre and right faced van der Maessen's ascending division, while Anson's men faced Maucune's on the col. Gauthier's brigade of Lamartinière's division clambered up the 'Spanish Hill', defended by the 40th and two Spanish battalions.

Taupin's first brigade, preceded by an exceptionally dense swarm of skirmishers, was able to push back the 20th, 23rd and 7th *Caçadores*, and had almost reached the crest when Ross's entire Fusilier Brigade charged, sending the French hurtling back. They eventually rallied, but were out of action for some time. The Fusiliers had not followed them far, and had returned to their position before advancing again, this time on the flank of the second column, aiming for the chapel. Having forced back the 10th *Caçadores*, this advance almost gained a foothold on the summit when the latter was attacked by the 7th Fusiliers and Campbell's 10th Line, and it likewise stumbled back downhill but was not pursued. It was now the turn of van der Maessen's division, in a single column preceded by skirmishers, to advance. It was met by Campbell's centre and left, but after a fierce exchange of fire it was able to reach the summit. George Stubbs's Portuguese were sent in to strengthen the line, about to give way on the left, exposing the flank of Ross's 7th Fusiliers. At the same time, the earlier French column, having rallied, returned to the attack, forcing back the right-hand of Ross's line; simultaneously, Maucune's brigade was launched against the col. It was at that instant, so Clausel reported to Soult, that, despite all the difficulties of the enterprise, he had some hope of success.

This hope was not to last long, although it appeared that several of Clausel's units had established themselves along the crest. Exhausted by their steep climb, and suffering severe casualties from the repeated volleys with which they had been met, they had lost most of their impetus. Maucune then found himself violently opposed by Anson's brigade, within ten minutes being driven back across the col with the loss of a colonel and 600 or 700 men of the 2,200 composing the attacking battalions. They were knocked out of the action entirely.

Shortage of ammunition now become a preoccupation. Sergeant John Cooper of the 7th Foot recalled that his colonel had ordered him to tell the brigade-major to send down ammunition immediately, otherwise they would be obliged to retire. By then they were taking cartridges out of the pouches of the wounded. Cooper scrambled up the slope and 'dragged a Spaniard, with his mule laden with ball cartridge, down to his company' and, having unladen the beast, he threw off his knapsack, smashed the casks, and served out the cartridges as fast as possible, while his companions continued to blaze away.

Having seen the repulse of the French from his position of vantage, Wellington took the bold step of ordering the 3/27th and 1/48th of Anson's brigade to fall on the flank of van der Maessen's division, which was slowly pressing back Campbell's and Stubbs's

Portuguese, and sent for Byng's brigade (in reserve, some 400 yards to the rear) to advance and support Ross. Anson's diagonal downhill charge drove back the enemy with immense losses, although Anson's own casualties were to amount to 389. Although sporadic fighting continued for another hour, isolated assaults by already exhausted and badly mauled troops were unlikely to succeed, and by 4.00 Soult had ordered them back to their original positions.

While the main assault was taking place, the 'Spanish Hill' was also being stormed by Gauthier's brigade, but, although supported by high-trajectory fire from his howitzers (which had little effect), his column, attacking frontally—Sympher's guns, not far to the south, may have deterred the enemy from trying to outflank the position—met with no success. Reille was directing the assault in person, but he may have been unaware of the steepness of the spur, and his massed troops, preceded by skirmishers, were not expecting such heavy and effective volleys as they approached the summit, only to be rolled back downhill. The assault was repeated, when two Spanish battalions gave way, but the 2,000 French were then met by a deadly fusillade from the 40th (reduced to ten officers and 400 men) posted higher up the spur and were driven back. A third resolute attack was made, but few could have withstood the intense fire, and, with mounting casualties, they turned back, picking their way past the dead and wounded strewing the descent to Zabaldika. One last but futile attempt was undertaken, but by then the French were completely 'fought out'.

In the Ultzama valley, the 6th Division had continued to bicker intermittently with Conroux's troops; but when Pack realised that Clausel's main attack had failed, he brought up his divisional battery closer to Sorauren, together with some light companies, and ordered Madden to push ahead along the far bank and try to break into the village from the rear. It was an unfortunate decision, because the place was held far too strongly. By the time Wellington had ordered the attack to cease—Cole's line was in no state to take advantage of such a thrust—Pack's battery had been drawn back, and Madden had suffered 300 casualties. Pack himself had been severely wounded in the head, the next day handing over his division temporarily to Edward Pakenham, who had only his coat sleeve 'much torn by a ball', according to Larpent, while the ever-resourceful Colonel John Waters (who had made a name for himself at the Passage of the Douro at Oporto in 1809) 'was shot in the head, through the hat, on the temple, but somehow was little hurt. . . . He was out again next day. Lord Wellington was near at the time, and told him that his head must be like a rock'.

Little movement, apart from slight skirmishing, had taken place on the extreme right wing, where Foy had been directed to keep Picton occupied. Pierre Soult had shown little intention of getting involved, while Sir Stapleton Cotton had been warned already by Wellington not to take the offensive but merely to protect his flank.

Although four more daylight hours remained, thus ended what is sometimes referred to as the 'First Battle of Sorauren', brought on before either side was fully prepared. Having overestimated the number of Allied troops facing him, Soult had delayed the commencement of the action until more of Reille's units had reached the field, while this gave Wellington sufficient time to deploy the 6th Division. Had this not been able to join Wellington's line, it is possible that he would have been obliged to fall back on Irurtzun: as he admitted to Larpent a week later, 'I hope we should in any case have beaten the French at last, but it must have been further back certainly, and probably on the Tolosa road [on which, north-west of Pamplona, stood Irurtzun].'*

While the battle was being fought, additional units of both armies were converging on the area, although the march of those of Hill and Dalhousie had been delayed considerably by the storm. Captain George Wood of the 82nd, one of Barnes's officers, when crossing the Puerto de Velate, describes the troops as being so entangled among carts, horses, vicious kicking mules, baggage and broken-down artillery lining the road that they could hardly extricate themselves:

> Some lighted sticks and candles only added to the confusion, for we were not able to see a yard beyond our lights, owing to the thick haze, which seemed to render darkness still more dark. In this bewildered state many who could not stand were obliged from fatigue to sit down in the mire: to attempt going on was impossible, except by climbing over the different vehicles that blocked the road. In this miserable plight, I seated myself against a tree, when weariness caused me, even amidst this bustle, mud, and riot, to fall fast asleep.

Two guns were lost over precipices, apart from a number of carts and mules. When daylight came, the soaked and bedraggled troops stumbled down the road and turned west near Lanz towards the village of Lizaso, which soon became congested. At Lanz, according to Larpent, they 'found General Murray and several officers, all looking very serious and gloomy.' The scene at Lizaso was dreadful: 'All the wounded . . . had just arrived there, on cars, on mules, crawling on crutches, and hobbling along: all those with wounds in their hands and arms, etc., walking'. Here Larpent, together with Colonel Scovell and his wife, found quarters in a village on the Pamplona road and climbed a neighbouring hill, but, although they could hear firing to the south, visibility was obscured by smoke.

Dalhousie's 7th Division, having only received their orders at 7.00 on the evening of the 27th, had hardly fared better. Dalhousie had kept his men trudging through the night over the Puerto de Arraitz or Donamaria Passes, due west of that of Velate, and entered Lizaso at noon on the 28th, having left a battalion of *Caçadores* to guard the passes. After

---

* Sorauren itself is now bypassed to the west by the busy N 121A, which allows one to visit the characteristic village more conveniently. From the medieval bridge (restored in 1987), one can well imagine Wellington scribbling down his orders to Murray while surveying the parallel ridges rising to the east. A closer view of both, together with the land-bridge joining them, may be gained by ascending to the cemetery overlooking the village, which is recommended to the less energetic.

six hours' rest they started off again along the side-road to Ollacarizqueta, which—as Dalhousie had advised Wellington—they should be able to reach by dawn on the 29th.

Hill had retired from Elizondo unobserved by Darmagnac during the stormy evening of the 27th and crossed the Puerto de Velate, followed by Ashworth's Portuguese. He had been occupied for hours since in sorting out his impedimenta—the wounded, baggage, wheeled vehicles, etc.—all of which, together with a horde of peasants with their possessions loaded on to ox-wagons, were sent off west on cross-roads towards Irurtzun.

It was not until dawn the next day that D'Erlon's troops, with Abbé in the van, were ordered to ascend towards the Puerto de Velate in Hill's wake, picking up some 400 Allied stragglers and wounded, but by dusk on the 28th both Abbé's and Darmagnac's men were bivouacking near Lanz; those of Maransin were some distance further north, near Irurita. D'Erlon was cautious, still preoccupied by the idea that he might be attacked by troops detached from Graham's corps or even by the Light Division, the exact whereabouts of which were unknown to him (and to Wellington). A battalion had been left at Elizondo to escort an expected convoy of food from France entering the valley via the Puerto de Otxondo. Abbé's cavalry reported that Hill had veered down the Ultzama valley to the west, but it was not until sunrise on the 29th that his cavalry were in communication with Soult's main force above Sorauren.

The 29th was spent by both armies in burying their dead and recovering their wounded. Allied casualties had totalled 2,652, of whom 1,358 were British, 1,102 Portuguese and 192 Spanish. Discounting Soult's mendacious understatement of his losses, it had been estimated that those of the French must have been between 3,000 and 4,000.

Captain Arthur Kennedy (18th Dragoons), traversing the battlefield three days' later, described it as 'incredibly horrid', for the ground

> . . . was literally strewed with dead and dying French, who have been lying there for three days without any food or any sort of medical aid. The poor wretches abandoned by their General and his surgeons crawled down the hills and collected as well as the could in groups, some without arms or legs, others dying every moment and hundreds among them lying dead under a scorching sun which had the most extraordinary effect of completely roasting the body the moment it expired. All the dead were completely black and swollen with the heat most enormously although not more than five minutes dead. . . . The numbers of our men wounded has been so great that we were not able to collect those of the enemy till yesterday evening. To-day the spring wagons are at work collecting as many as they can but hundreds have died for want of care . . .

It had been Soult's intention to send back his artillery and dragoons on the Roncesvalles road (they had started to file off during the night), while his infantry would wait to see what the next Allied move might be. However, learning that D'Erlon was—belatedly—at Lanz, on the spur of the moment Soult, recovering his confidence, decided on a entirely different but hazardous strategic plan.

Frustrated at being unable to relieve Pamplona, and knowing that the bulk of Wellington's army was now practically separated from Graham's corps, Soult, by using D'Erlon's divisions as his vanguard, would throw his entire force into the gap between the two, cut the road from Pamplona to Tolosa, and oblige Graham to raise the siege of San Sebastián. The manoeuvre, being so unexpected, would catch Wellington off his guard. But in making these nice calculations Soult had overlooked the risk entailed in extricating his troops from the Ultzama valley, which were so close to the Wellington's 4th Division that it would be almost impossible to withdraw them without exposing the rearguard to annihilation. However elaborate his plans, to take such a risk—and to underestimate Wellington's capacity to take the initiative and fall on him—was a gross tactical error.

In essence, the plan was as follows. D'Erlon, having been lent Treillard's dragoons, was to move from Ostiz and Lanz against Hill. Taupin's and van der Maessen's divisions would march behind Conroux's, which would continue to hold the village of Sorauren until they had passed. Conroux would then be relieved by Maucune's units, descending from the col, which in turn would be relieved by those of Lamartinière's. Foy's, evacuating its position near Alzuza, would replace the majority of Lamartinière's units north-west of Zabaldica, a battalion of which, together with the 18th Chasseurs of Reille's cavalry, would guard against any Allied attempt to follow the column of impedimenta, by now some distance along the road to Roncesvalles. All these movements would take place during the night of the 29th/30th, so that Wellington would be unaware of the danger in which he would soon be finding himself. This last instruction was entirely impractical: one cannot move tens of thousands of troops across unknown and mountainous country in the dark and in silence when still within earshot of an alert enemy.

Soult was in a precarious situation: he had run out of rations, the last brought with him having been consumed on the 28th, and he was also running short of ammunition. As far as food was concerned, his commanders would have little alternative but to ransack every village in their path (of which there were very few, and poor in these mountains), and this would apply also to those retiring up the Roncesvalles road (already plundered during their advance). Foy, more perspicacious and honest than many French commanders, had noted in his diary that these new orders were merely a pretext on Soult's part to conceal what was in essence a retreat: any idea of cutting the Allies' communications was unrealistic.

Meanwhile Wellington was taking precautions against any offensive movement on Soult's part. Those units which had suffered severely—notably Ross's and Campbell's brigades—were drawn back and replaced by those of Byng and Stubbs. The 6th Division, now commanded by Pakenham (Pack being wounded), occupied a height north-west of Sorauren, while Dalhousie's 7th Division, on entering the Ultzama valley after its night march, was to prolong the Allied line, two brigades taking up a position behind a ridge to the rear of the 6th and the third being deployed further west to defend a track which might be used by the enemy should he attempt to make a turning movement on this flank.

Hill was ordered to select a position of defence near Lizaso, to be held by two brigades of the 2nd Division and Ashworth's, while Da Costa's Portuguese were to proceed south-east to communicate with Dalhousie's third brigade. This alignment should protect the Allied left wing. Unfortunately, in the event, Wellington also sent a dispatch to Alten—of whose precise position he was still unaware—to move the Light Division west from Zubieta over the Puerto de Usateguieta towards the Irurtzun–Tolosa road. Thus Alten was to find himself near Lekumberri, where he was to serve no useful purpose. Henry Fane's cavalry brigade had also been instructed to ride north-west from its former position to a point on the Tolosa road not far north-west of Pamplona and to keep in communication with units arriving further along the road. These would include Hill's wounded, for Vitoria, further west, was still the main hospital base, and would continue to be so for some time.

At midnight, Taupin's and van der Maessen's divisions, facing Cole's line, moved off, leaving their fires burning, and were near Ostiz by dawn. Numbers of Maucune's men lost their way in the dark, and by daylight they had still not relieved Conroux (one of whose brigades was still holding outposts), although some were beginning to file behind his barricades at Sorauren, when the village received a barrage of shells.

Wellington was perfectly aware that Soult was moving his troops across his front, and had all his divisions under arms an hour before dawn: they would be equally ready to resist or fall on the enemy. Although it had been his intention to shell them out of Sorauren that morning, during the night his other guns had been appropriately sited, should Soult attack. Pakenham had succeeded in hauling six onto the hill dominating Sorauren, where they were mounted immediately in front of Madden's Portuguese, only 500 yards from their target. Two guns and a howitzer had been dragged up also and placed in positions near the pilgrimage chapel. Further east, three more guns from the 4th Division battery were trained across the trough towards van der Maessen's former position.

THE 'SECOND BATTLE OF SORAUREN'

Foy, on the far left flank, had only just succeeded in massing his division at Iroz by dawn, and from there his men ascended north-west behind 'Clausel's Ridge'; but by the time they had passed behind Lamartinière's troops and reached the col, they found themselves being shelled from the opposite heights by half of Sympher's repositioned battery. Foy had not been intending to fight, when, as he later wrote, '. . . suddenly we found ourselves massed under the fire of the enemy's cannon. We were forced to go up the mountain side to get out of range . . .' He very soon realised that there was no alternative but to retreat, for both flanks could be turned by the valleys to the east and west. While Foy might get out of range, it was the duty of both Maucune and Conroux to hold Sorauren.

The 6th Division started to advance directly on the village; a little later, preceded by skirmishers, Byng and Stubbs, with Ross and Anson forming a reserve line, descended from the Oricain heights, Ross making for Sorauren and Stubbs moving towards Foy's units on the far ridge. Meanwhile Picton had discovered that the French positions opposite him had been evacuated, and he started to push ahead up the Arga valley until receiving orders (at 8.00) to advance no further for the time being, although he might occupy the hills flanking the east bank of the Arga.

Madden's units were ordered to press ahead to the north-west of Sorauren, where they drove in a regiment left to defend the west bank of the Ultzama and pushed round to the rear of the village, now attacked frontally by light companies of Lambert's brigade and by Byng's from the east. Only Conroux's first brigade was able to escape being surrounded, making off towards Ostiz; his other brigade and units from Maucune's division, although obstinately resisting for almost two hours, and after an unsuccessful attempt to break out, could only surrender. A total of 1,700 unwounded prisoners were made, 1,100 of them from Maucune's division and the rest from Conroux's rear brigade. Maucune himself, together with about 1,700 survivors, joined Foy's units on the heights to the north-east: neither division could be thought of as a fighting force for the rest of the campaign.

Soon after 8.30, Dalhousie, having received orders to emerge from his concealed position, fell on Taupin's and van der Maessen's units assembling at Ostiz. While Inglis's battalions were engaged with the latter's units, the brigades of Le Cor and Barnes were firing relentlessly on Taupin's. Clausel sensibly disengaged and started due north up the road towards the Velate Pass, followed by Inglis's brigade, together with Byng's, which by noon had arrived from Sorauren. The other two brigades of the 7th Division kept to the western slopes of the valley, where they were able to turn each defensive position taken up by Clausel's rearguard. By dusk Clausel was at Olague, where he was joined by the vestige of Conroux's first brigade. There were very many stragglers, hungrily making their way over the hills. It is doubtful whether that evening Clausel had more than 8,000 men to hand of the 17,000 with which he had started out six days earlier.

Reille's fate had been no less agonizing. Having remained on the heights north of Clausel's former ridge, he realised that it would be impossible to maintain his position for long. He sent permission to Maucune to evacuate Sorauren, which was a dead letter, and gave orders at about 10.00 for Lamartinière's brigades to disengage and make their way north across country without further delay. Not only was Cole pressing hard on Foy's provisional position, but it was obvious that Picton was intent on turning Lamartinière's flank, if not encircling him.

The subsequent retreat became more disorderly as fugitives from Sorauren joined Reille's main body. A brief halt was made in the hamlets of Sarasibar and Etsain, further north, where Reille tried to work out a sensible route to follow—one that might enable him to join up with Clausel. He turned west to enter the Puerto de Velate road south of Olague, ordering Foy to work his way north-west along the higher slopes of the valley, which would take him to Lanz, beyond Olague. In the subsequent confusion, not surprisingly several units were following in the wake of divisions other than their own. By dusk Reille had reached Olague with probably fewer than 6,000 men.

Foy never reappeared, nor did he during the rest of the disastrous campaign. He later tried to explain his erratic retreat by claiming that he lost his sense of direction as his column worked their way through the thickly wooded hills, and that by dusk he had found himself at Iragui, on the east flank of an intervening ridge. With Picton's light troops hard on his heels, he had decided that it was hazardous trying to continue across country in the dark and so had veered north-east into the upper Arga valley. After crossing the Collado de Urquiaga, and marching for some hours more, he bivouacked, and the next morning descended via the Aldudes valley into France. He then sent all the stragglers which had attached themselves to him to St-Jean-Pied-de-Port—they had committed atrocities and sacked every village through which they had passed—while he led his own division in a leisurely fashion via St-Etienne-de-Baïgorry into the Nive valley and to Cambo, having lost only 550 men of his original complement of 6,000. It was not the first nor the last time that Foy was to put the safety of himself and his men first—and Devil take the hindmost. That it was not impossible for him to have continued due north into the Baztan is confirmed by the fact that stray battalions from Lamartinière's division, which had broken away at Iragui, had eventually reached it via Almándoz and Elizondo before traversing the Pass of Otxondo.

Thus ended the 'Second Battle of Sorauren'. As Wellington admitted, when writing to Bentinck six days later, the whole had been 'fair bludgeon work. . . . I never saw such fighting as we have had here.'

7

SOULT'S RETREAT

O NCE Sorauren itself was in his hands, Wellington distributed further orders. He assumed that, although the main body of the French army would be making its way due north towards the Velate Pass and into the Baztan—being the shortest and most obvious line of retreat—a large contingent would be retiring up the Roncesvalles road also. Picton's fresh division, taking his guns and being lent two squadrons of hussars, could now set off in pursuit. Cole was to proceed north, to sweep the hills between the two valleys but not engage in attacking any obstinate rearguard. The 6th Division, with its guns, Byng's brigade and some six battalions of O'Donnell's troops (brought forward from the San Cristóbal heights), was to advance on Olague, while Dalhousie would operate in the Ultzama valley: they should keep in close communication with each other.

Not yet appreciating how seriously Hill was threatened by D'Erlon, Wellington had sent him orders to move east from Lizaso towards Olague and Lanz. He would be sending him Campbell's brigade, that of O'Donnell's, which had been in waiting at Ollacarizqueta, and Morillo's Division. These 7,000 additional troops set off before noon but arrived too late to help Hill, overtaken by intervening events. Alten was advised that, wherever he might be, he should now return to Zurbieta.

Soult had meanwhile been urging D'Erlon to fall on Hill, and hoped to send him, in addition to cavalry, some of Clausel's units. He had left his east wing at Zabaldika so early on the morning of the 30th that he was quite unaware of subsequent events. He had passed Clausel's troops approaching Ostiz before 6.00. Although Soult must have heard Wellington's guns not long afterwards, he preferred to ignore them and concentrate on the complex operation he had set in motion. It was essential that D'Erlon should hurry, as Soult had understood from deserters that three Allied divisions were *en route* to reinforce Hill.

THE COMBAT AT LIZASO AND BEUNZA

Forewarned, Hill had taken up a defensive position with his four brigades. This lay along a wooded ridge half a mile south of Lizaso, with the hamlets of Gorrontz-Olano in his left front and Aróstegui behind his right. On his left wing stood survivors from Cameron's brigade, with Fitzgerald of the 5/60th in command (Cameron having been wounded on

7

the 25th). Next to them were Ashworth's Portuguese, with a regiment of Da Costa's brigade on his right, while battalions of Pringle's brigade (temporarily under O'Callaghan) was in reserve in the rear. Together with a thick skirmishing line before them, their numbers approached 9,000.

D'Erlon now ordered Darmagnac's division to demonstrate against the Portuguese while Abbé, with 8,000 men—comparatively unengaged earlier in the campaign—was to ascend a wooded height beyond Hill's left flank towards the hamlet of Beunza and sweep down on it from that direction, supported by Maransin. With such a preponderance in numbers, success was almost certain. However, Darmagnac was repulsed when attempting to break through the Portuguese line; but Abbé, who found himself attacking the 50th and 92nd frontally, by extending his line to his right, was able to turn the Allied left flank. This could have been cut off had not the 34th (in reserve) charged and held the French at bay long enough for the rest—less 36 taken prisoner—to retire. This caused the centre to swing back, when another 130 were cut off and captured, while the right wing, likewise withdrawing, pivoted on an isolated hill, on which Da Costa's men were able to maintain their hold. Hill was able to take up a new defensive position on a height in front of the hamlet of Egueras (Yguaras; south of Aróstegui), where he was able to repulse with loss a final attack by one of Darmagnac's regiments.

It was at about 4.00 in the afternoon that the arrival of Campbell's, O'Donnell's and Morillo's reinforcements was noticed by D'Erlon, who took no further offensive action: he had, after all, driven Hill back with heavy losses—notably among the Portuguese—and held the road leading west from Lizaso; but he had also suffered some 800 casualties in fighting which had lasted seven hours.

That evening Soult had to take stock of the very changed situation in which he now found himself at Olague, surrounded by the hungry, badly beaten and demoralised survivors of Clausel's and Reille's divisions. With only D'Erlon's remaining intact as a fighting force, it was pointless to attempt his projected break-through: an immediate retreat was the only way to save his army from further disintegration. It would make its way back to France with D'Erlon's troops forming a rearguard. Inexplicably, having 'bitten the bullet' and come to this decision, Soult then made a curious change in what would have been the most expedient routes north to be followed by his divisions. Instead of letting Clausel's and Reille's troops continue due north over the Puerto de Velate into the Baztan (where a convoy of food was expected), he ordered them to make their way north-west across the Puerto de Arraitz (or Donamaria passes) to Sanestéban, and from there to descend the Bidasoa valley. Did Soult still think there might be a chance of relieving San Sebastián by the convergence of such numbers towards the Bidasoa estuary, or was it because he expected that it was more likely that Wellington would thrust due north from Sorauren and attack his unprotected units than could Hill, exhausted by his engagement with D'Erlon?

At 1.00 in the night Clausel and Reille, with their depleted 'corps', set off, leaving countless stragglers in their wake. They were followed by Maransin's and Darmagnac's divisions, with Abbé's holding the heights north of Lizaso in their rear. Wellington, mis-led by some reports reaching him, had deduced that, although a large body of the enemy was taking the Roncesvalles road, his main force was following that climbing north over the Velate Pass. That Soult would order his surviving army *north-west* and into the narrow Bidasoa valley was a contingency so unlikely that it need not be taken into account. Thus Picton had been sent off on a wild goose chase, and the 6th Division, which had crossed the ridge to the east towards Eugi, on reaching Olague, was too late to intercept Foy.

Wellington himself, with Byng and Cole, marched up the Velate road, and orders were sent to Hill and his reinforcements to join them; only Dalhousie's 7th Division, still near Ostiz, was marched north-west past Lizaso towards the Donamaria passes to protect Hill's flank. Wellington was as yet unaware that the bulk of Soult's army—if it could be called such—was making its way helter-skelter over the Donamaria passes. Hill, being so close to Abbé's men, realised what had taken place and at about 10.00, knowing Dalhousie was coming up, took the initiative in starting in pursuit.

By noon on the 31st Wellington, on crossing the Puerto de Velate, had reached Almándoz, to discover to his exasperation that fewer than 1,000 of the enemy had passed that way and that the main body was descending through Sanestéban with Hill and Dalhousie on its heels. Should there be a chance that the Light Division might be able to fall on the enemy flank as it threaded the narrow Bidasoa valley, Wellington dispatched an aide to find Alten and instruct him to intercept them at Sanestéban or, if that were impossible, at Sumbilla, for the French were in the greatest disorder. The dispatch—which did not catch up with Alten for several hours—confirmed that Wellington's van-guard was at Irurita, over five miles due east of Sanestéban, and instructed Alten to pass on this information to Graham via the Goizueta road.* Meanwhile, as Wellington went on inform Alten, 'we are going to act immediately against a column which is retiring by the Dona Maria road. We have plenty of troops in the proper direction, and if we can overtake the column, I hope its rear will suffer considerably.'

Before the evening was out, news had reached Irurita that a large convoy of food, having crossed the Puerto de Otxondo, had just entered Elizondo. Byng made a forced march, and his flank companies surprised the one regiment left by D'Erlon to protect it and captured the whole. While the supplies of bread and biscuit were welcome, as a precaution Byng had the heads of the brandy casks stove in, although many men were later seen lapping up the spilt liquor with their hands. Years later, and with hindsight—and stating that he had been supplied with the facts by Wellington—Napier, vividly describing the subsequent incident which had deprived him of the chance of surprising Soult and cutting off his retreat down the Bidasoa valley, wrote that strict orders had been given

* In his previous dispatch to Alten, Wellington, when referring to a message received from Girón, who was worried about losing Bera, had stated that this did not matter too much: it was more important that Longa maintain his position on the hills dominating the Bidasoa between Bera and Irun. Since then, the situation had changed radically. But how could Wellington have known that, by placing a single division at Bera or Etxalar, he would have blocked entirely Soult's only line of retreat?

... to prevent the lighting of fires the straggling of soldiers or any other indication of the presence of troops; and he placed himself amongst some rocks at a commanding point from whence he
could observe every movement of the enemy. Soult seemed tranquil, and four of his *gens d'armes* [sic]
were seen to ride up the valley in a careless manner. Some of the staff proposed to cut them off;
the English general whose object was to hide his own presence, would not suffer it, but the next
moment three marauding soldiers entered the valley and were immediately carried off by the
horsemen. Half an hour afterwards the French drums beat to arms and their columns began to
move out of San Estevan towards Sumbilla.

Hill's movements will be described before Wellington's. Soult led the way up towards
the central of the three Donamaria passes (just west of the Putzueta; 1,061m), with two
cavalry divisions and the baggage, with Reille's and then Clausel's troops in his wake.
Seeing a pile-up developing ahead of him, Clausel veered off to the right, crossing the
ridge by the Puerto de Arraitz proper. Reille, and later D'Erlon, traversed the more westerly pass. Abbé's division, over 7,000 strong, gave ground under pressure from Hill and
took up a new position on the slope of a steep, wooded hill near what was known as the
Venta de Urrotz (named after the village in a valley on the north side of the main ridge).
It was now about 2.00, and Dalhousie's division was close to Hill's right flank; but instead
of waiting for it to come up and outflank Abbé, Hill pressed forward. William Stewart,
then commanding the vanguard, his wounded leg strapped to his saddle in a roll of
cushions, ordered Fitzgerald's brigade, by now reduced to under 1,000 men, to launch a
frontal attack on Abbé. Not surprisingly, it was repulsed with losses, and Fitzgerald
himself was wounded and taken prisoner.

A second assault, reinforced by Pringle's brigade, was equally unsuccessful, even
when supported by two guns shelling the woods. (Stewart was wounded again, and sent to
the rear.) Abbé withdrew in the face of a third attack and retired behind Darmagnac's
division, which now formed the rearguard. The action was halted at 5.00 by dense fog.
Having cleared the passes, Hill, not having received any further orders, then followed his
original instruction rather than waiting for the fog to disperse and continue the pursuit,
which was to join Wellington's concentration by crossing the Velate Pass. This he did by
traversing the ridge by a track over the so-called Puerto de Sangre, west of the Velate, from
which a ridge footpath leads east from the Velate, where stands the Odolagako Benta
('Inn of Blood').

By dawn on 1 August Wellington had time to reconsider his position *vis-à-vis* the bulk of
the enemy, which, several hours earlier, had started to file down the steep, wooded and
rocky banks of the Bidasoa valley. Larpent recorded two days later that the men—those
branded 'marauders' by Napier—had straggled, had been caught and had divulged
where Wellington had his headquarters, and it was this information—that the headquarters were too near for comfort—which had enabled Soult to decamp during the night
rather than the next morning, as had been his intention. The Allied presence at Elizondo
had been brought to him also by a cavalry patrol, making its escape from the village just
as Byng's units had swooped on the convoy.

Although Soult's contact with France had been intermittent, when next reporting to Paris he had complained bitterly of what he considered was criminal torpidity on Villatte's part for neither pushing forward and occupying Bera nor keeping in communication with him along the valley. One of Reille's battalions led the way, which was to turn right up a side valley three and a half miles short of Bera; beyond Etxalar, this track led to a pass into France.

By 7.00 Cole, with the 4th Division, was already attacking the French rearguard, with orders to press north along the east or right bank of the Bidasoa, while Dalhousie was shortly to push them down the opposite bank. Byng would remain where he was until Hill's units arrived from Almándoz. Van der Maessen formed the French rearguard on a hill on the north bank facing Sanestéban, with Taupin in support, while Conroux was threading his way through D'Erlon's baggage, which obstructed the riverside road. Seeing this, Clausel directed his brigadiers to march as best they could along the valley side.

Cole's skirmishers, further up the slope, were attempting to turn van der Maessen's flank. Although the French then extended their line uphill, the Allied troops were the first to reach the crest and thus retained their advantage. The enemy battalions disintegrated as they retreated below the line of cliffs and precipices, and only rallied on two of Taupin's regiments in a defile south of Sumbilla. Here Clausel found his passage blocked by Darmagnac's division, which had been unable to proceed ahead owing to trouble further north. After an hour of what Oman refers to as 'incoherent fighting on the slopes above Sumbilla', Clausel's three divisions retreated north-east in disorder across the trackless spurs of the Montes de Bidasoa, eventually converging on Etxalar. Cole continued to harass Darmagnac, who hardly attempted to make a stand, as is evident from scanning the list of Allied casualties that day: three men killed and three officers and 48 men wounded in the 4th Division, while the 7th Division had none.

While Soult's vanguard was 'running the gauntlet' more literally, Reille, with one infantry battalion, was followed by Treillard's cavalry, the main convoy of wounded and the baggage of his corps. In their wake tramped the rest of his units. Progress had been slow, and it was already almost noon by the time they were approaching the bridge 'of Yanzi', as it is usually referred to. This stone structure spanned the Bidasoa about one and a half miles east of Yanci (now Igantzi), on a side road from Lesaka, to its north. The village formed the extreme right flank of Longa's line of observation and was occupied by a battalion of the 2nd Regiment of Asturias, part of Barcena's division of the Galician Army, lent to Longa the previous day. Two of Longa's own companies had been placed as picquets on the bridge, which had been barricaded but not broken.

At a point 1,650m north of the bridge—not 'a little south of it', as stated by Oman, for the valley sides there rose abruptly from the road—a track led off to the east, round a spur, and ascended the Tximista valley towards Etxalar. As Reille's leading battalion filed through the steeply banked narrows, passing the bridge to approach this cross-track, it was fired on by the Spanish picquet and came to an abrupt halt. That Reille had not expected any interruption of his march is evident from the fact that he had not bothered to send any cavalry vedettes ahead to clear the way. A number of his dragoons took advantage of the halt to water their horses in the Bidasoa. On hearing a violent discharge of musketry, and not realising that it was merely the head of the column attempting to dislodge the picquet—out of their sight round yet another bend—the dragoons assumed that it was being assailed by the enemy in force. Panic ensued, and within minutes the majority of them were galloping back along the road, almost riding over Reille and his staff at the head of Lamartinière's division, and were only stopped by the solid mass of fugitive troops coming up behind them.

The picquet having retired, and the way to Etxalar being clear, the column moved ahead, but, as no guard had been left at the bridge, by the time Reille reached the spot the Spaniards had reappeared on the far bank, but further upstream, from where they were peppering his cavalry, causing confusion and loss. The next battalion to arrive was or-dered to ascend the almost precipitous banks at this point and direct continuous volleys against the Spaniards, while another battalion was sent across the bridge to dislodge them. The column continued to tramp up the track to Etxalar, along which they did not expect any further molestation, having left a battalion behind to guard the bridge.

Before long the Spaniards, now reinforced by the Asturian battalion from Yanci, drove the French from the bridge and started firing on the baggage train, then filing along the road, causing more chaos, for this, turning tail, collided with the convoy of wounded, followed by the wreckage of Maucune's division. The Spaniards continued to hold the bridge for another two hours, by which time Abbé's units had scrambled through the mass of baggage, much of it jettisoned into the river or pillaged *en route*. Abbé succeeded in reoccupying the bridge at some loss, after which, again leaving a couple of battalions to hold it, the rest of the column and the remaining baggage proceeded ahead. Eventually, the last of D'Erlon's divisions—Darmagnac's—reached the bridge and relieved Abbé's battalions, only to find itself the target of fierce firing from a swarm of green-coated skirmishers descending rapidly from the opposite heights: it was the Light Division, whose sudden appearance took the French entirely by surprise.

This narrative of events must now be briefly interrupted to explain the Light Division's movements during the previous few days. Alten received Wellington's dispatch of 29 July late that evening at Zubieta, and his division immediately started off though the night to the south-west, continuing along the mountain road traversing the Puerto de Usateguieta (695m) throughout the 30th within sound of the distant rumble of gunfire to the south-east (from Sorauren, and later from near Lizaso). Cooke described having to collect to-gether next morning the few women accompanying them:

> [They] dared not again encounter another toilsome night march along the verge of precipices. It was a droll sight to see this noisy group defiling from the forest. Many were dressed in soldiers' jackets, battered bonnets, and faded ribbons, with dishevelled locks hanging over weather-beaten features. They drove along their lazy *borricas* [donkeys] with a thick stick, and when the terrific blows laid on ceased to have the desired effect, they squalled with sheer vexation; lest they be overtaken by the enemy's light horse and fall into their hands.

By dark, after ascending the Alto Uitza (802m), Alten reached Lekumberri, on the Pamplona–Tolosa road, where he awaited further orders. These reached him the following afternoon (sent by Murray from Lizaso that dawn), when, 'more dead than alive from excessive fatigue', one of Wellington's aides reined up with orders to 'put his division in movement for Zubieta' and advising him that Dalhousie would be marching north over the Donamaria passes: no great urgency was enjoined. He brought news of Soult's defeat, and that it was supposed that he would be decamping by the Puerto de Velate. Alten set off back again over the Alto Uitza, halting that night at Leitza, where Wellington's next dispatch reached him belatedly during the early hours of 1 August, advising him that, as it was now apparent that Soult was in full retreat down the valley of the Bidasoa, would he 'head off' the enemy at either Sanestéban or Sumbilla or 'cut in upon their column' somewhere along his line of march.

At dawn the Light Division re-crossed the Puerto de Usataguieta and, on reaching Elgorriaga, learned that the enemy had already evacuated neighbouring Sanestéban. Under a blazing sun, Alten led his division due north across the hills overlooking and parallel to the left bank of the Bidasoa. By 4.00, when opposite Sumbilla, the dense enemy column came in sight, threading the valley road far below and pressed by the 4th Division. As it would take too long to scramble down the precipitous slope at this point, and as the French were past Sumbilla, the already exhausted troops, having covered over 30 miles of rough terrain that day, staggered on along the shaly mountainside. Descending the north flank of a ridge, the 2nd Brigade was told to halt and fall out near the village of Arantza (Aranaz), on the tributary Latza stream, while the 1st Brigade (the 1st and 3rd Battalions Rifle Brigade, 1/43rd and 1st *Caçadores*) turned north-east along a byroad, which, screened by woods, led directly to the bridge of Yanci. It was from the steep slopes rising above the river here that the 43rd and *Caçadores* opened a sudden and devastating fire on the hurrying mass on the far bank. As John Cooke of the 43rd vividly recorded,

At twilight [on the 31st], from the summit of a tremendous precipice, we overlooked the enemy within a stone's throw. The river separated us. The French were wedged in a narrow road, with inaccessible rocks enclosing them on one side, and the river on the other. Such confusion took place amongst them as is impossible to describe. The wounded were thrown down during the rush, and trampled upon. Their cavalry drew their swords, and endeavoured to charge up the pass of Echalar, the only opening on their right flank, but the infantry beat them back. Several of them, horse and all, were precipitated into the river; others fired vertically at us, whilst the wounded called out for quarter. They pointed to their numerous soldiers in bearers, supported on the shoulders of their comrades. The bearers were composed of branches of trees, to which were suspended great-coats, clotted with gore, or bloodstained sheets, taken from various habitations, to carry off their wounded, on whom we did not fire.

William Surtees refers to the enemy sending

. . . a pretty strong corps of light troops across, which got engaged with our people; but we soon drove down through the woods again towards the bridge. At length, we got two companies posted just over the bridge, in front of which all the rear of the French column had to pass. Poor creatures! they became so alarmed, that they instantly began to cut away, and cast off, all the loads of baggage, and both cavalry and infantry, &c. to make the best of their way. But the mountain on their right was inaccessible; consequently they had all, as it were, to run the gauntlet. Great was the execution done amongst the enemy at this bridge, and many were the schemes they tried to avoid passing. At length they got a battalion up behind a stone wall above the road, on the opposite side, from whose fire we received some damage . . .

Surtees goes on to remark that the French, to save themselves,

. . . were compelled to adopt the cruel alternative of either throwing their wounded men down to perish, or run the risk of being shot or taken themselves. I believe the former, shocking as it seems, was generally adopted; and I have reason to believe that the greater part of them were thrown into the river; for, from the point where we first came in view of them to near where this affair took place, the Bidassoa [sic] was literally filled with the dead bodies of Frenchmen, and they could have come into it in no other way.

While many escaped up the road to Etxalar, the surviving wounded, non-combatants and stragglers were taken prisoner: they amounted to about 1,000. The Light Division did not pursue those who had got away—they could not have stirred another step—while the 4th Division, now coming up, was hardly less weary. Surtees claims that, when considering that each man carried a weight of between 40 and 50lb, and some much more,

. . . probably never troops made such a march over such a country before. We travelled at least thirty-two miles over mountains . . . where you were sometimes nearly obliged to scramble upon your hands and knees. The day was exceedingly hot, and occasionally there was a great want of water. . . . I heard of one poor fellow, who, when he came to water and had drunk, lost his senses, fell to the ground, and shortly after expired.

We must now turn to the days' events further east. At 9.30 on the 1st, having occupied Sanestéban, Wellington had ordered Byng at Elizondo to cross the Puerto de Otxondo and descend to Urdax (now Urdazubi); Hill, at Irurita, should follow him to the pass. Once relieved there, Byng might advance towards Ainhoa. The 2nd Division, together with Silveira's Portuguese division, would follow him next day, while the 6th—by then somewhere near Eugi (across the mountains due south of Elizondo)—might also be able to join them. At 8.00 in the evening of the 1st, a dispatch was sent to Graham informing him that, as it was hoped that Byng would be over the frontier by next morning, Graham, together with Girón's troops, should prepare to cross the lower Bidasoa and attack Villatte, leaving only the minimum detachment to continue the blockade of San Sebastián. But within a few hours these orders—which might suggest a plan to encircle Soult—were countermanded, for several reasons. As was often the case with Wellington, he preferred to hold his cards close to his chest.

Byng was halted at Maya. Writing to Graham on the 3rd, Wellington explained that the 2nd Division had suffered enough and also lacked shoes and ammunition, that it could not have been used in an such offensive operation, and that Byng would not have had sufficient troops to support him.

In the morning of the 2nd, having ridden down the Bidasoa valley to join the 4th and Light Divisions (12,000 men together), followed by the 7th, Wellington had come to another decision, although at some hazard. Robert Blakeney describes how Wellington had

... hurried to Echallar to reconnoitre the enemy and consult his maps, taking a party of the 43rd ...
as a guard; but the enemy unobserved, discovering the party, sent a detachment to cut them off.
A Sergeant Blood of the 43rd with some men, being in front, perceived the enemy coming on at
speed; and ... dashed down from rock to rock roaring out the alarm. [Wellington] instantly mounted
and galloped off; the French came up, but only in time to fire a volley after him.

In spite of the exhausted condition of the 4th and Light Divisions, now short of
rations—Alten's men had been almost without any sustenance for two days—they were in
high spirits and keen to keep Soult on the run. The plan was for the 4th and 7th to attack
his positions on either side of the village of Etxalar, while the Light Division would turn
his right flank from the west, although this would entail a long detour down the Bidasoa
valley towards Bera. They would first have to ascend along the southern slope of the
heights of Santa Barbara overlooking the valley of the Arrequiko towards the Pic d'Ibantelli
(698m), approached by a track leading east opposite the road from Lesaka. It was a dull
morning, and the peak itself, on which the French were posted, was shrouded in a dense
mist. At this juncture, recalled John Cooke, 'an excellent commissary managed to overtake us, and hastily served out 1/2lb biscuit to each individual. This the soldiery devoured
while in the act of priming and loading as they moved on to the attack'. Then 'An invisible
firing commenced, and it was impossible to ascertain which party was getting the best of
the fight; the combatants were literally contending in the clouds.'

Meanwhile the 4th Division was busy extricating itself from the captured impedimenta blocking the defile between Sumbilla and the bridge of Yanci. As described by
Larpent, who was following Headquarters,

> For nearly two miles there were scattered along the road, papers, old rugs, blankets, pack-saddles,
> old bridles, girths, private letters, lint, bandages, one or two hundred empty and broken boxes;
> quantities of intrenching tools, rags, French clothes, dead mules, dead soldiers and peasants,
> farriers' tools, officers' boots, linen, etc. There were also the boxes of M. Le General Baron de St
> Pol [a brigadier in Maransin's division], and several private officers' baggage; the principal thing
> taken seemed to be ... the field hospital of the second division [Darmagnac's]. There were still
> more things worth picking up. ... This caused stoppage and confusion.

THE COMBAT AT ETXALAR

The 7th Division, which had ascended north-east from Sumbilla, after traversing the hills
over which Clausel's troops had made their escape the previous afternoon, approached
Etxalar from an unexpected direction, their advance screened by the mist, and, without
waiting for Cole's division to come up (this would have protected their left), made a
frontal attack which caught the French entirely unawares, 'cooking above, and plundering below in the village'. As Dalhousie, in justifying his rash action, later wrote, 'I thought
it best to be at them instantly, and I really believe Barnes's brigade was among them
before their packs were well on'.

Barnes, once his line was formed, launched his men directly uphill against Conroux's
front in spite of flanking fire from van der Maessen's men—and delivered the first volley.
The enemy simply melted away, running in upon van der Maessen's men. Confusion

followed, and Clausel was unable to stop the whole mass streaming back to the precarious shelter of Taupin's line in reserve.* At the same moment Ross, with the leading brigade of the 4th Division, belatedly appeared on Dalhousie's left and started to skirmish with Lamartinière's line, while five companies of the Rifle Brigade and four of the 43rd, having dislodged the enemy from the summit of the Ibantelli, swept down on Lamartinière's right flank. Reille spoke of himself as wandering about in the fog, taking advantage of which his troops had largely dispersed, stumbling down the northern slope of the range towards the French village of Sare.

Apart from Barnes's Brigade, which had 300 casualties, neither side lost heavily: the Light Division could number one officer and 26 men, and Ross had 37 in all. While both Clausel's and Reille's divisions retired on Sare, D'Erlon's, which had not been engaged, descended towards the village of Zugarramurdi, to the south-east, between Sare and the Puerto de Otxondo. There was no pursuit. Reille, in despair, remarked the next day that 'The spirit not only of the men but of the officers has been very bad during these last days. The absolute want of food must be the excuse for this state of things'.

Soult, in his exculpatory report to Clarke in Paris describing the ignominious disaster which had overtaken the army, admitted to his mortification and disillusion, and that he had deceived himself as to the state of morale of the troops he had led across the Pyrenees only nine days earlier, commenting that since he first entered the service he had seen nothing like it. He went on to insinuate that one of his generals had overheard men say, on approaching Pamplona, that they had 'better not fight too hard' because it would be preferable 'to get back to the frontier rather than to be led off into the middle of Spain'. Whether true or not, these were heartless words to describe an army which had fought with courage until 30 July, by which time it was convinced that Soult had seriously miscalculated and that the game was up.

Soult was left with a wreck of an army with which to defend French soil. In his infantry alone, 420 officers of the 1,318 with which he had set out were casualties. In his *official* returns of losses during the campaign in the Pyrenees, the total amounted to 12,563 (1,308 killed, 8,545 wounded, and 2,710 taken prisoner), but this does not include between 8,000 and 10,000 stragglers, which would take many days to re-join their regiments. It is doubtful whether, at Etxalar, he had been left with as many as 25,000 hungry and exhausted men of the 59,000 which had set out on 25 July. Allied casualties during the same period amounted to about 7,400, composed of 4,708 British, 1,732 Portuguese and perhaps as many as 1,000 Spaniards, but these would have included some stragglers later re-joining.

On 3 August Wellington halted his troops and started to redeploy them along the frontier. As he explained to Graham in a dispatch sent next day, while he was well aware of the objection to taking up a defensive position in the Pyrenees, it was too risky to advance into France. This was partly because of the still unresolved political situation, as is con-

* Wellington later referred to this as the most desperate and gallant charge he had ever seen.

firmed by Wellington's dispatch to Bathurst dated 7 August: 'as for the immediate invasion . . . I have determined to consider it only in reference to the convenience of my own
operations. . . . If peace should be made by the Powers of the North, I must necessarily
withdraw into Spain'. He would not be tempted to advance until quite certain that the war
had recommenced in Saxony. In the event, it was not for another month that news of the
rupture of the Armistice reached him. Meanwhile he must concentrate on taking possession of both San Sebastián and Pamplona: he could then reconsider taking the war into
France, should the international situation make that feasible. In the interim, he very much
doubted whether Soult would 'feel any inclination to renew his expedition—on this side at
least.'

On the 3rd, Headquarters were once again at Lesaka. Hill, with the 2nd Division, to
which Byng's brigade had returned together with Silveira's Portuguese, was at the Maya
passes; those at Roncesvalles were held by the 3rd Division; the 4th and 7th remained at
Etxalar; the 6th moved to the Aldudes; and the Light Division was placed along the
heights opposite Bera. Morillo's division occupied the lower Baztan behind Hill. Those of
O'Donnell's troops who had been engaged recently took up a position near the bridge of
Yanci, while the rest of his units, together with Carlos de España's army, continued to
blockade Pamplona.

Robert Blakeney, at Maya, records that there was often little in the way of demarcation between their advanced lines of sentries,

> . . . yet so well was civilised warfare understood that they never interfered with each other and
> scarcely ever spoke. The usual words, 'All's well', were never cried out . . . [being] superseded by
> 'stone chatters'—white polished stones, about two pounds' weight, were placed on the spot where
> each sentry was usually posted at night, and he struck them against each other twice in slow
> time. This was repeated along the chain of sentries. Should any sentry neglect this for more than
> five minutes, the next sentry instantly struck the stones three times and quickly; this rapidly
> passed along the line, and a visit from the piquet immediately followed. By these means we were
> sure that a sentry could not sleep nor be negligent on his post for more than five minutes at a
> time. It was rather remarkable that whatever signal our sentries made was immediately re-
> peated by those of the enemy.

Although not tolerated officially, a limited amount of circumspect fraternisation
went on, notably when exchanges of wine, brandy, tea, salt, tobacco, etc. were taking
place. Many pages of Brett-James's *Life in Wellington's Army* are devoted to the subject.

Lesaka, twice Wellington's headquarters, retains a number of characteristic old Basque
mansions, and it is assumed that his own quarters were in that known as 'Machicotenea',
a short walk from the church, while those named 'Juanamenea' and 'Zabaleta', in the
immediate vicinity, were also among the several buildings occupied by his senior staff.
Larpent described the town as a small, dirty place, as inevitably it was in the circumstances, crowded with fugitives, stragglers, with 'wounded and prisoners passing, with
mules and muleteers innumerable'. Although crossed by several rivulets, the place was
without drainage and the air heavy and oppressive.

General Longa was also there, 'looking like an English butcher in a handsome hussar dress'; but, as for his troops, nothing was 'safe at all from their fingers—from a horse or mule to a bit of biscuit.'

> Noises of all sorts, thrashing all going on in the rooms up stairs; the corn then made into bread and sold in one corner; aguardente [spirits of almost any sort, mostly brandy] being cried all about; lemonade (that is, dirty water and dark-brown sugar) the same; here is a large pig being killed in the street, with its usual music on such occasions; another near it with a straw fire singeing it, and then a number of women cutting up and selling pieces of other pigs killed a few hours before. Suttlers [sic] and natives with their Don Quixote wineskins all about, large pig-skins, and small ditto, and middling ditto, all pouring out wine to our half-boozy, weary soldiers; bad apples and pears, gourds for soup, sour plums, etc., all offered for sale at the same moment. Perpetual quarrels take place about payment for these things between the soldiers of the three allied nations and the avaricious and unreasonable civilian natives; mostly, however, between Spaniards and Spaniards. The animals eating green Indian corn almost against every house here and in the churchyard, which contains four tents, from the want of stables and quarters. Not the least curious or noisy in this confusion, are about fifteen men and women with fresh butter 4s. the pound, who are come from near St Andero and beyond it—a stout race dressed in a curious, peculiar manner, who contrive to bring butter on their heads in baskets for above a fortnight together, and sell it at last in a state that I am very glad to eat it for breakfast for ten days after it arrives. It forms a sort of very mild cream cheese, in fact.

Larpent records that Wellington 'could scarcely rise from the lumbago; but was in good humour and good spirits'; Cole was 'quite knocked up'; while Picton, 'attacked again with a violent bowel complaint . . . [had] fallen to the rear'. A few days later Larpent dined with Cole, who had the reputation of living very comfortably: even at this juncture, he had travelling with him

> . . . about ten or twelve goats for milk, a cow, and about thirty-six sheep at least, with a shepherd, who always march, feed on the road side, on the mountains, etc., and encamp with him. When you think of this, that wine and everything is to be carried about, from salt and pepper and tea-cups to sauce-pans, boilers, dishes, chairs, and tables, on mules, you may guess the trouble and expense of a good establishment here.

What Larpent found quite unaccountable was the fact that there were numbers of cases of desertion among the troops at this time, when they were quiet and well fed. Writing on 25 August, he confirmed that by then he had 'tried only five out of the sixteen sent for trial: they are all sentenced to death, and all shot!' One officer had tried to stop desertion by addressing his men and telling them that any who wished to do so would be sent over to the French with a flag of truce. Naturally, no one stirred, but Larpent had qualms about the legality of such a procedure. (He computed, when writing some four months later, that only 37 men had been executed during the previous twelve months.)

On the 23rd Larpent noted that Wellington, together with Murray and the Spanish staff, were busy comparing 'a dozen great Spanish drawings and plans of the mountains about them.' What was in the wind?

8

SAN SEBASTIÁN FALLS

HAVING thoroughly thrashed Soult at Sorauren, Wellington could now concentrate on extracting the thorn of San Sebastián from his flesh: if not at leisure, at least he did not intend to be hurried. In addition to those guns he had put ashore again at Pasajes, Wellington was expecting the remaining consignments of the long-promised battering train. They should have arrived from Portsmouth by 6 August but had been delayed by persistent contrary winds, the first ship of the convoy not sailing into Pasajes until the 19th, but—such are the inherent failings of administrators—without any ammunition; it was not for another four days that one carrying powder and shot for the 28 guns dropped anchor. The second convoy contained 23 new guns intended for a projected but cancelled descent on Cuxhaven, at the mouth of the Elbe, which had been re-routed by the Ordnance Board, but supplied with garrison carriages and traversing platforms—practically useless in siege operations—and with only 480 barrels of powder and hardly enough round shot for two days' bombardment. Providentially, the last vessels to arrive contained 62,000 round shot, 7,500 barrels of powder, etc.

Another cause of Wellington's dissatisfaction with the Admiralty's conduct of affairs was that they had persistently neglected to send an adequate squadron to assist him with the blockade of San Sebastián and St-Jean-de-Luz, from which the French continued to send reinforcements and *matériel* nightly to the besieged fortress. When the young Prince of Orange was sent to London with the dispatch reporting on the result of the battles of the Pyrenees, the only vessel to be found to take him, after some delay, was a cutter.

It was not until 3 September, largely because of the vagaries of weather and on account of contrary winds, that Wellington received news at Lesaka of the resumption of hostilities in Saxony on 12 August, at the ending of the Armistice of Pläswitz. This news had only reached Bathurst on the 27th, but it was sent on immediately by semaphore signal to Plymouth, where a swift vessel was waiting to sail for Pasajes. Wellington, apprehensive that the Austrians might make a patched-up peace, which would allow Napoleon to transfer considerable reinforcements to south-west France, had for over three weeks been left entirely in the dark concerning the latest political developments. To what extent he might have changed his policy if advised sooner is one more imponderable of many.

In mid-August young John Aitchison had been designated Military Commandant at Pasajes, a post directly answerable to Pakenham, and there he remained until early November, for the port 'from the want of a resident to make arrangements had got into a state of great confusion'. His duties were at first confined 'to finding quarters for the sick and wounded and seeing them forwarded to a hospital station', but his responsibilities were soon considerably extended to, for example, overseeing the embarkation of prisoners, among them the garrison of San Sebastián. Before long he was provided with a Provost to superintend the police under his command, while an Adjutant was promised. In late October, when writing to his father, he observed that, having many opportunities of conversing with French officers and men, he had been 'surprised to find so general a disgust at the War—all are for peace—they lament the blind policy of their Emperor tho' they seldom abuse him—but the feeling amongst the common Soldier is to prefer an English prison to being sent back in exchange to France.'

Among the continuing problems with which Wellington was pestered during this period was that concerning the command of Spanish troops. At last, under pressure, the Spanish government agreed not to dismiss Girón, who, together with General Manuel Freire (Freyre), would be responsible directly to him. Both were preferable to O'Donnell, who had far too good an opinion of himself, even proposing that he should command *all* the cooperating Spanish troops. When this was refused, he went off in a huff. Girón took over command of the Andalusian Army of Reserve and Freire the (4th) Army of Galicia. Together, including some of Girón's and Carlos de España's troops, still blockading Pamplona—and unlikely now to be relieved—and the divisions of Morillo, Barcena, Longa, Porlier and Losada, Wellington had some 24,500 Spaniards to hand by 8 August. He was under no illusion as to their capabilities; but he intended to keep them all—even those on which he could rely to a certain extent only—on a tight rein.

It was always possible that Soult's troops, concentrated behind the Nivelle, even if in temporary disarray, might make a desperate eleventh-hour attempt to relieve San Sebastián, and so the reinforcements Wellington was expecting (Matthew Aylmer's Brigade), together with the 1st Brigade of Guards, marching up from Oporto, where they had been detained owing to sickness, would be added to Graham's force. Among the units starting to disembark on 19 August were a company of sappers and miners wearing red coats, to the surprise of the engineer officers: they were the first to reach the Peninsula, replacing the blue-uniformed 'military artificers' Wellington had previously received in dribs and drabs. The 2nd Division, which had suffered severely in recent fighting, was sent to distant Roncesvalles, its place at Maya taken by the 6th, behind which, at Elizondo, were the 3rd.

Little of moment had occurred at San Sebastián since 27 July. There had been no further sorties, although a certain amount of intermittent sniping continued to take place. General Rey had been active in making further defensive measures in advance of the inevitable storm. On the Allied side, Fletcher was preparing positions for the siege artillery being disembarked. These would concentrate their fire on the riverside flank, again chosen to receive the main attack once the breaches had been further enlarged, but at the same time the horn-work and the demi-bastion of San Juan (at the south-east corner of the town) and curtain wall above it would be battered from the San Bartolomé redoubt. Burgoyne argued that such flanking fire would endanger storming parties at the nearer breach: it would be more sensible to make a frontal attack on the horn-work, particularly as it was apparent that Rey, having demolished the damaged houses behind the main breach, had run up internal fortifications and raised barricades in the streets, cutting off the area from the rest of the town and thereby making any projected attack from the east even more precarious. Fletcher pulled rank, and Wellington approved his decision to repeat the original plan, but on a larger scale.

Rey had indeed built up a formidable stone wall above the ruined houses, using the debris and paving-stones: it rose fifteen feet from the street level, and had been loopholed at intervals of a yard. He had repaired and scarped the town wall, leaving a sheer drop from the ramparts into what was now a virtual cul-de-sac dominated by the newly constructed wall. This extended north from the curtain above the San Juan demi-bastion. The counterscarp which had been blown down by the mine on 25 July had been repaired, and several new traverses had been constructed along the ramparts with beams and casks of earth, leaving only space for one man at a time to pass. Meanwhile, since the first assault, when receiving supplies of stores and ammunition by boat, Rey had shipped off all his transportable wounded. By 15 August —Napoleon's birthday, celebrated with illuminations and by running up in huge letters the words 'VIVE NAPOLÉON LE GRAND' on the castle walls—the garrison (according to Belmas) numbered 2,996 men.

Wellington was able to borrow 80 gunners from Collier's squadron and officers and artillerymen from the 3rd and 4th Divisions.* Two batteries were placed on the brow of the hill above the ruins of San Bartolomé to fire on the demi-bastion of San Juan, the greater part of the face of which 'came down with a crash' on the afternoon of the 27th, as did the adjoining curtain wall. North of the ruined bridge spanning the Urumea were fifteen guns, with another fifteen further north-east: these would play against the main breach and adjacent fortifications, while from the summit of Monte Ulia another battery would make life uncomfortable for Rey's men in the citadel. Several mortar batteries were also positioned on the sand hills east of the Urumea, which could shell the town and make it difficult for Rey to continue repairing the fortifications, although Wellington had admitted to Graham on the 23rd that he had serious doubts as to their utility, apart from causing 'general annoyance' to the Basque citizens of the place, who would be forced to seek shelter in their cellars. As he reiterated: 'If the general bombardment should set fire to the town, as it probably will, the attack on the enemy's entrenchment will become

---

* Augustus Frazer noted on the 27th that the batteries on that day 'were manned by seamen, Portuguese, Germans, and a few British artillerymen. Terribly confused work: half the number of good, well-instructed men would do twice the real service'.

impossible', adding: 'I do not believe that our use of mortars and howitzers does the enemy the slightest mischief, and the conflagration which it may occasion will be very inconvenient to our friends the inhabitants, and eventually to ourselves'.

Bombardment by the 63 pieces engaged commenced at 9.00 in the morning of the 26th and continued intermittently throughout the day. While Rey replied for some time, his counter-fire slackened as guns were dismounted or their gunners driven away by the tremendous battering they received. By evening, extensive damage had been done to the eastern fortifications. Much less had been brought about by the guns above San Bartolomé, so these were moved to a new position on the isthmus west of the broken bridge and near the parallels previously excavated in the suburb of Santa Catalina (only 250 yards away, rather than 800). A sortie made by Rey to destroy them during the night of the 27th was thwarted.

Meanwhile, at 3.00 in the morning of the 27th, an amphibious landing had been made on the island of Santa Clara, from which the west flank of the castle could be battered. It was led by Lieutenant Arbuthnot from the *Surveillant*, with several boats manned by sailors and marines, and soldiers commanded by Captain Hector Cameron. Four were killed and fifteen wounded before the small garrison was captured after putting up a strong resistance. Harry Jones, who had been taken prisoner in the earlier assault, refers to Wellington having written to Graham on that same day, intimating that it would be 'very desirable to have the back of the rock [Monte Urgull] closely examined by some Staff and Engineer Officers, and some of the Navy, in order to ascertain whether an attack there would be likely to be successful.'

At noon on the 29th, Wellington, Graham, Leith, Dickson and Fletcher conferred, when the decision was reached to storm the fortress at about noon on the 31st. By the 30th, gunfire had extended the main breach to a width of almost 300 yards, and had destroyed the *chevaux de frise* and other barricades which Rey had attempted to raise along its lip. Frazer, who could see the garrison 'like ants, toiling in adding to their defences', commented, when surveying the scene, that it 'may not be easy to persuade troops to attack breaches which have once been assaulted, without success.' A week earlier he had remarked that it was undoubtedly much stronger already, 'as the enemy has employed every means in adding to its defences, and in strengthening those he originally possessed', which was the natural consequence of the former failure. He had also made the ominous observation that 'It may be necessary to reduce the town to ashes', and had mentioned this possibility to Graham, who said he would obtain a specific answer from Wellington on that point, but of course the women and children would be permitted to leave the place first.

About 80 yards north of the main breach was a smaller breach, made very deliberately, should it be impossible to enter the town from the larger, with its interior retrenchment, which did not extend that far; but access to it was problematical, as it was the last place which could approached at low tide, and then only by scrambling along a narrow strip of slippery rock immediately below the ramparts. By the afternoon of the 30th, the letters on the castle walls had been almost entirely knocked away, and a large building, the Convento de San Telmo, 'under the Mirador' and dominating the lesser breach, had 'just burst out into flames; it was formerly an [*sic*] hospital: all this is very dreadful.'

Any guns not being employed were dragged towards Irun, as Soult had been moving troops into positions along the far bank of the Bidasoa during the previous night: an attack might take place at any moment from that quarter. In consequence, the 4th Division was marched to intermediate Oiartzun, on the *chaussée*, together with all the horse artillery, ready for this contingency.

Discussions had been taking place as to which division would storm San Sebastián. General Oswald, whose troops had failed to take the place five weeks earlier, did not hesitate to give his opinion that, if the assault was to be any repetition of the first, it would probably miscarry. Each general of his division felt the same and, as Graham remarked to Wellington, the very fact that such was the prevailing view would make it fail. When it was suggested that the 5th Division would be replaced by another, naturally Oswald and his officers rejected the idea as being a humiliation which would cause great resentment. Wellington therefore called for volunteers from the nearest three divisions to join in the storm 'and show the 5th Division that they have not been called upon to perform what is impracticable.'

In the evening of the 28th, 200 men from both the Guards' and K.G.L. brigades of the 1st Division, plus another 200 from the 4th and 150 from the Light Divisions, stepped forward. During the night of the 30th they filed down to the parallels, but not as the 'forlorn hope'. General Leith, arriving from England the previous day (having been invalided home after being wounded at Salamanca), refused to let them show the 5th Division how to mount a breach: they would act merely as supports. Oswald handsomely offered to act as a volunteer aide-de-camp to his successor, whose sudden arrival had deprived him of the opportunity of re-gilding what some had implied, unjustly, were tarnished laurels.

Leith selected General Frederick Robinson's brigade (1/4th, 2/47th and 2/59th) to lead the assault, supported by the 750 volunteers and with William Spry's Portuguese and Andrew Hay's brigades in reserve, while the 5th *Caçadores* from Bradford's brigade were to remain in the parallels to act as sharpshooters. Robinson's men were divided into two columns. From parallels in the sand hills to the east of the estuary—from which they would emerge on a broad front, avoiding the mistake of the previous assault—one column would traverse the exposed bank of the Urumea and then wade across it to storm the main breach; the other would make for the ruined corner of the bastion of San Juan, which, if they could clamber over its debris, might enable them to outflank the secondary defensive wall. The main attack was scheduled for noon on 31 August at low tide, for there was a mean difference of some sixteen feet in height here between tides.

Leith had planned what might well become more than a diversionary attack for Bradford's Portuguese, since during recent nights several officers had been investigating the sites of possible additional fords. The first to discover one was Captain Robert Macdonald, R.A., while Major Kenneth Snodgrass (of the 52nd, but seconded to the Portuguese) had waded across the river near its mouth, when the water had hardly reached to his waist, and, eluding the vigilance of a sentinel, had clambered up to the lip of the lesser breach and looked down into the town; a third officer is said to have even climbed some way up the rock face below the Mirador battery. This subsidiary assault would take place once the main attack had developed.

Rey's attention would be distracted also by sending out two cutters serving as gun-boats and 29 launches carrying companies of the 85th Regiment to simulate a seaward disembarkation, although they would keep well out of range of Rey's guns. Harry Jones had added an editorial note to the 3rd edition of Jones's *Journals of Sieges*, suggesting that, from personal observation, an actual amphibious landing would have been successful, for

> The appearance of the boats of the squadron with troops in them, at the back of the castle, created considerable consternation among the few soldiers who had been left in it, more as a guard over the prisoners than from any idea of an attack from the sea. Had the boats pushed in rapidly, there were no defences to have prevented the troops from landing; the effect of their having done so would, in all probability, have caused the surrender of the garrison. There were 150 English prisoners anxiously looking out to be released, who would have formed a great addition to the number landed from the boats.

Bradford would have in readiness some 300 volunteers from his 13th and 24th Line regiments. These would cross the shallowest of the fords—some 200 yards broad and immediately below the disabled guns on Monte Urgull—and take the lesser breach by surprise. From there they could outflank the main breach and defensive wall and pour into the town.

While awaiting the storm, Rey's men had been desperately removing all the debris falling inward from the main breach, although under continuous fire from mortars. There was a perpendicular drop of anything between seventeen and thirty feet from the lip to the foot of the internal wall, and behind it rose the newly erected barrier. While most of his guns had been disabled, Rey had kept three pieces concealed, two in the high curtain and one behind the horn-work, and these could be brought out to enfilade the breach at short range once the assault had begun. In addition, Rey had placed perhaps as many as five mines, which had not been unnoticed by the British engineers, among them one of 12cwt of powder secreted below the middle of the main breach, which would certainly blow to pieces the head of the assaulting column.

A false attack had been delivered at 10.00 on the night of the 29th in the hope that it might induce Rey to explode the mines prematurely, but he did not take the bait. Stores of bombs and live shells were piled in positions from which to hail the assailants. The 2,500 men remaining of the garrison (less 250 left as a reserve) were deployed wherever they might cause most destruction, notably behind the loopholed counter-wall, but they would be kept under cover until the last moment. Picked men, each with three loaded muskets at hand, held the traverses on either side of the breach.

The Allies made their last-minute preparations at 2.00 during the night of the 30th, when three mines were run out from the advanced sap near the battery in the suburb of Santa Catalina to a point below the sea wall, which impeded a direct approach to the beach: when fired, a 70-foot stretch was demolished.

Frazer recorded that the evening had been very stormy, with violent rain, thunder and lightning, but that at 8.00 next morning the sun had just forced its way through the haze, which a gentle sea breeze was dispersing. Graham was waiting at the battery just north of the east end of the ruined bridge, from where he would direct operations. As soon as there was reasonable visibility, the batteries started firing, which continued until 10.55, when the assault began. Providentially, during the bombardment, a chance ball or falling stone had broken or cut the fuse to the mine by the main breach, which never exploded.

> It is curious at such moment to watch the countenances, and endeavour to read the minds of men [observed Frazer]. Hope, solicitude, anxiety are to be seen; frequently apathy and indifference, the effects of a continuance of scenes of danger; and now and then, though rarely, open fear. None here seem more praiseworthy than the good-humoured Portuguese infantry, who serve our batteries with shot and powder. They toil all day in a slavish way, yet retain their composure and good temper through all our urgent endeavours to make them do more than human strength is equal to.

At 10.55 Lieutenant Francis Macguire of the 1/4th, leading the 'forlorn hope' of twenty men from his regiment, sprang out of the trenches and reached the foot of the main breach, only to be shot dead. Seconds later a French mine, known to exist under the sea wall north of the horn-work, blew up before a party sent to find and cut its train could reach it; they all perished. By now the French defences were black with men, while their hidden guns were run out and opened up with canister. The debris from the breach was found to be composed of large slippery blocks of stone or concrete rather than rubble— smaller fragments had been washed away by high tides—and difficult to clamber over to reach the lip, where Robinson's men were faced by repeated volleys from the loopholed counter-wall directly facing them. Below them was a sheer 20-foot drop into the dry moat, into which one man jumped and broke his neck. Those who attempted to break through the traverses on either side of the breach—the only exits—were shot down immediately. Successive waves of troops attempted to gain a foothold on the rampart, but as each party surged towards the traverses it was met by canister fire from guns trained directly or diagonally on the approaches and the survivors could only reel back. Further reinforcements were sent in and, although the buglers kept on sounding the advance, the movement was entirely checked. No lodgement could be made on the approach to the breach since most of the masonry was too heavy to move, although it provided some cover. Sir Richard Fletcher, the commanding engineer, was shot through the neck and killed early in the action, while Oswald, Robinson and Leith were all severely wounded, the last by a splinter of shell breaking his arm in two places.*

---

* Fletcher was buried near San Bartolomé at first, together with other engineer officers, and only much later transferred to a small graveyard on the seaward slope of Monte Urgull.

At 11.35 Bradford's Portuguese units set off at the double across the sand hills, slip-pery rocks and pools of the tidal flats, deployed in two columns. The first, of 300 volun-teers from the 13th Line, led by Snodgrass, had 900 yards to cover and reached the foot of the lesser breach within ten minutes, during which time they received only two salvos, one knocking over fourteen men. Those too badly wounded to crawl away were drowned in the shallows through which their companions had waded thigh-deep when crossing the estu-ary. The column was not immediately successful in carrying the breach, but the men soon established themselves there. As had been calculated, their position did outflank the internal defensive wall, and they looked down directly into the town. The second col-umn—six companies from the 24th Line under Major William MacBean—found itself nearer the right flank of Robinson's men.

It was at about 12.15, when matters looked desperate at the main breach and the impetus of the attack had slackened, that Graham took an unusual decision from his position with the forward battery. He gave the order—by semaphore to more distant guns—to resume fire on the French defending the curtain wall, even if that meant firing imme-diately over the heads of the storming units, the survivors of which were now taking what-ever cover they could among the debris. The range was known from long practice, but the margin of error was less than 40 feet vertically. However, such was the accuracy of the new guns that the only Allied casualties were from flying fragments and ricochets. The bom-bardment continued for some twenty minutes, after which the guns were turned on to more distant targets. The firing was effective enough, causing great slaughter among those attempting to fire over the parapet—long lines of headless dead were seen next day under it—while the artillerymen of the two guns which had caused so many casualties among the storming party were found mangled beside them.

Once again, the assaulting troops clambered up the wide-mouthed breach, there turning left to pass through the traverses, now battered to pieces, and got a footing at the near end of the curtain wall, although the central bastion still resisted. Suddenly a store of cartridges, grenades and live shells there caught alight—probably accidentally—causing a terrific explosion which scorched or killed at least sixty of the defenders. This enabled the 3/1st, the leading regiment of Hay's brigade, which Leith had just ordered up (indeed, it was his final reserve) to press ahead and dominate the horn-work, which was now evacuated by its garrison to avoid being cut off. After a desperate resistance, the surviving French in the bastion being bayoneted down its steps into the town, the storm-ing-party reached the far end of the curtain and were enfilading those that had taken refuge behind the retrenchment wall.

Simultaneously, 300 yards to the north, volunteers of the Light Division discovered a ruined house built against the back of the ramparts, but not sufficiently cut away from it, and were able to slide and jump down into the street below. Other units, pressing north, drove the French from a stockade delaying Snodgrass's men, who likewise swarmed into the town together with those from the 5th Division straying north from the main breach. Fire from the Mirador and nearer San Telmo's bastion were still being troublesome and, as Frazer noted at 1.20, 'must be silenced'. This was not so easy, as a high wind was now blowing clouds of sand in front of his guns, almost blotting out the view, while during the next hour and a half the temperature dropped, it started to rain again and the lowering sky blackened. By 1.30 numerous prisoners, caught in cul-de-sacs, were being escorted out: Wellington was later to report 750, of whom 350 were wounded. Heavy musketry was still being heard within the town, where two more mines exploded, but this gradually decreased as Rey retired his men from positions tenaciously held there, among them in the upper floor of the convent of Santa Teresa, at the north-west angle, until dislodged by the 9th Regiment. They then withdrew to their upper defences, the Mirador bastion and the citadel, which now came under fire from 68lb carronades, 8-inch howitzers and 10-inch mortars.*

At 2.15 Graham ordered his guns in the batteries to cease firing, for the lower town, at least, was now in his hands. General Wilson's Portuguese brigade, which Wellington had requested earlier, with which to reinforce his front near Irun, was already marching away. Clouds of smoke were now obscuring visibility, for a large fire had broken out already near the main square, and two others were soon alight. The fact that Rey was now rolling down shells into the town must have started additional conflagrations, but although it poured with rain again all afternoon and night, half-filling the parallels with water, the deluge was not strong enough to extinguish the flames—it had more of an effect on the actions taking place along the banks of the Bidasoa, as described in the following chapter.

On 1 September Wellington rode back to survey the sorry scene and decide on those measures which, he considered, would most rapidly reduce the citadel. While his surrender was inevitable, Rey was apparently determined to procrastinate, although already suffering further casualties by mortar fire: no fewer than sixteen mortars were now in operation against the upper defences of Monte Urgull.

While the storming may have looked very grand when seen from such a distance as the commanding height of Monte Ulia by the crowd which had gathered there the previous morning, the reality was very different. John Cooke of the 43rd, having obtained permission to ride across the mountains from Bera to San Sebastián to witness the assault, well described the scene, for all the world knew that it was to take place that day, and numerous non-combatants—commissaries, doctors, orderlies and servants—together with hundreds from neighbouring villages, dressed to kill and intent on seeing the show, were already seated when he arrived. Cooke found himself between two sprightly young girls sucking sweets, which they shared with him. He records that while shedding a few pearly tears, and unfolding the little papers containing their sugar-drops, they ejaculated '*Pobre Sebastiano! pobre Sebastiano*'; and when he asked them why they did not rather say 'Poor soldiers!', they replied '*Oh, si, si! Pobres soldados también!*'

---

* Frazer complained about the quality of the 'wretched shells' of the 8-inchers, nearly half of which burst in leaving the howitzers.

The next day Captain Andrew Leith Hay, after visiting his wounded uncle, Sir James Leith, made his way towards the main breach, the whole ascent of which he described as being

> ... covered with dead bodies ... stripped and naked ... they now lay on the ground where they had fallen, but in such numbers, that on a similar space was never witnessed a more dreadful scene of slaughter. Behind this impressive foreground rose columns of smoke and ashes, and occasionally, through the vapour, was to be distinguished the towering castle-keep.... I proceeded along the curtain, which presented a scene of indescribable havoc and destruction. The heat from the blazing houses was excessive ... [for] the buildings all having communication, and being very closely arranged, ensured the conflagration becoming general; roofs falling, and the crashing of ruined walls that rolled down, and, in some cases, blocked up the passage in the streets, it was rendered more impressive from the obscurity occasioned even at midday by the dense cloud of smoke that shrouded the scene of ruin and desolation ... in the centre of this chaos, I found General Hay, blackened with smoke and dust ... still busily employed in restoring order ... or in vainly endeavouring to obstruct the unquenchable flames that surrounded him in every direction.

Having stormed the place, the troops had taken advantage of the immemorial privilege of sacking what remained of the town, and few would contest the fact that even if the unfortunate inhabitants, who had been cowering in their cellars for days, were friends and allies, this would not hold back the more brutal soldiery from revelling in every form of excess. Certainly there was much drunkenness, and there were isolated cases of rape. Captain John Harley, of the 47th Regiment, describes intoxicated men lying incapable between corpses (and, when in that state, being relieved of their loot by the Portuguese), and soldiers' wives sitting in circles, dividing between them the watches and silver brought to them from pillaged churches and private houses. Major Frederick Hoysted, of the 59th, reporting to Hay, maintained that 'As to plundering having been *permitted*, I can assure you that every exertion was made by me and my officers to prevent anything of the kind, and that I sent frequent patrols, by your order, to arrest any man found in the town, and to afford assistance to any inhabitant who might ask for it'. Colonel William Maynard Gomm, 9th Foot, recorded in his diary four days later that

> ... although many of the excesses committed at Badajoz were avoided here, St Sebastian is a more melancholy story than either Badajoz or [Ciudad Rodrigo]. For, with the exception of ten or twelve fortunate buildings, there is nothing left ... but the blackened walls of its houses ... How the fire was started is uncertain—I think there is little doubt of it having been done intentionally by the enemy. In a town so constructed as this, there was little chance of its being got under [control] when kindled—particularly by our soldiers, who were busy about anything else'

Gomm continued:

> We have been driven almost to the ramparts by the fire, while the people rushed in crowds where certain destruction seemed to threaten them, in search of their property, [the] great part of which they had concealed and buried. Much certainly has been saved: we have done what was in our power to assist them: a great deal however has been plundered, and a vast proportion must lie buried under the ruins. Never surely was there a more complete picture of desolation than the place presents.

George Gleig, when exploring the site several days later, found the streets still

... choked up with heaps of ruins, among which were strewn about fragments of household furniture and clothing, mixed with caps, military accoutrements, round shot, pieces of shell, and all the implements of strife. Neither were there wanting other evidences of the drama which had been lately acted here, in the shape of dead bodies, putrefying, and infecting the air with the most horrible stench.

Worse was to be seen in the breach, which was still covered 'with fragments of dead carcases, to bury which it was evident that no effectual attempt had been made'. Gleig afterwards learned that 'the Spanish corps which had been left to perform this duty, instead of burying, endeavoured to burn the bodies; and hence the half-consumed limbs and trunks were scattered about, the effluvia arising from which was beyond conception overpowering.'

As Oman has remarked in a footnote, if Graham had followed up Wellington's suggestion that Aylmer's brigade should replace immediately after the storm those units which had been engaged in it, fewer excesses would have taken place: but in the heat—literally—of the moment, this might not have been so easy to organise: street-fighting was still going on, and so few officers were left to control the plundering. As confirmed by the casualty lists, in the 5th Division alone, out of 200 officers present at the storm, 37 were killed and 70 wounded; five only survived in the 47th, and four in the 59th. Allied casualties in this second assault on the fortress amounted to over 2,300 (865 in Robinson's brigade alone, of the 1,500 men engaged), of which some 870 were fatalities—a very high proportion of killed to wounded, largely caused by canister or grape firing into a compact mass at close range.

While naturally distressed at these heavy losses, Wellington was also infuriated by the mendacious Spanish manifestos now being printed, insinuating that by his order, or with his connivance, San Sebastián had been deliberately set alight by the British, who they claimed were jealous of the town's economic prosperity, having formerly traded exclusively with France.* The civil prefect of the province of Guipúzcoa, of which San Sebastián was the capital, had accused Graham likewise. While Wellington would have been the first to admit that it was virtually impossible to lay siege to and storm a town without destruction taking place, and there was always the chance of fire breaking out, he would never deliberately start a conflagration. In this case, high winds were fanning the flames, which, with street fighting still taking place, no one was in a situation to extinguish. In his Dispatch of 9 October, he firmly denied the calumny, reiterating:

Every thing was done that was in my power to suggest to save the town. Several persons urged me, in the strongest manner, to allow it to be bombarded, as the most certain mode of forcing the enemy to give it up. This I positively would not allow for the same reason as I did not allow Ciudad

* Neighbouring Pasajes had been the chief home port from the mid eighteenth-century of the flourishing Caracas Company, trading with Venezuela.

Rodrigo or Badajoz to be bombarded; and yet if I had harboured as infamous a wish as to destroy a town from motives of commercial revenge, or any other, I could not have adopted a more certain method than allow it to be bombarded.

Meanwhile Rey still remained in the citadel, perched on the summit of Monte Urgull, where, with about 1,250 men but hampered by 450 or more wounded and almost 350 Allied prisoners, he awaited developments. Offensively, there was little he could do. Of his artillery, only four small guns and three mortars remained on his land front, while his four heavier pieces faced out to sea. The vaults of the old castle now served as his main powder magazine, but no other structure could resist the impact of an 18-pounder ball, and by the evening of 3 August every building that had survived that long had been smashed, and even the upper works of the castle were pulverised, although the walls of the Mirador bastion were so hard that balls split on striking it. There were no casemates, and his prisoners (38 of which had been killed or wounded, as Rey had refused to let them construct any stone shelter), together with the garrison, had to lie in the open unless they could find clefts among the rocks in which to hide.

On that same day Graham sent up a flag of truce and a formal summons to surrender; but Rey, although aware that Soult's attempts to raise the siege had failed, and that there was no likelihood of relief, defiantly refused to accept defeat. Wellington determined that he could only be brought to reason by stepping up the bombardment, battering him into submission. On the 5th, and in pouring rain, seventeen 24-pounders were man-handled across the fords by several hundred men and 70 or 80 pairs of bullocks (one gun got lost in quicksands *en route*). They were moved in full daylight, without any reaction from Rey, and positioned in the centre of the horn-work, while another three were placed further back, where the French 'Cask Redoubt' had stood. Two guns were later ferried across to the island of Santa Clara, from which they could enfilade the citadel's sea front.

At 10.00 in the morning of the 8th, 61 guns, including those in Graham's former batteries on the Chofres and Monte Ulia, opened fire. At noon Rey hoisted a white flag. Providentially, Wellington arrived back at San Sebastián soon afterwards, which pre-vented any delay discussing details in the articles of capitulation. Rey was granted the usual terms. Twenty-four hours later, descending from their demolished defences, the 1,234 effectives of the garrison marched out from the Mirador gate and to the still smoul-dering ruins of the Plaza Vieja to lay down their arms, some breaking them as they did so. Officers were allowed to keep their swords, while one was permitted to convey Rey's last justificatory dispatch to Soult. According to Frazer, besides the effectives, there were about 600 non-combatants, many disabled by former wounds, among whom 272 were severely wounded. On the 11th, the garrison was shipped off to England as prisoners, while the few women and children still there were sent to France. Apparently Rey was anxious that he and his men be embarked at Pasajes under British protection: they feared Spanish reprisals.

Frazer went up to inspect the relics of Rey's defences later in the day, where he found every single gun carriage shattered and the castle entirely ruined. He noted that, apart from 37 guns remaining on Monte Urgull, another 56 pieces of artillery had been taken—a total of 93. It was generally estimated that, prior to its surrender, the siege had cost the French in killed and wounded (and including some few deserters) about 2,400 men, remembering that many wounded earlier in the siege had been evacuated by boat.

Harry Jones, who had been among the prisoners released, recorded that the scene

... which the interior of the hospital and castle [presented] that night was beyond description: the numbers of unfortunate men laying in rows, suffering the most excruciating agony, black, and scorched from head to foot, were the unfortunate sufferers who had been wounded by the explosions which took place in the rear of the breach. From what was communicated to [him] ... previous to the assault, of the great quantity of combustibles which had been distributed by the French among the houses, he has very little hesitation in attributing to that circumstance the destruction of the town; nor did he ever hear the garrison accuse the British of having it set on fire.

On 25 September Frazer noted that the temporary Portuguese garrison at San Sebastián was being replaced and that 'a Spanish one has arrived, or rather is arriving: for their troops straggle in, as it were, by a kind of accident.' About two companies of Allied artillery were to remain with them. On the 30th Frazer rode south from Oiartzun, where he took leave of Sir Thomas Graham, who had been suffering from an eye complaint for some time and was about to sail home, being replaced by Sir John Hope. Hope arrived on the 6th; Graham embarked on the 9th.* Frazer missed seeing Beresford, who had sailed for Lisbon some days earlier. After inspecting artillery units under Ross, Ramsay and Smith, Hope made his way to Headquarters at Lesaka, where his presence would be required very shortly.†

---

* In November, while on sick leave, Graham was approached by Bathurst to take command of a small force making a descent on Holland, which he reluctantly agreed to do. It was a decision he was to regret. His surprise attack on Bergen-op-Zoom during the night of 8 March 1814 was a failure: although he was entirely acquitted of all blame, it was a mortifying close to an otherwise distinguished military career.

† Jones's Journals of Sieges (3rd edn) provides a deal of detailed information concerning the siege, in which the amount of shot and shell expended came to 27,719 for the earlier operation, and 43,112 for the second—a total of 70,831 projectiles, together with 5,579 90lb barrels of powder. The engineers had expended 2,726 gabions, 1,476 18-foot fascines, and 20,000 sandbags!

9

THE ACTIONS AT SAN MARCIAL AND BERA

THE sound of the preliminary bombardment of San Sebastián by Allied artillery on 31 August had drowned the thunder of gunfire along the lower Bidasoa at precisely the same moment as Graham's troops were engaged in storming the main breach. Listeners at either Oiartzun or Pasajes would have been confused, although the cannonade to their west was the heavier. At dawn that day Soult had attempted what turned out to be no more than a token relief of San Sebastián by a show of force at two points on the frontier, the first being at a series of fords across the Bidasoa between Béhobie and the hamlet of Biriatou, where the river makes a sharp turn to the west, commanded by the ridge of San Marcial (249m), which extended south-east from the village of Irun.

Almost a month had passed since Soult's demoralised troops had stumbled back across the frontier. Indefatigably, he had spent the intervening time rehabilitating and reorganising his army yet again. The much reduced divisions of Maucune and van der Maessen were strengthened by the inclusion of intact regiments from Villatte's reserve, while his most depleted units were sent back to Bayonne to do garrison duty until they could be built up to a reasonable strength by new recruits. Soult intended to make his next stroke with men who had suffered least during his Pyrenean campaign: together, discounting flank guards, he could muster almost 45,000, among them some 8,000 stragglers who, piecemeal, had re-joined their colours since their precipitate dispersal among the wild and intricate Pyrenean passes.

Soult realised that a break through to San Sebastián—although only twelve miles away—could only be made by means of a rapid thrust on a narrow front, and the lower Bidasoa was the only place from which this offensive could be launched. Beyond an arm of the estuary there was a stretch of level land and a comparatively accessible gap in a range of low hills between the frontier and the beleaguered fortress. To the north extended the long coastal ridge of Jaizquibel (543m), and to the south rose the rugged spurs of the Peñas de Haya massif (832m), which, like La Rhune (900m) on the frontier, dominated the area. From the bridge at Béhobie, destroyed two months earlier, the *chaussée* from Bayonne traversed this plain and, after crossing a low col, entered Oiartzun and then Hernani, bypassing both Pasajes and San Sebastián, before continuing up the Urumea valley to Tolosa. The lower reaches of the Bidasoa from Béhobie to a point below the

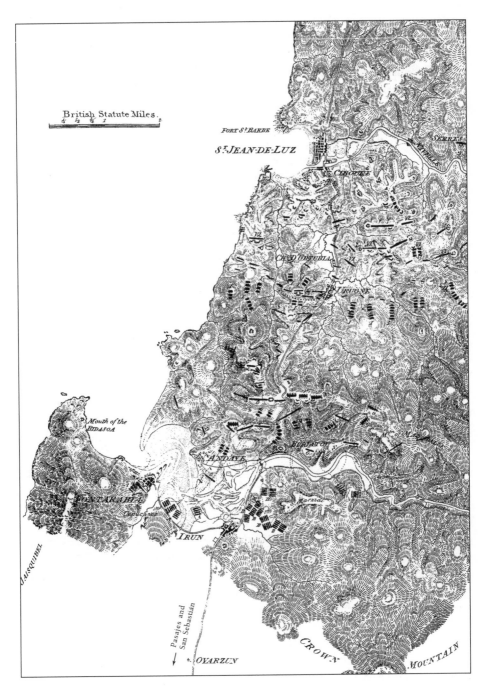

The Mouth of the Bidasoa: A Reduced Section of Batty's Map

hamlet of Biriatou were fordable at several places at low tide, and this was the most obvious stretch over which to make the advance in any strength.

Soult had ascertained that Wellington's forces were again strung out from Fuenterrabia to Roncesvalles, and that the two-mile-long ridge of San Marcial, rising immediately south-east of Irun and dominating his main area of attack, was occupied by Freire's 'Army of Galicia' and Longa's Cantabrians. Between Biriatou and Bera, the Bidasoa flowed in a ravine difficult to cross. As far as he could tell, further to the south-east, the front from the heights of Santa Barbara—rising just south of Bera—to the Col de Maya was held by the Light, 6th and 7th Divisions, with probably the 3rd and 4th in their rear. These would be a threat to his left wing, which would require a strong flank guard—the more so as it was Soult's intention to make the left half of a 'pincer movement' from Bera, as had General Moncey some twenty years earlier.

When circling towards the coast, Moncey had circumvented the Peñas de Haya— also known as the Cuatro Coronas (Four Crowns) by the Spanish and Les Trois Couronnes by the French (only three of its peaks could be seen by them)—and, approaching the San Marcial ridge from the rear, had routed the Spanish defending it. Why should he not do the same? It would first be necessary to take the San Marcial ridge, commanding the chaussée, which ran for a mile between the river and its lower slopes. It should not be too difficult to take.

By 27 August, having brought up Foy's outlying division from St-Jean-Pied-de-Port, Soult had nine divisions concentrated between Espelette and St-Jean-de-Luz. His plan was that Reille, with three divisions (those of Maucune, Villatte and Lamartinière), with Foy in his rear as a reserve, would cross the Bidasoa fords at Béhobie and deliver a frontal attack on San Marcial. Four divisions under Clausel (those of Taupin, Darmagnac, van der Maessen and Maransin) would cross further upstream, just below Bera, break through the Allied line, traverse the hills in the rear of the Peñas de Haya and descend on the highway at Oiartzun. As Clausel's thrust would pass diagonally in front of the Allied divisions known to extend south-east from the heights of Santa Barbara, D'Erlon, with Abbé's and Conroux's divisions, would take up a defensive position between the village of Sare (immediately east of La Rhune) and Ainhoa (some distance due north of the Otxondo or Maya Pass) to oppose any movement against Clausel's flank.

Wellington was well aware that Soult had concentrated his troops towards the coast, ready to launch a frontal attack against the San Marcial ridge, and as aware that Clausel would be making a simultaneous thrust towards his centre from Bera. On 30 August Q.M.G. Murray had distributed dispatches to the commanders of each Allied division, advising them that 'the enemy appears to have assembled a very considerable force towards Irun, opposite our left, and also to have added something to their strength near Vera, opposite the position of the Light Division. All rumours from them also agree that they mean to make an attempt for the relief of St Sebastian.' This was followed by orders detailing what counter-dispositions should be made.

On Wellington's left, from near Fuenterrabia, some of Mendizábal's Biscayan units watched the broad estuary of the Bidasoa, where they were unlikely to be attacked. Freire's Galicians—from left to right, those of Juan Díaz Porlier's (near a hermitage chapel on the summit), with Francisco Xavier Losada's units in the centre, and flanked by Pedro Barcena's Division opposite Biriatou—would bear the brunt of any attack on the San Marcial position, which they had taken up some weeks before and where they were well installed. They would be supported by the 1st Division and Aylmer's behind their left, while to the rear of their extreme right, high on a spur of the Peñas de Haya, were two brigades of Lowry Cole's 4th; also partly behind them were Francisco Longa's Cantabrians, brought up from further upstream and from Lesaka. These were deployed on the Descarga–Pagogana ridge, which, after a slight dip, extended that of San Marcial to the south and rose steeply from the gorge of the thickly wooded Bidasoa valley, which it overlooked from the west.*

The river banks along the next reach rose so abruptly that it was very unlikely that any attempt would be made to cross there, but the situation would need to be watched. Further upstream, between a bend of the river at the hamlet of Endarlatsa and Bera, were four fords, the most accessible being near Endarlatsa, which was normally only a foot deep. These were guarded by the Portuguese brigade of the 4th Division, now commanded by Colonel James Miller as Stubbs had been wounded at Sorauren. They had taken up their position there on the 26th, and had been reinforced four days later by Inglis's Brigade of the 7th Division.

On a meander of the Bidasoa, immediately south-west of the village of Bera, was a narrow bridge, the only one surviving on its lower reaches, now barricaded and defended by Captain Daniel Cadoux's company of the 95th, installed in a group of adjacent houses which they had fortified. A brigade of the Light Division, commanded by John Skerrett, was deployed along the heights of Santa Barbara overlooking Bera from the south. A detachment of the division (a wing of the 43rd, three companies of the 1/95th and three battalions of Pedro Girón's Andalusians), provisionally under James Kempt owing to the temporary absence of Alten, were later to move up from Lesaka, cross the bridge, and deploy to the west.

The 7th and 6th Divisions, on the Puertos de Etxalar and Otxondo, respectively, were to demonstrate against D'Erlon's forces near the villages of Sare and Zugarramurdi (between Sare and Urdax), while Girón's men and the 3rd Division, now commanded by Charles Colville, would be ready to support them if necessary, but this right wing was not to commit itself to any serious attack—generally to 'disquiet' the enemy and keep him occupied would be enough.

It had been Soult's original intention to cross the Bidasoa on the 30th, in view of Rey's insistent calls for help, but he had to delay this for a day, as neither had the bridging material—constructed and ready to throw across the river once a foothold on the far bank

---

* All these Spaniards, numbering less than 15,000, had been starved by their inefficient commissariat, particularly the Galicians, and Freire had been obliged to request rations from the already overstretched Allied magazines.

had been made—yet arrived from the rear, nor had the alerted divisions yet received the two days' rations ordered for them. Meanwhile Reille's units were to remain behind the hills immediately north of Béhobie and Biriatou, while Clausel's were to be kept out of view behind the crest of the so-called 'Bayonnette Ridge', descending from the Mandale (573m) towards Bera. To conceal such concentrations of troops was virtually impossible, and they were duly observed and reported on by officers placed on the commanding heights of the Peñas de Haya and Pic d'Ibantelli.

Before dawn on 31 August Reille led his divisions down towards their forward positions.* As at San Sebastián, it was a morning of dense haze, which enabled Reille's columns to descend towards the Bidasoa and Soult's artillery to be moved into position unnoticed, although it is hard to believe that no sounds of movement were heard by Spanish picquets across the valley. Soult had chosen the old redoubt of Louis XIV† as a convenient place of vantage from which to direct operations. Some of the 36 guns on this front to protect the crossing were sited on the redoubt ridge; others were placed below hills to the east, and on another height further west (north of the destroyed bridge at Béhobie). An additional twelve guns had been positioned by Clausel to command the fords at Endarlatsa, south of the gorge of the Bidasoa.

At 6.00 the van of Reille's columns started across the fords, but it was not until they began to drive in the Spanish picquets that any alarm was given. On account of the morning mist, it was not easy either for the French to re-form in an orderly line or for the infantry and their supporting artillery to see their objectives or targets. It was almost impossible to advance for another hour and a half, by which time the Spaniards had ample time to deploy in line along the upper slope of the ridge, where a trench had survived from the battle of 1794.

Lamartinière's division was the first to wade through the three fords below Biriatou, which they did without loss before occupying a wooded knoll situated above a meander of the river, from there ascending to fan out below the southern end of Freire's position. They were ready to resume the steep climb—the mean gradient was almost 1 in 4—once the other divisions were over. Maucune's, using the same fords, then crossed and veered to Lamartinière's right while sappers began to erect a trestle and/or pontoon bridge (or bridges) between two fords to enable them to keep in communication dry-foot with their base after the tide had risen.

When the mist had lifted, Villatte's units could be discerned waiting to cross near the broken bridge, as soon as the falling tide had made the deeper ford there practicable. It was only 8.00, and the full ebb tide would not be for another four hours, during which period there would be time not only for Villatte to pass over but also for Foy's troops to do likewise. Meanwhile Soult's artillery started to shell both Irun on its knoll and the San Marcial ridge, only to find that the main Spanish positions there were out of effective

---

* By the present *péage* (toll-gate) of the A 63 motorway, and along the riverside flats immediately below Biriatou.
† On a hill rising abruptly north-west of the present *péage*.

range. Freire had only twelve guns with which to make a comparatively feeble reply: most of the gunners from Graham's batteries were fully occupied at San Sebastián.

Soult became impatient. At 9.00, without waiting for his other divisions to cross, he ordered Lamartinière to storm the centre of the ridge, while Pinoteau's brigade of Maucune's division attacked further north-west, where the pilgrimage chapel stood, leaving Montfort's brigade to guard the bridge-builders. The undergrowth on the ridge, which rose steeply from the Bidasoa, while providing occasional cover, also broke up any orderly advance in column behind *tirailleurs* as intended, and before long the whole had become one confused mass swarming breathlessly uphill. Freire had sent some of his light companies down to skirmish but kept his main line two-thirds up the slope. As the French approached, after giving them a volley Freire ordered his whole force to charge with fixed bayonets, which sent them streaming back to the river bank, not coming to a stop until almost colliding with Montfort's men, while their pursuers—their success so far having given them renewed confidence—clambered uphill to regain their former position. By now it was about 10.00.

Within an hour Villatte's troops would be across, with the exception of St Pol's Italian brigade, which remained behind on his right flank near Hendaye. At noon Soult repeated the attack, this time with a superior force—Lamartinière, having rallied his men, on the left, with Maucune's in the centre and Villatte's fresh units on the right wing—but with little better result. Again they found themselves being rolled back, the centre and left predictably giving way before the rest. Only General Guy's brigade, on the extreme right, was able to get a brief foothold near the chapel, gallantly defended by Porlier.

Meanwhile Wellington, intensely preoccupied by the progress of events at San Sebastián, in his rear, had, on learning of Soult's attack, sent a message there to instruct Bradford's brigade to join his front urgently, but it had arrived too late for Graham to countermand his own order to Bradford to take the smaller breach. Wellington was also as intently watching the action at San Marcial from the Peñas de Haya. He had already instructed Aylmer to support Freire, should it be necessary, but his brigade had not yet climbed up from near Irun when one of Freire's aides reined up, requesting the support of the 4th Division also. This was refused, for, as Wellington remarked to the Spaniard, passing him his telescope, he could see for himself that the enemy were dislodged already and in full retreat downhill. Oman discreetly repeats only part of Stanhope's record of his conversation with the Duke (which took place some eighteen years later), who, when being questioned about the Spanish troops, had replied:

> Oh, poor devils, they never won a battle. I made them win one though at San Marcial. They were standing an attack, and sent me pressingly for succour. Meanwhile the French finding my troops at hand on their side [presumably Aylmer's units] were beginning to withdraw. This the officer who came to me did not see with his naked eye, but I could through my glass. Look, I told him. Why, he said, they do seem to be retiring. Well, I said, if I send you the English troops you ask for, they will win the battle; but as the French are already in retreat you may as well win it for yourselves. So they accordingly did; and now I see that in their accounts this is represented as one of their greatest battles—as a feat that does them the highest honour.

Wellington had observed that the rest of the attack had failed entirely, and that it would be impossible for Guy to maintain his position on the ridge. This was indeed the case, for, seeing themselves abandoned by their comrades, they likewise recoiled when the Spanish counter-attacked, having by then suffered as many as 37 officer casualties. The French descended with such impetus that the press of men broke their bridge(s). Captain Thomas Henry Browne later recorded the day's action with the words, 'Their conduct on this occasion was good, & this was the only time I ever saw the Spanish Army behave like Soldiers'; while Private William Wheeler, on visiting the ridge a week later, had testified: 'a desperate job it must have been . . . for the contending parties lay dead bayonet to bayonet. I saw several pairs with the bayonet in each other'.

Having regained the north bank in utter disarray, Reille's brigades were in no state to be rallied in a hurry—indeed, it took three hours for him to get them sorted out. Any idea that Soult may have entertained of sending in Foy's division to deliver a third assault on the ridge cannot have been considered for long. By then Soult's casualties were at least 2,500; the tide was beginning to rise; and he had received such disquieting news from D'Erlon that Foy's units were sent hurrying towards his left wing. Meanwhile Clausel was reporting that the same rainstorm which had deluged San Sebastián and was now soaking Soult's dispirited men had fallen in torrents further upstream, not only blotting out the landscape but making the fords they had crossed that morning quite impassable.

Clausel's operations that day had been equally ineffective. At dawn his long columns were marched from their places of concealment towards the Bidasoa, unobserved in the morning mist; but, as Kinkaid remarked, as soon as this was dispersed by a passing breeze, the opposite hills were seen to be bristling with bayonets, as the enemy descended towards the river. Bugles instantly sounded the alarm, and the riflemen hurried to their posts. Taupin's division waded across the Bidasoa at Endarlatsa, and Darmagnac's, followed by van der Maessen's, crossed at another ford further north. George Hennell states that it was not until 2.00 that they were all over. Maransin's division was to remain on the French bank, should there be any attempt by the Light Division, deployed along the Heights of Santa Barbara, south of Bera, to cut Clausel's communications with D'Erlon. Van der Maessen's troops had been halted soon after crossing and remained on the defensive, in case Allied units advanced from Lesaka against Clausel's thrust.

Once the haze had begun to lift, Clausel's guns started to shell Bera, from which the Light Division picquet withdrew, allowing some of Maransin's units to enter the village and take possession of the bridge. When Harry Smith, Skerrett's aide, saw this happening, he remarked that unless the 52nd were sent down to support the battalion of riflemen still there, they would be unable to maintain their position for long, to which Skerrett had merely replied: 'Oh, is that your opinion?' Smith had then impertinently commented: 'And it will be yours in five minutes. Indeed, as soon as the enemy was in possession, Skerrett agreed reluctantly and Colborne was ordered to send down the 52nd. The bridge and a group of houses facing its eastern end were soon recovered, after which the 52nd returned to its position on the ridge of Santa Barbara. Maransin's men retired also to take up a position on a low hill just south-east of Bera, where they remained for the rest of the day anxiously watching the Light Division opposite them.

Meanwhile Taupin's skirmishers, which with those of Darmagnac were cautiously moving ahead after crossing the Bidasoa, found themselves being shelled briefly by another French battery when aiming at Miller's Portuguese ahead of them. Before long Miller was driven off the lower wooded slopes and retired uphill out of artillery range towards a stronger position, along which Inglis's brigade was already deployed. It was now about 11.00. Stiffer fighting commenced when Darmagnac's men, approaching through the woods, engaged with Inglis's right; and although the 51st and 68th launched a counter-attack (in which eleven officers of the former were disabled), the two brigades had to abandon the position and rallied on another ridge further south. Private Wheeler records that

> General English [Inglis] had ridden to the front to become better acquainted with the ground, when by some unforeseen accident he became separated from his men and would have been made prisoner but for the little band who at a great disadvantage rescued him. Captain Frederick saw the danger his General was in, ordered his buglar [sic] to sound the charge, the sound was answered by three cheers, and off his company went accompanied by Lieutenant Bayly's Company and one company of the C.B. [Chasseurs Britanniques] Regiment. In a moment they were mixed with the enemy and down the hill they went together, pel mel [sic], into the wood. The General was rescued. Our company was now ordered to the front, we soon got into action but as the enemy had [been] joined [by] their reserves and the large trees completely covered them, we fell back on our reserves. This soon drew them out from cover and brought us all together by the ears. I never remember to be under so sharp a fire in an affair of his kind before.

By now Clausel, hearing gunfire in his rear and seeing Kempt's units approaching from Lesaka, with which van der Maessen was soon to be bickering at long range, was becoming uneasy. By 2.00 Taupin's division found itself engaged with the flank skirmisher of two brigades of the 4th Division, which had deployed on a shoulder of the Peñas de Haya north of the Risco de San Antón, towards which they had been sent once Wellington was satisfied that Soult's second assault on San Marcial had failed. Clausel, getting increasingly nervous and anticipating that he would get cut off from his reserves if he pressed ahead into the tangle of steep, trackless and thickly wooded hills, brought his troops to a halt below Inglis's hill. Not long afterwards, Lemonnier-Delafosse arrived there with a dispatch from Soult, in which he conceded that he had been checked at San Marcial, directing Clausel to re-cross the Bidasoa as his flank might be endangered. As when frustrated by Soult at Sorauren, Clausel displayed apparent annoyance, the order reaching him precisely at the moment when his own half-completed operation showed every sign of being successful! Even had that been true, there was not the slightest chance of making any further advance, for the whole battleground was now deluged by the same thunderstorm which had so darkened the sky over San Sebastián. It was with the greatest difficulty that his exhausted troops slipped and stumbled downhill through the trees under the downpour, several units getting lost, while Soult's aide had a narrow escape from drowning in the Bidasoa on his return ride.

Meanwhile, opposite Soult's left wing and fulfilling Wellington's orders of the 30th to keep D'Erlon pinned down by a series of sham raids, Dalhousie, the moment the mist had lifted that morning, had sent Carlos Le Cor's brigade to demonstrate against Rémond's brigade of Abbé's division at Zugarramurdi. Colville, at the Puerto de Otxondo, had sent down Madden's Portuguese to probe likewise near Urdax, further east; to the west, Girón's Andalusians bickered with Conroux's outposts south of Sare, within its wide bowl of hills. In each case, supporting troops made their presence noticed, which was enough to convince D'Erlon that his two divisions were to be attacked in force; he thus sent Soult an urgent demand for reinforcements. He might not have been so worried had not Dalhousie launched—or, at least, sanctioned the advance of—Le Cor's men directly against Zugarramurdi, where they were successful in driving out Rémond's troops, who retired north-east towards Ainhoa, upon which the rest of Abbé's division, pressed by Madden's brigade at Urdax, likewise concentrated. Whether or not with Dalhousie's approval, Madden and Le Cor then attacked, but were driven back, whereupon British battalions from Barnes's brigade were fed in, and the Portuguese rallied. Abbé remained on the defensive, having lost 325 men, while Allied casualties in the action were about 250.

Although entirely contrary to Wellington's orders, which were to demonstrate only, the attack had more than served its purpose and, together with Colville's movements further east, which were duly reported to D'Erlon, strengthened the latter's supposition that it was his section of the front which was in serious danger. He repeated his request that Foy's division be sent back urgently, otherwise he would not answer for the safety of the army. By the time D'Erlon was reporting that the Allied attack seemed to be slackening, the action at San Marcial was over and Foy's troops were well on their way.

At 10.00, on receiving a dispatch from Wellington directing him to break off his demonstrations against Abbé and march to join Inglis east of the Peñas de Haya, Dalhousie found his units so entangled with those of the enemy that it was difficult to extricate them, and it was not until 4.00 that Barnes's brigade was able to proceed west towards Lesaka, leaving Le Cor's men only opposite the French. By then the rain had started to fall in earnest.

Ordering van der Maessen's division to cover their passage, Clausel's two sodden fighting divisions, having picked their way down through the woods, at dusk started to reassemble near the fords they had waded across that morning, only to find that the water level had been rising so rapidly that the river was becoming impassable. Clausel himself, and the leading brigades of both Taupin's and Darmagnac's divisions, found their way across. Many men were swept away and drowned in the torrent, however, and each rear brigade, together with the whole of van der Maessen's division, found itself cut off: by then the fords were covered by six feet of water, which was overflowing the banks. Van der Maessen now took charge, and, realising that he would be overwhelmed entirely unless he got away by morning, led his troops east along the river bank towards Bera, where they could cross by means of the bridge (that of San Miguel) immediately south of the little town. After groping their way round a wide meander of the flooded stream, their path lit fitfully by lightning, at about 2.00 in the night they suddenly came upon two British sentries, who were promptly bayoneted before they could give the alarm, the rain having wet the priming of their rifles, which misfired.

Van der Maessen was staggered to find the bridge not in friendly hands but barricaded against him. How was it that Maransin had neglected to occupy such a vital crossing that morning when he had had the chance? Harry Smith states that earlier in that rain-drenched evening, when again urging Skerrett to send down additional reinforcements to hold the bridge, he was told to send back the battalion already there, leaving only 'a picquet of one officer and thirty men at the bridge'. Smith could hardly believe his ears and, when he remonstrated, Skerrett confirmed the instruction. Smith thereupon galloped down to the houses to carry out the order, where Captain Daniel Cadoux, after first abusing him for not supporting him earlier that morning—not realising that Smith was in no way to blame—remarked that although his company was by then reduced to not many more than 50, he and Captain John Hart would remain with them, barricading the bridge and further fortifying and loop-holing the neighbouring houses meanwhile, and would resist as best they could until supported, for surely reinforcements would be rushed down on the next occasion any enemy units made a serious attempt to occupy the bridge.

Cadoux's men, under cover in their 'blockhouses', had remained on the alert and immediately opened on the head of van der Maessen's column with a volley, bringing down numbers, and the whole to a halt. Cadoux himself soon fell, having made himself conspicuous by imprudently mounting his horse at the first alarm when leading his company towards the bridge. Both Lieutenants Travers and Henry Llewellyn were wounded, the latter's jaw being shattered while repulsing the desperate rushes being made towards the narrow stone structure and resisting vain attempts to break into the fortified houses. The sound of continuous firing could be heard from Skerrett's position above the thunder and lightning pealing around the hills.

Skerrett, only half a mile away, failed to take advantage of the critical situation in which the French now found themselves and obstinately refused to send down the reinforcements at hand to the hard-pressed picquet until too late, in spite of messages reaching him that, although able to hold their own, without more men they could not maintain their position for long. Nevertheless, the combat continued for over an hour without the enemy making any progress—van der Maessen himself being shot and killed—until, superior numbers eventually prevailing, the picquet was overwhelmed. Including Cadoux, seventeen men were killed and 43 wounded. The few survivors were brought off by another company, sent down belatedly by Skerrett, whose callous sacrifice of Cadoux's men was never forgiven by members of the 95th.

A single battalion could have blocked the passage until daylight, forcing four enemy brigades, with Allied units converging on them from the west, to surrender. As it was, the whole, three or four abreast, were able to file over during the early hours of the 1st and make their way to the security of Sare before Skerrett was aware of the opportunity lost.* It is difficult to verify to what extent they continued to be fired on while crossing, but at least 200 killed and wounded Frenchmen were found lying near the approaches to what has since been known as 'Cadoux's Bridge', now with an appropriate memorial plaque on it.†

So ended Soult's last 'battle' on Spanish soil: he was now to remain on the defensive. He had been foiled ignominiously in his attempt to relieve San Sebastián, and by minimal forces. A mere 8,000 Anglo-Portuguese and 12,000 Spaniards had succeeded in checking his army of 45,000; indeed, a good proportion of it had not even been seriously engaged, being 'contained' by mere tactical threats on Wellington's part.

During that day Soult must have suffered over 4,000 casualties —1,643 alone in Lamartinière's division in his own report of losses—while Lamartinière himself was mortally wounded also. The 350 men listed as 'missing' may be accounted for by those lost in the Bidasoa. George Simmons, when examining the site of Cadoux's gallant exploit two days later, noted that numbers had been drowned close to the bridge and also at the fords even before the downpour. Although the wounded had been removed, the dead 'were still laid out about the bridge', and some of the latter may have been consigned to the river already. Simmons could not help noticing that 'Trout of a large size were feasting upon the Frenchmens' carcases in the water'. This did not seem to deter the angling fraternity, for both William Surtees and Jonathan Leach frequently cast their lines into that stream, where 'some uncommonly fine trout' were caught!

Anglo-Portuguese casualties in the above-described actions were just under 850, and those of the Spaniards no fewer than 1,679 when defending San Marcial. Wellington, not often given to praise, certainly felt justified in offering congratulations in his official dispatch on this occasion, and his less critical opinion of the Spaniards' capacities was conceded later when he added a number of Spanish units to his forces before the advance on Toulouse.

---

* Skerrett appears to have succeeded in concealing several salient facts of the action from Wellington for some time. Although he had been able to evict Soult's rearguard from Seville on 27 August 1812, Colonel Thomas Bunbury later referred to Skerrett as being 'brave to rashness' as an individual, but 'At the head of troops, he was the most undecided, timid, and vacillating creature I have ever met'. Not long afterwards, Skerrett applied for leave, having just inherited a considerable estate, which he was not long to enjoy—he re-joined the colours and the following March was killed at Bergen-op-Zoom.
† The Pont de Cadoux, partly hidden by vegetation along the river banks, may be seen by following the former main road south from the west end of Bera—now with a bypass—for about 200 yards, there turning briefly right along a narrow lane and then a few paces to the left.

10

THE PASSAGE OF THE BIDASOA
AND THE ASCENT OF LA RHUNE

WHICH of the two commanders—Soult or Wellington—had the most uncomfortable night is impossible to determine. It was not until early on 1 September that Soult was advised that van der Maessen's divisions and the rear brigades of Taupin's and Darmagnac's divisions were safe and had not been encircled and taken prisoner; he was aware already that San Sebastián had been stormed, even if Rey still held out, and that there was no chance now that he could be relieved.

According to Captain Thomas Henry Browne's *Journal*—slightly confused at this point—Wellington had descended from the Peñas de Haya once assured that Soult had failed to take the San Marcial ridge and, as the rain started to come down in torrents, as it continued to do through the night, took shelter in an iron foundry (that of San Antón), to which a Basque peasant had guided his party, before proceeding—if Browne is correct—to the hamlet of Artikutza (Articuza), south-west of Lesaka, which he re-entered next day. Lesaka remained the headquarters for the rest of September. It had been a distinctly unpleasant progress: for two hours Wellington and his staff picked their way down 'a steep and winding path so narrow we were obliged to dismount, & lead our horses in single file … & such was the darkness & insecurity of the path, that we took hold of the tail of the horse in our front' before reaching the foundry. In trying to avoid a cascade, several officers, including Pakenham, slipped and fell down a slope of shingle, and, 'having been stopped in their descent by trees, clung to them, until day broke.'

Browne was correct when he went on to say that there was little else Soult could do but employ his troops 'night & day in raising works & batteries, destroying roads & bridges, & fortifying every knoll & spot of ground that they supposed would impede the entry of our Army into France.' These redoubts, abatis and entrenchments were thrown up along the line of hills rising from the north bank of the lower Bidasoa, together with others east of the commanding height of La Rhune.

Soult could not understand why Wellington had not immediately pushed across the frontier once San Sebastián was in his hands—the more so after the poor showing of his own troops at San Marcial. He had not realised that there were more complex reasons causing Wellington to hold back. One, referred to earlier, was political. It was not until 3 September that he first learned that Austria had declared war on France, and another twelve days passed before reliable news reached him of the defeat of Vandamme at Kulm.

123

As Rory Muir has stressed, as far as the Northern Allies were concerned, the defeat over 20,000 French troops at Kulm had far more immediacy and impact than the fact that many times that number were pinned down on the Spanish frontier, and although they were quite willing to acknowledge the fact that Wellington's engagement with Soult was contributing towards the eventual overthrow of Napoleon, it was a perfunctory acknowledgement: it was, for them, a distant, remote struggle, about which they had read in the papers for years, and it meant little to them personally. They had even signed capitulations allowing French garrisons to be released without making conditions which prevented them from fighting on the Spanish front. This was largely due to delays in communication and the lack of any assertive British representation at the headquarters of the Northern Allies: as these delegates were chosen by Castlereagh, he has been held responsible for their not having sufficiently emphasised the unremitting British partici-pation in the continuing conflict.

In writing to Bathurst on the 19th, Wellington announced, in an unusually convoluted way, that he would shortly put himself in a situation

> ... to menace a serious attack, and to make one immediately if I should see a fair opportunity, or if I hear that the allies have been really successful, or when Pamplona shall be in our power.... the Allies are very anxious that we should enter France, and ... [as] the Government has promised that we shall do so, as soon as the enemy has been finally expelled from Spain.... I think that I ought, and I will, bend a little to the views of the Allies, if it can be done with safety to the Army.

On the same day, when acknowledging the receipt of a bundle of French large-scale maps from the Horse Guards, he also requested more maps covering the Upper Garonne and of the Bordeaux region, adding: '*I wish I may not require them*—but it is as well to have them, at all events', which suggests that Wellington had hopes that the Emperor might be brought to heel before he had invaded France that far.

Wellington was preoccupied with several complex logistical problems, vital to re-solve. The cooperating Spanish troops, in spite of their recent performance, were in a physically weak condition. As he explained, to get the necessary superiority of numbers with which to enter France, he would require about 25,000 Spaniards; but, as they were neither being paid nor properly fed by their own people, they would undoubtedly plun-der and set the whole country against the Allies in general. Eight thousand of Freire's men were in hospital, many suffering from malnutrition because of the apathy, if not worse, of their wretched commissariat and malingering officials. They had been subsist-ing on half-rations of bread and eight ounces of rice for several days and had not seen meat for weeks.* Many men had been left on the San Marcial ridge and had died with their wounds undressed, as Freire had no means of getting them back to the hospitals, no great distance behind the front. While reluctant to allow inroads to be made on his own magazines, Wellington had given permission that the Spaniards might receive limited

---

* Gleig mentions that they were then subsisting on heads of Indian corn, which they gathered from the fields, and roasted over their fires.

supplies from food convoys entering Pasajes and from his depots at Vitoria and Tolosa; but he could not allowed this to continue for very long, and extra pressure had to be exerted on the incompetent Spanish administration. As it was, Wellington would never permit more than three days' rations to be issued at any one time to his own troops, who otherwise were quite likely to consume the whole lot immediately or sell their surplus supplies.

Writing in mid-October, John Cooke described several hundred Spaniards he had seen bivouacking on the summit of La Rhune, where 'from want of good clothing and owing to the cold nights, they were in the most miserable and forlorn state . . . [with] barely a sufficiency of provisions to keep life and soul together'. This was particularly so in Longa's units:

> Their clothing was as ragged and miserable as their fare, uniforms of all countries and all colours of the rainbow: French *chakos* [sic] without peaks, leather and brass helmets, rusty muskets, and belts which had never been cleaned since in their possession. Some had old brown cloaks, with empty knapsacks and hempen sandals, and others were with torn shoes and almost bare footed. At the solitary roll of a drum, they sometimes issued from their burrows, or cavities of the rocks, like so many rabbits.

On one occasion, when Cooke was standing on a large slab of rock, it suddenly moved and, when he stepped aside, it slowly lifted. Smoke and the sound of voices issuing from it were followed by a dozen Spaniards, who had been crouching in a cave 'enveloped in the fumes of *cigarras* which they smoked to keep themselves warm, to drive away hunger, and to beguile the tedious hours'.

At a later date Larpent recorded an anecdote concerning the Spaniards, and why Wellington valued Colonel Dickson, his chief artillery officer, so much. The incident had taken place on 9 November, immediately prior to the Battle of the Nivelle, when Freire's troops at Bera were to march to the attack at 4.00 next morning. Although it had been known for some weeks that this was likely to happen, it was only at 9.00 that evening that Freire sent word that they were 'without any ammunition, and could not get any up in time'. Within an hour Dickson was sent for, 'just as he was going to bed. Instead of saying nothing could be done, or making difficulties, he proposed giving the Spaniards immediately the reserve ammunition of the nearest English division, and said that he would send out orders instantly, and undertake to get the English reserve replaced in time, and this was done.'

Soult's system of fixed fortifications—redoubts supplemented by elaborate entrenchments—was about a century out of date, yet he persisted in their construction. Meanwhile, since mid-August, he had been in correspondence with Suchet in Catalonia, floating impractical collaborative schemes, which Suchet sensibly rejected, partly because the two commanders were mutually antipathetic. By the time an alternative plan might have been agreed upon and received Napoleon's sanction, the disaster of Leipzig had intervened and Soult was left to his own devices: indeed, before long Napoleon was demanding that both commanders send troops to the northern front.

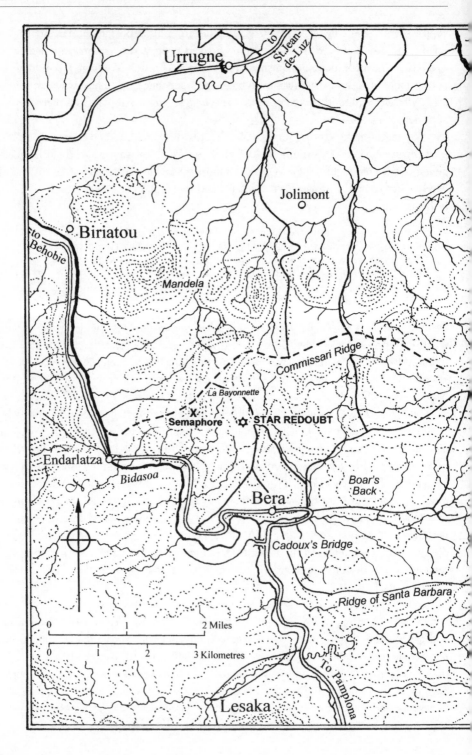

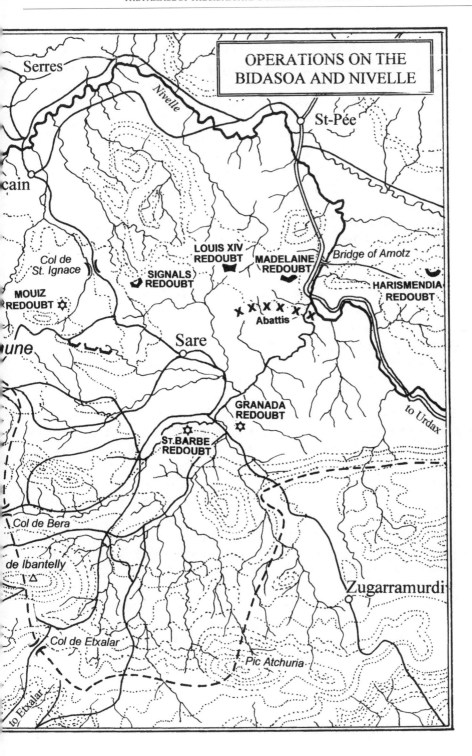

OPERATIONS ON THE
BIDASOA AND NIVELLE

Serres

Nivelle

St-Pée

cain

LOUIS XIV
REDOUBT

MADELAINE
REDOUBT

Bridge of Amotz

Col de
St. Ignace

SIGNALS
REDOUBT

HARISMENDIA
REDOUBT

MOUIZ
REDOUBT

X X X X X X
Abattis

une

Sare

GRANADA
REDOUBT

to Urdax

St.BARBE
REDOUBT

Col de Bera

de Ibantelly

Zugarramurdi

Col de Etxalar

Pic Atchuria

to Etxalar

Soult had assumed that the inevitable Allied attack would be confined to the area between Hendaye, near the Bidasoa estuary, and Cambo, on the upper Nive, a stretch of some twenty miles as the crow flies. With winter coming on, it was unlikely that he would be attacked on his left wing near St-Jean-Pied-de-Port, as the Pyrenean passes there were often snowbound at that season. This stretch was divided into two by the La Rhune massif, rising to 900m north of Bera and commanding the area closer to the coast. It was a formidable height, composed of several spurs and secondary ridges, and had wide areas of scree on its southern slope. One can well imagine the laboriousness of an ascent made by men carrying muskets and accoutrements, whatever the weather. There were also wooded areas on its lower slopes, and a few rocky outcrops closer to its summit, notably that known as the Lesser or Petit Rhune to its north-east.*

A chain of much lower and more accessible foothills of the range extended east. Many among them, as far as the Pic du Mondarrain (749m), were not far south-west of Cambo—from which a road partly skirting the Nive approached St-Jean-Pied-de-Port— and were crowned with Soult's line of static defensive positions. Beyond the Nive stood Foy's division, should the Allied 2nd Division threaten the left flank from their position near Roncesvalles; if necessary, Foy could call on Paris's garrison, but this was still at Jaca, south of the Somport.

It was in the twelve-mile (17km) section east of the Rhune that Soult now deployed the larger half of his army—six out of nine fighting divisions. Those of Abbé, Darmagnac and Daricau (commanding van der Maessen's men), together 14,000 men under D'Erlon, manned the five closed redoubts and lines of entrenchments between the Mondarrain and Ainhoa, north of Urdax. Secondary defences had been constructed behind them, between Espelette and the bridge of Amotz. Clausel, with the divisions of Conroux and Maransin in the vicinity of Sare, held the next sector, from the Nivelle to La Rhune, together with units of Taupin's division in fortifications thrown up below the northern flank of La Rhune. This central sector was defended by 15,000 men. Behind them stood Soult's reserve of 8,000 under Villatte. The most westerly sector, between La Rhune and the coast, commanded by Reille, had Maucune's weak division (4,000 men) deployed along the hills immediately north of the lower Bidasoa, with that now commanded by Joseph Boyer (formerly Lamartinière's) in reserve some three miles to the rear, encamped at Urrugne and Bordagain, not far west of St-Jean-de-Luz. Together they provided another 10,000 men at what Soult considered would be the least likely part of his alignment to be assailed—probably more than enough, as the site was naturally protected by the broad expanse of the estuary.

Unfortunately for Soult, it was here, precisely at the weakest point in his defensive line, that Wellington was preparing to attack, after one of his staff had made elaborate

---

* It should be pointed out that the IGN map (1254 OT at 1:25,000) prints the Petite Rhune as being a slight rise to the west of the summit at 699m rather than the rocky ridge to the north-east at 624m, marked as the Altzanga, which has led to confusion. The summit of La Rhune may be reached by the energetic pedestrian from a number of points, but since 1924 a rack-railway has operated during summer months from the Col de St Ignace (further north-west on the Ascain–Sare road), making a steep, 780m climb and taking some 35 minutes. The peak—now disfigured by a wireless and meteorological stations, bars, etc.—still provides splendid views.

preliminary investigations as to the viability of wading across the Bidasoa estuary from near Fuenterrabia as early as 15 September. In the words of Captain Robert Batty, this officer had been

> ... employed in ascertaining the situation of the fords, by which columns of infantry might pass the river near its mouth. With this view, and to avoid exciting suspicion, some of the Spanish fishermen were prevailed upon to undertake the wade through the channel at low water: and, under the appearance of being occupied in their usual employment of fishing, they proceeded a considerable distance across the river.

Soon afterwards, one of them was induced to make the entire crossing and return, which he did without having excited suspicion: in due course three fords were found, by which troops might wade over at low tide between Béhobie and deep water, in addition to those further upstream recently traversed by Soult's divisions.

Pamplona had yet to surrender, but, as it was impossible that it could hold out for very much longer, Wellington determined to cross the Bidasoa at the first practical opportunity, which would be at dawn on 7 October. At the same time he would assault and occupy the commanding height of La Rhune: this would enable him to dominate entirely Soult's defensive positions, which he would attack and take at leisure. Wellington had also ascertained that, although there was a picquet or two near the bar of the estuary,* Soult had no fortification further downstream than that at the 'Café Républicain' redoubt, on a ridge behind Béhobie.†

Wellington's plan was as follows. Three brigades of the 5th Division were to march from their camp at Oiartzun during the night of 6 October towards deserted Fuenterrabia, where one brigade would be concealed in the ditch of the old fortifications and the other two behind a long dyke further south, built to keep the sea water from the low-lying meadows to the west.‡ At 7.15 next morning, when it had been calculated that the three fords discovered in the vicinity would be covered by only three feet of water, they would make a dash across the estuary to occupy the village of Hendaye, not much more than a heap of ruins (having been largely destroyed by the Spanish in 1790) surmounting a knoll above the far bank.§ They would be followed by their divisional battery and a squadron of the 12th Light Dragoons, and would press forward and swing round and along a line of low hills to take in flank and rear the Croix des Bouquet position, known to be a rallying point for the French.

The 1st Division would likewise advance to Irun during the night and wait behind a lower ridge below the heights of San Marcial. On seeing the 5th Division move out of its concealment, the 1st would approach and wade across the ford opposite Béhobie and two just below it and storm the hill on which stood the Louis XIV redoubt. It would be accom-

---

* Beyond the sandy bay of Chingoudy, now flanked by the villas and hotels of Hendaye Plage, and where nod the masts of its marina or yacht basin.

† Not far west of the present N 10 at the Croix des Bouquets junction.

‡ This dyke may still be recognised, as along the top of it extends the main road from Irun to the airport, the runway of which has been laid out on land reclaimed from the shallows of the estuary.

§ Below this bank is another stretch of reclaimed land, now entirely covered by railway sidings.

panied by Wilson's Portuguese brigade, two squadrons of the 12th Dragoons and two batteries, with another three in support from the lower slope of San Marcial, which would fire on the French hill. Both the artillery and the pontoons, which the engineers would then throw across the river, would remain concealed until the infantry had started their advance.

Freire's 3rd and 4th Divisions, now commanded by Del Barco and Barcena, would cross further upstream below Biriatou by the same fords the French had used. The first column was to seize the Lumbaberdé (otherwise known as the 'Green Hill') behind Biriatou; the second would occupy the lower slope of the Xoldokogaina (or Choldocogagna; 486m), an extension of the Mandale massif further south-east. Once the far bank had been secured, they would be provided with a pontoon bridge. They would also be supported by Bradford's Portuguese brigade, which would cross the river later. Aylmer's brigade, only recently arrived from England, was to support the 1st Division, having left its tents in view of the French picquets still standing, to mislead them, before moving down to the forward positions assigned.

Thus on his left wing Wellington had some 24,000 men—45 battalions—ready to unleash against the thinnest part of Soult's extended line. To deceive him into believing that the danger was further east, on 1 October Wellington had ridden over to Roncesvalles to inspect the 2nd Division outposts, by now experiencing flurries of snow. Archibald Campbell's units in the Aldudes had received orders already to drive in the French further down the valley, a successful demonstration which had also enabled them to capture a flock of 2,000 sheep but which caused alarm along that sector. Soult hurried to St-Jean-Pied-de-Port to warn Foy to expect a more serious attack and to throw up additional earthworks. On the 5th, the 2nd and 6th Divisions—the latter on the northern flank of the Maya Pass, threatening Urdax—received orders to remain where they were, but that Campbell's and Da Costa's Portuguese (again commanded by John Hamilton) should hand over 'their outposts' to Francisco Espoz y Mina's irregulars, cross the Col d'Ispéguy, and relieve Picton's 3rd Division at Maya. Picton would lead his men north-west towards Zugarramurdi to replace the 7th Division. This would move south-west behind the hills (Atxuria; 759m) to the Puerto de Etxalar, where some of Girón's Andalusians were posted. Girón would assemble his units and be ready to drive in all enemy outposts below the south-eastern flank of La Rhune, which he would then assault: behind him, if required, would be the 7th Division in reserve and, not far to the east of the latter, the 3rd.

The southern flank of the massif would be ascended by the Light Division, already deployed on the Santa Barbara ridge, south of Bera, together with 2,500 of Longa's Cantabrians. Alten—Skerrett was no longer in evidence—was ordered to attack in two columns: Kempt's, abutting Girón's men, would ascend from Bera and drive off outposts on the Col de Insola (or Intzola) Pass* and try and outflank La Rhune from that direction; the other column, Colborne's, was to attack positions on the so-called 'Bayonnette Ridge',

---

* Not far east of the present Col d'Ibardin, where a more modern road ascends north, following a mule-track climbing to what was referred to the Puerto de Bera.

a spur descending from the Mandale towards Bera, and others immediately east on the Commissari or Erintsi Heights. Two of Longa's battalions would act as a thick line of skirmishers between the two columns; the other two would guard Colborne's left flank and, if possible, outflank the redoubts at a higher level. The 4th Division was brought across the Bidasoa to act as a reserve, relieving the Light Division at Bera.

Communications between the French on the Mandale or Bera front and those at the Croix des Bouquets, behind the Béhobie front, were difficult on account of the rugged intervening terrain. However, they had placed a semaphore on the Xoldokocana with which to keep in touch, although this would be useless in wet, foggy or misty weather and after dark. No attack would be made further east, where Colville's 6th, with the 3rd and Hamilton's Portuguese within supporting distance, would demonstrate only against D'Erlon, who would hesitate to leave his lines and counter-attack the flank of the Allied advance.

Thus the comparatively isolated central or La Rhune front, defended by Taupin's and Conroux's divisions in the first line, was to be assaulted by three Spanish and one British division (the Light, two of Girón's and one of Longa's), with five more (the 3rd, 4th, 6th, 7th and Hamilton's Portuguese) in support in their rear. Facing them were Clausel's three and D'Erlon's three, with Villatte's in reserve. Their numbers were fairly balanced; but towards the coast there was an immense preponderance in favour of the Allies.

The storm of the previous night had cleared the air on the coast and the sun was up when the state of the fords was examined by General Andrew Hay (in command in the absence of Oswald and Leith, both wounded at San Sebastián). At precisely 7.25, ten minutes after the appointed time, the Allied troops sprang out of their concealed positions and started towards the fords. Everything went according to plan.

The French were taken so entirely by surprise that the light companies of the 5th were across the Bidasoa before a shot was fired against them, while the 1st (the Guards and the K.G.L. brigade), wading the wide estuary, were also by then half way over. Gleig, with the 85th Regiment—part of Aylmer's brigade—remarked that the water reached considerably above the knees, and that those crossing the estuary had to 'hold their firelocks and cartouche-boxes over their heads, to keep them dry.'

Hardly any resistance could be made to what was an overwhelming force. There was only a picquet of 50 Frenchmen at Hendaye, very soon disposed of as the 5th circled round behind the village towards the Croix des Bouquets position. Frederick Robinson's left-wing brigade, keeping near the corniche should enemy troops be advancing from St-Jean-de-Luz, captured an old seaward-facing battery on the Pointe Ste-Anne and pushed back a battalion sent down from the Croix des Bouquets as far as the 'Sans Culottes' redoubt, surviving from 1794, on a hill north-east of the Croix des Bouquets. The two other brigade columns—those of Charles Greville and Luiz de Regoa—having occupied desolate Hendaye, veered south-east, driving a battalion before them along the crests of hills past the Café Républicain redoubt to attack in flank the Croix de Bouquets, already being assaulted frontally by the 1st Division.

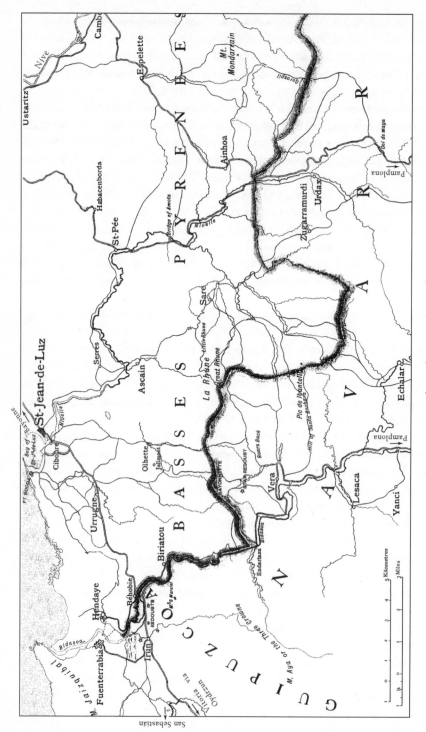

Operations on the Bidasoa and Nivelle (ii)

The latter, together with Wilson's Portuguese, on reaching the right bank of the Bidasoa, had spread out, and the battalion defending Béhobie, to avoid envelopment, had immediately left its positions and fled to the Louis XIV redoubt. Here a battery was in action, but it was overwhelmed within a few minutes. Both units retired on the Croix des Bouquets, where Reille, riding up in haste from Urrugne, now took command, hoping that Boyer's troops would arrive before the position was stormed; but the four advance battalions did so only in time to cover the retreat of fugitives, hustled back by the 1/9th to the skirts of their fortified camp at Urrugne, where they were joined by Boyer's other brigade, belatedly starting from its billets at Bordagain (then a hamlet adjacent to Ciboure, on the left bank of the Nivelle opposite St-Jean-de-Luz). By noon Reille had been reinforced by the leading brigade of Villatte's reserve, hurrying across the hills from near Ascain with Soult in person, in what might be best described as 'a lather'. However, it had not been Wellington's intention to push forward any further: a foothold had been secured, and that was sufficient for the time being.

As Soult, trying to explain away the disaster in his report to Paris dated the 18th, remarked, 'I had many reasons to think that the enemy's main attack would be on Ainhoa, and was there at 7 a.m. when the action commenced. But finding that there was but a demonstration in that quarter, I hurried to my right—only to find that everything was over.'* Indeed, it was all over, and quickly: the Croix de Bouquets position had been taken by 9.00.

Freire's Spaniards, further east, had been as successful, although at first their left-hand column had met strong resistance from two battalions and a redoubt above Biriatou, which prevented them from crossing the Bidasoa until the right-hand column, ascending the north-west spurs of the Xoldokocana—which then becomes rugged—had turned north and dislodged the enemy by attacking his flank and rear. Both columns then spread out: one brigade met the Guards at the Croix des Bouquets; and the other climbed further south-east, up the Osingozela (392m), to a position guarded by only one battalion, soon evicted, and pressed on to the Col des Poiriers, below a spur of the Mandale, where two isolated enemy battalions made off east in haste to avoid encirclement, followed for some distance by Freire's gleeful troops.

Wellington had taken possession of the whole of the heights commanding the lower Bidasoa at an absurdly low cost in casualties. But they were to be much heavier in the fighting taking place simultaneously on the southern face of La Rhune.

THE ASSAULT OF LA RHUNE

As explained earlier, to distract Soult, Colville's troops—at 7.00 that morning and as noisily as they could—drove in a French picquet at Urdax. It had the desired effect. At the same time Girón's, Alten's and Longa's men started to climb through the wooded

---

* The distance between Ainhoa and Urrugne, as the crow flies, is a good 10½ miles (17km), but over intricate, hilly country.

lower slopes of La Rhune, in the hope of ascending as far as possible unseen by using dead ground or under cover of intervening spurs and ridges. The bulk of Girón's division, deployed in two columns with deep skirmishing lines ahead of them, clambered up the Faague (or Fagadia; 552m), a south-eastern spur but before long ran into opposition from four of Conroux's battalions. However, they were able, gradually, to force them uphill towards the eastern extension of the massif. The crest further west had already been occupied by Alten, who had set off from Bera with Kempt's and Colborne's two columns, the first making for the Col de Insola, east of the Commissari, and the other having first to evict an outlying battalion defending the 'Hog's Back' (the Ttipittarri in Basque), a partly isolated hill rising to 309m north-east of Bera.

Colborne's brigade had a tougher assignment, for there was more than one line of fortifications to be taken on the ascent, the first being the star fort of St Benoît, at a junction of two subsidiary spurs. There was an entrenchment higher up and, on the summit of the Mandale (573m), the Redoute de la Baïonnette, giving its name to the descending spur. Two battalions of Longa's men ascended the wooded, intervening valley between the British brigades while two of his units veered off to the west of Colborne, and three companies were detached with orders to work their way round the steep slopes of the Askop and Faalegi spurs, descending west from the Mandale, and to destroy the sema-phore at the south end of the Xoldokocana.

Taupin's division of 4,700 men, well-entrenched in successive positions, commanded the slope up which Kempt was ascending, but each one was carried by flanking attacks by dispersed units, leaving the 43rd to deliver a direct blow. John Cooke confirms that the mountain 'was fearfully difficult' to ascend, largely because it 'was so intersected with rocks, trees, brushwood, and prickly briars, that our hands and limbs were pierced with thorns, and the trousers were literally torn in shreds from our legs'.

Eventually the brigade reached the crest of the Commissari at several places; but its defence had been half-hearted. Flanking movements were more difficult to make up the steep sides of the narrow Bayonnette spur, and Colborne suffered heavy casualties while storming the star redoubt, the garrison of which gave way on the second attempt to take it when charged frontally by the 52nd and pursued uphill by the light corps past subsidiary entrenchments as far as the Bayonnette redoubt. As with those manning the fortifications along the Commissari ridge, they did not keep up their fire for long: once the swarm of skirmishers, together with the 52nd in their immediate front, had bounded over their parapet, they enemy broke and fled in disorder down the far slope.

Both brigades having reached the crest within sight of each other, their nearest units converged to cut off the retreat of the battalion below, which had been holding back the ascent of Longa's men in the valley. Some tried to escape, but 300 were forced to surrender.

'Among other incidents of the day' chronicled by John Kincaid had been the birth of a son and heir to one of the men,

> ... presented to him by his Portuguese wife, soon after the action. She had been taken in labour
> while ascending the mountain; but it did not seem to interfere with her proceedings in the least,

for she, and her child, and her donkey, came all three screeching into the camp, immediately after telling the news, as if it had been something very extraordinary, and none of them a bit the worse.

Although Girón's Andalusians were by then far up the eastern slope of La Rhune, they were unable to establish themselves on the summit in spite of repeated attempts to do so during the afternoon and evening. Clausel had sent five battalions in succession to strengthen the formidable position, and it was not until next day that Wellington had the whole summit of La Rhune in his hands. This was not by storming its heights, but by turning its flank.

The morning of the 8th was misty, but once the mist had dispersed, at about midday, Freire was ordered to push his troops along the northern slope of the hills extending west from the La Rhune massif, towards the villages of Olhette and Ascain, where the enemy reserves were concentrated. This advance, only feebly resisted by Taupin's defeated units, reached as far as the farm of Yolimun (Jolimont), just west of Olhette. Simultaneously, the 6th and 7th Divisions were ordered to demonstrate again against Clausel's left and D'Erlon's right: the French might think this was the actual attack that they were expecting to be delivered the previous day. Colville appeared to be moving on Ainhoa, while Dalhousie advanced towards the redoubts of Ste-Barbara (or Barbe) and Grenade, both just south of Sare.

Meanwhile Girón's reserve brigade in the valley below the Faague, together with the right wing of his troops on the lower east slope of La Rhune, advanced against Conroux's outposts to occupy a redoubt at the Chapelle d'Olhain on an under-feature east of the Faague, which was captured by Colonel Hore, and moved against the Ste-Barbe redoubt further east. This, together with the Grenade fort, was then evacuated, without orders (Clausel implied), and their garrisons retired on other defensive positions immediately south of Sare, on its low hill. Girón made another unsuccessful attempt to gain the summit of La Rhune, but as night came on the two colonels commanding the eight battalions defending it, aware that they were in danger of envelopment, decided that it was sensible to evacuate their posts and retire from the trap while there was still time; and so they picked their way in the darkness down the north-eastern flank to the Col de St-Ignace. According to Clausel, they gave up this vital position entirely on their own responsibility, contrary to his intentions and without orders; but he made no attempt to reoccupy it.

Before dawn on the 9th, Girón's Andalusians were in possession of a hermitage on the summit of La Rhune, followed later by Wellington in person. It provided a very extensive panorama over France and a marvellous plunging view over almost all the lines of fortification run up by Soult during previous weeks, stretching from the coast to the Pic de Mondarrain, east of Ainhoa. It had been a remarkably successful operation, undertaken with comparatively few casualties—a total of about 1,600, of which half were among Spanish units, particularly those of Girón's, who had fought so valiantly in the capture of La Rhune. French casualties, mostly among Taupin's division, were probably not many more, for the rest had retreated rather than put up much of a fight. Nine guns of small calibre had been taken, together with heavier artillery found in the redoubts.

Naturally, Soult, in making his report, blamed everyone except himself for the serious reverse, for allowing the enemy to topple his defences along this vital stretch of frontier. Maucune, habitually casual and relaxed, became a scapegoat and was sent to the rear in disgrace—although in the following spring he was again serving, in Italy. What Soult found hard to admit was the fact that he had been entirely misled and outsmarted by Wellington's strategic deployments. He had kept no concentrated force to hand with which a counter-attack might have been made, preferring to disperse his troops along the length of his line. Here they had remained in the deceptive security of his static defences, which had led to their defeat in detail. As Villatte put it in a letter to General Pierre Thouvenot at Bayonne, written immediately afterwards, when requesting quarters to be found there for himself and his staff, the army was 'bien décousue' (well unsewn), and he confirmed that the men had been fighting badly. Meanwhile Soult, obviously shaken by his reverse, sent an urgent order to Thouvenot:

> . . . the line of the entrenched camp in front of Bayonne must be strengthened by every imaginable means. Throw up works commanding all the roads, so that the troops which may . . . have to form up upon them, may find shelter behind them without delay. This is of the highest importance. Every one must be set to work, even the civil population, and work even at night. Arm all the recently arrived conscripts, and make them dig in also.

While professing that he was confident that the works at Bordagain, defending Ciboure, would keep the Allies at bay, Soult anticipated a serious confrontation the next day.

11

THE BATTLE OF THE NIVELLE

OTHER than those few officers in the confidence of Wellington, none could understand why the general advance was not pursued further, at least as far as the Adour at Bayonne. Certainly Soult expected it, but Wellington had forbidden any further offensive operations. Already he had had to rebuke George Madden for having allowed his Portuguese—with Dalhousie's tacit approval or otherwise—to make a lodgement on the outskirts of Sare on the 7th, from which, when Clausel moved to eject them, they were extracted with difficulty, covered by Girón's battalions. On the 12th a more serious incident had occurred, when two companies of Andalusians occupying the Ste-Barbe redoubt, not having placed any outlying sentries, were surprised by a night raid in which three of Conroux's battalions encircled them, escaladed the strongpoint and carried off 200 prisoners. Only the day before this incident, Larpent had heard it said that their officers were never seen there with the men to keep them on the alert, and that the men were cooking, quite unconcerned and without arms to hand, within twenty yards of the French sentries. A brigade of La Torre's Division then counter-attacked to recover the salient position, only to find themselves beaten off, and when five of Girón's battalions repeated the attempt they were obliged to retire. Wellington had refused to allow a brigade of the 4th Division to get involved in any action to assist them, as in his opinion the outpost was not worth keeping. In addition to those taken prisoner, the Spaniards lost some 300 men; Conroux's casualties were half the number.

Another month was to pass before any further advance was ordered, for which delay Wellington had his reasons. On 18 October we find him reiterating to Bathurst that he was

> ... very doubtful indeed about the advantage of going any further here at present. I see that Buonaparte [sic] was still at Dresden on September 28th, and unless I could fight a general action with Soult, and gain a *complete* victory, which the nature of this country scarcely admits of, I should do but little good to the Allies.... It is impossible to move our right wing (Hill, &c., at Roncesvalles) till Pamplona shall have fallen, which I think will be within a week. I shall then decide according to the state of affairs at the moment.

Wellington was not aware of the details of the débâcle at Leipzig on 19 October until after going on the offensive again, although he heard rumours of it from a French colonel captured at the Battle of the Nivelle on 10 November.

The fall of Pamplona was essential, for it was always possible, if unlikely, that Foy might try and make a sudden dash in that direction. Once in Allied hands, Carlos de España's troops, still blockading it, could be used reinforce Mina's units, which would allow Hill's divisions to be redeployed on the main front.

Wellington was preoccupied about the behaviour of the Spanish troops—and even some of the Portuguese—once they set foot in France. So many French atrocities had taken place in the Peninsula, and no one knew to what extent they might wish to settle scores and take their revenge whenever inevitable temptations were offered. It would also be extremely difficult to restrain them from plundering for food whenever an opportunity occurred, unless they were strongly disciplined. Even Soult's troops, so used to plundering, found it hard to stop doing so, even when back in France. By keeping his British and Portuguese troops under an iron grip, enforcing discipline by the stringent use of punishments, Wellington found that after a few weeks the Basque or French peasantry became increasingly more friendly towards them, as they were paid for what was wanted, than towards their own countrymen. When retreating through Urrugne and Ascain, Maucune's and Taupin's men had apparently caused a deal of wanton damage, and Soult was constantly receiving complaints from local mayors of their marauding proclivities, which were hard to control. Wellington could not risk exciting any form of reprisal, and had determined to send back to Spain any units responsible for acts likely to instigate them, for the natives would not differentiate among the British, Portuguese or Spanish. Larpent records that, as early as 9 October,

> Plunder has begun, and disorders in French villages, and Lord Wellington is exceedingly angry. He says, that if officers will not obey orders, and take care that those under them do so also, they must go home, for he will not command them here; many of our officers seem to think that they have nothing to do but to fight.

Wellington was still engaged in a running battle with the perverse Spanish government, who seemed to have deliberately and persistently turned down promotions he had made as Spanish Commander-in-Chief and had placed in positions of importance those whom he had dismissed in disgrace. They had also virtually ignored all his suggestions for the improvement or reorganisation of their commissariat, etc. As his position had become meaningless, he might as well resign the empty title: but instead of being scared into sitting up and taking notice when he did so, the Regency merely acquiesced, saying they would refer the matter to the *Cortes*. It was not until 8 November that the latter body issued a report stating that the original conditions agreed would be adhered to, and O'Donoju, the Minister of War with whom Wellington had long been at loggerheads, was forced to resign—only to be promoted in rank by the Regency (which insult to the *Cortes* did not go unnoticed). Meanwhile Wellington's position *vis-à-vis* control of Spanish troops had been in a state of suspension.

Spanish libels concerning San Sebastián continued to proliferate, and it was at about this time, according to Napier, that Wellington, writing privately to his brother Henry, terminated a letter thus: 'It will rest with the king's government to determine what they will do upon a consideration of all the circumstances of the case, but if I was to decide I would not keep the army in Spain for one hour'.

On a more practical level, and closer to the front, Wellington's officers had plenty of reasons to be exasperated by the Spanish petty officials. Their customs officers were holding up the landing of essential supplies at Pasajes with the excuse that they were searching for contraband concealed among powder barrels and flour sacks; they refused warehouse space for stores when there were empty buildings in plenty; and they had stripped a requisitioned hospital in Fuenterrabia of every convenience, even burning the plank beds and tables, before handing it over to Allied medical staff. In Bilbao, they had left wounded men to starve in a ropewalk without bedding or any utensils of any kind: several men had died from privation, due to either the intransigence or the inefficiency of arrogant petty bureaucrats. In Bilbao, also, the movement of wagons had been prohibited, with the excuse that they would break up the surface of its streets, while at both Vitoria and Santander the local authorities had adopted a policy of passive resistance when it came to providing any form of accommodation for the Allied wounded. Then, with the pretext that a contagious fever had broken out in the British military hospital, they did their best to place the entire port of Santander under quarantine. It was here that, under pressure from James McGrigor, prefabricated buildings transported from England had been erected, which gave the wounded essential shelter from the elements. Santander was preferable to Pasajes, 'the most murderous place' according to Sergeant John Douglas, invalided there to await transport home: if any British subject were 'foolhardy enough to venture out after night, 'twas next to a miracle if he escaped being stabbed. Almost every morning brought with it fresh proofs of villainy, as the bodies would be found in the streets, and floating in the tide.'

Beresford had returned from Lisbon to report that he had done his best to energise the Portuguese government, which so far had supported the British as much as it could, but with the tide of war and immediate danger ebbing from their frontiers, in recent months regular drafts of recruits, or convalescents ready to return, were failing to reach the Allied army—admittedly now distant—to replace losses among their units, which had fought so well but were now becoming seriously depleted. It would appear that with having only the expense of maintaining an army and not the profit of having one on its doorstep any longer, the government had become sullen and recalcitrant. Beresford's perhaps patronising presence during continuing discussions did not endear him in their eyes. Since British transports supplying Allied forces had been directed to harbours such as Pasajes on the Biscay coast, the quays of Lisbon were comparatively deserted, and with the consequent diminution of trade the financial burden of carrying on the war seemed to press more heavily. The government was also complaining that Portuguese troops did not receive the mention in Wellington's dispatches that it felt they merited.

A more unrealistic demand was that the ten Portuguese brigades at the front should be separated from the integrated Allied divisions and placed under Portuguese command, a proposal soon quashed, for, as Wellington remarked when writing to Sir Charles

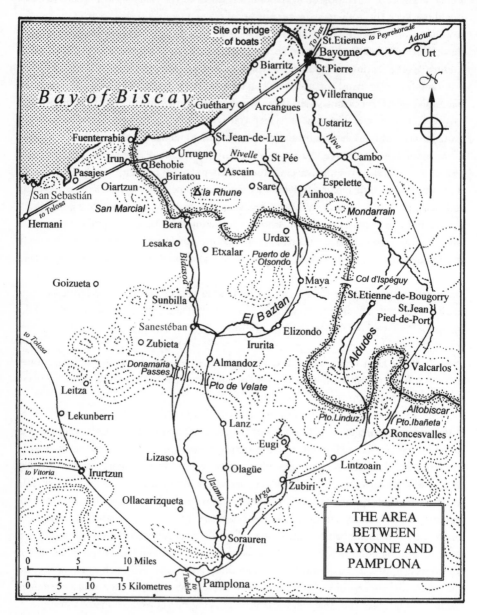

Note: The contour/contours on this map has/have been simplified and is/are only shown above a certain level, but note that the whole area is dislocated by a jumble of steep and often densely wooded lower hills, ramifications of the main Pyrenean range, and numerous streams.

Stuart on 11 October, 'Separated from ourselves they could not keep the field in a respect-able state, even if the Portuguese government were to incur ten times the expense they now incur.' Should they have to rely on their own staff and commissariat, they would soon come to grief. However, he was prepared to commend their merits further in future dis-patches, whenever deserved, if that would content them.

Apart from having to pour oil on troubled waters stirred up by his Allies, Wellington was still having a vexatious time as far as his relations with the British Admiralty was concerned. The Royal Navy had shown themselves to be quite capable of sending trans-ports into the insignificant Cantabrian port of Santoña while it was still in enemy hands, when some vessels were captured (although it was said that they were forced to take shelter there in a storm), and of unloading uniform coats at Pasajes but knapsacks and cross-belts at Corunna; and—with the excuse that ships lacked a convoy—a supply of greatcoats left at Oporto in May had not reached the front by November, by which time it was freezing. Even in his correspondence with Bathurst, Wellington was frequently pro-voked by the British administration's—and that included the Duke of York's—apparent lack of comprehension concerning many of the problems facing him. He was pestered by Bathurst to send back seasoned troops to form 'provisional battalions' and let them be replaced by battalions of militia—this a whimsical expedient of York's—which caused him to reply sarcastically:

> I have never had under my command more than one regiment of English militia. I found that, however, to be so entirely divested of interior economy and real discipline, that however well the soldiers may be disciplined as regards their exercises and movements, I should very much doubt that a large militia army could be useful in the field for more than a momentary exertion. My notion of them is that their officers have all the faults of those of the Line to an aggravating degree, and some more peculiarly their own.

Wellington went on to say that members of the militia volunteering for active service might be acceptable as drafts to regiments at the front, and that this might be stimulated by promising a sustenance allowance for their wives. In his experience when in Ireland, the wives would do their utmost to prevent their men from volunteering, knowing that the moment they enlisted 'they themselves went not "upon the parish" but upon the dunghill, to starve.' He went on to observe that he was astonished that any Irish militia soldier was ever found to volunteer: if such men did so, 'they must certainly be the worst members of society; and I have often been inclined to attribute the enormity and frequency of crimes committed by the soldiers here, to our having so many men who left their families to starve, for the inducement of getting a few guineas to spend on drink.' Court-martial statistics merely confirm this supposition—that there was a surprising predominance of violent crimes and robbery having been committed by men with certainly Irish names, 'even when it is realised what a considerable percentage of the whole Peninsular army was Irish', to repeat the words of Charles Oman, himself a Scot.

The lack of guineas had become an additional problem, for, as the Bank of England had not coined any since 1799, they were becoming increasingly scarce. As a result of

Wellington's insistence, Bathurst had put pressure on the Bank to release some of its reserves of gold. Quantities of gold coins were sent from Madras to London, where they were melted down and re-struck in 1813 to produce what was generally known as the 'military guinea' for the benefit of the Peninsular army, several regiments in which, even by that November, had not received their pay for June.

On 10 October Headquarters was moved a few miles east from Lesaka to Bera, for Lesaka had 'grown very unwholesome, like an old poultry-yard, and the deaths of the inhabitants are very numerous. . . . there is no reason to regret the change.' Bera, having been a sort of neutral ground for about two months, was 'a little deranged': several of the better houses had been destroyed, while many of the others were largely gutted of doors, shutters and furniture by the French. But, as Larpent noticed, the inhabitants—somewhat used to these events—having also carried them away and concealed them, were now returning, and the place looked much improved. Wellington occupied one which was sufficiently capacious to admit comfortably 25 to 30 people to dinner, under the aegis of Colonel Colin Campbell, who had long been responsible for the smooth running of the Headquarters establishment. In addition to Wellington's own staff, Bera now accommodated those of Cole, Alten and Beresford (just back from Lisbon, accompanied by Colonel Howard Elphinstone). Apparently, on his arrival at Lisbon, Elphinstone had written asking what Wellington wished him to do and where he was to go as Chief Engineer in the Peninsula. Not surprisingly, he was told in no uncertain terms that he should best know where his proper place was, which had brought him sailing in within a week.

Among others installed at Bera at this time was the artist Thomas Heaphy, busy painting half-length water-colour portraits of the Commander-in-Chief and two dozen or so generals, some of which in Larpent's opinion (and in that of many others) 'were excessively like' and for which he was now charging 40 guineas.* Among those sketched were Surgeon-General James McGrigor and George Scovell.

With a surfeit of officers, prices naturally increased, should they wish to vary their menus, for the 'ration beef' was like shoe-leather. Larpent (whose narrative is full of interest, the more so as being written by a civilian and thus free from any military rhetoric) complained that 'mutton I can scarce ever get; fowl are 9s. each, and are snapped up before my man can resolve to give that price for them. Pork, ham, sausages, salt-fish and bacon alone abound.'

They were certainly better off than the French at Pamplona, the fall of which was now expected daily. Since the end of September, Cassan's garrison had been on half-rations. Although it had been sufficiently provisioned for a garrison 2,500 strong, this had been augmented by another 1,000—including wounded—retreating from Vitoria, while a number of 'strays' had later entered. By the time the place was invested, Cassan had about 3,200 effectives at his disposal, together with another 500 sick or wounded. He had made

* They are now in the vaults of the National Portrait Gallery, London, but deserve to be better known and reproduced without a fee imposed.

several sallies since, largely to plunder the neighbouring market gardens, which, together with nearby wheatfields, the Spanish troops blockading the place had neglected
to destroy as Wellington had ordered. If they had done so, the garrison may well have
given in several weeks earlier. Cassan missed a possible opportunity of breaking out in
late July, while the Battle of Sorauren was taking place so close, but, since Soult's failure
to relieve the fortress, he had been almost entirely isolated. Desertions became more
frequent, while, in an attempt to reduce the number of mouths to be fed, Cassan tried to
expel the remaining civilian population, but Carlos de España had fired on the fugitives
and driven them back. Scurvy broke out and his hospitals had filled. By mid-October the
place of the garrison's horses and mules as the common ingredients of stews was taken by
the canine, feline and rodent population. Cassan started to negotiate a surrender, but De
España would not accept any of the conditions stipulated. Cassan then threatened to
blow up all the works and cut his way free, to which the Spaniard answered that if he did
so, he had Wellington's express permission to give no quarter, prisoners would be deci-
mated, etc.; but this was all part of their game of bluff. In the end Cassan had no alternative but to capitulate unconditionally, which he did on 31 October, when his famished
garrison was marched away to waiting transports at Pasajes. Those permanently disabled
might be exchanged; French civilians over sixty were allowed to return to France; Allied
deserters found skulking there would be handed over to the proper authorities; and some
executions took place.

The October days 'passed tediously', wrote John Cooke, and the troops indulged in

> . . . the most simple pastimes whenever the weather would admit of a ramble. Sometimes we
> fired with ball at eagles and vultures, and at others, chased herds of wild ponies which browsed
> in the sequestered valleys. . . . They were hardly beyond the size of wolf-dogs, with wiry coats and
> long shaggy manes and tails. It was astonishing to see these sure-footed little animals, with
> small heads and wild eyes, capering, prancing, and darting through the underwood, and up and
> down steep acclivities.*

Indeed, the weather at the main front deteriorated. Writing up his *Journal*, Larpent had
recorded that it had turned very cold one day, and that the thermometer had got down to
36° Fahrenheit 'close to where I was shaving three morning since [the 28th]; but it soon
turned to wet—raw, constant, violent cold wet; north-west wind, and rain in repeated
stormy torrents. In camp our poor soldiers have their tents torn, and almost washed away;
then we have had hail followed by snow.' The 85th Regiment may have been luckier,
having seized a French encampment near Urrugne, although it was described by Gleig as
being 'exceedingly exposed . . . stretching along the ridge of a bleak hill . . . [and] the
only fuel now within our reach, consisted of furze', the lower branches of which were 'very
indifferent material for our fires'. Here, before long, 'crowds of sutlers, and other camp-
followers, began to pour in . . . taking possession of such of the enemy's huts as had
escaped the violence of our soldiers, opened their shops . . . and soon gave the spot . . . the

---

* These little ponies—*pottoka* in Basque—may often be seen in these districts today.

appearance of a settled village during the season of a fair . . .' Inland, at Roncesvalles, the snow was now so high that one picquet had to be dug out, and some men had perished. None of this helped when it came to deploying the artillery: 'The work of getting guns along over a clay-road, up a mountain, in the dark, without being allowed to use lights, is no trifling undertaking', while the artillery horses were 'living upon dried fern and corn— no hay, no straw, and very little coarse grass'.

On 6 November 'our great men were all at the front, peeping to-day into France from the mountains which surround this hollow [at Bera].' Three days later, as the weather had improved, and with the thermometer up to 52°, Larpent was anticipating a forward move-ment. Coincidently, he had just heard news

> . . . from the French side, which is believed by every one here, and by the French army as we are told; namely, that Bonaparte is beaten back to the Rhine, with the loss of three divisions cut off by blowing up a bridge too soon, &c.; one General taken, and one drowned, &c. This puts our party in spirits for to-morrow, and will, I hope, damp the French if believed by them, as the deserters report it to be.

That evening he dined with Wellington, who was 'all gaiety and spirits'. He remained until almost 10.00, when Wellington, on leaving the room, only said, 'Remember! at four in the morning.'

On the previous occasion Larpent had dined at Headquarters, Wellington had got into a conversation with him 'for nearly two hours about the poor-laws, and the assize of bread, about the Catholic question, the state of Ireland, etc., just as if he had nothing else on his mind.' On many points they were in agreement, 'particularly as to what would be necessary to be done in Ireland—if anything; but he thinks nothing should be done at all.' Wellington was 'still alarmed at the separation spirit which he thinks exists there, and the remains of a Jacobin feeling in the lower classes in England.'

It was on one of those fine bright days when Wellington was 'peeping' at the French that Harry Smith (attending, as Colborne's aide) described a scene, which in so many words was as follows. Wellington, extended on the grassy summit of La Rhune, after surveying the future field of battle through his telescope, where the French, like ants, were busy toiling away at their fortifications on ridges some distance below, turned on his elbow to remark to Colborne:

> 'Those fellows think themselves invulnerable, but I will beat them out, and with great ease.'
>> 'That we may beat them out, when your lordship attacks, I have no doubt, but for the ease . . .'
>> 'Ah, Colborne, with your local knowledge only, you are perfectly right; it appears difficult, but the enemy have not men enough to occupy all those works and lines. I can direct a greater force on certain points than they can concentrate to resist me.'
>> 'Now I see it, my lord,' Colborne conceded.

Wellington continued in earnest conversation for some time with Alten, Kempt, Colborne and then George Murray, who, taking out his writing materials from his sabretache, began noting down the plan of attack outlined for the whole army. So clearly had he understood the essence of the design that on reading back what he had written, Wellington, eye still glued to his glass and face displaying great concentration, could only smile and say, 'Ah, Murray, this will put us in possession of the fellows' lines. Shall we be ready tomorrow?' 'I fear not, my lord, but next day,' was the reply, meaning that he would require two days to draw up and distribute the orders. In the event, the forward movement was contingent on the fall of Pamplona, and it was further delayed due to appalling weather. Leaving the complicated instructions entirely in Murray's hands says much for the confidence the C-in-C had in his Q.M.G., but by then they had worked closely together for several years.

The operation planned was to extend over a distance of some sixteen miles, to cover which Wellington had arranged his forces into what may be conveniently referred to as 'corps', although the term was not used. That on the right wing was commanded by Hill, abutted by Beresford's. Wellington placed himself next, with Sir John Hope to his left, by the coast. Hope had just disembarked to replace Graham, who had sailed to England. Should any untoward accident have befallen Wellington, Hope would have been left in command since he outranked his other lieutenant-generals. Even if Wellington deprecated the drafting out of generals without recent Peninsular experience—almost five years had passed since Hope had accompanied Moore on the retreat to Corunna—he welcomed Hope's arrival as he was wary of placing Beresford in such a position of responsibility since his showing at La Albuera in May 1811, whatever other sterling qualities he possessed. Neither of them approached Hill as far as strategic insight was concerned, but unfortunately Hill was junior to both.

Hill was made responsible for the 2nd and 6th Divisions (the latter again commanded by Clinton, who had been absent since June), Hamilton's Portuguese and Morillo's Spaniards. Beresford commanded the 3rd (Colville; Picton being on leave), the 4th and the 7th (Le Cor, as Dalhousie had gone home in October), the Light Division, Bradford's independent Portuguese brigade and Girón's and Longa's Spaniards. Hope was responsible for the 1st and 5th Divisions (Hay commanding the latter since Leith had been wounded), Aylmer's Independent British brigade and Archibald Campbell's Portuguese brigades (John Wilson having been wounded at the Bidasoa), and Freire's two Galician divisions.

The infantry now available to Wellington now totalled 82,000—38,000 British, 22,000 Portuguese and 22,000 Spanish. He ordered up from their cantonments three of his nine brigades of cavalry—those of Grant, von Bock and Victor Alten—should they be of use in any pursuit. Already, on 7 October, 60 pieces of artillery had been conveyed across the Bidasoa during the night and positioned near Urrugne, but the churned-up state of the roads had made their further movement difficult. Only seven batteries were brought forward, one of them of mountain guns. As described by Cooke, their

> . . . carriages, guns, ammunition boxes, and iron balls, were strapped separately on the backs of a string of powerful mules. These guns could be, therefore, conveyed, so as to bear on the enemy from cliffs, or craggy elevations. The sure-footed mules would ascend and descend steeps, dried

water-courses, or crooked goat-tracks; and would pick their steps from rock to rock, planting their feet cautiously for the good foundation, or a firm hold.

Facing Wellington, Soult commanded approximately 62,000 men, largely installed in his complicated system of redoubts and entrenchments, in which, in spite of his recent experience, he still had faith and although—unaware of the precise situation in which he now found himself—Napoleon and Clarke, the Minister of War, had repeatedly urged him to counter-attack. He had been forced to give up the hills overlooking the Bidasoa, together with La Rhune, but we nevertheless find Soult writing to Paris stating that in fact it had been advantageous rather than otherwise to have lost them, and that Wellington would find it hard to hold and difficult to keep such heights supplied in winter. The continued occupation of the Petite Rhune was just as useful: the army 'is now more concentrated, and has its right wing resting in a much better position than before.' Soult reiterated to Paris that he would 'rather fight a general action in a good position, than to take the risk of making partial attacks upon ground which I could not hold if I succeeded in winning it, on account of the broad spaces involved', etc.

From the seventeenth-century fort at Socoa—still conspicuous—defending the bay of St-Jean-de-Luz, Soult's deep lines of redoubts stretched south-east. The seaward section, beyond an area flooded just south of Socoa, consisted of three redoubts along the hill of Bordagain, beyond which was that of Ste-Anne, together with another two on hills to the west; overlooking the right bank of the Nivelle, on the hill of Bailiaenea, south-east of Chantako and near Serrès, dominating Ascain (where there was an ancient bridge, possibly Roman), were three more.* Several redoubts had been built or strengthened below the north flank of La Rhune, among them those of St-Ignace, on hills north-east of the col), three along the rocky Altxanga ridge (north-east of the summit, and always referred to as La Petite Rhune), and the Mouiz redoubt (between the Col de St Ignace and the Altxanga. Apart from the Ste-Barbe and Grenade redoubts, south of Sare and already referred to, there were four more aligned along the hills rising north and north-east of that village—the Signals redoubt and those of Louis XIV, the Madelaine and, on a height overlooking the Nivelle and bridge of Amotz from the east, the Harismendia. Further north there was yet another on a hill within a meander of the river at St-Pée, while at the far end of the entrenched ridge extending east of the Harismendia stood the Pinodieta redoubt, dominating a depression in the hills crossed by the road between Espelette and Ainhoa, and another just beyond. One more stood on a height overlooking a loop in the Nivelle no great distance west of Ainhoa. While these were the main forts, there were numerous earthworks on many defensible positions between them, including a cluster on the low hills south-east of Ciboure, between what the French referred to as their 'fortified camps' of Bordagain and Serrès.†

---

* Bordagain is now a suburb of Ciboure, on the south bank of the tidal Nivelle opposite St-Jean-de-Luz;, while St-Anne is south of the A 63 motorway. The two hills to the west are near the present-day D 704, leading south from Ciboure to Olhette, and that of Bailiaenea is just west of the motorway on crossing the river.

† Many of these fortifications are overgrown by vegetation, or have been partially obliterated since, but remains of a number may still be found with perseverance by the more energetic with a 1:25,000 map in hand.

Soult deployed 11,000 men in the Bordagain positions and another 12,000 (including Villatte's reserve) about Serrès, concentrating 23,000 along the shortest stretch of his extended line. The adjoining sector—from Ascain to the bridge of Amotz, overlooked by La Rhune—was defended by Clausel's three divisions, with a brigade from each of Maransin's and Conroux's in the front line of defence and with the other brigades and Taupin's division in the second line. Although these amounted to 15,000 men, half of them garrisoned his several redoubts or were tied down within entrenchments or other works. D'Erlon, on Soult's left wing, had 11,000 men, but eleven of his sixteen battalions were likewise immobilised. He was assured by Soult that he could count on Foy's division whenever necessary, and on 8 November this was marched from St-Jean-Pied-de-Port to Bidarray, on the Nive, where it guarded D'Erlon's flank but could also threaten the rear of any Allied force attacking D'Erlon frontally.

The severe weather conditions, with snow blocking the higher lying tracks, meant that Hill was unable to start redeploying the majority of his troops near Maya until 7 November, the rest setting out the next day. Hill had taken the precaution of leaving one of Morillo's battalions and two of Mina's to watch the Col d'Ispéguy, east of Maya. The rest of his corps remained south of the Puerto de Otxondo, apart from outposts of the 6th Division below the north slope. By the evening of the 9th, the Allied army was ready to take the offensive next day.

HOPE'S DEMONSTRATION

Hope, on the coast, had been ordered to demonstrate with every show of force, but without committing himself to a general action, against the entrenched camps between his front and St-Jean-de-Luz. This he succeeded in doing with the minimum of casualties—174 in all ranks— the most serious being among the K.G.L. Ensign Wheatley records that, well before dawn on that starlit, frosty, morning,

> . . . the different groups around several fires, together with the distant lights of the enemy, had a most superb appearance. A distant approaching clashing and murmur announced the signal. Nothing was heard but the unhooking of muskets. The fires stood deserted, excepting a solitary drummer boy shivering with apprehension and cold, or a soldier kneeling to the fire, lighting perhaps his last pipe. We now silently groped down the hill, crossed the high road and, breaking through a hedge, skulked along the ditches, no one daring to speak according to orders. The men were ordered to carry their muskets horizontally to prevent the gleaming of the bayonets from betraying our approach. Some fires being on our left, we crawled slowly and silently taking a circuit to the right, when suddenly whirling in a circular manner to the left, we pounced upon the dozing French piquet at the fire and seized them all without a shot's expense. In the same crafty manner we crept along the bye paths, and through the hedges with a country guide until we arrived under some trees, where we halted and drew up in a close column. We were ordered to lay [sic] down quietly without speaking a word.

Wheatley was now close to Urrugne, which, with Aylmer's brigade to his right, was stormed soon afterwards. Gleig, with the 85th Regiment, vividly described the scene on the evening of the 10th, where in the village church his battalion, piling their arms in the side-aisles, took possession of the nave while a party of officers occupied a gallery. Gleig and a friend found space by the altar, on which, lighted by tapers, were spread their cold salt beef, brown bread, cheese and grog, and here they ate and drank 'in that state of excited feeling which attends every man who has gone safely through the perils of such a day' before sinking to sleep on the paved floor, wrapped in their cloaks.

During the same day, Freire's two divisions had been demonstrating against the Yolimun position, making itself obvious to Villatte's units across the Nivelle at Serrès. Some skirmishers of Freire's eastern column, on approaching Ascain, unfortunately found themselves too closely engaged with Villatte's outlying picquets, but their casualties hardly amounted to 100.

These displays of force on his left wing enabled Wellington to tie down two-fifths of Soult's army with one-third of his own (only three of Hope's eight brigades had been lightly engaged; he had amply reserves, had the French facing him emerged from their fortifications and counter-attacked).

Wellington's main offensive thrust was made against the centre of Soult's line. Although a proportion of Hill's corps took part in the complex operation, the rest were to 'contain' D'Erlon's troops by demonstrations in force further east, as were Hope's near the coast. Longa's Spaniards were to keep in touch with both Freire's men to the west of La Rhune and Girón's—whose main objective was the lower eastern slopes of the Lesser Rhune—but without committing themselves to any serious fighting. East of Girón's stood Cole's 4th Division, which was to recover the Ste-Barbe redoubt and occupy the fortified village of Sare, on which Le Cor's 7th Division further east would converge, having taken the Grenade redoubt. The 3rd Division, marching from Zugarramurdi, further in the rear, would follow up these movements and then attack the enemy positions near the bridge of Amotz, spanning the Nivelle; the 6th, the nearest of Hill's divisions, which had a long march to make, would aim for those east of the bridge. Behind them, advancing in echelon from Maya, Hamilton's Portuguese would attack the works further east, while the 2nd Division (with three brigades) made for Ainhoa and the redoubts in its vicinity. Morillo's men, extending the Allied line, were to threaten the enemy on the flanks of the Atxulegi (Atchulegui) and Mondarrain further east but were not to press their advance unless the French abandoned those heights. The only unit held in reserve was Bradford's Portuguese brigade, which took up a position behind the Light and 4th Divisions. With the exception of the Light Division and the 2nd, which had three brigades, each division advanced in two lines and, as Oman has explained, the second line of each formed in fact the reserve of the first, as is evident when perusing their casualty lists (several of such 'reserves' were never engaged). There were five intact brigades to hand should Soult counter-attack; and in the event over half the battalions in Beresford's and Hill's columns never fired a shot.

The signal for the general advance was given by three guns firing at daybreak from the height of Atxuria (Pic Atchuriabia), south-east of the Pic d'Ibanteli. This was shortly after 6.00 on that bright morning of 10 November. By the time Larpent was awake at Bera, he found that almost everyone had already 'gone to see the glorious attack—even the doctors and the two parsons.' He followed by the route recommended to him by Cole, and remained on the summit of La Rhune for about six hours.

THE ASSAULT ON LA PETITE RHUNE

At 2.00, well before dawn, the men of the Light Division, after a very early breakfast, had silently clambered down the steep north-eastern slope to positions close to the outlying French picquets and lain down muffled in their blankets to await the signal. Their assignment appeared formidable. They were to traverse a gully between La Rhune proper and La Petite Rhune, the precipitous side of the rocky crest of which, crowned by an alignment of three redoubts, faced them, behind which was another, the Mouiz, on a knoll at a lower level than the eastern end of the outcrop.

Having studied the ground in minute detail through his telescope during previous days, Wellington concluded that, to carry this ridge, the Light Division could turn its western extremity from a small boggy level (Les Trois Fontaines) west of the Col d'Argaïneco, a narrow land-bridge, from which the gully between the two descended steeply east. If the defences were pierced by a sudden and resolute assault and their positions overrun, the enemy would have no alternative but to make a rapid retreat: if continuing to resist for long, he would soon find himself surrounded.

Alten, in discussion with Kempt and Colborne, worked out a detailed plan of attack. The 2/95th, having descended to the gully, would rush a strongly placed outlying picquet below the col from the right. From here it could occupy the attention of and 'contain' the French defending their ridge. This would be stormed by the 43rd, supported by the 17th Portuguese, ascending from the level to its south-west. As the attack developed, the 1/95th and 3/95th would push forward as far as possible, while the 52nd, followed by the 1st and 3rd *Caçadores*, bypassing behind them and turning uphill towards the Mouiz, would outflank the main enemy position. To the west, Longa's men would protect their flank from any possible move by Villatte's troops near Ascain, who, in the event, never left their entrenchments.

William Napier, the future historian of the war, who happened to be leading the 43rd, dramatically described the ensuing action. Although the French in the lower strongpoint were surprised by the 2/95th suddenly leaping up at them and soon gave way, a battalion on the col held up their advance for some time, although the French were also under fire from three mountain guns which had been hauled up into position on the lower slope of La Rhune. The 43rd, at a run, during which they were exposed to a heavy fire, had reached the level peat bog meanwhile, their skirmishers having driven in some enemy picquets near it. From here, five companies in line, with three other in column in reserve, charged uphill towards the sheer stone wall of the most westerly redoubt, referred to as the 'Place d'Armes', from which its garrison kept up as spirited fire. This did not stop the storming party clambering up wherever they could get a toe-hold, many being hoisted up on the shoulders of their comrades or otherwise dragging themselves up and over the edge amongst the astonished enemy, unable to stay the determined onrush, in which Napier himself narrowly escaped being bayoneted.

After a brief pause to gather their breath, the members of the storming party scrambled up towards the second fort (the 'Magpie's Nest'), partly an irregular rock face, partly breastwork; its garrison, demoralised by the retreat of their colleagues, with certain exceptions put up a half-hearted resistance and were looking to ways of escape. By now the 43rd, over half-way along the Petite Rhune positions and exhilarated by its success, pressed ahead, only to find a deep cleft in the rock between it and the 'Donjon', the easternmost fort on the crest; but as the men were deliberating how this might be best traversed, the problem was resolved.

In the meantime Kempt, noticing the fall of the 'Place d'Armes', had led the 17th Portuguese round to the northern slope of the Petite Rhune and attacked a thinly manned wall extending between that and the Mouiz. During this action, in which Kempt himself was wounded, the 52nd, with Colborne leading, had worked its way north unnoticed, partly along dead ground below the Mouiz. From there, having outflanked the breast-works being attacked by the 1/95th and 3/95th, they climbed up behind the defenders, who, seeing themselves turned and in danger of being cut off entirely, abandoned their trenches and even the adjacent star fort, and stumbled downhill to the north, as did those holding the wall.Seeing this taking place, the garrison of the 'Donjon', realising that their own retreat was at risk, likewise absconded without putting up more than a token resistance. Only the battalion on the Col d'Argaïneco retreated in good order, at the same time providing some cover for the fugitives, although there was little pursuit: the riflemen were too exhausted by their exertions, and so few prisoners were taken, and the defeated troops were eventually rallied behind their positions north-east of the Col de St-Ignace. Once they had re-formed, the whole Light Division followed them, and deployed ready to push ahead once again, although this depended on the success of fighting to its right. Their casualties so far that day had been a few over 100, of which the 43rd, in carrying the redoubts of the Petite Rhune, lost eleven officers and 67 men killed or wounded.

THE CENTRAL THRUST

To the east, the Allied thrust against Clausel was irresistible. His right flank was exposed by the capture of the Petite Rhune; Soult had failed to provide him with any reserves from the camp at Serrès; and he had fewer than 16,000 deployed in his lines of redoubts, etc., to withstand the onslaught of some 33,000 men. The outlying redoubts of Ste-Barbe and Grenade were overrun at the first rush, after the parapet of the former had been cleared by a round or two of shrapnel from the three guns brought into action—almost the only pieces dragged to the front that day because the ground was so rough and boggy. Its garrison made off in haste on seeing Girón's troops well to their right rear on the lower slopes of the La Rhune massif. One battery also shelled the Grenade redoubt from the flank, and, attacked by Inglis's brigade frontally, it was evacuated shortly after to avoid being surrounded. By 8.00 that morning the fortified village of Sare had been carried after only slight bickering. Those detailed to defend it retired in some disorder and attempted to rally behind the Signals and Louis XIV redoubts on the line of hills in their rear.

Further east, Colville's troops, emerging from the hills, crossed low-lying ground threaded by the Harane rivulet to approach a mile-long abatis of felled trees, defended by Baurot's brigade of Conroux Division. Power's *Caçadores* had some initial difficulty here but then forced their way through in the vicinity of the riverside hamlet of Cherchebruit. On a hill behind it stood the Madelaine redoubt. In the Nivelle valley, to the east, the bridge of Amotz was the main means of communication between Clausel and D'Erlon. Although guarded by breastworks, it was soon in the possession of the 94th Regiment, pressing ahead of the rest of Keane's brigade, other regiments of which swarmed up the hill overlooking the bridge from the west and, after a sharp struggle in which Conroux himself was killed, captured the Madelaine redoubt. Power's Portuguese, crossing the Nivelle, were soon to be in touch with Hill's troops, converging on the bridge of Amotz from the south-east.

Although Clausel's front had been turned even before its western end had been attacked, he was determined to hold on, in the expectation that reinforcements from Daricau and Villatte would reach him at any moment. But their units remained paralysed by what were merely demonstrations in their front on the part of Freire's Galicians. Soult would not move them. Clausel could only order the survivors of Conroux's division west towards the Louis XIV redoubt, garrisoned by Maransin's two brigades, which were also defending the neighbouring Col de Mendionde, further west, beyond which stood Taupin, holding the strongly entrenched line from the Signals redoubt on the hill of Suhalmendi to the two dominating the Col de St-Ignace. Unfortunately for Taupin, half the troops at hand had been those recently seeking asylum there after their retreat from their positions on the Petite Rhune.

At about 10.00, Beresford having re-aligned his units, disordered during their swift advance, with their skirmishers followed by one brigade and another two in support, the 4th, 7th, and 3rd divisions were ready to move forward again. Girón's men had come up between the Light and 4th, while Bradford's Portuguese were within supporting distance of the former. Longa's units had veered off to the west, and were by now in evidence opposite the entrenchments defending Ascain.

The Louis XIV redoubt put up a stronger resistance than most. This was partly because, although it had not yet received any guns of position, on its flank were a number of field guns whose enfilading salvos of canister caused at least one Allied attack to falter, and it was only after a battery of Ross's horse artillery had been brought up with difficulty and answered their fire that it was carried. Maransin, who had led the defence in person, was briefly taken prisoner but escaped in the ensuing confusion. He attempted to mount a counter-attack with his reserve, but this failed and he withdrew to the north-west.

Taupin's division had received a draft of 1,300 conscripts not long before, which he had placed with old cadres in part of the line he assumed was less likely to be attacked. To support Clausel, he had already sent one of his regiments (the 47th) from his extreme right, where he could see no enemy threat. Unfortunately for Taupin, when Alten's Light Division continued its advance, it was against this sector, defended by the conscript units and only five seasoned battalions. The descent from the Mouiz had been slow, for in many areas the slope down was precipitous. On reaching a deep gully at the foot of Taupin's position the line spread out, as there were few points where the re-ascent could be conveniently made. The 52nd found a stone bridge by which they could cross, but three enemy guns had been trained on it. By making sudden dashes by platoon immediately after every discharge, and then taking cover, the whole battalion got across. As soon as the rest of the very rough line of battalions was able to form lower down the hillside, the 95th and 52nd bounded ahead towards the breastwork not far above them, which, much to their surprise, was evacuated after its defenders had fired only a few hasty volleys. The officer commanding, aware that the 47th Regiment had been marched away from his right, realised that his position had been turned and that he must retreat or be cut off; indeed, Longa's troops were not far from his rear.

This left the rest of the line of defences extending to the Signals redoubt—at which both Taupin and Clausel were anxiously watching the caving in of their front—exposed to attack (which was to cause recriminations as to whom was responsible). The only thing to do, before being entirely enveloped by the Allied units swarming towards them, was to abandon their line and join the general retreat north, Clausel having first ordered the commander of the Signals redoubt, by then almost surrounded, to hold on at all costs.

Colborne, presumably misunderstanding an order received from Alten, started to storm these fortifications, a closed work much stronger and more complete than others carried that day. Several unsuccessful attempts were checked by a deep ditch surrounding it, where the assailants were met by heavy fire. After half an hour had elapsed, by which time the routed French divisions were well away, Colborne, with a bugler to sound a parley and at some risk even with a white handkerchief on his uplifted sword, presented himself at the gate, where the commander, whose name was Gilles, came to meet him. Colborne explained to Gilles that he had been left in the lurch by his comrades, who had fled, and that between him and safety were several thousand Spaniards. The Frenchman acknowledged that he must surrender, but asked that they might *not* be handed over to Spaniards, to which request Colborne consented. The garrison of 350 effectives was marched out with the honours of war before the 52nd drawn up in line, and then escorted down to Sare and placed under the protection of Victor von Alten's hussars. Four-fifths of the casualties of 32 killed and 208 wounded suffered by the 52nd that day occurred during this exploit.

Clausel made one more attempt to rally his troops on the redoubt of Aróstegui on the Bizkarzun hill, rising due east of Ascain, but his attempt to do so was frustrated by a vigorous thrust by the Light Division in full pursuit, in which Colonel Andrew Barnard of the 1/95th was severely wounded. Taupin's demoralised troops crossed the Nivelle by the bridge at Ascain; that at Ibarron, further east, was already in the hands of Power's Portuguese, who had turned downstream from the bridge of Amotz and were now threatening another bridge at adjacent St-Pée. The bulk of Conroux's fugitives had already retreated towards Habantzenborda, in the hills north-east of St-Pée.

Larpent, who had remained until the early afternoon on the summit of La Rhune, where he met, among other spectators of the battle, Thomas Heaphy and Lord Edward Somerset—for the cavalry did not take part in the battle—describes

> . . . hearing and seeing fire and smoke all away along the hills from St Jean de Luz to near St Jean Pied de Port. The whole was visible at once; and I could see the men even with the naked eye, by the glitter of their arms, for a considerable way. The French redoubts crowned the tops of all their positions with deep ditches; and they had full shelter in woods and houses; but our men slowly beat them on and on, from place to place, forcing their way until all the right of the position seemed ours. Two redoubts on the hill below me [the Petite Rhune] I saw abandoned shamefully, when our men got round them. A large Star fort on the top took more time.

HILL'S ADVANCE

The day's events on the right wing, east of the Nivelle, had started later than the momentous operations described and had little influence on them. Hill's four divisions had much further to march, and, although they had left their respective camps at 6.30, it was already 9.00 by the time they first engaged those of D'Erlon, who had only two divisions to hand. Foy, whose division was expected to remain 'on call', preferred to play his own game, as usual, and had led it away on a wild goose chase, as will be described below.

One brigade of Abbé's division held works on the Erebi (583m), rising east of Ainhoa, and on the Mondarrain, further east (and not far south-west of Itxassou on the Nive). The positions were formidable and their approaches steep. Wellington merely demonstrated against them with Morillo's five battalions. Due north of the former height was the Col de Pinodieta, to the west of which, overlooking Ainhoa, was D'Erlon's main position, a series of trenches extending towards the Harismendia redoubt overlooking the bridge of Amotz on the Nivelle. The eastern section was held by Abbé's second brigade; one of Darmagnac's divisions defended the western. The main body of the other, commanded by Chassé, was deployed just north of Ainhoa, some units being detached on both banks of the Nivelle further south.

From the Harismendia redoubt, dominating the bridge of Amotz, D'Erlon had a wide view of much of the battlefield, from La Rhune to the south-west to beyond Ainhoa to the south-east. As Hill's columns wound their way down from the hills he had every reason to feel nervous: he was being faced by numbers double his own. Although Chassé's outlying units were intended to detain any advance forces, it was very evident to D'Erlon that the Allied columns could not be detained, so Chassé was sent orders to let them be driven in, to abandon Ainhoa and to retire to the main defensive ridge. Before long all D'Erlon's thirteen battalions were redeployed there in single line: he had no reserves in his rear.

Clinton's 6th Division had, like Colville's 3rd, the bridge of Amotz as its immediate objective, to reach which it would first have to wade across the Nivelle and storm the Harismendia height. To Clinton's right were Hamilton's Portuguese, who were to make for the next redoubt to the east. The 2nd Division, again commanded by William Stewart (recovered from his wound at Maya) and which had descended the right or east bank of the Nivelle from Urdax, was to push through or skirt Ainhoa and veer north-east up a side valley to attack the redoubts at the Col de Pinodieta once Clinton and Hamilton had gained the ridge to the west.

Clinton, before reaching the Nivelle, drew up his division in fighting order, with a thin skirmishing line in advance. Two fords were discovered, almost out of sight of the enemy, hidden by a copse. Clinton crossed unobtrusively and waited for Hamilton to do likewise further east, but the latter ran into some picquets on the far bank and was also receiving enfilading fire from a distant battery on Abbé's positions further east. Clinton then sent a detachment to chase off the picquets and Hamilton was able to cross and form in two lines abutting his own. Both divisions now pushed forward, Clinton's in advance, to approach the Harismendia redoubt and its neighbouring breastworks and trenches. It was a stiff climb to the summit, but, when it was reached, the French flinched and abandoned the whole works. Hamilton's Portuguese were hardly resisted further east, although de-layed by flames and smoke from the straw-roofed winter hutments of a French brigade, set alight as they filed off along the crest; and, such was there haste to escape, the French had left six unspiked guns in the next redoubt. In fact D'Erlon had ordered the whole of Darmagnac's division not to delay their evacuation of these positions and to retire rapidly north towards Habantzenborda before their line of retreat was cut. That little resistance was offered is confirmed by the fact that the whole division of 5,000 suffered only 400 casualties, less about 30 taken prisoner. Those of Clinton and Hamilton together were about the same.

Stewart's division had waited until the west end of the ridge was in Allied hands before launching his own attack with Byng's brigade. Resistance here was more reso-lute—it could hardly be otherwise—but, once the Pinodieta redoubt had fallen, Abbé ordered his brigade to retire east, towards Espelette and to the bridge over the Nive at Cambo, being joined en route by his other brigade left on the Erebi and Mondarrain, hurrying north to avoid isolation, with Morillo's units on their heels.

It had been Wellington's intention, once the defile and bridge of Amotz were in his hands, to circle to the west along the valley of the Nivelle in an endeavour to cut off Soult's divisions near the camp of Serrès and even those in the defensive works near the estuary at St-Jean-de-Luz. It might have been possible in summer, but in early November dusk fell early; moreover, his men had been in action for ten hours and were exhausted, and it would have also been difficult to redeploy his scattered units appropriately while still daylight. Reluctantly he 'drew stumps', which enabled Soult to evacuate all his seaward redoubts and entrenchments and get well away under cover of darkness. When writing next day to Graham, now back in England, to keep him informed of events, and describ-ing the considerable achievements of the 10th, Wellington assured him: 'Soult had a very narrow escape. If I had had an hour or two more of daylight, or two fresh divisions in reserve, I could have caught his right before they could have got back into the entrenched camp at Bayonne.' Whether that could have been possible is a matter of speculation; but, indisputably, if Clausel had not continued to hold out as long as he did—allowing his own divisions to be shattered in consequence—the envelopment of many more units of Soult's army would have taken place.

FOY'S EXCURSION

It remains for Foy's wayward little expedition to be excused—not that his appearance on the main battlefield would have made much difference. Foy had made up his mind several days earlier that when Wellington took the offensive again, it was unlikely that his sector would be involved; intuitively, he reckoned it would take place precisely where it did. Therefore, as he noted in his diary, 'If I am not attacked myself, I shall move against the enemy's flank and rear, to draw off troops against me. If the centre gives, it will be difficult to hold on to St Jean-Pied-de-Port.' On 9 November Soult informed him that he was under D'Erlon's command, and late that night D'Erlon ordered him to send back one of his brigades urgently to Espelette, but the aide bearing the dispatch got lost and it was not until 7.00 next morning that Foy received and ignored it, as he had already set his mind on making this diversion and was about to march his division from Bidarray via the Gorospil Path, or Chemin des Anglais, towards Maya.

At 11.30 Foy's vanguard found itself engaged with Mina's units guarding the Puerto de Otxondo, which he forced back. Brigadier José Andrade sent down to Maya for reinforcements and was able to hold the pass with 2,000 against 5,000 for two hours before retiring downhill. Foy was impressed by such resistance. On approaching Maya, he captured some impedimenta left by a brigade of the 6th Division before marching for the front on the previous night. James Anton, with the 42nd, recorded that, the alarm having been given, 'hospital orderlies, convalescents and stragglers in the uniforms of a dozen corps turned out in something like military order, weak as they were, to show a fight.' However, by then, after noon, Foy realised that he had led himself on a wild goose chase: the bird—in this case, the Allied units he had hoped to have surprised—had flown hours earlier. A dispatch from the front stating that all was going badly must also have caught up with him. Foy promptly turned on his tracks, having lost 28 killed (among them a colonel) and 192 wounded: all he could show for the expedition were 100 Spanish prisoners, 20 British stragglers and 150 horses and mules laden with plunder collected from the Allied camp. Soon after regaining Bidarray, Foy set off towards Cambo to take his place on the left flank of the redeployment Soult would have to establish if he intended to hold the line of the Nive.

Soult, taking stock of the state in which he found his army at dawn next day, must have been under great stress: it was not for some time that he was aware of the precise whereabouts of the dispersed units surviving the inglorious defeat—which, naturally, could not be laid at his door. Daricau's division, not even in action the previous day, had marched off and halted at Bidart, half way between St-Jean-de-Luz and Bayonne. Before dawn he had been followed by Villatte, after leaving Ascain to the mercy of Longa's troops, and abandoned the camp at Serrès. Reille had extracted his two divisions from positions defending St-Jean and had partly wrecked the bridge spanning the Nivelle there, but had left all his batteries behind him. Clausel had reached Ahetze, inland from St-Jean, with most of Maransin's division and some of Taupin's, while survivors of Conroux's were north-east of St-Pée. D'Erlon had retreated to Ustaritz, on the Nive, taking with him Darmagnac's division almost intact, while Abbé's, not badly hit, had retired to defend the bridgehead at Cambo, further upstream, where he was joined later by Foy. Numbers of stragglers would be converging on their units during the next few days, and until then Soult would not have any clear idea of what effectives he would have at his disposal.

The Allies bivouacked wherever they had halted at dusk. Among the first to be redeployed next morning were the 5th Division and 2nd Brigade of Guards, which advanced towards the banks of the Nivelle, but according to Batty the repair of the bridge at Ciboure 'and the construction of a flying bridge to assist in conveying the troops over, occupied the artificers a considerable time, so that it was mid-day before they were rendered passable for artillery.' The 1st Division and Wilson's Portuguese brigade were able to ford the river further upstream, although it had rained all morning, but

> . . . the spectacle of the allied columns descending from the fortified position in files to the banks of the river, and then forming columns in the most perfect order; with the grand style in which the troops forded the river and ascended the opposite bank, was remarkably striking . . . Many of the soldiers' wives were seen wading through . . . and dragging themselves through the muddy banks and swampy ground of the opposite shore by the sides of the companies to which their husbands belonged . . . On the following day tents and camp equipage arrived, but the rain of the 11th was only the commencement of bad weather, which continued without interruption until the 18th of November, rendering the cross roads so muddy and bad, besides swelling all the rivulets into broad and deep streams, that any attempts to advance further at that period must have failed.

In their hurry to get away, the French had left behind a magazine entire at St-Jean-de-Luz, while a fleet of luggers and fishing boats still lay at anchor in the harbour; these would come in useful. By the evening of the 11th, the enemy units facing them having retreated to the vicinity of Bidart, the Allied left wing were able to take up a position on a ridge of hills leading inland from Guéthary, where they bivouacked. In their rear, Sir John Hope had occupied St-Jean-de-Luz without incident, having (so Larpent was informed) 'flogged the two first men he caught taking some wine—this instantly.'

Larpent's impressions of his tramp from Sare to St-Pée, crossing the line of French redoubts and positions in the wake of the battle, with 'our wounded and the stripped dead lying about as usual', were distinctly bleak. Were it not for the fact that he passed all the wounded and prisoners 'going to the rear, instead of marching with them', it had almost the appearance of a retreat. Also on the hoof were the Spanish oxen, likewise a melancholy sight:

> . . . so starved, and thin, and weak, that during the first league I counted probably about eleven lying down to die, whilst every now and then a sergeant with his pike, or a soldier, gave them a stab, half

out of humanity, and half to see the effect, and from a sort of love of mischief. Then there were ten
or fifteen poor women belonging to the baggage of the division lamenting over their dying donkeys
and mules, whilst others were brutally beating some to death, because they would not go further.
In every direction baggage was falling off, and the whole formed a glorious scene of confusion.

Larpent had found shelter from the rain in what appeared to be a *curé*'s house, where,
looking out onto the garden, a Portuguese lad, 'with a dragoon broadsword [was] cutting
down cabbages and apples . . . for his brother Portuguese, who has his apron ready to
receive them', while 'a dirty, brown, snuff-coloured Spaniard is looking about on the other
side with an old French musket trying to shoot something eatable.' This, with the 'occasional riotous noise of muleteers and stragglers . . . as well as a few swearing English', he
found depressing, for

> . . . to a person not actively engaged in what is going on, by which all minor considerations vanish
> in the dangers and anxiety of the scene, there is a sameness of misery and starvation, of wounds
> and of death, which . . . becomes very unpleasant, especially without any rational companion to talk
> to on what is passing.

Should Batty's description of the sudden change in weather require further substan-
tiation, Larpent's *Journal*, written up on the afternoon of the 13th, states that, as it had been
raining incessantly, he had not stirred from his hole, and, although he had seen no one,
he understood

> . . . that all the grandees were to have gone to the front at five this morning, but from the state of
> the weather, they have all stopped at home—not for the fear of wetting themselves, but most likely
> from the impossibility of getting through the country, and across rivers, when in such a state.

The Battle of the Nivelle, less dramatically spectacular than either Salamanca or Vitoria,
was, of all Wellington's large-scale offensive operations, perhaps that in which the su-
premacy of his army over the French was most evident, although this is rarely acknowledged. It is debatable whether or not he could have taken more immediate advantage of
the situation in which Soult found himself. Had the elements been kinder, it is possible
that Wellington might have followed up his success by thrusting ahead through the gap
left in the centre of Soult's line of defence, but he remained wary, preferring not to
continue the advance until all his divisions were appropriately redeployed.

Allied losses in the battle had amounted to fewer than 2,450, 2,000 being British, but
with an abnormally high ratio of officers to men, due probably to their intrepidity when
leading their units against such formidable positions as those on the Lesser Rhune.
Casualties among officers alone were 32 killed and 145 wounded. Spanish losses must
have been about 800, including those among Andrade's men at Maya. Without taking
into account their widespread demoralisation, those of the French had been about 4,350,
of which 2,900 were among Clausel's divisions. Soult had also lost not fewer than 59
guns—largely those of position supplied by the arsenal of Bayonne with which he had
armed his redoubts. These, with the exception of one or two only, had proved virtually
useless.

12

THE BATTLES OF THE NIVE

AS these separate actions took place over an extended area and during a period of four days, this chapter has been divided up accordingly; the next is devoted entirely to the separate battle of St Pierre, on the east bank of the river.

After reviewing the few alternatives open to him, Soult decided that the most effective method of containing Wellington's army would be to align the divisions of Darmagnac, Daricau and Abbé along the east or right bank of the Nive, itself a formidable natural defence. Once he had assured himself that Bayonne was sufficiently garrisoned, he would move the rest of his forces across the river, retaining only the bridgehead at Cambo, now occupied by Foy. In this way Wellington would find himself constricted within the triangle of land between the Nive and the coast. It was unlikely that he would advance towards Bayonne, leaving both his flank and rear threatened by 50,000 men: he might well retreat to the Spanish frontier. If he divided his army by crossing the Nive and investing the fortress from the south-east as well, Soult, with the bridges at Bayonne at his disposition, could fall on either part and crush it before the other could traverse the river further downstream in time to offer support. Soult made the necessary deployments with the minimum of delay.

Several officers were court-martialled for cowardice—as an example to others. Taupin's division was disbanded, conscript units being sent to strengthen the Bayonne garrison and the rest distributed amongst other divisions. Taupin himself was given command of Conroux's division, which, together with those of Leval's, Boyer's, Maransin's and Villatte's, would remain with Soult for the time being. D'Erlon would be responsible for the others, including Paris's division, brought up from St-Jean-Pied-de-Port—unlikely to be attacked from the now snowbound Pyrenees—to Bidarray to cover his flank. Pierre Soult's light cavalry division would be stationed between Urcuray (east of Cambo) and Hasparren, keeping in touch with both Paris and Foy.

Meanwhile, inexplicably to Soult, Wellington had merely advanced as far as a line extending inland from Bidart to Arrauntz, opposite Villefranque on the Nive, and had then halted. Hope had placed his corps in winter cantonments at Bidart and Guéthary; Beresford's units had established themselves in and around Arcangues, further east; and Hill's troops had settled near Espelette, where they were able to keep a close watch on Foy.

News of Napoleon's defeat at Leipzig on 19 October had just reached Soult: this was discouraging enough, even if the full gravity of the disaster had been toned down in the Emperor's 'Erfurt Bulletin' (also known to Wellington). In addition, Soult was exercised by information received from Captain Pomade, one of Cassan's aides, who had been allowed to pass through the lines on 12 November to bring him details of Pamplona's surrender. Naturally, Pomade had been detained by Wellington for several days at Bera until the projected offensive had got under way. Larpent, who had met him—'a gentle-man-like man'—at Wellington's table, had noticed that, when asked whether he would be willing pass a message to a banker in Bayonne for him, Pomade, while replying in the affirmative, had remarked that he would have preferred to avoid Bayonne 'as he was not ready yet to be shut up again in another town': it was obvious to him that something was in the wind, and he had a hunch of what was likely to be the result. Apparently Pomade had arrived at Soult's headquarters with a rumour which he had picked up—or had been fed— at Bera, to the effect that it was Wellington's intention to break through Soult's lines between St-Jean-Pied-de-Port and Bayonne and, after leaving his less reliable troops to invest those fortresses, to advance directly inland towards the Garonne.

Soult now had serious misgivings as to whether or not his original plan was viable, and on 14 November, together with D'Erlon, he rode along the full length of his defensive line behind the Nive. Stretches of the river were commanded by hills on the far bank, but, in spite of recent rains—the weather had been miserably cold and wet for three or four day— several fords were still passable. Would it not be more sensible to make the Nive merely a first line of defence, withdraw to Bayonne the bulk of his troops at present distributed along its river bank and make that fortress his *point d'appui*, on which his forces could rally, and from which they could fall on the Allies' rear should Wellington be so foolish as to thrust inland, as now seemed likely? The extensive *tête de pont* at Cambo would be of little value in the changed circumstances: in due course Foy would be ordered to evacuate it.

The crossing point there had already been the object of a reconnaissance in force on Hill's part two days earlier, when skirmishing had taken place. On the 14th Wellington had written to Hope saying that he intended to deprive the French of their bridgehead as soon as the weather improved, or the Allies would have no peace during the winter. On the night of the 15th the accidental firing of a gun caused Hill—on the alert should Foy attack—to order up a brigade to threaten the French outworks. Foy, assuming that it was Hill who was attacking him, and in earnest, immediately withdrew his garrison and guns, blew up the bridge and its fortifications and deployed on the far bank, enabling Hill to occupy the bridgehead without any loss of life.

Meanwhile, on the 12th, Wellington, with reluctance, had come to the decision to send back across the frontier all his Spanish auxiliaries with the exception of Morillo's, for the moment that Longa's troops had entered Ascain two days earlier they had started to plunder and commit atrocities. This was no surprise to many of Wellington's officers. In

July George Hennell, when writing home, had stated that Longa's nephew had told a British officer that 'his men swore they would kill every Frenchman & destroy every town they came to in France', and in mid-October Hennell had remarked that, however impatient the Spanish troops might be to advance into France, it would 'require all Lord Wellington's management to prevent them murdering the inhabitants. Plundering I am sure he cannot'—which proved only too true. Wellington could not afford to allow the peasantry, provoked by such outrages, to start any form of 'guerrilla war' against his troops.

By supplying the forlorn and famished Spaniards with huge quantities of food from his own stores, he had brought them to the battlefield of the 10th, where in general they had behaved well, but in the present circumstances he would have no compunction in sacrificing his numerical superiority over Soult's army by dismissing them. They had been warned, and now would have to find food and shelter in their own country, where they would be the entire responsibility of their wretched government: he had had enough. On the 21st Wellington wrote to Bathurst, having already made his decision: 'I am in despair about the Spaniards', continuing two days later:

> They are in so miserable a state that it is hardly fair to expect that they will refrain from plundering a beautiful country, into which they are entering as conquerors—particularly adverting to the misery which their own country has suffered. I cannot, therefore, venture to bring them into France, unless I can feed them and pay them. If I could now bring forward 20,000 good Spaniards, paid and fed, I should have Bayonne . . . Without food and pay, they must plunder; and if they plunder they will ruin us all.

Longa's troops were sent back out of the Basque provinces, Girón's to the Baztan and Freire's Galicians across the frontier to find what food and lodging they could along the coast and further inland. Together with his marching orders, Freire, as their commander, received a scorching reproof:

> Indiscipline is general in your corps. Undoubtedly it was guilty of grave disorders on the evening of the 10th and the morning of the 11th—the soldiers of all three nations misbehaved. Now I do not enter France to plunder: I have not had so many thousands of officers and men killed and wounded merely in order that the survivors should be able to rob the French. On the contrary, it is my duty, and the duty of us all, to stop pillage, especially if we intend to make our army live on the resources of the country. The only way to stop pillage is to keep the troops under arms. Individual punishments are no good; for one man punished there are a hundred who escape detection. If you keep the troops under arms, pillage is prevented. I have tried this device with my own troops frequently, so I must beg you to explain to your officers that I have no intention of insulting any one. If you want your army to do great things, it must submit to discipline, without which nothing can be accomplished.

Their behaviour had made Wellington disinclined also to risk bringing into France any other Spanish forces—among them those of Carlos de España's, or Mina's—which might be at his disposal. For the time being, to be without them would be one less worry with which to contend. The main Allied army, with the Pyrenees behind them, had a firm foothold in France. It need not suffer from exposure, now that winter quarters had been found, for the weather continued to be bad; and it was still a very formidable force—some

Above: Gen. Sir Thomas Graham, Lord Lyndoch.
Below : Sir Galbraith Lowry Cole.

Above: Gen. Sir John Hope, 4th Earl of Hopetoun. (Private Collection)
Below: Gen. Miguel de Alava.

Above: Gen. Sir Denis Pack.
Below: Col. John Colborne.

Above: Gen. Sir Rowland Hill.
Below: Gen. Sir Thomas Picton.

Above: Gen. Sir Edward Barnes.
Below: Col. Sir Augustus Frazer R.A.

Above: Gen. Pedro Girón, when Marqués de las Amarillas.
Below: Gén. Maximilien Foy.

Above: Gén. Bertrand Clausel.
Below: Gén. Honoré Reille.

Above: Gén. Jean-Baptiste D'Erlon Drouet.
Below: Marshal Nicolas Soult.

Above: The Vitoria Gate, Tolosa, c. 1836. (T. L. Hornbrook)

Below: A French blockhouse between Tolosa and Hernani. (Gén. Bacler d'Albe)

Left, upper: A view from the pass of Maya, looking north-east.
Left, lower: Sorauren forty years ago—the bridge and village looking east.
Above: The bridge at Sumbilla on 19 October 1813. (Edward Hawke Locker)
Right: One of the tower houses at Lesaka.

Left, top: San Marcial—the
bridge, seen from Biriatou.
Left, centre: San Sebastián
from Monte Ulia. (Published
by Edward Orme)
Left, bottom: San Sebastián
from the east, several years
later. (Henry Wilkinson)
Right, upper: Gén. Rey's
plan of the defences behind
the main breach at San
Sebastián.
Right, lower: Camping in
the Pyrenees, from *Military
Discoveries or the Miseries of Cam-
paigning*. (1819, Henry Thomas
Alken)
Below: The inlet from the
sea at Pasajes. (Gén. Bacler
d'Albe)

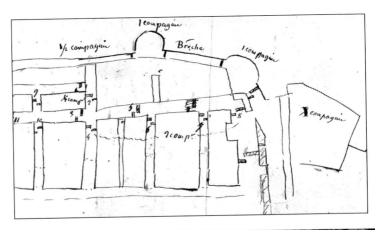

Above: A view across towards a British frigate at
Pasajes, c. 1836. (T. L. Hornbrook)
Below: An old photograph of the Bidasoa, looking to-
wards Fuenterrabia.

Right, upper: Commissariat mules descending towards
the Bidasoa. (Robert Batty)
Right, lower: The Guards wading into France, 7 October
1813. (Robert Batty)

Left, upper: The monument on Cadoux's bridge, Bera.
Left, lower: La Rhune—a view from the summit towards the ridge of La Petite Rhune.
Below: Pack-mules being unloaded at Irun. (Robert Batty)
Right, upper: Urrugne—a former French hutted encampment, looking west, with the Bidasoa estuary in the distance. (Robert Batty)
Right, lower: The quay and House of the Infanta—Wellington's headquarters—at St-Jean-de-Luz. (Robert Batty)

Above: The Château de Larraldia, St-Pierre, as it is today.
Right: Wellington's residence—2 rue Mazarin, St-Jean-de-Luz.
Below: The bridge of boats over the Adour. (Robert Batty)
Opposite page, top: Bayonne, seen from the wooded sandhills to the west. The citadel may discerned top left. (Published by Edward Orme)
Opposite page, centre: A mid-nineteenth-century view of the Capitole at Toulouse.
Opposite page, bottom: The citadel at Bayonne, seen from the south. (Gén. Bacler d'Albe)

Above: The Coldstream Guards' cemetery, Bayonne.
Below: French wounded leaving Spain. (Gén. Bacler d'Albe)

63,500 infantry (deducting recent losses), comprising 36,000 British, 23,000 Portuguese and Morillo's 4,500 Spaniards. According to the 'morning states' of 1 December, Soult still had 54,500 men with him, without counting the 8,800-strong sedentary garrison at Bayonne.

Morillo's men were the only ones not ordered back across the frontier, although Wellington was obliged to send him a strongly worded rebuke on several occasions for failing to enforce stricter discipline. Morillo had then complained to Friere, from whom Wellington received a letter of remonstrance. In his reply, Wellington had reiterated that he would not tolerate any pillaging of the French peasantry, terminating his reproof with these words:

> One would think that I am your enemy, in stead [sic] of your best friend, because I take decisive measures to prevent pillage. I repeat once more, I am quite indifferent whether I command a large or a small army; but large or small, I will be obeyed; and I will not suffer pillage.

On 23 November the picquets of the Light Division, misunderstanding orders received from Kempt, had pushed too far forward and had attacked Soult's outposts north of Bassussary (north-east of Arcangues) and were repulsed with the loss of some 80 men. Captain Hobkirk was taken prisoner. He was a great dandy, and his splendid uniform and equipage made the French assume he was a general at least. Napier, writing to his wife four days later, mentioned having heard that Hobkirk was not badly wounded, and that he had been 'as usual very well treated by the French, who, I'm sorry to say, exceed us considerably in their attention to officers who are made prisoner'. It was hoped an exchange might be made before long.

Before indulging in any further advances of consequence, Wellington had to 'test the temperature' of the civilian population in the territory already under occupation. In general, on the evidence of almost all personal narratives of the time, the Allies were received with equanimity; indeed, a good proportion of the inhabitants had shown undisguised relief whenever French troops were withdrawn from any town or village, where they had treated the locals with scant ceremony.

At about this time, in an attempt to incite desertion, the French had printed leaflets in English, and in Spanish on the verso, which were stuck on sticks near the Allied advanced posts. The text—as spelt—was as follows:

ADVICE.

The soldiers of all Nations, French, Italian, German, Polanders, English, Spaniards an Portugese who are in the English service are advised that the deserters coming to the french imperial Army are perfectly well received; they are paid for the arms and the horses they bring with; none of them is obliged to serve; pass-ports are delivered to them to return to their native country, if they chuse, or to go to inner parts of France where they may freely exercise their professions; the are moreover treated with all sort of regard. They are warned that the whole French Nation is armed, and that in the case of the English, Spaniard and Portugese armys should tread his territory, they would not find any where but death and destruction.

On 17 November Wellington moved his headquarters from St-Pée to St-Jean-de-Luz, where it was to remain for the next three months. He must have been relieved to find the Basque citizens, once confident that his commissaries were able to pay cash for all requisitions (although his troops were still months in arrears of pay), flocking back to their vacated homes. Although Batty described the small port as having 'rather a gloomy appearance when the troops first went into cantonments', before long markets were flourishing and local fishermen, or anyone with a boat, were busy assisting with the transhipment of goods and supplies from Pasajes and other neighbouring Spanish ports to St-Jean, and then up the Nivelle to Ascain, which served as a centre of distribution to the units dispersed in villages further north and east.

In his *Campaign of the Western Pyrenees*, Batty, a good amateur artist, reproduced his sketch of 'The Quay, St Jean de Luz', in which the 'Maison de l'Infante' is depicted, the exterior of which has little changed since occupied by the heads of Wellington's Commissariat.* Edward Pakenham, the Adjutant-General, was accommodated in the adjacent house, while Wellington's personal quarters were close by, at 2 Rue Mazarin, the street parallel to the quay, conveniently approached directly from the Place Louis XIV. Other departments had established themselves in neighbouring buildings, while the headquarters' printing press was set up on an island site between St-Jean and Ciboure. The hamlet of Socoa, at the mouth of the bay, its harbour defended by a 'Martello tower' (still extant), was the entrepôt for supplies of corn and biscuit.

At first the majority of the inhabitants had shut themselves up in their houses, expecting to be plundered, as they had been told they would be; but gradually, learning that their property would be respected, they reappeared and reopened their shops. Batty records that it was amusing to observe 'with what amazement they regarded the affability of manner, and the unassuming style of dress, of the Commander-in-Chief; so different to what they had been accustomed in the French generals, strutting about in splendid uniforms, attended every where by the staff-officers and their aides-de-camp'. Wellington's favourite walk was along the summit of the sea wall, where he might be seen 'in a plain grey coat, devoid of all military parade and attendance, enjoying a momentary relaxation from the bustle and cares of the camp'.

Before long the port witnessed an influx of Spaniards bearing provisions, some from as far afield as Santander, from which women, wearing 'very singular and gaudy' costumes, carried 'in truck-baskets slung over their shoulders, butter, chocolate, honey, &c.' On 3 December, their confidence increasing, about 3,000 Frenchwomen with their children crossed the Allied outposts facing Bayonne to return to their villages. Batty noticed that 'Many young men were amongst these, disguised as women, to avoid being detained by the French authorities for the new conscription. Their fears were ludicrous when detected . . . apprehending that they would be sent back . . . or treated as spies.' There must

---

* The turreted mansion, the *grande salle* of which may be visited during the season, has been so named since being the residence of the *infanta* María Teresa of Spain prior to her marriage with Louis XIV, which had taken place in the church of St-Jean-Baptiste at St-Jean-de-Luz in June, 1660.

have been a certain amount of complicity on the part of the guards at the gates of Bayonne, who might well have enjoyed the chance of frisking the party! In Larpent's words, this influx added to 'our female stock' of

> ... seven hundred Portuguese women and four hundred Spanish, who are already in this place and the environs as suttlers, *vivanderas*, washerwomen, etc. In short, here we are in quiet winter-quarters, for a time at least, with head-quarters within seven miles of the French, and yet we are all so at our ease, even in France, that the baggage animals of head-quarters are gone now beyond Tolosa, forty miles and more to the rear, for straw to feed the horses.

There was a serious lack of forage. On 24 November Larpent lamented that, as 'every field is eaten close down, and all straw and maize consumed', on the previous day he 'had sent twelve miles for straw ... and the mules returned today empty.' He now intended 'to try bruised furze, to mix with their Indian corn, so as to hold out until some more hay shall reach us from England.' Meanwhile the sutlers,

> ... by the great profit they make, can pay the muleteers as high as two dollars a day for each mule to carry up their produce, making us pay for it in the end. This evil increases, for our muleteers, who have only one dollar a day for each mule (and enough in all conscience), are tempted to desert and get into the service of the suttlers [*sic*], who thus supply the men with rum only at a dear rate, when we cannot do it. The pay of our muleteers is now over-due twenty-one months for each mule: they have, therefore, their own way, and are under no control at all. Nothing but a sort of *esprit de corps*, and the fear of losing all claim to the debt, makes them keep with us at all; and we submit to their fraud and carelessness, for we have no remedy.

This state of affairs was partially remedied shortly afterwards by acknowledging that all arrears were a debt, by giving a month's pay 'by bills on the Treasury at a great discount', and then beginning 'a sort of new score'!

The bad weather returned just as the roads were becoming passable again. As Larpent added—after remarking that Wellington and his gentlemen had been out with the hounds—'You have no conception how soon fifteen thousand sharp-footed heavy-laden mules in rain, cut up a road in this country, even when at first tolerably good.'

Wellington was still waiting for Bathurst to inform him what the latest political situation might be since Napoleon's defeat at Leipzig. Weeks seemed to be passing without any decision being reached. It was essential that he be told the Allies' intentions. Was Napoleon to be deposed or not? Was he to make up his own mind as how he should treat the royalist emissaries who were now pestering him for support? As yet, he had taken little notice of claims he had received—from the Duc de Berri among others—that 20,000 royalists would take up arms the moment he had crossed the frontier. Although most people were in favour of getting rid of their present ruler, there appeared to be negligible enthusiasm for the return of the House of Bourbon; nevertheless, the Allies ought to agree on some future sovereign for France. In the event, it was not until 22 December, after Napoleon had refused to come to an accommodation, that the vanguard of the Allied armies crossed the Rhine; but Wellington only received this news officially on 10 January.

THE PASSAGE OF THE NIVE: 9 DECEMBER

Meanwhile Wellington, rather than remain in a cul-de-sac south of Bayonne, had decided to extend his front beyond the Nive. If he then rolled up the enemy divisions defending the river front and swung his right wing round to reach the Adour and face Bayonne from the south-east, Soult would be obliged to move away. With the Allies commanding all river traffic on the Adour, by which means a great part of his food and munitions were at present reaching the fortress, it would become impossible for Soult to keep both the garrison and his army of over 50,000 men—let alone the citizens of Bayonne—supplied for long, other than by the one road traversing the desolate pine forests of the Landes extending to the north. There was always the risk that Soult might sally out in strength while the Allied forces were separated by the Nive. But it was a risk Wellington was prepared to take: even if divided, they should be able to hold their own.

The operation was to be carried out as follows. Hill, with the 2nd Division and Hamilton's division (now commanded by Le Cor), together with Morillo's Spaniards and two brigades of light cavalry (those of Hussey Vivian and Victor von Alten, the latter only recently ordered up to the front from Navarre), would cross the Nive by several fords which had been discovered adjacent to Cambo and repair the bridge there. Morillo's men would then turn upstream and remain opposite Itxassou as a flank guard with Vivian's hussars, which would fan out as a reconnoitring arm and to keep a watch on possible enemy movements towards Hasparren (north-east) or on that part of Paris's detached brigade to the south near Louhossua, which was very likely to find itself cut off. The rest of Hill's force would turn north-west and follow the river bank, turning the flank and rear of any troops they met.

Meanwhile Beresford, with an advance guard of the 3rd and 6th Divisions, would cross the Nive by a ford at Ustaritz and there construct a pontoon bridge, across which the rest would follow. Having driven off any French in the vicinity, they would join up with Hill's men and continue the advance on Bayonne. Their place on the west bank would be taken by the 7th and 4th Divisions, moving up from their cantonments, the left of their line being abutted by the Light Division. Towards the coast, Hope would advance on a broad front with his corps—the 1st and 5th Divisions, together with Aylmer's brigade and those of Bradford and Archibald Campbell—and demonstrate in force against, but not attack, the French outposts wherever they might be in that quite thickly wooded area (their positions were not exactly known). Thus five divisions would cross the Nive, and the equivalent of six—counting the three independent brigades as one—would remain on the left bank, with the fords and bridges at Ustaritz and Cambo being the lines of communication between the two sectors. Between Cambo and Bayonne the main crossing-points of the Nive were being kept under observation by the divisions of Foy at Cambo, Darmagnac opposite Ustaritz and Daricau at Villefranque, with Abbé's being in reserve at Mouguerre, on a nearby ridge south-east of Bayonne.

A signal fire was kindled on the hills near Cambo at dawn on 9 December and the 2nd Division, followed by Le Cor's, waded into the Nive. Only Pringle's brigade, the most north-erly, after some trouble crossing (the water-level having risen slightly) found Foy's picquets resisting, but not for long. Foy, having noticed that the 6th was already over, had started to retire up the road winding north-west down the Nive valley. He was later joined by Berlier's brigade, which, after opposing Barnes's brigade south of Cambo, on finding that Pringle had cut the riverside road, had been forced to retreat by tracks among the hills behind him. Hill, as a precaution, had detached Byng's brigade to advance towards Urcuray, to cover his flank should Berlier return to attack his rear, perhaps together with Paris's troops.

William Keep, writing home from Espelette while recuperating from a wound, records that units of the 28th (part of Pringle's brigade) were at one time put into any house they could find, to shelter from the rain, and that officers were ordered to remain in the same buildings as their men—an unusual but precautionary measure, for the cellars were full of wine casks. The poor woman remaining in the building in which Keep found himself came complaining 'of the excessive bad behaviour of the men, who had broken open her cellars, and taken the shoes off her feet.' Keep descended to the cellar to take control of the delinquents, having first sent one of his men to acquaint the Adjutant. When the guard arrived to arrest them, the corporal leading the file informed Keep that no further assistance could be sent 'as the same and worse conduct was going on with the other companies of the Regiment'. 'The Corporal, though a powerful man, was levelled to the ground immediately with his men, by these intoxicated soldiers, and I found there was nothing to be done, except by remaining myself among them, being a check upon their committing further mischief, as they professed to be willing to obey my orders in this respect.' Once they were all somnolent, Keep left them snoring until advised at dawn that the French appeared to be advancing, which information 'had the most surprising effect upon the men, who turned out with the greatest steadiness, and fell into their ranks, so that when I marched them up to the Regiment they were in perfect order.'

Beresford's crossing had gone remarkably smoothly. There was a small island in the river at Ustaritz, where the nearer channel was spanned by pontoons, leaving only the far one to be forded. Darmagnac's picquets were soon driven in by Clinton's brigades, and pontoons were thrown over. Once the 3rd Division had occupied the right bank, they were to guard the crossing and repair the wooden bridge which had been destroyed on Soult's instructions. Gruardet's brigade, defending the sector, was pushed slowly back by Clinton, who, advancing ankle-deep in mud along the riverside road winding between rain-sodden banks and fields, did not near the enemy positions overlooking Villefranque from the north until the early afternoon.

Meanwhile, on hearing of the passage of the Nive to his south-west, D'Erlon had ordered Abbé's division at Mouguerre to move south towards Foy, who was waiting near Larréburua,* east of Villefranque, for Berlier to re-join him, which he did at 2.00: together, they might make a stand against the Allies advancing north. However, there was a three-mile gap between them and Daricau and Darmagnac at Villafranque. Seeing Hill's

* On the 1:25,000 map, on which Oman's Lorminthoa does not appear.

troops advancing in force to join Clinton's, D'Erlon redeployed Abbé's and Foy's divisions closer to his others.

Hill, on approaching, noticed that the village of Villefranque itself was defended by two of Darmagnac's battalions only and decided to evict them before dusk, on what until then had been a miserably wet day, by sending in Douglas's Portuguese brigade. D'Erlon countered by ordering down reinforcements, with which they were expelled. Hill renewed the attack, with Pringle's brigade in support, and reoccupied the place. D'Erlon retired for the night. Allied casualties that day on the right bank of the Nive had been very slight—fewer than 300—and it is unlikely that the French would have lost more.

It would appear that both Wellington and Soult had incorrect intelligence concerning the numbers opposing them. Soult had overrated, assuming that six divisions, not four—Morillo's not included in the calculation, as being distant—were advancing against his left wing. Wellington had underrated, assuming that there were fewer enemy divisions in Clinton's and Hill's front, otherwise he might not have risked the chance of Clinton being attacked while only half across the Nive, at least until he was quite certain that Hill was close enough to give him adequate support. As it was, only two of D'Erlon's four, at Villefranque, were anywhere near.

Hill noticed the enemy's watch fires being built up during the night on the hills before him and to his right, and it was not until dawn, when his vanguard reported that the French positions were virtually deserted, that he realised that the had been duped. With scant resistance, his reconnoitring parties—resumably including some of Victor von Alten's cavalry—were able to approach quite close to Bayonne's outworks. What was Soult up to?

THE ACTION AT ANGLET: 9 DECEMBER
Before explaining the combats taking place in the vicinity of Bayonne, it may be convenient to describe that fortress in general, although additional aspects of it will be covered in later chapters.

Bayonne, as Lapurdum, the main port of the Roman province of Novempopulania, gave its name to the old Basque province of Labourd. It appears as Baiona (Ibai-ona, 'good river' in Basque) in the twelfth century, and whaling, deep-sea fishing and shipbuilding flourished while under Plantagenet and Lancastrian occupation between 1154 and 1451, but the port later silted up and trade declined. Its medieval defences, which resisted a Spanish siege in 1523, were extended later and entirely remodelled by Vauban between 1679 and 1691 and to a lesser extent during the following century. It had a reputation for its armourers, and the bayonet is said to have been invented here, while by 1757 Bayonne and St-Jean-de-Luz between them were responsible for arming as many as forty-five privateers. It was at the Château de Marracq, which stood just south of the *enceinte*, that Carlos IV of Spain was constrained to surrender his crown to Joseph Bonaparte on 6 May 1808. In 1787 its civilian population had been about 12,000, and in the interim had probably increased very little.

The walled town stood on the south bank of the broad and sandy tidal Adour at a point some three miles from its mouth, where it is joined by the Nive, which flows right through its centre, the two halves being spanned by several narrow bridges. The bastions and curtain walls on the west bank of the Nive were known as the Front d'Espagne, and those on the east as the Front de Mousserolles. On the far bank of the Adour rose its formidable Citadel, its guns commanding the whole of the comparatively low-lying town. To the east of the Citadel lay the riverside suburb of St-Esprit. At a higher level to the north stood the village of St-Etienne and the hilltop crossroads of the *chaussées* entering from Dax (for Mont-de-Marsan and Bordeaux) and from Peyrehorade (for Orthez and Pau). The *chaussée* to Spain left the town in a south-westerly direction towards the village of Anglet and, skirting that of Biarritz, veered parallel to the coast through Bidart, Guéthary and St-Jean-de-Luz towards the frontier.

Soult had ordered the construction of an outer ring of entrenchments, beyond Vauban's fortifications.* These ran south from a flooded area (where a brook had been dammed at its confluence with the Adour) before circling east to the Château de Marracq, close to the Nive. Another stretch of outworks, with two strong redoubts, lay between the Nive and the banks of the Adour, within which stood the camp of Mousserolles. Between the inner and outer fortifications were another two entrenched camps, those of Beyris to the south-west and of Marracq near the château. From the latter a minor road left the ramparts:† this, after crossing the Urdainz rivulet and skirting the Château d'Urdainz, led through the villages of Arrauntz and Ustaritz to Cambo. From the south-eastern perimeter, another road (later given the name 'Route Impériale des Cimes') climbed beyond the village of St-Pierre-d'Irube on to a plateau between two valleys and wound south-east along a ridge before swinging away to the east, eventually leading to St-Jean-Pied-de-Port.

A boat-bridge had been placed over the Nive just outside the old walls to facilitate communication between the camps of Mousserolles and Marracq, but Wellington had received only limited intelligence as to the extent of the camps and the completion or otherwise of the entrenchments thrown up by Soult to defend them, so the advance to be made by Hope was as much one of reconnaissance as a demonstration in force.

Regrettably, almost the whole area between the west and south-western suburbs of Bayonne and those of Biarritz, further west, is now built over, making it difficult to follow precisely the actions taking place here, although most of them occurred further south. It is mainly a rolling plateau (on a stretch of which the runway of the airport has been laid out), large tracts of which were (and some still are) thickly wooded. It is dissected by several deep valleys, formed by rivulets descending towards the coast or entering the Nive. The watershed is narrow, and along this ran the *chaussée* from Anglet to Bidart, passing between the Etang de Brindos (east of La Négresse, and now isolated between runway and railway) and the larger, pine-fringed Lac de Mouriscot, further west, skirted by the same railway and the N 10 road. West of the latter, on approaching La Négresse from Anglet, is the smaller Lac Marion. According to Batty's map, another piece of water, named the Etang de Rousta, lay in the depression in which the railway station of La

* Still conspicuous on the south-west side of the *enceinte*.
† Following approximately by that of the present N 263.

Négresse now stands. Some 550 yards immediately south of the Lac de Mouriscot (but now almost entirely encircled by an approach to or exit from the A 63 motorway near a toll point) is the Château de Barroilhet (or Barrouillet), the scene of heavy fighting.*

Biarritz, now an urban sprawl, was at the time of the battle an insignificant hamlet and watering place which lay in the vicinity of the church of St-Martin, some distance south-east of the present centre. John Murray III's *Hand-Book for France* (1843) invitingly described it then as

> . . . a group of whitewashed lodging-houses, cafés, inns, traiteurs, cottages, &c., generally of a humble character, scattered over rolling eminences and hollows bare of trees . . . [where] French ladies and gentlemen 'en costume des bains,' consume hours in aquatic promenades. The ladies may be seen floating about like mermaids, being supported on bladders or corks, and over-shadowed by broad-brimmed hats.

More heavy fighting took place around the hilltop church and churchyard of the hamlet of Arcangues,† further south, as will be described below, while John Cooke also refers to units stationed further east, 'at a cottage half a mile to the right, situated close to a lake, on the other side of which, on a rising ground, was the chateau of Chenie, enclosed by the small plantation of Berriots through which a road runs towards Ustaritz.' The château is now known as that of Berriotz.‡

Hope, with the 1st and 5th Divisions and Campbell's and Bradford's brigades, together with the 12th Light Dragoons, lent to him for the purpose, advanced on a broad front from their cantonments at Bidart and Guéthary early on 9 December, while the Light Division at Arcangues were ordered to cooperate by sweeping the plateau in front of Bassussarry as far north as the Aritxague valley.§ In their rear were Aylmer's Brigade and the 4th Division, the latter brought up over the hill from Ascain to take up a position just

---

* Although private property, the former 'Mayor's House' of numerous narratives—a small farm then belonging to Jean Commamalle, the mayor of Biarritz—may still be approached discreetly from the verge of the N 10, walking a few yards towards the buildings of a small enterprise and passing the entrance to a neighbouring house. The owners may obligingly allow one to traverse their garden to enter the adjoining one—that of the Mayor's House—there to stretch the imagination.

† By referring to the 1:25,000 I.G.N. map 1344 OT, or their *Plan de Ville de Bayonne* (not contoured) one may either follow by-roads to the east or turn on to the D 3 from the D 932 driving south from central Bayonne immediately after passing below the A 63 , to approach the hamlet of Arcangues from the north. The site also provides quite extensive views. The château—which had been loopholed—lying 300yds to the east of the church, is now of no interest apart for its situation, having been entirely rebuilt a century ago.

‡ The château of Berriotz is between the D 932 and the Nive. It was this—mentioned as that of Herroritz—that General Colville occupied as his headquarters, and where he was visited by his nephew Frederick Frankland, who related that the proprietor, a fine old gentleman, 'had wisely remained in his house and gave us the use of his kitchen garden, which abounds in vegetables of all sorts. He was very sociable and dined sometimes with the General and his staff, and once or twice he gave us a dinner. I, indeed, lived in clover here, having a nice bedroom and a good French bed to myself.' Again, map in hand, one may traverse the village of Bassussarry on its ridge north-east of Arcangues to approach the Château d'Urdainz, otherwise referred to as 'Garat's House' (having been the residence of Dominique Garat, the Revolutionary politician), between which and the Nive was swampy ground by the Urdainz rivulet, crossed by the bridge of that name. Further south, conveniently approached from the village of Arrauntz, rises the hill of Ste-Barbe, a good viewpoint, commanding also the neighbouring village of Herauntz and the position—on the Nive to the north-east—of the vital bridge of communication between Beresford's and Hill's corps when it was isolated during the earlier stages of the battle of St-Pierre (see the following chapter).

§ A depression through which railway and motorway now run.

south of the village of Arbonne (west of Arcangues), while the 7th Division was deployed on the hill of Ste-Barbe, with an advance guard occupying 'Garat's House'.

The 5th Division advanced between the Lac de Mouriscot and the sea, with the two Guards brigades of the 1st Division marching along the *chaussée*. After skirting the lake, the K.G.L. Brigade veered away, spreading out past the hamlet of Pucho (then just north of La Négresse) and towards the present Tour de Lannes.* Enemy outposts were encountered at Anglet, where skirmishing took place, until the position was turned by the K.G.L., when units of Boyer's and Leval's divisions occupying the village retired to the camp at Beyris, the front of which was then reconnoitred. On his left, Hope had sent forward a patrol of Light Dragoons, together with Major John Burgoyne of the Engineers. Passing through the *pignada*, a belt of pine woods between Biarritz and the mouth of the Adour, Burgoyne cursorily surveyed the area, on which he was able to report in detail after a later visit. The Light Division pushed ahead to occupy a line between the bridge of Urdainz and Etang de Brindos. Allied casualties on this front on the 9th were about 350.

At dusk, having left a line of picquets, supported by only Campbell's and Bradford's Portuguese near Barroilhet, Hope ordered the 5th Division back to Bidart and Guéthary, and the 1st and Aylmer's men as far as their cantonments near St-Jean-de-Luz, ten miles south and a long and wearying trudge (presumably without advising Wellington that he had sent them back so far!). The Light Division, leaving picquets on the ridge of Bassussarry, returned to Arcangues. It does not seem to have occurred to Hope that Soult might make a counter-attack, which was his intention, almost exactly as he had outlined to Clarke at Paris three week's earlier.

Having left men to build up the watch fires opposite Clinton and Hill, at midnight all four of D'Erlon's divisions were ordered to retire discreetly towards the boat-bridge awaiting them and cross to the west bank of the Nive. Three of the four divisions—Foy's had hardly recovered from hours of marching in the rain the previous day—had filed across by dawn, although in the darkness several units had got muddled up with those of other regiments. Soult left four battalions of the garrison together with conscript units to man the outer defences of the Mousserolles camp, and had ordered gunboats from his small flotilla on the Adour to fire on any enemy troops seen to be approaching them.

THE ACTION AT ARCANGUES: 10 DECEMBER

Soult was to make a two-pronged attack: Reille's two divisions were to move against Hope's picquets south-west of Bayonne, while those of Boyer and Leval were to advance directly down the *chaussée* (which will be described later). His main thrust was made by Clausel with Taupin's division, followed by Maransin's, but not until 9.00 did they march out of the entrenched camp of Marracq and work their way towards the Bassussarry ridge. Massed behind them were three of D'Erlon's divisions, waiting for Foy's to cross the Nive and the order to advance to be given.

---

* Rising immediately north of the east end of the airport runway.

At first, the day—'cold and raw, and after 2 o'clock very rainy'—promised to be quiet. During the night John Cooke, with a salient picquet in front of Bassussarry, had heard only 'confused sounds, like the rumblings of artillery, intermixed with a good deal of hallooing and barking of dogs, but two hours before daybreak all the sounds died away and everything was hushed and tranquil.' The suspicion of the field officer being awakened, Cooke was ordered to feel his way towards the house of Oyhenart (Oihenart, between the village of Bassussarry and the Château d'Urdainz), usually held by the French, to check whether they had reoccupied the ground from which they had been driven the previous day. As Cooke and his party, to avoid an abatis, turned into an adjoining field, they almost walked into a dozen of the enemy but were able to retire unnoticed. At 8.00 Kempt visited the picquet but did not appear preoccupied, and he was about to order the 1st Brigade back to Arbonne when Colonel Beckwith advised him to cancel the order until there was more certainty regarding the enemy's intentions, while Major John Tylden rode off to warn other advance companies to be on the alert.

Before leaving the outpost, Beckwith accompanied Cooke on a tour of the sentries, one of which, soon afterwards, beckoned to him. He had noticed a mountain gun on mule-back passing a gap in the hedge ahead and being placed behind a bush. A few minutes later Soult himself, with a group of officers, was seen at point-blank range. On climbing an adjacent tree, Cooke caught sight of a whole enemy column lying down, 'in readiness to pounce'. Within seconds he was riding back at speed and luckily met Kempt, who sent on a message to Alten and ordered up a party to support Cooke's picquet. Within a few minutes a group of French nonchalantly appeared, bidding his sentinels to retire. As was the custom, they would not be fired at while they did so; but, realising the seriousness of the intended attack, Cooke had no compunction in directing his own men to 'fire away', the volley precipitating a general engagement, with the enemy skirmishing line charging uphill. During the subsequent confused action one or two outposts were cut off, but all the others retired on the church and château of Arcangues, both having been fortified and provided with abatis some days previously. Although two brigades had by now been deployed opposite them, with others coming up, the French advance slowed up on approaching the strongpoint, manned by the Light Division. A ravine to the west of it was defended by the 52nd, while the centre of the position, east of the church, was held by the 3/95th and the Caçadores.

At first Clausel tried to break through the centre, but both here and on advancing towards the church his men were met with such a tremendous fire that they soon retired out of range, for the 1/95th were not only firing from the encircling churchyard wall but also from two tiers of windows lighting the north side of the wooden galleries on all three sides of the interior.*

When Clausel later placed two batteries at a lower level some 400 yards away, the incessant fire being kept up against his gunners—not accurate, but a hail of balls fired at a high trajectory—was causing sufficiently heavy casualties that they were withdrawn.

---

* Still their typical position in many Basque churches.

Apart from knocking about the tombstones and chipping off a few pieces from the solid stone structure, his artillery did little damage to the church, and a later attempt to bring the guns into play was likewise unsuccessful.

Further east, at the château and its outworks, held by the 1/95th, the action had been equally heated. John Kincaid, who described it as 'large, well-furnished, and unoccupied, except for a bed-ridden grand-mother, and young Arcangues, a gay, rattling young fellow, who furnished us with plenty of wine (by our paying for the same)', relates that the enemy had advanced 'in formidable numbers . . . blazing away at our windows and loopholes, and showing some disposition to attempt it by storm; but they thought better of it and withdrew their columns a short distance to the rear, leaving the nearest hedge lined with their skirmishers'. In the words of George Hennell, on first seeing the French within range, they had 'opened one of the most tremendous fires I, & many older than myself, ever beheld. I have since been to the house & trees around it, where the French appeared, & there is scarcely one tree without 20 balls stuck in it'.*

In the rear of this narrow front, the 2/95th and the 17th Portuguese had been placed in reserve, together with two mountain guns to command the road close to the château. By 1.00 the 4th Division had moved up to support the Light and were deployed on a hillside some 600 yards to the rear, should they be needed, but in the event Clausel never delivered a general infantry attack on the Arcangues position, although by now Daricau's Division had reached him. Abbé's Division had been diverted towards the bridge of Urdainz, as units of the Allied 7th Division had been seen in the vicinity of its château. Darmagnac's Division remained in the rear to support Abbé's or follow Daricau's; but Clausel's men seemed rooted to their positions: the Light Division could never understand why they had not pressed their attack.

One excuse may be that Clausel had received intelligence that the 3rd and 6th Divisions were marching up from Ustaritz, for the moment that Wellington was aware of Soult's latest ploy and that they would no longer be required to support Hill's thrust he had ordered them back across the Nive and to advance down the near bank to relieve the 7th, which then moved west toward Arbonne. It was not far north of Arbonne, and west of Arcangues, that violent and costly fighting was also taking place. At Arcangues itself, the combat was virtually over by 3.00. The Light Division had suffered 150 casualties, apart from 73 taken prisoner at the onset of Clausel's attack. The French may have lost 400 during the day along this sector of the front.

THE ACTIONS AT BARROILHET: 10–12 DECEMBER

Initially Soult had intended that his main attack would be by Clausel's units, but this eventually petered out, as we have seen. Those commanded by Reille, further west, were to demonstrate against Hope's outposts only, but the battle developed otherwise. Boyer's

---

* The grandmother, sitting in an arm-chair mounted on mule-back, was later sent to the rear, while Kincaid described the two remaining fruit trees as being cut down to prop up a floor likely to give way with the weight of bricks they had used to make a fireplace, the weather having become so bitterly cold.

and Leval's divisions, together with a brigade of cavalry (Sparre's) had left the camp at Beyris before dawn. They advanced along the *chaussée* to a point between the lakes of Brindos and Marion, a narrow front across which one of Leval's brigades was to push towards the Allied picquets—from Robinson's brigade of the 5th and Campbell's Portuguese. These picquets appeared not only to have been taken by surprise but also, according to Frazer—the 5th Division having been separated from the ammunition mules during the night—had very little ammunition left. After conferring with Hope, Frazer had ordered up 150,000 ball cartridges from the reserve near the Bidasoa, but 'There was nothing to be done but to hold our ground as well as we could, till more troops and ammunition should arrive.' Frazer also described the ground as being 'little favourable for bringing many guns into action at the time. To our right, and close to the road, was low thick wood; to the left a rugged heath, intersected with gulleys and ravines.'

The first onrush took place at about 9.30, once Leval had heard firing from Clausel's troops to the east. The centre of the Allied line of picquets broke at once and those on either flanks had to beat a rapid retreat, many being cut off and taken prisoner in the ensuing confusion. Their officers had great difficulty in checking their flight and getting their units to turn about, and it was only on reaching the bulk of Campbell's brigade, a mile to the rear and which had formed up meanwhile, that the French were brought to a temporary halt between the Lac de Mouriscot and woods to the east of the *chaussée*. By then Reille had deployed Boyer's brigade to the east of Leval's and had ordered up Sparre's dragoons, a squadron of which, charging forward unexpectedly, caused havoc among the 1st Portuguese Line, which suffered 135 casualties within minutes. Campbell fell back on the little château of Barroilhet—the 'Mayor's House'—and its dependencies a short distance to the south. By now Bradford's and Robinson's brigades, hurrying up from Bidart, had reached the scene of action, but not yet those of Greville and De Regoa from near Guéthary. Bradford's *Caçadores*, among other units, were deployed to cover the right flank.

Boyer's division was now ordered into the woods east of the Mayor's House to cut off the retreat of units defending it, and in confused skirmishing both contending forces found groups of their men being surrounded and captured without any decisive movement having taken place.

Soult, realising that Clausel's attack on Arcangues was running out of steam, and that nothing very positive was likely to happen in his front, decided to reinforce Reille, who appeared to be having far more success. Foy's division, having belatedly reached the camp at Marracq, together with Villatte's reserve, were both hurried west across the comparatively level part of the plateau, and, on arrival, Foy's troops were ordered into line east of Boyer's front with the intention of turning the flank of Hope's line.

This they did, pushing it back towards the Mayor's House, nearly reached when they encountered Greville's brigade. Meanwhile Robinson's, in and around the building, being attacked frontally by Boyer and with Leval's troops edging forward along the *chaussée*, was in a hazardous situation. Berlier's and Gauthier's brigades (of Foy's and Boyer's divisions, respectively) were almost at its walls when the vanguard of Aylmer's brigade, closely followed by the 1st Division—breathless after a four-hour slog along muddy roads—came up.

Seeing ahead of him the desperate situation at Barroilhet, Hope ordered Aylmer's brigade to veer right. Hurtling ahead, it caught Berlier's in flank, which gave way, as did the rest of the enemy line, being rolled back into the woods. It only remained unbroken because Reille threw in the German brigade of Villatte's reserve to cover the withdrawal. (Villatte himself had been wounded by a chance shot.) The fighting flagged, even if some skirmishing continued as Reille redeployed to hold the ground from which Hope's picquets had been evicted. It was now mid-afternoon, but neither the Guards nor the K.G.L. brigades had been brought into action.

Hope himself was conspicuous everywhere, doubtless desperate to recover a position which would have been easily lost, largely due to the withdrawal to an unreasonable distance of troops which should have remained much closer to his too lightly manned front. When forced to leave the farm buildings, which could have fallen to the enemy at any moment, he galloped from a side door under fire from their skirmishers. Although his horse was shot, Hope got clear, having only three musket balls through his hat. As Wellington later reported to Torrens at the Horse Guards,

> We shall lose him if he continues to expose himself to fire as he did . . . indeed his escape has been wonderful. He places himself among the sharp-shooters, without (as they do) sheltering himself from the enemy's fire. This will not answer; and I hope that his friends will give him a hint on the subject. But is a *delicate* subject.

As Oman remarked of Hope's rash behaviour on this occasion, 'the whole mentality of this gallant officer . . . makes us ponder on what would have happened if Wellington had fallen sick, and the command of the whole Allied forces had devolved on him.'

An unexpected incident took place during the following night. Colonel Krüse, commanding the 2nd Nassau Regiment in Villatte's reserve division, after secretly negotiating with an old friend in the K.G.L. that his regiment and any others he could bring over would be transported back to Germany to join the Northern Allies, walked over from the French lines at the head of three battalions. A fourth—the Baden battalion—failed to follow as its commander had been wounded that afternoon and his second-in-command, not being in the secret, could not understand why on earth the others were marching off in such an eccentric direction. Next day these troops, numbering some 1,400 veterans and with their colours flying, embarked at Pasajes and sailed for home.*

Although the Allies had been able to cling on to their two bulwarks at Barroilhet (just) and Arcangues, 10 December might also be remembered as the day on which they lost more men as prisoners, mostly from the overrun picquets, than in any other throughout the Peninsular War—over 500 in all (some 150 British and over 350 Portuguese).

---

* This wholesale desertion prompted Soult to disarm not only the Baden battalion forthwith but also several other units composed of 'foreign' troops—Swiss, Poles, Italians and also *Afrancesados* (who had fought for France but could no longer be relied on), and many of them were sent away from the fighting line to inland Toulouse or merely turned adrift.

John Cooke records that, during that night,

> ... the whole of our regiment [at Arcangues] were hard at work throwing up a formidable battery in front of the churchyard. Before morning it was finished, with embrasures, *épaulements* [breast-works] (filled up with small bushes, to make the enemy believe that it was a masked battery) and traverses. Both our flanks were secured by felled trees strewn about, even at the back of the burial ground, which was now impregnable against any sudden assault. I do not believe 6,000 men could have taken it. So much for the ingenuity of infantry soldiers, with their spades, shovels, pickaxes, bill-hooks, and hatchets.

The morning of the 11th found the adversaries holding more or less the same lines as on the previous evening, and both waited for the other to renew the offensive; but no movement of consequence occurred that day. When ordered to push back some of Reille's outposts, the 9th Regiment, in Greville's brigade, went too far, was counter-attacked on both flanks and suffered casualties. In retaliation, at 2.00 Soult sent Daricau's and Boyer's divisions to assault Hope's line east of the *chaussée*, caught the picquets and supports unawares, pushed them back towards Barroilhet and even briefly occupied some of the dependencies. This time Hope, who was slightly wounded in a leg, had sufficient troops at hand to redress the balance, and the fighting petered out; but, again, there had been unnecessary casualties in the 5th Division, which was later withdrawn from the front, its place taken by the 1st.

On that very morning Soult had sent a dispatch to Paris confirming that, having attracted the bulk of the Allied troops on the coastal front, as planned, he would fall on Hill's depleted corps on the 13th, having conveyed the bulk of his own troops across the Nive unobserved during the previous night; meanwhile, they would have a day's rest after their recent exertions.

Wellington, however, had guessed what game Soult was playing and had already ordered Beresford to place one or more bridges across the Nive at Villefranque to improve communications between the two Allied sectors, although this proved more difficult than expected owing to a rise in level of the Nive after heavy rains in the mountains. It was vital also to have at least one bridge closer to Bayonne than that at Ustaritz, so that reinforcement could be sent over whenever necessary.

During the morning of the 12th there was a noisy exchange of fire when each thought the other was about to attack, causing Wellington to move the 7th Division from near the hill of Ste-Barbe towards Arbonne, more centrally placed. This was observed by Soult, now more eager than ever to carry out his plan, which he started to put into operation as soon as dusk fell. Six divisions were in readiness to cross the Nive, leaving only those of Boyer and Leval and Villatte's reserve behind, with orders to retire to the entrenched camps of Beyris and Marracq if pressed.

13

THE BATTLE OF ST-PIERRE

O N the morning of 10 December, as we have seen, Hill was able to reconnoitre the outer fortification thrown up by Soult to defend Bayonne from attack from the south-east, between the Nive and Adour. These, enclosing the Camp de Mousserolles, lay across the neck of land between the two rivers, approximately where it is crossed by the present railway. A convenient position from which Hill could dominate this sector was provided by hills rising a mile or two away from the outworks, along which the Allies were soon deployed. Their line ran south from the hill of Mouguerre, overlooking the Adour to the north-east, occupied by Byng's brigade, with one battalion (1/3rd; 'The Buffs') pushed forward along the ridge of Partouhiria,* rising steeply from the river bank. Cantonments were found in the village of Mouguerre (then known as Vieux Mouguerre, with its twin-turreted château and Romanesque church).† Between this ridge and another to the south was a deep valley in which lay the Etang d'Ecoute Pluye (Escouteplo[u]ya), a former mill pond.‡

The brigades of Ashworth and Barnes were stationed from a point just south-east of the lake and across another ridge to near the hamlet of Gélos. Along this second ridge, ascended the main road from Bayonne to St-Jean-Pied-de-Port,§ first traversing the sub-urban village of St-Pierre-d'Irube and the farm of Hiriberry before ascending past the hamlet of Harrichury (Marichurry in contemporary narratives). Hill had placed ten guns on the summit of the hill here, facing down the road and along both sides of the ridge. The road continued through Loste (Losterenea) to reach crossroads near the knoll of Horlopo. Le Cor's Portuguese Division was positioned below this knoll, on which Hill had his headquarters, together with two more guns.

South-west of Gélos was a boggy valley in which lay another mill pond—after rainy weather developing into two—through which a stream descended to the Nive, but the valley bottom has been drained since. To the west rose another hill, crossed by the road

* Not named on the 1:25,000 map.
† From near the Adour, a road climbs this ridge to Mouguerre, passing near a conspicuous obelisk, 'erected by modern piety'—Oman's words—in memory of Soult and his troops and known as the Croix de Mouguerre. The site, commanding fine panoramic views towards Bayonne and the distant Pyrenees, is worth visiting on a clear day. Naturally, several of the viewpoints have been partially built over in recent decades, but in general the area has changed comparatively little since the time of the battle—certainly less than that between Bayonne and Biarritz.
‡ Its banks are now skirted by both an extension towards Bayonne of the A 64 motorway and the D 936.
§ The present D 22 or 'Route Impériale des Cimes'.

from Bayonne to Villefranque, which later wound south along the right bank of the Nive towards Cambo, passing, on the far bank, Ustaritz. On the wooded western slope of this hill stood the Château de Larraldea, fortified and occupied by Pringle's brigade. Marshy meadows abutting the banks of the Nive lay to the north-west.

More concisely, Hill's front lay across three ridges, between which were two water-logged valleys. The nature of the ground made communication between each ridge diffi-cult for both assailants and defenders. They had to fight on three separate fronts, and could only feed in reinforcements frontally from reserves placed some distance to the rear, not laterally.

On 11 December Soult sent over a brigade of Sparre's dragoons from the Barroilhet front, together with a small infantry support, to reconnoitre Hill's position, but otherwise this front remained quiet that day and the next. However, Hill had been warned by Wellington that Soult might well try and surprise him in force during the next few days and advised that Beresford was busy bridge-building near Villafranque: indeed, the bridge had been laid by late afternoon on the 11th. Unfortunately, within twenty-four hours it was broken by a frechet caused by heavy rain upstream, although that at Ustaritz held firm.

The only incident of consequence on the 12th happened far to Hill's rear, when Pierre Soult's cavalry, together with Paris's division, advanced west, pushing Vivian's cavalry back towards Urcuray, where Morillo's infantry was on the alert for any such movement. After some skirmishing with the 14th Light Dragoons, in which the impetuous Major Brotherton was taken prisoner, Soult retired towards the village of Bonloc, south-east of Hasparren. This diversion caused Hill to send Barnes's brigade to support Morillo—a wild goose chase, for by the time Barnes had reached the area Paris had already with-drawn. The brigade trudged back north-west, reaching its position facing Bayonne long after dark and feeling very weary.

During the frosty moonlit night of 12/13 December the advance picquet on the Partouhiria ridge reported that it had heard suspicious sounds, like the rumbling of wagons or artil-lery, emanating from the Mousserolles camp, which was illuminated by more fires than usual. Glimpses had also been caught of columns crossing the new boat-bridge span-ning the Nive between the inner and outer fortifications. It was very probable that Soult was massing troops there; indeed, he had been packing four divisions into this con-stricted area in readiness for his dawn offensive. Two others (those of Maransin and Taupin) had yet to file across the Nive from the camp at Marracq.

Little could be seen at dawn until the mist dispersed, although unusual noises continued to be heard. Then, at 7.00, the head of the first enemy column could be made out debouching on a narrow front from the Mousserolles Gate. This was Abbé's division, perhaps the strongest of those under Soult's command with over 6,000 men, which started up the *chaussée* ascending the central of the three ridges being defended. The second division to advance was Daricau's, which veered right along the Villefranque road, while a third column—Chassé's brigade of Darmagnac's division—turned towards the Adour and the Partouhiria ridge; the other brigade, Gruardet's, followed Abbé's column. Behind Chassé, Foy's division ascended the northern ridge. Maransin's division, now being brought across the Nive, was to remain in reserve for the time being, and Taupin's was not ordered over until late in the day, and then only to cover Soult's eventual retreat.

Several batteries of artillery—22 guns in all—had been brought forward and placed on the southern slope of the low hill on which stood the village of St-Pierre-d'Irube, and shortly they started to fire against Ashworth's Portuguese, less than 800 yards distant. All this deploying had taken some time—longer than Soult had estimated—and it was not until after 8.00 that any serious fighting took place. This delay was disturbing, for it was essential to deal Hill a crippling blow before he received reinforcements from the left bank of the Nive. Apparently Soult was aware neither that Beresford had placed a form of pontoon-bridge—described by Frazer as 'of seventeen country boats'—across at Villefranque nor that three of Wellington's divisions were within striking distance on the far bank. In the event, as it was impossible to repair the bridge displaced by the freshet until shortly before noon, the 6th Division had to make the long detour south to the bridge at Ustaritz, but it still managed to reached the battlefield in time to tilt the balance in Hill's favour when for a moment it seemed precarious.

At first Hill had only 14,000 men at hand to contain Soult's massive attack. The first troops to become engaged were Ashworth's Portuguese, their thick skirmishing line opposing Abbé's. William Stewart, commanding this central sector, started to feed in light units from Barnes's brigade to support Ashworth, followed by the 71st, who placed themselves on the ridge slope near the farm of Gélos, and then the 92nd in front of Harrichury, west of the *chaussée*. But pressure from the French was strong, and the farm of Hiriberry was lost, although a copse to its east was held, becoming the pivot of Stewart's right. It was at this point that Sir Nathaniel Peacock, the recently arrived colonel of the 71st (replacing the much-respected Cadogan) not only ordered the regiment to retire but galloped off to the rear himself, where he was seen beating forward Portuguese ammunition carriers—an exhibition of courage which is said to have caused Hill, who led the 71st forward again in person, to swear for the second time in the war! (Peacock was cashiered.)

On the right flank, Colonel William Bunbury (who later resigned his commission) lost his nerve and withdrew The Buffs, admittedly hard-pressed, and before long Chassé's men were swarming through Mouguerre, until brought to a halt by seven companies of the 1/92nd, which had been re-formed behind some houses by Colonel Cameron of Fassifern. An anonymous contributor to Maxwell's *Peninsular Sketches*, described them as suddenly appearing

> . . . on the high road in close column, bayonets fixed, and the bagpipes [two of their three pipers were killed in this action] playing in its front, marching steadily down towards the column of the enemy, although at least four times its number. At the same time the skirmishers also again pushed forward on the flanks. The French column halted, perhaps wishing to deploy; this the broken ground on its right scarcely admitted, and on the left a hedge prevented it. They remained

steady; and it appeared that the very rare event in modern warfare—personal conflict—would take place, that bayonets would be used. But on the 92nd getting half-way down to the enemy, or within about fifty yards, the officer on horseback at the head of the column suddenly wheeled round, waving his sword, evidently giving the order to retire.

Abbé's battalions, although repelled temporarily by the counter-attack, rallied and, together with their reserves, ascended to the brow of the hill, their skirmishers picking off the Allied gunners, who were about to retire. Barnes—wounded minutes later—then rode up and called upon them to maintain their fire at all costs, for it was vital to hold the line.

Meanwhile Hill, just advised that the 3rd Division was now crossing the Nive at Villefranque, had brought forward Le Cor's Portuguese from the Horlopo hill, with Hippolito Da Costa's brigade in the centre to support Stewart, who had led the 71st to charge again, and sent John Buchan's to his right to support Byng. Cameron, on foot—his horse had been shot—mustered the remnants of the 92nd and counter-attacked again from Loste, east of the Harrichury position. The French started to give way all along the line, Abbé's division withdrawing down the *chaussée* but turning to fire sporadically. One shot disabled Ashworth, who had taken over the command of the centre from Barnes. His place was then taken by Colonel Currie, who re-formed the 50th and led them in a downhill charge: the enemy were hardly able to retain their ground.

It was already too late when Soult, in an attempt to staunch the flow of retreating men, ordered back Gruardet's Brigade to support Abbé's and take the offensive once again. All impetus had been lost, and they refused to face the salvos which continued to pour down on them from the Allied guns.

Foy's division, occupying the Mouguerre heights, to which he had brought up some guns from his horse artillery, still threatened Hill's right wing. It was not until Byng, leading the 1st Provisional Battalion in person and supported by Buchan's Portuguese, had assaulted the Croix de Mouguerre position that Foy was driven downhill to the bank of the Adour after a running fight along the ridge.

While the fiercer fighting had been taking place in the centre and on the right wing, Pringle's brigade (1,900 men), on lower wooded hills to the south-west, had been maintaining its position centred on the Château de Larraldia.* Daricau (with 5,000) had advanced cautiously, skirting the boggy ground in the valley below the central ridge before skirmishing in the woods in a desultory fashion, in which he gained only half a mile of ground in two or three hours. At about noon, on approaching the fortified château and finding it so strongly held, Daricau seems to have despaired of taking it and started to retire, at which Pringle, by now reinforced by a brigade of the 3rd Division, came out into the open and severely mauled his rear battalions. A number of stragglers were picked up, and Pringle's skirmishers were almost at the outer defences of the Camp of Mousserolles

---

* Sadly, the Château de Larraldia, which presumably was restored at a later date—when it must have been a most attractive country residence—together with its dependencies, has been permitted to deteriorate to a serious extent; but even in its present state of neglect, standing forlornly in the trees, it stirs the imagination. It may be approached from the north, by turning left off the D 137.

by the time the fighting had petered out. Daricau's total casualties were between 400 or 500; two of Pringles battalions (the 1/28th and 1/39th) had 120 between them but his reserve (2/34th) five only.

Wellington himself had crossed the Nive at Villafranque ahead of the 3rd Division (the Portuguese brigade of which had been left to defend the bridge) and had reached Hill's position just as the 6th had gained the Horlopo hill. By then the French had almost given up the struggle, and Wellington was able to turn to Hill with the words, 'The battle is all your own.' It had been a serious confrontation, which Hill had conducted remarkably well considering the odds against him and the fact that two of his commanders had behaved shamefully. His total casualties were 1,775, of which seventeen officers and 340 men were killed, while, apart from Barnes and Ashworth, Le Cor was also wounded, together with Colonel Tulloh, commanding the Allied artillery, three Portuguese colonels and seven aides-de-camp. It has been estimated that French casualties were about 3,300 and included three generals.

Larpent records that at Wellington's table a few days later, a certain 'Major D——', who made out the returns, was made the butt of jokes by Wellington 'because he wanted to make a grand total of wounded' after the recent fighting. Wellington intimated that he would prefer not to have any more such figures until he had fought another Vitoria without more loss,

> ...always great enough in all conscience, without displaying it in this ostentatious manner, and that he would not have every drummer and every officer, etc., killed or wounded in the last five days, all added up in one grand total, but that at least the croakers should have the trouble themselves of adding up all the different losses, and making it out for themselves.

Soult's direction of his forces at St Pierre had been undistinguished: any advantage he had gained by concentrating his troops was wasted by his procrastination, by not ordering them all into an overwhelming attack before Hill had begun to receive reinforcements. Unaccountably, two and a half divisions were held in reserve by Soult at a moment when Hill had thrown in his last man. Soult's direction of the battle merely confirmed Wellington's opinion that, however brilliant he may have been in moving up his men, 'Soult never seemed to know how to handle his troops after a battle had begun.'

Oman has suggested that Wellington must have felt the lack of his Spanish troops during the Battle of the Nive, for now—as reluctantly as he had ordered them off the field—he instructed Freire to send up one Galician division to St-Jean-de-Luz and O'Donnell (no longer 'convalescent') to bring forward two brigades of the Andalusian reserves, formerly commanded by Girón, and deploy them into positions near Itxassou.

Soult could not do otherwise than accept the fact that he was now on the defensive: all his offensive operations had failed, his troops were discouraged and his losses had been heavy. Even with 24 gunboats at hand, Soult could not keep Wellington's artillery from

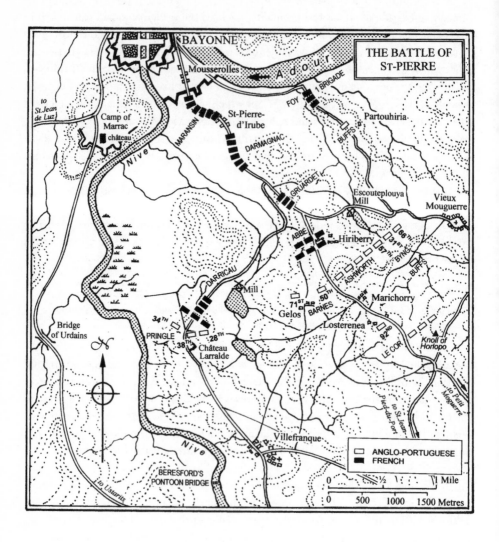

commanding the Adour, and it would become increasingly difficult to keep his troops at Bayonne provisioned: indeed, it was vital to transfer the majority of his troops further east before Wellington crossed the river and threatened his communications with the interior, even if this meant leaving Bayonne to be besieged. Wellington was perfectly aware that Soult had a serious problem of logistics on his hands. If his field army of 60,000 remained in the vicinity of Bayonne for even a week, it would reduce for almost two months the length of time the garrison could hold out.

The divisions of Abbé, Leval, Maransin and Taupin remained at Bayonne under Reille for the time being but ready to march upstream if the Adour seemed threatened. Foy, with his headquarters at St-Martin-de-Seignax, would spread his units along its right bank east of Bayonne. Boyer's and Darmagnac's divisions would be deployed further east near Port-de-Lanne, on the left bank of the Adour just north of its confluence with the Gave de Pau, its largest tributary. Soult himself would establish his own headquarters at Peyrehorade, near the confluence of the Gave d'Oloron with the Gave de Pau. Soult's left wing, commanded by Clausel, consisted of Daricau's division at Hastingues, together with a new division, given the number '8' (replacing Taupin's, dissolved after the battle of the Nive) and commanded by Jean-Isidore Harispe, and all the cavalry (both Pierre Soult's and Treillard's dragoons). This 8th Division—7,000 strong—incorporated Paris's troops, the French brigades of Villatte's reserve and battalions of the National Guard from the department of the Basses-Pyrénées. Harispe, himself a Basque, had been seconded from service under Suchet as it was assumed that he would have an intimate knowledge of his native country and might inspire the local population to take up arms in its defence. Soult thus had no fewer than seven divisions facing south, with another two and his cavalry, threatening the Allied right wing should Wellington attempt to force a passage across the Adour.

This, however, was not Wellington's intention—which was to lure Soult into marching his troops as far east of Bayonne as possible. He would hope to do this by dispersing Soult's left wing—the two divisions south of the Adour—and when that was done he would cross downstream, between Bayonne and the sea, a manoeuvre the possibility of which apparently had not occurred to Soult. Meanwhile, apart from sending Hill to expel enemy troops garrisoning the hilltop village of Urt (their only remaining foothold on the south bank), which took place on 16 December, there was a lull in hostilities while Wellington reviewed the situation in which the Allies now found themselves and planned the next campaign.

To guard against future surprise attacks, and to give timely notice to Headquarters at St-Jean-de-Luz of suspicious activity, Wellington set up a series of telegraphic signal stations. According to Robert Batty, these were places on the church towers of Guéthary, Arcangues and Vieux Mouguerre, which communicated with another on a height just north of St-Jean. Then,

> By an ingenious combination of flags, and barrels suspended from high signal-posts—it was found that notice could be almost instantaneously given . . . of whatever movement the enemy

might undertake; whether against the advance posts of the left wing at Barouillet, the centre at Arcangues, or the right wing under Sir Rowland Hill between the Nive and Adour. To save time, the telegraphic sentences were so arranged that each separate signal would at once explain the nature of the communication it was meant to convey.

Edmund Wheatley, writing on 29 January, gives details of his 'written orders'— together with a sketch—as far as the telegraph at the Barroilhet was concerned:

> . . . if a disturbance appeared among the enemy to lift one flag; if the French piquets retired, two flags; if they fired at me, three flags. At night if they began to be clamorous or retreat to hoist a tub of pitch and set fire to it. If they endeavoured to advance, to fire my tent and a bonfire near it and retreat as well as I could to the rere piquets. On any signal made thus a cannon, half a mile back, fired and was answered by another to Guéthary and so back to St Jean de Luz where Lord Wellington lives.

A divisional telegraph officer and assistants were appointed to each, to carry the apparatus, together with a 'dictionary of signals', to wherever the division might move. On 12 January, George Simmons was appointed to superintend a station near 'Garat's House', where a log cabin was erected to shelter the group. This system may have facilitated local communication while the army remained in the vicinity of Bayonne, but it was difficult to operate when troops were on the move or over longer distances, or if left in the hands of incompetent officers. In February General Colville received a tart reprimand from Wellington concerning the telegraph at Arcangues, which had been put in charge of one

> . . . known to be so stupid as to be unfit to be trusted in any way . . . when I call upon a General Officer to recommend an officer to fill a station in the public service, I mean that he should recommend one fit to perform some duty, and not one so stupid as to be unable to comprehend that which he is to perform; who is recommended only because he is a favorite with such General Officer.

Nor was it easy to explain to the civilian government in London that a war could not be carried on with the same speed and momentum in all weathers: some people there seemed to be expecting an instant march on Bordeaux. When writing to Bathurst on 21 December, Wellington had reiterated: 'In military operations there are some things which *can not be done*: one of them is to move troops in this country during or immediately after a violent fall of rain. Our operations, then, must be slow: but they shall not be discontinued.' Most of the roads were knee-deep in mud. General Sir Stapleton Cotton, whose splendid dress and appointments were said to be worth £500, had fallen into a deep puddle near Ascain, together with his mount, where he lay almost submerged until dragged out by his orderly and Major James Hughes (18th Hussars), who was with him. Captain Thomas Browne, writing up his *Journal* on the 13th, confirmed that the weather had

> . . . become so very severe, as to prevent all ideas of operations for the present. The roads, except the main road to Bayonne, became almost impassable, & in the transport of provisions, on Mules, from the Port of Passages & from St Jean de Luz to the several divisions on the right of the Army, a great number of these animals perished . . . & the dead bodies of the Mules in all directions added to their difficulties.

It was still possible to ride across higher ground, and several officers took advantage of the lull, among them—as described by George L'Estrange, captain in the 31st, while writing from Vieux Mouguerre—Sir Rowland Hill, traversing his recent battlefield 'with his pack of hounds at his heels. In his invariable kind and bashful manner, Hill reined up and turned to him, exclaiming: "I am going to put my hounds into this little wood; they may perhaps flush a woodcock, and you get a shot." '

To while away the time when the men were sheltering in their cantonments, 'the great work of Shoemaking & mending, & repairing Clothes began. Grey watch-coats that were worn out, & in holes, were cut up to mend red coats. The Army was in a terrible plight for want of Clothing, & the Men had every Color on their backs, that would have done Harlequin credit,' wrote Browne. According to Larpent, watching a party of the 57th Regiment escorting prisoners through St-Jean, the British were 'absolutely in rags and tatters, here and there five or six inches of bare thigh or arm are visible through the patches; some have had only linen pantaloons all winter through.' They must have been frozen. However, huge stocks of new uniforms were being landed at Pasajes and brought round to St-Jean, as different regiments were marched there successively to be re-equipped and then back to the lines, an operation which took several weeks, 'until nearly all the Army were clothed'. As Browne described it:

> The scene of this operation was not a little amusing, & the wit of the Soldiers, at thus changing as it were their skins, was exerted to the utmost. Caps, Jackets, Trowsers [sic], everything old, was thrown away . . . The men were comfortable & warm, & the quantity & quality of vermin, they thus got rid of, was sufficient . . . to cause their becoming fat & plump in a very short time. The town of St Jean de Luz, became thus a sort of depot of the Stores & clothing for the Army. Shops were established in every House, & every sort of comfort & necessary very soon arrived from England, & so great was the number of Speculators who arrived, that their competition rendered the price of Articles much more moderate . . .

Unfortunately, a vessel transporting a cargo of uniforms had been captured by the French under Lameth at Santoña, and Mr Drake, one of the Commissaries, had been sent there by Wellington, with Soult's agreement, with a proposal to exchange them for cash with which to pay the garrison. Drake was able to purchase the jackets only, the rest being too useful to relinquish. After hospitably entertaining Drake, Lameth offered to have him rowed back to Santander. Drake thereupon received a formal complaint from the Spanish authorities for having dared to allow a French boat enter the port without their leave and a pass. The governor of Santander was additionally incensed by the fact that Drake and his party were mobbed by the local children, shouting 'Viva los Ingleses'.

John Cooke, taking the opportunity of revisiting St-Jean-de-Luz one day, found it now presenting 'a gloomy aspect, being filled with muleteers, cars loaded with biscuit-bags, bullocks, rum casks, ammunition, idlers, and all the disagreeable encumbrances attached to the rear of an army', and he was

> . . . exceedingly surprised at the numerous dilapidated houses and empty chateaux, with the orchards and all the fruit trees having been cut down and converted into abattis by the French army. Every article that had been left by them in good order, the followers of our army ransacked. How

often do the soldiers of armies bear the odium of enormities and plundering committed most frequently by the non-combatant wolves in the shape of men, whose crimes are of such long standing,
and so frequently executed under the cloak of night … They devour the rations on their way to the
hungry army; they steal the officers' horses; they extort exorbitant prices for small articles which
they have stolen from the peaceful inhabitants; they strip the deserted and expiring wounded on
the field of battle, and would willingly sell their bodies could they find purchasers.

Wellington was still preoccupied concerning the state of peace talks with Napoleon. His
own opinion was that the Emperor was so convinced of his invincibility that he would fight
on, refusing all reasonable terms offered. Perhaps the time was ripe to foment civilian
opposition, for he had recently received several proposals from crypto-Royalists and even
émigrés from England that the White Banner of the Bourbons should be raised, for discon-
tent with the military regime was almost universal. Not only were the Anglo-Portuguese
troops accepted amicably, but Wellington was now being constantly supplied with valuable information from behind Soult's lines. The local peasants were keen to supply his
Commissaries with cattle, while the mercantile members of the community were glad to
procure brandy, wine, timber, corn and a variety of other commodities for them. Naturally,
they wanted payment in hard cash.*

On 25 December, having been given permission by Soult, and with the excuse of
settling the accounts of officers who were imprisoned in France (but also with the intention of doing some profitable business), Monsieur Batbédat, the leading banker in
Bayonne, turned up at Wellington's headquarters. He offered to find French *napoléons*
(gold 20-franc pieces) and francs in exchange for British Treasury bills, but on certain
conditions. One of them was that he be given leave to transport from St-Jean-de-Luz to
Bordeaux and other ports, as a commercial speculation, some of the goods which were
been unloaded. Wellington agreed, licensing twenty vessels on condition that they
carried only English merchandise, not colonial produce.

However, the peasantry were still reluctant to accept silver dollars, so the problem was
solved by letting it be discreetly known that anyone in the British ranks who had been a
professional coiner in civil life would be indemnified and well paid if he came forward. In
the event, no fewer than forty did so, and were set to work melting down dollars and casting
them into five-franc pieces dated earlier in the century. These were so well made that
when mixed with the genuine articles from the Paris mint they circulated freely. A great
deal of the coinage changed hands later while the British troops were in or near Bordeaux
awaiting transport home, with the French even buying up guineas and Portuguese gold,
turning them into *louis*, having set up a mint at Bordeaux in addition to one in Paris.†

Doubtless Monsieur Batbédat was suitably regaled on that Christmas Day. The previous evening, Edward Costello of the 95th, positioned near 'Garat's House' (the Château
d'Urdainz), describes his friends having 'clubbed half a dollar each' and sending one of
their company to the enemy picquets to purchase brandy. Alarmed by the passing of

* Even the Americans, with whom Britain was at war, continued to export vast quantities of flour as long as the British
remained willing buyers.
† That at Pessac, a suburb of Bordeaux, is still in operation, turning francs into euros.

time, a search party was sent out, which, on emerging from the French lines after having recovered him there dead drunk, ran into General Kempt, who was riding past to inspect the post. The tippler was fortunate to escape with only a slight punishment on that occasion. On the 31st, as Jonathan Leach recalled, 'we got together some females, French and Spanish, and danced in the new year at the Château d'Arcangues, in spite of our proximity to such queer neighbours as the French advanced posts consisted of.'

Writing in mid-January, Larpent describes the daily scene at St-Jean-de-Luz, where the British officers could be seen 'wearing their morning great coats; Lord Wellington in his plain blue coat, and round hat, or perhaps his sky-blue hunting dress'. Often, between four and six, there was a promenade along the sea wall,

> . . . for all the great men . . . including Lord Wellington himself, generally appear there at that time, and the Guards also, though the exertion of walking, to which we men of business are accustomed to take at a true twopenny postman's long trot, is too great for them; yet they are formed about in knots and groups, sitting on the wall, or gently lounging on it, and add to the gaiety of the scene.

The narrow streets are described as being

> . . . full of Spanish mules, with supplies, and muleteers, &c. all running against you, and splash-ing you as you walk; every shop crowded with eatables—wines, sauces, pickles, hams, tongues; butter, and sardines. The quay is now always a busy scene, covered with some rum casks, and flour casks, and suttler [sic] stores; the sailors all in our pay, at work constantly and making fortunes; the pilots in full hourly employment, bringing in vessels here or at Sacoa. The latter is full of masts and sails from Passages, Bilbao, Lisbon, or the West of England. The prices are still enormous, and of course the activity is the result. The French peasants are always on the road between this place and Bayonne, bringing in poultry, and smuggling out sugar in sacks on their heads.
>
> The Basques must have been a very happy race twenty years since, for though generally a poor country, there is plenty of their usual food—Indian corn, and excellent meadows by the rivers, which are numerous. Fish is easily procured—the houses are spacious and comfortable, and the children seem numerous, well-grown, intelligent, and healthy. The men are tall, straight, and active; the women, stout and useful, and rather good-looking. Nor was any great deficiency of young men observable . . . though certainly there are not so many tall idle fellows about as in Ireland. The town, however, had evident marks of a tendency to retrograde and decay.

On 19 January Larpent, among other senior officers, were out watching experiments be-ing made with Congreve rockets, which 'certainly made a most tremendous noise, and were formidable spitfires . . . but . . . none went off within half a mile of the intended object, and the direction seemed extremely uncertain.' However, in spite of their unreliability, as Larpent commented, 'Where guns could not be got up without great difficulty, these rockets could be carried by hand, or on mules; and being let off near, would have tremendous effect even upon infantry when in column.' Wellington, who had been sceptical of their utility, could not well refuse to have them sent out, hearing that they had proved so successful at Leipzig.

It was not until 10 January 1814 that Wellington was aware that the Austrian, Prussian and Russian armies had crossed the Rhine on 22 December and that a general invasion of

France was in progress. While he did not approve of the plan already in operation, it was a *fait accompli*; his opinion had never been asked, but at least his own hands were now no longer tied—that is, except by the weather (which, although mild, continued to be appalling) and by the perennial problems with which the Commissariat found themselves faced. It was additionally provoking that during one recent storm several vessels fell into the hands of the French, having sailed into the mouth of the Adour, one 'with fifty-two Irish bullocks', one with 700 trusses of hay, and others with cargoes of biscuit, etc., a list of which the mayor of Bayonne then had the gall to send across the lines.

The loss of cattle on the hoof had been frightful. Store cattle in the depot at distant Palencia (south-west of Burgos) had died by the fifties 'the moment they marched', 300 out of 500 getting as far as Vitoria, while only 60 head of these 'convalescent bullocks' sent forward from there had reached St-Jean-de-Luz. In addition to the mules and men, it was also the continuous trample of cattle that poached up the byways.

While on the subject of bullocks, Larpent recalled Wellington having ridiculed several notions held at home concerning the maintenance of army in the field: for instance, a 'corporate body or Society in England had once made him an offer of twenty bullocks for the army, which would last head-quarters only about a week; General M——said it must have been a mistake—the offer must have been for his table only; not for the army.' And, doubtless, the Horse Guards would be mortified to observe the unmilitary bearing of his men,

> . . . now all so round-shouldered and slouching in their gait, that he was sure, if his regiment here was in its present state to pass a review at Wimbledon Common, the whole would be sent to drill immediately, and declared quite unfit for service. Indeed, he added, that the men had now got into such a way of doing everything in the easiest manner, that he was often quite ashamed of the sentries before his own quarters.

Wellington himself remained

> . . . remarkably neat, and most particular in his dress, considering the situation. He is well made, knows it, and is willing to set off to the best what nature has bestowed. . . . He cuts the skirts of his own coats shorter, to make them look smarter: [one day, Larpent, on going to him on business] found him discussing the cut of his half-boots, and suggesting alterations to his servant. The vanity of great men shows itself in different ways, but in my opinion always exists in some shape or other.

Among many referring to his invariably dapper appearance was William Keep, who, on seeing him at close quarters, described him as being 'the neatest man I had seen for some time, with small cocked hat, blue coat, and white muslin cravat, and his horse furniture in the finest order; and I thought he had somewhat the look of a Statesman or General of Engineers.'

14

THE ADVANCE ON ORTHEZ
AND THE PASSAGE OF THE ADOUR

ON 16 January 1814, less than a week after Napoleon had dictated relevant orders to his Minister of War, half of Soult's cavalry—Treilhard's three brigades of heavy dragoons, together with their horse batteries—was already making its way north on the *chaussée* to Orléans. Three days later, marching from Peyrehorade, Leval's and Boyer's infantry divisions (11,000 men) were following them. This surprising movement of troops may be explained by outlining Napoleon's latest scheme to outwit the Allies. On reaching Paris after his defeat at Leipzig, in his wisdom the Emperor had decided that a certain way to recoup his losses was to draw heavily on Soult's and Suchet's armies: with these reinforcements he could face with equanimity the forces of Schwarzenberg and Blücher.

Fernando VII of Spain, still in confinement at Valençay, would be a very convenient pawn in his game. He would free Fernando and allow him to return to Spain on certain conditions. The sixth of the fifteen clauses in 'The Treaty of Valençay', to which Fernando had ostensibly agreed on 10 December, would formally oblige him to order all British troops from Spanish soil forthwith. Wellington's army could not survive long without Spanish support: the ports of Pasajes and Santander would be closed to him, and he would lose all his Spanish troops. What Napoleon had not taken into account was that Fernando, a profoundly devious character, would not hesitate to repudiate the treaty the moment he set foot in Spain, which was precisely what happened. But Napoleon, with his incurable optimism, was so sure that his ingenious scheme was foolproof, and that the war in the Peninsula, at least, would be soon over, that he had issued instructions for the withdrawal of men from Soult's army without even waiting to hear whether or not the treaty had been ratified by the Spanish *Cortes* and Regency in Madrid. Moreover, so convinced was Napoleon that Fernando would fall in with his plan that he had ordered Soult to have another 10,000 infantry ready to start for Paris 'by post' the moment the Spanish armies collaborating with Wellington had crossed back into Spain; the rest of his cavalry and other large contingents of infantry could march towards Orléans as soon as the coast—or, rather, the Pyrenean frontier—was clear.

Hearing that such a treaty was in the wind, Joseph Bonaparte had written to his brother offering to abdicate his throne formally if that would make things easier, to which proposal Napoleon had heartlessly retorted: 'I do not require any abdication of yours: you are no longer King of Spain. I have given up the country altogether, and only want to get it off my hands, and to be able to utilise my armies.' Suchet, in Catalonia, had received similar orders to those dispatched to Soult, and on 24 January had confirmed that 8,000 infantry, over 2,000 cavalry and twelve guns were already making their way north along the road from Perpignan to Lyon.

Soult, on receipt of his orders, reported that, although he was keeping his ear to the ground, he had neither heard nor seen any sign of the withdrawal of Spanish troops as yet. Meanwhile he was left with seven infantry divisions, only one cavalry division and 77 field guns at his disposal for active operations, not taking into account the 8,000-strong garrison of Bayonne and another 2,400 at St-Jean-Pied-de-Port. Clarke had agreed that, if necessary, having been deprived of his veterans, he could call on the reserve battalions being assembled by General Travot at Toulouse, which, although raw recruits, would be some slight compensation.

It was soon very evident that the treaty with Fernando was unlikely to be ratified in any hurry, but already Soult was becoming distinctly nervous—the more so because after having written to Paris for contingency orders, depending on the progress or not of events, he was bluntly informed that, although not required to supply more men for the time being, he would have to make the best of the position in which he had been placed. Whether Napoleon, writing to Clarke from Troyes on 25 February, was yet aware that Wellington had started to take the offensive again on the 12th is uncertain; but by the time Soult received the strategic plan prepared for him by Napoleon, events had overtaken him. Among several other measures proposed, Clarke was directed also to advise Soult to 'leave a minimum garrison in Bayonne' but to keep in touch with it; but on 27 February Soult's communication with Bayonne had been severed by his defeat at Orthez, and on that same day Hope, having crossed the mouth of the Adour, had completed the investment of the fortress, as described below.

Although the Allies had been busy throwing up their own line of defensive positions not far beyond the outer southern perimeter of Bayonne, little movement had taken place in the vicinity during the weeks since the battle of St-Pierre, although on 16 January Captain Francis Gualey had decided to 'beat up' a picquet in his front, stationed in a barn behind a dry moat, and was given permission to do so. The outlying sentries, led into believing that a group of deserters was approaching, were bayoneted, the picquet surprised and some 200 prisoners taken, for which enterprise Gualey received the brevet rank of Major.

On two occasions—and without Wellington's permission—Mina's irregulars had made plundering forays against St-Jean-Pied-de-Port but had been repulsed by local levies and its garrison. Morillo also made an unauthorised incursion towards Mendionde (east of Cambo) and Hélette (further south-east), borrowing two squadrons of the 18th Hussars from Victor Alten. Having driven in enemy outposts under Major Charles Hughes, they had found themselves under attack by Pierre Soult's cavalry and had rapidly retreated, suffering slight casualties. Both Morillo and Alten were severely reprimanded, the former ordered to keep his undisciplined men under arms for five days in bitter weather as a punishment.

Commissary Schaumann, when describing the Hussars' advance on Hasparren on 30 December, records that, while seeking fodder for their mounts, he had come across a 'rustic of the district', who pointed out to him that if he

> . . . chopped up the prickly thistles that flourished on the heaths . . . into chaff, and mixed them with corn and hay, they made very good fodder . . . and that the horses would like them. The matter was immediately reported to the general, and having tried it, it was approved; but owing to the prickles the thistles had first of all to be crushed, otherwise the horses would not touch them. The crushing process was performed as follows: our men would lift a barn door off its hinges, lay it on the ground, and then beat the thistles upon it with clubs until they were flattened out. And the sound of this curious threshing operation could soon be heard in all directions.*

Schaumann remarked that conducting foraging parties, which took place almost daily in front of the Allied lines, was a hazardous occupation. On one occasion, his route

> . . . led through Hasparen, past our remotest hussar picket, and then along sunken roads to various farms scattered about in the small villages below. We went in search of maize. As, however, the French, who were opposite us, did the same, these expeditions were very dangerous, for in the thousand and one ramifications of these hill-clefts it was an easy matter to be cut off, attacked, or surprised. Very often I would find on reaching a certain farm that a French commissary and his escort had only just left it. The town of Hasparen is tastefully built, clean, and breezy. Monsieur le Maire was a friendly, obliging man, an anti-Bonapartist, who had fled and had now returned, and did everything to further our interests.

A more serious action than that at Mendionde took place between 3 and 6 January, when Clausel, with Taupin's division (brought out of Bayonne), together with Daricau's and in cooperation with Harispe's units and Pierre Soult's cavalry, attempted to drive in the Allied line; but they were only able to push Buchan's Portuguese brigade out of the advance post of Labastide-Clairence (north-east of Hasparren) and back towards Briscous. This provoked Wellington into counter-attacking with the 3rd (again commanded by Picton) and 7th Divisions and the rest of Le Cor's units, and also bringing up the 4th and 6th in support if necessary. Two days of incessant rain delayed this movement until 9 January, when the French were thrust back to their former position on the Joyeuse river. Neither side had many casualties.

This confrontation had taken place a fortnight before Napoleon had requisitioned two of Soult's divisions and half his cavalry, after which Soult had to redeploy his troops. He had now fewer that 38,000 infantry at hand, of which Abbé's 5,300 remained at Bayonne together with the garrison. Under Reille were Maransin's division, replacing Foy's in guarding the right bank of the Adour, together with Darmagnac's further east. Foy's, Taupin's and Daricau's divisions lay south of the Adour, their line extended by Harispe's, near Hélette. As Daricau himself had been detached to the department of the Landes (north of the Adour, and of which he was a native) in an attempt to build up resistance there and activate the National Guard, his division was commanded temporarily by Villatte.

---

* It is recorded that some horses, having their tongues punctured by prickles, and unable to eat, had died.

On Clausel's extreme left were Pierre Soult's cavalry, facing Morillo's Spaniards on Wellington's extreme right near Itxassou.

One day a French unit advanced towards Morillo's men, who naturally fired at them. The enemy then sent ahead an officer to parley, saying that they had not expected a hostile reception as they had understood that, a treaty having been signed, they were now at peace with the Spaniards. Morillo was sufficiently astute to reply that he did not know of it, and even if the *Cortes* or the Spanish Regency had signed such a thing, until he received orders to the contrary from Wellington he would continue to do as the English did, which was to fire on them. Whether it was an attempt to trick the Spaniards or not is uncertain. More deliberate was the stratagem devised on 18 January, when British units approached a French picquet and, when challenged, an old Highlander called out 'deserter'. The sentinel held his fire until too late, and the whole picquet was surprised and taken prisoner. Whether Larpent was aware or not of Captain Gualey's similar stratagem, he remarked at the time: 'I am not very glad of this, for I fear it will lead the French to try and return the compliment, and make the outpost duty much more dangerous and troublesome than it has been. If it only leads to their shooting our next deserter, so much the better.' Soult continued to have trouble with his foreign contingents. Those on outpost duty, having their necessaries, knapsacks, etc. taken from them, were placed amongst the French and carefully watched: it was said that a German was so posted only after having his shoes taken from him.

Wellington had now 67,000 Anglo-Portuguese troops to hand; but in order to take the offensive he would have to draw on his more reliable Spanish units to reinforce the blockade of Bayonne. Morillo's, together with those of Carlos de España's, the Reserve of Andalusia and Freire's Galicians, amounting to 30,000 men, might be used, but he would be obliged to fed and supply them otherwise he would be plagued again by their plundering proclivities. General Colville, writing on 24 January—and reflecting the general opinion of the British higher command as far as any Spanish troops were concerned—had remarked:

> O'Donnell's army would be sufficient for the investment of Bayonne should Lord W. on any account feel inclined to bring a Spanish force forward, but there is so much intrigue and ill disposition among that people that it is the common talk that we shall have to thrash them into a proper sense of their insignificance before we embark.[*]

Pakenham, the Adjutant-General, had been visiting the hospital stations at Fuenterrabia and near Pasajes in person and had 'routed out' about 1,400 convalescents and malingerers, who passed through St-Jean on 17 February *en route* to their regiments; every man was wanted, the more so because the expected reinforcements had not yet

---

[*] The reference to embarkation was because Colville was then under the impression that it might have been Wellington's intention to push ahead to Bordeaux, although, knowing how stormy the Bay of Biscay could be at that season, this was unlikely to take place for several weeks, even if the Navy were lucky enough to find an intermediate anchorage along the coast.

arrived from either England or Portugal, apart from some 500 horses urgently needed by
the artillery. The transport of mounts was often wasteful: 22 out of 100 had died during a
recent voyage.

Ever since the Allies had left the Pyrenees behind them, the majority of the advanced
troops had been Portuguese, who, as Larpent had noticed, 'not only stop our deserters, but
go off very much less themselves'. A few days later he was discussing with Pakenham the
idea of forming a French royalist corps out of the prisoners and deserters, for 'the idea that
all deserters must be sent away from their own country to England deters many from
deserting, who would otherwise be willing'. Naturally, any such project would have to be
carried out very circumspectly, but in the event it was not followed up.

The days passed by: with inaction, the army was becoming restless, impatient to be
on the move again; and rumours were rampant. On 23 January Colonel Sir Henry Bunbury,
Under-Secretary of State at the War Department, arrived from England, and we find
General Colville writing that 'Curiosity is on tiptoe to know the purpose of his trip, but it
will most likely for the present be a secret between him and the Lord'—which it remained.
Bunbury had come to confide that a British warship was to be expected shortly, sailing
from Holland with a shipment of specie. Nathan Rothschild had been commissioned by
the government to get his agents on the continent to collect up to £600,000 sterling in
French coins, in addition to any being 'minted' locally, with which to pay for all the food
and fodder the army would need when advancing further into France. Considering the
amount of specie required and the secrecy and speed with which this *coup* had been
undertaken, Rothschild well deserved the two per cent commission he would be receiving.
Bunbury returned to London with a long list of other essentials Wellington was requiring
in the immediate future.

Meanwhile, more of Soult's units were being transferred further away from Bayonne—
much to Wellington's satisfaction, for it was his intention to invest the fortress by passing
troops across mouth of the Adour once Soult's main army had been pushed far enough
east to make any interruption of the complex operation unlikely. Having the numerical
superiority, this could now be done.

Wellington had determined to march east against Soult with seven divisions (2nd,
3rd, 4th, 6th, 7th, Light and Le Cor's Portuguese), together with Morillo's Spaniards, and
Fane's, Vivian's and Somerset's light cavalry brigades. These amounted to about 43,000
infantry and 2,500 cavalry. The four heavy cavalry brigades were not ordered up from their
winter cantonments in Navarre until later. Several infantry units had been left behind at
St-Jean-de-Luz to be re-clothed and equipped. There had been unaccountable delays,
and the uniforms of the 34th, 43rd and 79th, and the 1/95th, among other units, were not
to arrive until the winter was virtually over.

Hope's corps—the 1st and 5th Divisions, Aylmer's brigade, Bradford's and Campbell's
Portuguese and Vandeleur's cavalry, left to occupy a series of fortified positions south of
Bayonne—amounted to another 18,000 men. Carlos de España's units and Freire's three

divisions—an additional 16,000—were ordered back into France to take their place in the blockading force: these numbers were necessary to protect the Allied ports and maga-zines at Pasajes and St-Jean, on which the rest of the army depended for its ammunition and food supplies. Wellington did not intend to live off the countryside by requisitions: it was essential to keep in the good books of the civilian population through which he would be advancing, and whose property must be respected. Cattle, forage, or any other provisions, if offered, would be gratefully accepted, but also paid for promptly. The troops were in fine fettle.

John Aitchison had remarked on this several weeks earlier, correctly ascribing it 'to being well fed', for they had 'never been without meat and biscuit since July and seldom without rice, two ounces of which was last year [1812] added to the ration; being near the sea too they get plenty of potatoes to buy which have come in great quantities from Ireland and England . . .'

After a week of fine weather, which dried the roads, the forward movement commenced on 12 February. It was not easy country through which to advance on a broad front, being remarkably hilly and cleft by several rivers flowing from south to north from the Pyrenees into the Adour. These, from west to east, were the Joyeuse, the Bidouze, the Saison, the Gave d'Oloron (which joins the Saison near Sauveterre) and the Gave de Pau. The plan was to force Soult back by a series of outflanking movements to turn his left wing, an operation left in Hill's capable hands. With his left flank protected by Fane's cavalry, units with-drew from their cantonments opposite the Mousserolles camp and deployed on the ex-treme right wing, there being joined by Morillo's Spaniards from Itxassou. In echelon with Hill was Picton's 3rd Division, to the north of which Beresford commanded the 4th and 7th and Vivian's and Somerset's cavalry. Four days later the Light Division and, on the 21st, the 6th Division moved up behind Beresford, while during the last few days of Febru-ary the heavy cavalry brigades commanded by O'Loghlin, Manners, Clifton and Arentschildt reached the front and took their place on Wellington's left wing, abutting the Adour.

Hill's corps, disposed in two parallel columns, set off from Urcuray (just east of Cambo) on the 14th. Meanwhile Harispe, from near Hélette, had sent one of his brigades on a forced march in an attempt to relieve the isolated garrison at Jaca, about to be starved into surrender: it was, on the 17th. The brigade, in danger of being cut off by Morillo, was recalled. After some skirmishing, Harispe abandoned the line of the Joyeuse and re-treated through the village of Méharin towards St-Palais, on the Bidouze, followed by Hill.

Picton had meanwhile pushed east towards the village of Bonloc, from which Villatte, seeing that Harispe had retired, did likewise, via Orègue, with Picton in pursuit. Clausel was aware that if both Harispe and Villatte were retreating, Taupin's division had to follow, otherwise Picton would outflank it, even if Beresford's 4th and 7th Divisions had only just reached the Joyeuse. The river's east bank was then evacuated by both Taupin and Villatte. On the 15th, having avoided any engagement, they took up new positions on the east bank of the Bidouze at Ilharre and Bergouey respectively, both communes being north of St-Palais.

THE COMBAT AT GARRIS

On that same day, on approaching St-Palais, Harispe, having recovered his brigade and being reinforced by three cavalry regiments, determined to make a stand at the village of Garris. The main street lined a ridge immediately west of which was a gully—a fine defensive position if only he had more men. Harispe's 7,000 were faced by Hill's 12,000, leisurely deploying in their front, while Morillo was hovering further south. Hill seemed to expect Harispe to retire after receiving a few rounds of long-range artillery fire. At this point Wellington rode up to confer with Hill and, after a cursory survey of the French positions, ordered the leading brigade, Pringle's, to take the Motte de Garris before dark, for dusk was already falling.

This was more easily said than done, for although Pringle's two battalions (the 39th, with the 28th following in echelon) crossed the gully to storm the ridge and Le Cor's Portuguese pushed down the road to St-Palais further south, they met with stiff resistance from units of Paris's brigade, which, having been in garrison at St-Jean-Pied-de-Port, had never been confronted by British infantry before. On ascending the steep slope towards the ridge, Pringle, leading the foremost battalion himself, was severely wounded. Harispe's musketry brought down the horses of every mounted officer present, among them Robert O'Callaghan, at the head of the 39th. They were twice charged on reaching the hill top, and it was not until the 28th was able to join them, when stiff hand-to-hand fighting took place, that Harispe's men gave way. Harispe was also in danger of having his retreat across the bridge at St-Palais blocked by Morillo: Le Cor was pressing his centre, and three more brigades of the 2nd Division were coming up. Harispe left it too late to extricate himself from his position without heavy loss—some 500 men, 200 being taken prisoner. Allied casualties amounted to about 170 only. As night fell the French poured back across the Bidouze at St-Palais, where Harispe was unable to rally his men, who then ineffectually blew up the bridge before continuing their retreat for another ten miles.

Hill's engineers had repaired the bridge by noon next day, the 16th, and, having sent Fane's cavalry ahead, his corps crossed during the afternoon. Harispe, now aware that he was heavily outnumbered, had fallen back and during that night crossed the Saison at Osserain-Rivareyte (Arriverayte). On that same day Soult, unaware of the rout at Garris, was writing to Clarke at Paris that the Bidouze would provide a good line to defend; but now it would have to be the lower reaches of the Saison and those of the Gave d'Oloron, with his left wing at the old fortress of Navarrenx, to the south-east, and his right at the fortified bridgehead at Peyrehorade. The distance between them was over 30 miles—an extended front which Soult, with four divisions, could not possibly hold against the eight which were in motion towards it. By the 16th, the 7th Division was occupying hills to the east of Labastide-

Clairance and the Light Division was close behind them; by the 21st, the 7th Division would also be reaching the front. Foy sensibly retired his advance post at Bardos, crossed the Bidouze at Came and bivouacked at Hastingues, near the Peyrehorade bridgehead. The 4th Division moved ahead to occupy Bidache. Somerset's and Vivian's hussars had likewise pushed forward, their vedettes searching for the enemy's latest positions.

Soult soon realised that he was likely to find himself in 'a tight spot' unless he withdrew additional troops from further west—which was precisely what Wellington had intended he should do. Darmagnac was ordered east across the Adour at Port-de-Lanne, where he would be closer to Foy. Maransin's division, now under General Rouget (Maransin had been sent off to Tarbes to activate the National Guards in that area, as had Daricau in the Landes), was marched away towards Dax, leaving only Abbé's division with the garrison at Bayonne.

Reille, deprived progressively of most of his command, had already, on 17 January, protested to Soult, saying that he did not wish to be shut up in Bayonne with Thouvenot, his junior although governor by Imperial patent, and the correspondence became more heated until on 15 February he sent in his resignation to Clarke, together with a letter of complaint. The Minister of War took Reille's part and told Soult that he should not have appointed a senior general over Thouvenot's head and that Reille must be kept with the field army. Soult, submitting to this snub, placed Reille in command of Rouget's and Taupin's divisions, but relations between him and Reille continued to be strained.

On 17 February Hill's corps were facing Harispe on the Saison near its confluence with the Gave d'Oloron, with Morillo further south-east at the village of Nabas, on the road to Navarrenx. Picton, who had found the roads ahead of him near the Bidouze virtually impassable, had veered south towards St-Palais and fell in behind Hill's main column.

The bridge at Osserain-Rivareyte had been fortified, and the fords on either side of it, although said to be deep and dangerous, were seized without too much difficulty; a third ford, not far upstream and left unguarded, was crossed unopposed by the 92nd, who then took in the rear the units defending the bridge, causing them to retire in haste to avoid capture. The bridge, hardly damaged, was now in Hill's hands: the line of the Saison was won with the loss of three killed and fifteen wounded only, but there remained the Gave d'Oloron to be crossed, at this point, near its confluence with the Saison, dominated by Sauveterre.

There was now a brief lull in the offensive, with Soult reporting to Paris that he had ordered all the bridges on the Gave d'Oloron to be destroyed and his magazines moved to the rear. If forced back, he would retire across the Gave de Pau at Orthez and concentrate behind that line, having called in Foy's and Darmagnac's divisions.

THE PASSAGE OF THE ADOUR

After riding over 30 miles through miserable weather across hilly country from Garris, Wellington reined up at St-Jean-de-Luz during the afternoon of 19 February to verify with Admiral Penrose and Colonel Elphinstone the state of their preparations to cross the

Adour. During previous weeks, 48 *chasse-marées** had been hired with their crews and collected in the harbour at St-Jean and Socoa, together with cables, planks and beams with which to construct a bridge of boats, the design of which was entrusted to Henry Sturgeon of the Engineers. Lieutenant Douglas was left to supervise the fabrication of a flexible boom, made by fastening together a number of masts: this should protect it against any vessel or material likely to be floated downstream from Bayonne to destroy it.

The bridge, once placed across the 300 yards broad Adour near its mouth, would allow Bayonne to be entirely blockaded rather than merely besieged from the south bank only. A pontoon train was also in readiness, as was a small contingent of sappers. It only remained for the weather to calm down, for the Biscay rollers were being driven hard against the coast, causing a 100-foot long spit of gravel to be thrown up almost across the narrow harbour entrance at St-Jean during a storm on the 14th; fatigue parties of the 1st Division were still busy shovelling it away at low tide.

Writing on the 14th, Larpent noted his astonishment that apparently neither the engineers nor the Navy had been supplied with any charts of the river mouth. Although Elphinstone had requested to be sent out anything available some four months earlier, all he had received from England was a miserable little printed plan of Bayonne, but showing no soundings, which was of scant use.

Elphinstone, when discussing the bridge-building operation with Wellington, had remarked that to saw an adequate number of planks would take some time, to which excuse Wellington retorted that then he should cut up the platforms already sent out for the siege guns, which were lying idle. When Elphinstone reasoned that he would then have no platforms when it came to proceeding with the siege, was bluntly told: 'Work your guns in the sand until you can make new ones out of the pine-woods near Bayonne'; so all the platforms were sawn up. Wellington approach to resolving a problem was invariably pragmatic.

It appears from what Larpent has written that Wellington may not have consulted with Sturgeon in advance nor told him exactly *where* he wanted the bridge of boats to be placed, assuming that Elphinstone would do so. Sturgeon had not taken the initiative of making measurements of the width of the river anywhere near its mouth, with the excuse that his engineers would require a strong guard while doing so and he had no orders to that effect; and yet it would have been easy enough to get permission from the Adjutant-General for a guard to be supplied without worrying Wellington and to get the thing done. It must be to Sturgeon that Larpent was referring acidly as seeming 'to be too much of the English official school; has too much regard to forms and regular orders. All this *entre nous*.'†

The wind continued to blow across the bay during the morning of the 20th as Wellington and Penrose stood on the sea wall of St-Jean discussing the chances of its

---

* A *chasse-marée* was a local variety of two-masted lugger, mostly between 30 and 50 tons burden and between 40 and 50 ft in length.
† The following month Sturgeon replaced Scovell in charge of the Post Office, but he was not up to it. As John Rous remarked: 'Unluckily for us, our Post master is a clever fellow, and amuses himself with constructing bridges instead of attending to his office. The consequence is that our letters came in a bullock car ... [taking] six days to perform a journey

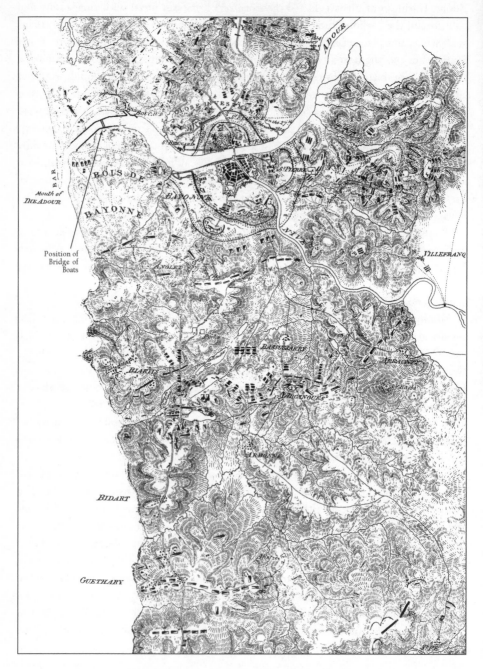

Actions near Bayonne: A Reduced Section of Batty's Map

direction shifting, for the boats in the flotilla, tugging at their anchors, were all set to sail. Several days before, Freire's troops on the Bidasoa, where they had been drawing rations from British magazines, had been warned to have their baggage packed, and Freire was now ordered to be ready to march at an hour's notice to replace Hope's troops on the south side of Bayonne. Once his staff had settled with Hope the exact redeployment of the Allied troops after the Adour had been spanned, there was little left for Wellington to do. As he could not wait and supervise the crossing himself, he returned on the 21st to Garris, beyond which Hill had resumed his advance towards the Gave d'Oloron.

It is of interest that Arthur Young, the eminent author of *Travels in France* (first published in 1792), when passing through Bayonne in mid-August 1787, had specifically visited the embankment being built near the river mouth and had described it as 'a work of great expense, magnificence, and utility'. They were driving piles of pine 16 feet deep, for the foundations of 10 to 20 foot-wide embankments, with the top stones cramped together with irons. It was on these that both extremities of the bridge of boats would be anchored.

Meanwhile the 5th Division had replaced the 6th opposite the Mousserolles defences when the latter marched to join Beresford's column. The stretch between the châteaux of Urdainz and Barroilhet was now held by Aylmer's Brigade, Carlos de España's Spaniards and Campbell's Portuguese. The 1st Division, which was the first to cross the bridge of boats, with Bradford's Portuguese in its rear, was positioned opposite Anglet, in the villages of Bidart and Biarritz, and in the pine woods extending north to the mouth of the Adour. Also hidden in the woods were the pontoon train, the engineers and the site prepared for a battery of 18-pounders. These were to open up against any gunboats approaching from upstream (a corvette was known to be in the vicinity) and a two-gun battery on the far bank by the village of Boucau, where the French had a small outlying post. Fortuitously, these two guns had been retired on the 17th, and the two companies stationed there were ordered back to Bayonne, so sure was Thouvenot that no enemy would attempt to traverse the river in that unlikely direction.

With the wind falling during the afternoon of the 22nd, the flotilla sailed out of St-Jean-de-Luz's harbour with orders to try and make the mouth of the Adour. At midnight the 1st Division trudged north through deep sand, in which one 18-pounder and several pontoons got stuck until hauled out by the infantry. The leading brigade— Stopford's— approached its place of crossing at dawn, but no sign was seen of the *chasse-marées*, blown out to sea by another change of wind. This was disconcerting, for if the French became aware of the impending operation they could rapidly march a considerable force from Bayonne to the sand hills at Boucau, opposite, which would seriously impede any crossing. Hope waited anxiously, until at about 11.00 he decided it was worth trying to ferry some troops across on the few pontoons and jolly-boats he had to hand, and to get a

---

which mules would do in one.' Sturgeon's apparent incompetence in managing the postal service—although one entirely foreign to his unquestionable capability as an engineer—naturally incurred Wellington's displeasure, but, although it has been so insinuated, it is implausible that he therefore deliberately put himself in a position to get killed, as he was by a chance bullet at Vic-en-Bigorre a month later.

foothold on the far bank before they were noticed. At first this equipment had been dragged forward overland on carriages, using relays of horses borrowed from the field guns, but as the wheels had then sunk deeply into the sand they were eventually hoisted on to the shoulders of troops and carried bodily over the dunes.

In order to distract Thouvenot, Hope instructed the investing units facing the entrenched camps to simulate a concentric attack by pressing the enemy picquets and displaying formed battalions in their rear, as if in preparation to surge forward, while a K.G.L. brigade of the 1st Division crept out of the pine woods and stormed a strong picquet at Anglet. The masked battery in the woods started to fire with red-hot shot, badly damaging the corvette patrolling the river, which limped away upstream, as sailed likewise the enemy gunboats positioned there, though not before several had been sunk. The anonymous author of a chapter in Maxwell's *Peninsular Sketches* stated that Congreve rockets were also tried out against them: they

> . . . went skipping about the river like mad things, and dancing quadrilles in every direction but the right one . . . The only one which took effect—and this seemed quite an accident—stuck in the bow of one of the boats, and sank her. The French soldiers, at that period wholly unaccustomed to that arm, were so frightened, that they jumped overboard with all their accoutrements, and were drowned. The practice from our battery was not good at first, from the want of platforms; but this was soon rectified, and the corvette got a most handsome pommeling, and was glad at last to sheer off with the loss of her captain, and more than half her crew killed and wounded. One of our shots cut her flag-staff in two, and the tri-colour flag was seen floating down the stream. An artilleryman, stripping off his clothes, swam in, and brought it out, and it was soon seen waving on our battery as a trophy. Captain M—n, of the artillery, was walking about that evening a most ridiculous figure. A shot had shaved off the skirts of his coat, and being rather Dutch-built, he looked just like a fat cock-pheasant, whose tail had been shot away by a bungling sportsman.

Perhaps there was some exaggeration here, for Batty describes the flag being recovered by the French and nailed to the remains of the mast.

However, Thouvenot, convinced that his southern front was about to be attacked in earnest, sent forward his reserves to his southern line of defences. He had about 14,000 men at his disposal, including Abbé's division, although not all would have been effectives. Thus Hope's demonstrations completely fulfilled their object.

The jolly-boats, which had been brought up with the pontoons, were launched. They each held between eight and a dozen men, and were rowed across without opposition, taking with them a long hawser to secure to the north bank. Before noon five rafts constructed with the pontoons, each containing 50 men, were working their way across, but with the tide turning this had become more difficult and the ferrying operation was suspended until 2.00. By 5.00 only five companies of Guards and two of the 5/60th had been placed by Stopford among the sand hills to defend the point of passage.

Just before dark, troops were seen approaching them from Bayonne, soon to be halted by the well-directed fire of musketry and a steady cannonade from the south bank. Together with the Guards, a party of 'rocketeers' had crossed ('each with a rocket ready in his hand, and three on his back in a case, with three poles on his shoulder'), and it is said that the discharge of a flight of Congreve rockets—these missiles were entirely new to the enemy—threw the head of their column into such confusion and dismay that before long they had turned tail and retired to the shelter of the Citadel. No further attempt was made to oust the Allies from their foothold during that frosty moonlit night, when at slack tide several more pontoon- and boat-loads were conveyed across to support Stopford, as it was likely that he would be attacked again next morning.

At sunrise, much to Hope's relief, the whole flotilla, escorted by a frigate, a brig and five gun boats, was seen off the mouth of the Adour, waiting for high tide, for there was a dangerous bar to be crossed. Although there was a navigable channel, its position was liable to shift after a gale. Some of the larger ship's boats were sent ahead to find it, where the surf was not flying so high. After a mishap or two, the passage was located, but it was now too late to bring in the flotilla until the next high tide—another six hours' delay— for the fall of the tide here was no less than nineteen feet. This was exasperating for Hope, who was impatient to get the bridge of boats in place.

Meanwhile the jolly-boats, and additional pontoons substituting for the rafts, con-tinued to ply over, with Vandeleur's dragoons, holding on to the reins of their horses, swimming behind them. By noon 3,000 men were over; by evening the number had risen to 8,000, including three brigades of the 1st Division, several of Campbell's Portuguese units, two guns and a troop of horse. They dug into the sand hills, but there was still no further reaction from Thouvenot, whose attention had been distracted meanwhile by an-other false attack, this time on the Mousserolles front by two brigades of the 5th Division.

It was not until late in the afternoon of the 24th that Admiral Penrose was able to authorise Captain O'Reilly, in charge of the flotilla, to let them enter. Unfortunately the man-of-war boat leading the procession was wrecked with the loss of all hands, but 34 vessels, together with two others carrying the boom, eventually passed the bar success-fully, their Basque and Spanish crews exhorted by the naval officers and British engineers in charge of the complex operation (which was not made any easier by the French having removed the *balises*—marker buoys or staffs—indicating the normal entrance channel). Two other *chasse-marées* foundered and a few others boats were upset, with a total loss of life of about 35 men. Twelve vessels sailed back to St-Jean-de-Luz, having failed to make the passage before the tide turned again.

The boats were now moored parallel to each other, anchored both at bow and stern and connected by a series of five strong 13-inch cables stretched by capstans from deck to deck across the whole. To the outer cables, thick planks, placed transversely, were fas-tened by cords. Ten iron 18-pounder French guns (taken at the Nivelle) anchored the cables on the right bank. On the left, a series of strongly secured capstans held the cables taut: by these, the tension of the platform of the bridge was increased or relaxed as the rise and fall of the river required. On the upstream side, a boom was laid across the Adour, formed by a double line of masts held in place by chains, should the enemy send down fireships or rafts. Lieutenant Cheshire was in command of five gunboats, their broadsides facing Bayonne, anchored there ready to engage those of the French should any attempt be made to destroy the bridge.

That the whole structure survived several months, providing a remarkable example of military engineering, must be credited not only to the British naval officers superintending the entry into the estuary and aligning the boats but also to the ingenuity of Sturgeon, his fellow engineers and Major Todd of the Royal Staff Corps.*

While the bridge of boats was being assembled, the rest of the 1st Division and Campbell's units continued to be ferried over, together with Bradford's brigade and two more squadrons of Vandeleur's dragoons. By the afternoon of the 26th, Carlos de España's Spaniards, together with most of the cavalry and the artillery, were deployed on the Adour's north bank. It is difficult to understand why Thouvenot and Abbé, apart from making a half-hearted sortie against the sector held by the K.G.L. on 1 March, did not try again to disrupt the bridging operation or make another attempt in force to dispossess Hope of his foothold on the right bank of the Adour before he was too strongly established there.

Freire's Divisions now replaced those of España's units, and a brigade of the 5th Division was transferred to the west bank of the Nive, while Aylmer's brigade was marched to Anglet. By the 27th the investment of Bayonne had been completed, with 16,000 men on the south bank and 15,000 on the north, although the occupation of the hilltop suburban village of St-Etienne, north-east of the Citadel, had been a costly affair: the enemy had first to be driven out of several fortified houses and earthworks, in the storming of which the K.G.L. brigades had suffered no fewer than 328 casualties, among them General Heinrich von Hinüber, their senior officer, who was slightly wounded.

From the convent of St-Bernard, to the west of the Citadel, the blockading line circled round to the suburb of St-Esprit.† Houses were loopholed, as was the church of St-Etienne, and roads were barricaded with earthworks.

Vandeleur's cavalry spread out to search for enemy units to the north-east, but all they could find was a post of National Guards defending the Adour bridge at Dax. On the 27th they pushed east, crossing the river close to the broken bridge at Port-de-Lanne, and entered Peyrehorade, where they met a patrol of Somerset's hussars. It was apparent that Soult had withdrawn some distance further east, leaving Bayonne completely isolated. Once the bridge at Port-de-Lanne was repaired, Hope would be in direct touch with Wellington.

The operation of last few days had been a great success: the only disappointment was that, owing to the difficulties of entering the estuary on account of its shallowness at the bar, Bayonne could not be used by men-of-war and transports as a supplementary port of supply to those at St-Jean and Pasajes but only by small boats at high tide and in favourable weather.

---

* More technical and detailed descriptions of the operation may be found in the second volume of the 3rd edition of Jones's *Journals of Sieges* (1846), Batty's *Campaign of the Western Pyrenees* (1823) and Browne's *Napoleonic War Journal* (1987).
† Between the present bypass and motorway.

15

THE BATTLE OF ORTHEZ

O N 22 February, after a tiring ride back from St Jean-de-Luz to Garris the previous day, Wellington resumed his planned manoeuvre to turn Soult's left wing entirely. Hill's corps was now reinforced by the Light and 6th Divisions, brought forward from their positions in Beresford's rear at Labastide-Clarence and Hasparren to converge on St-Palais, directly behind Hill. The 4th and 7th Divisions were redeployed to positions from which they were to demonstrate against Darmagnac and Foy, whose detachments were driven from Hastingues to his bridgehead on the Gave de Pau opposite Peyrehorade. On Hill's right flank the Gave d'Oloron at Sauveterre was defended by a line of Harispe's troops, but it appeared that the fords between there and Navarrenx were being watched by cavalry picquets only. To Harispe's right on the Gave, the line was extended by Villatte's division, but with some distance between it and Taupin's units further north-west near Caresse (west of Salies-de-Béarn). There was another gap in the enemy defensive line between Taupin's troops and those of Foy and Darmagnac.

Wellington planned to force the Gave d'Oloron south of Harispe's position while at the same time demonstrating against both Sauveterre and Peyrehorade to the extent of making Soult unsure where his main stroke would be directed. The operation commenced on the 24th with Hill's columns advancing towards a number of fords between Sauveterre and Navarrenx, where Morillo was to threaten to cross at Dognen, further south, but actually cross at Bastanès, downstream from Navarrenx. Hill laid his pontoon train at Viellenave-de-Navarrenx, west of Bastanès, over which the 2nd Division and Le Cor's Portuguese crossed, while the Light Division, approaching from Nabas, waded the river north of Viellenave and the 6th, from Montfort, further downstream. Hardly any resistance was offered, the enemy cavalry retiring when fired on. By the evening 20,000 Allied troops had established themselves on the north bank of the Gave d'Oloron, Hill's central column having only two men drowned, but it had been a time-consuming operation and there was little chance of getting into Harispe's rear as had been intended.

While this outflanking movement was taking place, Picton had exceeded his orders— as usual—and instead of merely demonstrating, once a party of hussars had discovered an unguarded but inferior ford some 1,000 yards from the Sauveterre bridge he ordered four companies of Keane's brigade to wade over. Having done so, and climbed the steep far bank by a path between stone walls, they found themselves driven back in disorder by one of Villatte's battalions. Seventy-nine unnecessary casualties were the result of this little fray, including several drowned on the return and 29 made prisoner; and their losses might well have been heavier had not a British battery started shelling their pursuers.

Once Harispe was aware that Hill had a foothold across the Gave further upstream, he retired north-east to the village of Orion, whereupon Villatte destroyed the Sauveterre bridge and followed him in the direction of Orthez, on the far bank of the Gave de Pau, here almost parallel to the Gave d'Oloron.*

John Cooke recorded that, as the central arches of the fine stone bridge at Sauveterre had been blown up, it was necessary

> . . . to ford the river, which was more than 100 yards in breadth. Although hardly three feet deep
> below the bridge, the current was so extremely rapid, and the bottom so intersected with loose
> stones, that it was thought advisable for the strongest men to throw off their knapsacks and join
> hands to form a strong chain. Thus, with their faces to the current, they could pick up any soldiers
> who might chance to turn giddy or lose their foothold, for if an individual wavered on either side,
> the probability was that he would be whirled round by the force of the stream and lifted off his
> legs, sinking to the bottom like a lump of lead, loaded as he was with knapsack, accoutrements,
> and sixty pounds of ball cartridges!

Little fighting took place further downstream. Some of Vivian's cavalry were drowned when trying to pass reconnoitring parties across in deeper water. When several men of the 4th Division were drowned also by missing a ford at St-Dos (half way to Peyrehorade), Beresford directed them to cross further north at Sorde-l'Abbaye. For a moment, Walker, with the 7th Division, thought Foy might take the offensive, as Rouget's troops from Dax had arrived to reinforce him; but once Soult was aware that his left wing had been turned, Darmagnac, Foy and Rouget were ordered to retire east towards Orthez, on the Gave de Pau, where he intended to make a stand.

All Soult's divisions were now converging on Orthez, some crossing there while Taupin's men traversed a bridge further west at Berenx, which they then blew up. Both Harispe and Villatte had reached Orthez early on the 25th; by that afternoon Soult had concentrated all his available forces in the vicinity. Darmagnac, Rouget and Foy, having marched through the frosty night (Foy leaving a detachment to watch the site of the ruined bridge at Berenx), had by then had reached Baights-de-Béarn, some four miles west of Orthez. Soult had some 32,000 infantry and 3,000 cavalry to hand to deploy on the several intervening ridges extending from the north. As he had promised Clarke in Paris, from this position, on which every man would be massed, he would attack any isolated column of Wellington's army which exposed itself.

Although Wellington was aware that Soult was concentrating, he may not have realised at first that Soult had intended to bring on a battle. When this appeared likely, a redeployment was put in hand. The 4th and 7th Divisions, together with Somerset's cavalry, were to cross the Gave de Pau near Peyrehorade and follow Foy along the road towards Orthez. On reaching Berenx, where the bridge had been replaced by Hill's pontoon train,

---

* A bypass now circles to the west of Sauveterre, but it is worth crossing the old bridge and making the steeper ascent to the village.

they would be joined by the 3rd, 6th and Light Divisions and Vivian's cavalry. There would then be five divisions and two cavalry brigades on the north bank of the Gave de Pau, the line of which Soult had intended to hold.

Meanwhile the 2nd Division, Le Cor's Portuguese and Fane's cavalry would move forward to menace the bridge at Orthez itself. The passage below its imposing medieval tower having been blocked, and the arch over the rocky narrows of the Gave partly demolished, it was pointless to try and force it; but once Beresford's columns were approaching the enemy's right flank, Hill was to ford the river slightly further east, where the banks were lower and the stream broader and shallower. On the far bank here lay the hamlet of Les Soarns (not Souars).*

The only Allied troops not involved in the ensuing encounter were three battalions commanded by Morillo, investing the small fortress of Navarrenx. St-Jean-Pied-de-Port, by now entirely isolated but with a garrison under General Blondeau of three regular battalions and some National Guards, was left to the tender mercy of Mina, who had orders to gather together as many battalions as he could to ensure that it remained *hors de combat*.

To make up for the loss of Morillo's men, who had contributed to his fighting force since Vitoria, Wellington ordered Freire to being up two divisions from Bayonne, replacing them with Girón's 8,000 men from the Baztan, having issued a severe warning of the punishment awaiting any troops found plundering and promising them that they would be fed from Allied magazines. Freire and his troops reached the front promptly, but, as the divisions were weak, another commanded by Espeleta was also ordered up, together with a 'provisional division' made up of picked units from other battalions in the best order. However, these did not arrive until long after the battle at Orthez was over. The rest of Friere's force at Bayonne was handed over to Carlos de España.

Hill's column reached its positions during the afternoon of the 25th, having cleared Soult's outposts from the transpontine suburb of Départ, and kept up a threatening posture. Apparently Wellington and his staff had been seen surveying Orthez from the hill of Magret, rising further south, and a French battery had even sent a salvo towards them. Picton's division was approaching the broken bridge over the Gave de Pau near Berenx. Beresford, having crossed the Saison at Sorde-l'Abbaye, and leaving the 51st Regiment to occupy Peyrehorade, found practicable fords on the Gave de Pau immediately to the north and further east near Lahontan, across which the infantry waded in the wake of Vivian's hussars. They then turned east, finding to their surprise that the whole north bank had been evacuated by the enemy. They had not even left outposts to report on Allied movements, of which they were unaware until Vivian's hussars, far in advance, on approaching Puyoô, ran into a French squadron commanded by Colonel Faverot. (The rest of Soult's cavalry were miles to the east, watching the fords between Orthez and Pau.) Vivian, who happened to be in the van, led a charge in person, driving them back some distance until counter-attacked by their supports. Soon rallying, Vivian's squadron pressed

---

* A modern bridge spans the river almost precisely where Hill crossed, but the former hamlet is now hemmed in by an industrial estate.

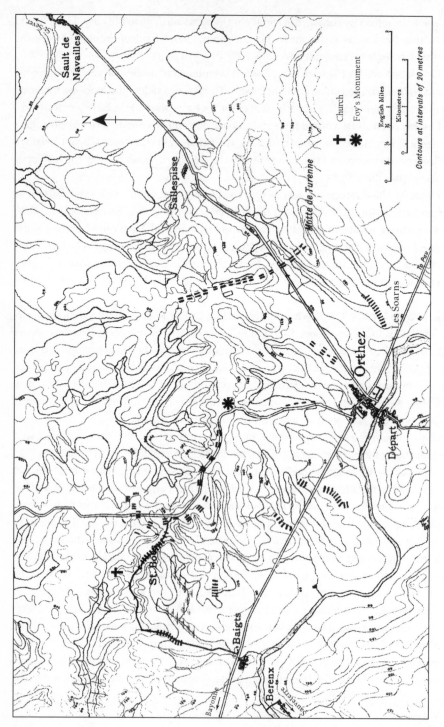

St-Sever

Sault de
Navailles

Sailespisse

Motte de Turenne

Church
Foy's Monument

Contours at intervals of 20 metres

English Miles

Kilometres

Le Pau

Les Soarns

Orthez

Départ

St-Boes

Bayonne

Baigts

Berenx

The Battle of Orthez

them beyond Berenx. According to George Woodberry, Captain Sewell, one of Beresford's aides taking part in this action, having lost his sabre, had wielded a broomstick—'tho it may well have been a stake pulled from a hedge'—with some effect!

The battalion left at Berenx by Foy was driven away by the 3rd Division, which then crossed by a ford downstream from the broken bridge, both Allied columns meeting during the afternoon of the 26th. Once this had taken place, Wellington ordered the Light and 6th Divisions, who were in the rear of Hill's corps, to march on Berenx, bringing with them Hill's pontoons, by means of which they crossed and followed Picton. By dawn on the 27th Wellington had five divisions and two cavalry brigades on the north bank of the Gave de Pau: Soult's line of defence had been completely turned.

Aware of his hazardous situation, Soult had called a council of war on the 26th, at which only Clausel—as he had at Sorauren—advocated an immediate attack before the Allies had time to concentrate. As every other divisional general opposed the idea, Soult, himself on the defensive ever since the débâcle at St-Pierre, ordered his troops to be redeployed during the night, facing west and aligned along the road to Dax, where they would await the Allied onslaught.

Orthez was a ancient stronghold of the counts of Béarn, whose castle, the Tour Moncade, overlooked the town from near the Hagetmau road, which ascends north-east from the centre. To the south-east, the road from Peyrehorade continues up the valley towards Pau. Climbing due north is the Dax road. Passing, after about one and a half miles, a insignificant monument to the battle and referred to as the 'Monument de Général Foy', this veers north-west along the narrow plateau of a ridge overlooking the rolling countryside to the west, from which three spurs descended towards the Peyrehorade road and the river. Their intervening valleys, marshy at a lower level, are threaded by rivulets. Along the main ridge, facing down each spur, Soult had placed his artillery.

After another one and a half miles, near the Plassotte farm, a by-road forks left through the hamlet of St-Boès and eventually circles to the south towards Baigts-de-Béarn. The old church of St-Boès sits on a knoll, reached by turning right off this by-road after about 650 yards. (The original hamlet stood nearer this church, but, having been virtually destroyed during the battle, it was rebuilt further east.) The main road to Dax bears north from the fork, between which and the turning for the church another lane descends south-west towards Baigts, after half a mile passing (left) an isolated, flat-topped hill, once the site of a Roman camp.

The only access to the main ridge from the west is by the roads from Baigts climbing the two spurs, the more easterly of which has a lane ascending it from the old Peyrehorade road—which should be followed from Baigts rather than the N 117, skirting the Gave de Pau—to meet the Dax road south of the monument to Foy. More hill spurs rise east of Orthez, the most defensible position there being one between the steep hill known as the Touroun de Toury (Motte de Turenne on older maps) and a line bearing north-west across the Sault de Navailles or Hagetmau road and past the hamlet of Parouilles.

Soult's dispositions were as follows. Reille held the north-west or right wing with Taupin's and Rouget's divisions, with Paris's brigade as a reserve. One of Taupin's regiments held the churchyard knoll, while the main force extended along the ridge to the east and the Plassotte farm. Rouget's troops continued this line to the south-east, facing the former Roman camp. Further east was D'Erlon, with Darmagnac's division at the head of the adjoining spur, followed by Foy's division, aligned west at the summit of the easterly spur,* with his left-hand battalion established in the convent of the Bernardines on the north-western outskirts of the town. Clausel was responsible for the defence of Orthez itself, with two of Harispe's battalions guarding the bridgehead and another two watching the fords of Les Soarns; both could be reinforced by his reserve near the Tour Moncade. Villatte's division formed the general reserve, placed between the Hagetmau road and Foy's troops, ready to support Harispe should Hill's corps—very much in evidence—attempt to cross the fords; otherwise, Villatte could move north-west should Reille need additional men to defend his sector. While some of Soult's cavalry were behind Darmagnac and Foy, and a regiment watched the fords, two regiments had been sent north-east to the village of Sallespisse and to guard the bridge over the small river Luy at Sault-de-Navailles 'in case the troops should be obliged to make a retrograde movement'—which would seem to substantiate the fact that Soult, who had overestimated the numbers opposing him, contemplated having to withdraw even before the battle took place.

Soult had to hand about 36,000 men including 2,000 cavalry, and 48 guns, and was expecting to be 'reinforced' at any moment by 3,750 half-trained conscripts, who turned up in the late afternoon, short of both uniforms and cartridges! Wellington had 38,000 infantry, 3,300 cavalry, 54 guns and about 1,500 gunners, sappers, etc. A superiority of only 7,000 hardly justifies the excuses made by certain French authors that Soult was greatly outnumbered and had little chance of success in holding a strong position. Some contemporaries stated that Wellington had as many as 70,000 men with him!

With the exception of the Light Division, which had not quite reached its place behind the Roman camp (remaining Wellington's headquarters throughout the battle, providing as it did a good view of almost the whole field), the Allied columns were in position by 8.30 on the slightly frosty morning of 27 February when the action commenced. Although Captain William Verner, 7th Hussars, remembered it as being a calm day, 'with a bright sun, more like summer than the month of February', according to Ross-Lewin two of his officers procured an umbrella to shelter Wellington from the drizzling rain when sitting on the grass, writing, which he was glad of although he did not approve of their use on the battlefield, making 'the gentlemen's sons' among his officers look ridiculous in the eyes of the rank and file.

The 4th Division, having ascended the track from Baigts, had already passed Reille's flank at St-Boès and the 7th was in its wake. The 3rd and 6th Divisions were making their way in two parallel columns towards the lower slopes of the two spurs descending from the

---

* More or less where the Dax road ascends from Orthez.

main ridge but were still screened from Soult by undulations of ground near Baigts. Hill's corps was blatantly demonstrating meanwhile on the far bank of the Gave opposite Orthez, but ready to dash across the fords when required.

Having established himself along the heights west of St-Boès, Cole opened the attack on Reille's flank by sending Ross's brigade to eject the enemy from the church, which was done without difficulty. However, when Ross advanced towards Taupin's line further east, he was checked by his battery at the Plassotte farm, which swept the road and narrow dip to its north, and Ross had to fall back with loss to the shelter of neighbouring cottages. Cole brought up Sympher's K.G.L. battery, but before this was able to open up, Taupin's fire had dismounted two guns and Sympher himself was killed. The area was also raked by fire from one of Rouget's batteries on a knoll further south-east.*

Ross's Brigade, having rallied, and now reinforced by Vasconcellos's Portuguese on the right, where there was a steep slope to climb, repeated its attempt to carry the enemy position, but this was no more successful. Ross himself was wounded. His men fell back to find more cover, for Taupin's guns fired a salvo whenever they showed a compact group. Sergeant John Cooper describes his own company as replying by 'firing in rapid bo-peep fashion from behind the corners of a large building'. Cole preferred not to bring up Anson's brigade, left as a reserve, should the French counter-attack. This they then did, recovering several houses, before the action petered out into intermittent skirmishing. Ross's men found wine in some cottages and plied bottle and musket alternately: 'drink and fire—fire and drink'. Meanwhile Vasconcellos's men, wavering under the cannonade, fell back to find shelter, as did Ross's brigade, losing all the ground they had gained. Wellington, who was watching this repulse anxiously from the Roman camp, sent forward the 1st *Caçadores* from the Light Division, who then got mixed up with their compatriots and appear to have retired entirely from the main field of action.

Wellington's plan for turning the French right having failed, at about 11.30 he sent forward Anson's brigade, still intact, and the 7th Division, which had now reached the front, together with Colonel Barnard's brigade of the Light Division. Simultaneously these were to ascend the height on which Taupin's left flank stood, while the 3rd and 6th Divisions, which had been intended merely to demonstrate, were ordered to move ahead in two columns up the spurs further east. Only a small reserve remained on the Roman camp.

Keane's brigade, followed by Power's Portuguese—together nine battalions—climbed the northern spur towards Darmagnac's line, while Brisbane's brigade, with the 6th Division behind it, ascended the more southerly to attack Foy's position. In both cases light companies were sent ahead as a screen, but, the spurs being comparatively narrow, they were unable to advance on a broad front. The enemy skirmishers were driven back on their own line without much difficulty, but Soult's batteries then opened on the heads of the columns. Picton then halted them, sending forward a powerful skirmishing line only, but this was brought to a stand on approaching the main French line defending the ridge top, which showed no sign of giving way.

* Marked 'Luc' on the 1:25,000 map.

Brisbane's brigade slowly forced Fririon's brigade of Foy's division uphill until it found itself on the same level. As described by William Brown of the 45th,

> Our brigade had to pass along a narrow path directly in front of the enemy's centre, from which they kept up a heavy cannonade, by which we were sorely annoyed, and had many killed and wounded. We dashed on, however, at double quick time, and soon got under cover of the height on which the enemy was placed. Being then secure from the destructive fire . . . our general halted, and . . . seemed to get into a kind of quandary, and not to know what to do . . . until . . . [General Pakenham] . . . came galloping from the left exclaiming, 'Good God! General Brisbane, why stand there while the brigade gets cut up? Form line, and send out the 45th skirmishing.' . . . The bullets flew thick as hail, thirteen men of my company alone fell within a few yards of me on the brow of the hill. Notwithstanding we pressed on, and the enemy after dreadful carnage gave way, and left us in the possession of a ditch, which we held till the brigade came up in line. We then gave three cheers, charged the enemy's light troops, and drove them from another ditch . . . Having repeatedly charged, and charged in turn, we got on the height, from which we had a complete view of the dark masses of the enemy in column, one of which was moving against us . . . By this time we were greatly diminished—nearly a half down or disabled—and might have given way, if a staff-officer had not come up at the critical moment and encouraged us to hold our ground, as we should be relieved in a minute. Two brigades of the 6th Division . . . formed immediately in our rear, and we retired through their line, which advanced and encountered the French on the summit of the heights, where a most desperate conflict ensured. Our troops fired a volley at a distance of a very few yards from the enemy, and instantly closed and pushed on with the bayonet. Their adversaries rolled downhill in the greatest haste and consternation.

Meanwhile the divisional battery, which had followed the 88th further to the left, came into action: a squadron of *chasseurs*, charging down the road from the north, fell upon the guns, only to be met with such a well-directed volley by the 88th that almost every horseman was killed. Soult, who was nearby, ordered another squadron to ride down a British regiment in a vain attempt to silence the guns, only to be annihilated in turn. Foy himself, who had been conducting the defence of his position from behind Fririon's brigade, was struck by shrapnel from a shell which exploded six feet above him, badly wounding his shoulder, and he was carried to the rear after receiving first aid.* This had a disastrous moral effect on his troops, who began to give way almost immediately, their retreat uncovering Berlier's brigade to their left, at a lower level, which likewise withdrew before the onslaught of the 42nd of Pack's brigade of the 6th Division. Harispe's two battalions in the town, seeing Foy's units retreating in disorder, hastily retired to avoid getting cut off, leaving the bridge undefended.

To the left of Brisbane, Keane's and Power's brigades had by this time reached the summit of the ridge facing Darmagnac's line in Soult's centre, although a detachment Picton had ordered to the left to occupy a tongue of land was driven back in confusion and lost 23 prisoners among other casualties. After severe fighting, Darmagnac, with Foy's Division disintegrating on his left, retired to a parallel ridge further east, between Villatte's reserve Division and Harispe's re-deployed units, facing west. This re-formed line now sustained some destructive artillery fire from Picton's and Clinton's batteries in a com-

---

* The location was probably near the insignificant monument raised to commemorate him.

manding position along the main *chaussée* ascending north from Orthez, under cover of which the 6th and 3rd Divisions prepared to advance against it.

Further north-west, at St-Boès, Anson's brigade, together with the three brigades of Walker's 7th Division and that part of the Light sent to reinforce the left wing, were pressing Taupin's troops back along the saddle of the ridge, thickly strewn with the dead and wounded of Ross's and Vasconcellos's brigades. Their advance was greatly helped by two British batteries to their left, by the church, trying to silence the French guns, with two battalions of infantry pushing ahead through hollows along the side of the ridge; to the right of the 7th, Doyle's Portuguese brigade was advancing where Vasconcellos's had failed earlier. Taupin's men, having been fighting for four hours without receiving reinforcements from either Paris in their rear or from Rouget, both of whom had retired east once Darmagnac's troops were forced back, gave way before this onslaught, although the 6th Regiment, leading the centre of Walker's attack, suffered severely. On reaching the Plassotte crossroads, the battalions of the 7th Division were able to spread out in line and continue their steady advance east, with the Light Division coming into the gap between Taupin's left flank and where Rouget had been. Colborne, who led the 52nd from the Roman camp, well describes the scene:

> Lord Wellington was standing dismounted on the knoll, with Fitzroy Somerset. When I rode below him he called out, 'Hallo! Colborne, ride on and see if artillery can pass there [for the marshy ground was in general impassable].' I galloped on, and back, as fast as I could, and said, 'Yes—anything can pass.' 'Well then, make haste, take your regiment on and deploy into the plain, I leave it to your disposition.'
>
> So we moved in column from the Roman Camp up the road towards St Boès. There we met, at the ridge, Sir Lowry Cole coming back with his division. He was much excited, and said, 'Well Colborne, what's to be done? Here we [the 4th Division] are coming back as fast as we can.' I was rather provoked, and said, 'Only have patience and we shall see what's to be done.'

Having seen Picton's division scattering to the west, Colborne ordered the 52nd to deploy into the lower ground, which they did,

> . . . as evenly and regularly as on parade, accelerating their march as we approached the hill. The French were keeping up a heavy fire, but fortunately all the balls passed over our heads. I rode to the top of the hill and waved my cap, and though the men were over their knees in mud in the marsh, they trotted up in the finest order. As soon as they got to the top I ordered them to halt and fire. We were soon supported by the other divisions [the 4th and 7th] and the French were dispersed.

It was at this point in the battle that Wellington himself was disabled briefly. When riding near the 3rd *Caçadores* of the Light Division, a bullet struck his sword hilt and forced it against his thigh, breaking the skin and injuring the muscles, which made him fall back in great pain. Although he did not dismount, he was unable to ride ahead. Larpent noticed that he was still limping a little several days later, on 6 March, and saying that he was 'in rather more pain than usual, but that it was nothing'.

Once his flank had been turned by the 52nd, Taupin had no alternative but to escape north-east down a deep cut in the far side of the ridge past the Laborde farm on a track parallel to the Dax road, leaving behind only two of the guns which had produced so much destruction earlier in the day. But his infantry was never able to rally, and continued to retire across country towards the bridge spanning the Luy de Béarn at Sault-de-Navailles.

It was now 2.30 in the afternoon, and although the French right and centre were broken, Soult made an attempt to redeploy his less-engaged troops across the Sault de Navailles road to cover the withdrawal. However, when he rode to the far left of his line and found to his consternation that Hill was not only across the Gave de Pau in force and driving back Harispe's scattered units but was also already threatening the flank of his new position, he ordered a general retreat.

Hill had received his order to cross the Gave de Pau at 11.00, and the two battalions and one cavalry regiment left to resist him gave way at once when his horse artillery opened on them, allowing the five infantry brigades and one of cavalry—12,000 men—to traverse the deep fords at Les Soarns undisturbed. Buchan's brigade, finding the bridge at Orthez by then undefended, pulled down the barricades and marched through the town and up the Sault road. Harispe, with two brigades facing five, after briefly attempting to hold a line through the hamlet of Rontrun, retired up the Sault road.

Soult's withdrawal was a difficult operation, for each successive line of battalions was harassed continually by Wellington's artillery on the ridge and by Hill's horse artillery thundering in its rear, and what at first had been a reasonably orderly retirement became a confused flight, with survivors from Foy's and Taupin's units in the van and Harispe's and Villatte's bringing up the rear. The latter tried to hold the village of Sallespisse but were soon driven out by the 42nd (Black Watch), not without loss. Converging on the bridge at Sault, the wreck of Soult's army disintegrated.

Although the ground was too broken for the cavalry to act earlier in what until then had been largely an infantry battle, Somerset's 7th Hussars were now able to move ahead and capture one of Harispe's battalions and another of National Guards. Although the rest of the cavalry was well up, it were unable to deal many effective blows, partly because of the configuration of the ground, partitioned as it was by numerous walled enclosures.

Captain Thomas Wildman, with the Hussars, recorded that

> ... the French no sooner gave way than they ran like mad, our infantry running out of breath after them, all open to avoid the shells, and the squadrons of cavalry moving on in the midst of them. The French however rallied and three times made a stand upon very strong positions, but our artillery soon got at them, and when the infantry advanced they ran.

General Tirlet had placed twelve guns to defend the bridge, backed by companies of sappers and two more battalions of conscripts which had just arrived (many without cartridges) to receive their baptism of fire, shelling from horse-artillery accompanying Fane's cavalry. They stood with grounded arms while a mass of veterans, their pouches full, fled past them pell-mell. Luckily for their cavalry and for some of Reille's units, fords were found across the Luy de Béarn near the bridge, which was blown up by Villatte at

10.00 at night, leaving some of Harispe's units on the southern bank to escape as they may. Soult's army did not draw breath until the town of Hagetmau was reached, some sixteen miles north-east of the battlefield.

Neither the Allied infantry nor the cavalry attempted to cross the Luy in pursuit of the rabble: this has been attributed to the lack of initiative on the part of their senior officers, now without Wellington at hand to direct them. Had he sufficient confidence in his cavalry—once the bit was between their teeth—to allow them to pursue, he might have been able to turn the French retreat into a rout. Most of the exhausted infantry bivouacked on the heights above Sallespisse, first lighting fires to broil their ration beef before sinking to sleep.

Allied casualties were some 2,175 (including 80 missing, largely Vasconcellos's men), of which 519 were Portuguese. Soult's losses were just over 4,000, including 1,350 taken prisoner.

Colonel John Keane, commanding John Colville's former brigade, when describing the battle to Colville in a letter of 17 March, very matter-of-factly commented that the French had 'got off cheap', and, as there was little shelter on the heath,

> . . . we got well pounded, the 45th, 83rd and 87th particularly, as also the 88th . . . Poor Parker was cut in two by a cannon shot close to the God of War. Taylor was wounded in the neck but is up again. Greenwell severely, Carr ditto—ball entered the chin and lodged in the roots of his tongue. It has been cut out and he is doing well. Elliott severely in the belly, but also doing well. Poor Nugent dangerously in two places, but there are some hopes. Baldwin severely, right arm broken. Capt. McDermot, 88th, only joined the day before, with his Vitoria wound open, was killed.*

---

* Those officers referred to were Captain Edward Parker RE, Lieutenant-Colonel John Taylor, Major Leonard Greenwell, Major Henry William Carr, Captain Gilbert Elliott, Ensign Pierce Nugent, Lieutenant Connell James Baldwin and Captain Henry McDermott.

16

THE ADVANCE ON TOULOUSE

IT had been a frosty night, and the next morning, the 28th, in Oman's words, 'it was a very stiff and rheumatic army which fell slowly into its ranks, after the uncovenanted mercy of a tot of rum, served out by a thoughtful order from head-quarters. Head-quarters was late in rising itself—the commander-in-chief was abominably stiff from his contusion of the previous evening, and suffered considerable pain for several days; he found riding difficult.'

The French were already on the move from around Hagetmau towards St-Sever, over-looking the Adour another eight miles further north, where Soult tried to bring some order into his divisions and plan his next move. Desertion had been rampant, particularly among the National Guards and newly levied battalions, many of whom had made them-selves scarce, stealing back to their homes before any attempt was made to round them up. This was practically impossible, however, although the close-cropped hair of many young men in the villages passed through by the Allies during the next few weeks gave away the fact that they had bolted from the conscription.

Of the two alternatives, Soult chose to retire on Toulouse rather than Bordeaux, be-cause, by doing so, that would cause Allied lines of communication with their ports of supply to be lengthened and bring him nearer to the main military base in the south. He would have to risk Bordeaux falling to the Allies, although if Wellington sent a sizeable detachment there Soult might still be able to attack the remainder with his own reduced army. He could have retired on Bordeaux via Mont-de-Marsan, where there was another large depot, but he had no means of transporting it, while further north extended the inhospitable forests of Les Landes, where he could not have managed to feed his troops; and, once at Bordeaux, he might find it difficult to pass the Garonne. It was far more sensible to retire east towards Aire-sur-l'Adour: from there, if Wellington were rash enough to move towards Bordeaux, he could fall on his flank. Dax would have to be abandoned: as it was, Daricau, who had been sent there, had found the place untenable, and the National Guards he had collected to defend it had deserted by escalading the ramparts to the rear of the town, leaving him only a weak regular battalion with which to re-join Soult.

One can well imagine Soult's exasperation, when three days after the battle at Orthez, he received peremptory orders dictated by Napoleon at Troyes (whence the Emperor was about to march against Schwarzenberg's army), 'to resume the offensive at once, and fall upon one of the wings of the enemy; even if he has but 20,000 men, by seizing the opportunity boldly, he ought to be able to get the advantage over the English. And he has talent enough to understand what I mean.'

Wellington's cavalry reached the outskirts of St-Sever during the afternoon of 28 February. Soult had retired east to Grenade on their approach, having first blown up the bridge spanning the Adour. George Simmons records that the Light Division, after encamping near the hamlet of Bonnegarde, advanced parallel to the main road through Doazit and forded the river near St-Sever, from which Beresford's units thrust north-east towards Mont-de-Marsan. This had been evacuated by the French, allowing a large accumulation of provisions intended for Bayonne to be captured, which Soult had no time to destroy. Simmons found that the place abounded 'with wine and eatables of all description': it was 'quite droll to see the French people treating us as if we were friends instead of enemies. We certainly paid for everything, and now it was found necessary to pay us regularly.' Kennedy, with his squadron of the 18th Dragoons which had forded the Adour opposite Montaut on the 29th, found comfortable quarters in the mansion just vacated by the *préfet* of the *département*, and much appreciated both his 'fine claret' and library, in which letters were found from Soult telling the *préfet* 'how to raise the *levée en masse* as his army would not be able to oppose us without their assistance', which revealing correspondence Kennedy handed to Colonel Vivian to pass on to Wellington. Cavalry patrols were reporting that the enemy were in force at Nogaro and Manciet, north-east of Aire.

On the 29th Wellington himself entered St-Sever, which remained his headquarters for the next eight days. Several entirely new dispositions had to be made in view of Soult's movement east, for Wellington was now faced with the problems inherent in occupying a large area. He had to decide also in which direction the Allies should make their next move. It was obvious that the main object was to knock Soult's army out of the ring, now that Bayonne was entirely isolated. If he could engage more Spaniards to continue blockading the place, he could withdraw some of his Anglo-Portuguese units and then would have enough men to hand to be able to detach a sufficient number to march on Bordeaux without weakening the force opposing Soult. Yet it was essential to leave Hope in control on the coast with enough Anglo-Portuguese units: he dared not risk leaving the blockade of Bayonne in Spanish hands alone.

Freire had been ordered to bring his two best divisions to the front, and these were replaced by men of the 'Reserve of Andalusia', who had been kicking their heels in the Baztan. Wellington's heavy cavalry—von Bülow's K.G.L. brigade (formerly von Bock's), the Household Brigade (O'Loghlin's) and the dragoons (Clifton's, and those of Charles Manners', formerly Ponsonby's, who had gone on leave)—which had ridden from their cantonments in Navarre during the last week of February were expected to start reaching the front by 10 March together with five regiments of Portuguese light horse under Barbaçena and Campbell. The Allies would then have 8,000 cavalry instead of the 3,500

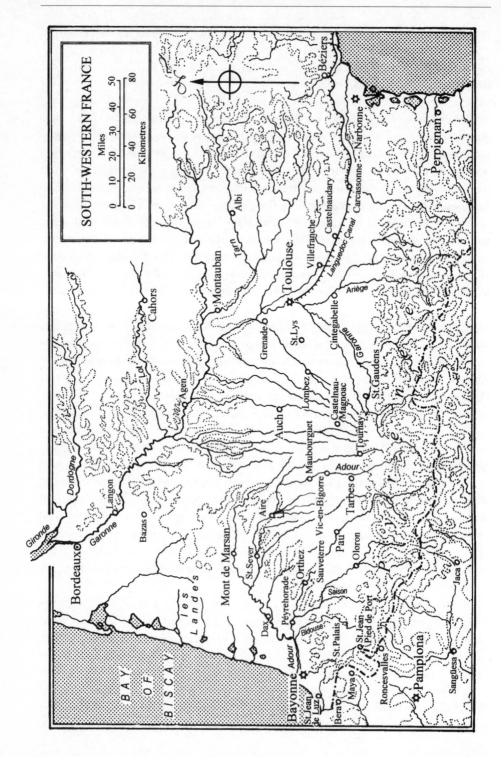

SOUTH-WESTERN FRANCE

then to hand. The further they advanced into France, and the further they were from the coast, the more useful this arm would be.

On 4 March two confidential agents of the mayor of Bordeaux rode into St-Sever to confer with Wellington. Jean-Baptiste Lynch, who had held that post since 1808, was the grandson of an Irish Jacobite exile of 1688 who had become a prosperous wine merchant. Jean-Baptiste himself had been a member of the 'Parliament of Bordeaux' and later a prominent 'Girondist'. Under the Directory, he was on the Council General of the Gironde, had been partly responsible for the afforestation of the Les Landes and, in 1809, had been created a 'count of the Empire'. Late in 1813 he had been called to Paris. While there, he had come to the conclusion, as had many others, that Napoleon was ruined, and that the only way to save France from further desolation was to topple the emperor. On returning to Bordeaux, Lynch had started to undermine the imperialist organisation there, making ineffective all the measures being taken by the Commissioner Extraordinary and the Military Governor, General L'Huillier, and to foment an underground royalist conspiracy. Lynch had not been the first to promise such a rising should Wellington support it.

Wellington, in his dispatch to Lord Liverpool dated the 4th, confirmed what he had already intimated to Bathurst—that the further he advanced into France, the less enthusiasm he had found for Napoleon and the more in favour of the Bourbons: but he was certain that the French people would not rise unless the Allies declared themselves. The government should not remain sitting on the fence, even if some ministers were hesitant to sponsor a rising which, if things went badly, they might be forced to abandon. Wellington reiterated: 'I cannot discover the policy of not hitting one's enemy as hard as one can and in the most vulnerable place. I am certain that he [Napoleon] would not so act by us, if he had the opportunity. He would certainly overturn the British authority in Ireland if it were in his power.'

Already, on 2 February, an incognito visitor to St-Jean-de-Luz, officially known as the 'Comte de Pradel' (or Pradelles) but in fact the 38-year-old Duc d'Angoulême, had offered his services to head a rebellion. Angoulême was not an impressive leader, and many felt the same as Larpent:

> I do not think much of the little Duke; his figure and manners are by no means imposing, and his talents appear not very great. He seems affable and good-tempered, and though not seemingly a being to make a kingdom for himself, he may do very well to govern one when well established. Lord Wellington was in his manner droll towards them [the Duke's slender entourage, among them Count Etienne de Damas]. As they went out, we drew up on each side, and Lord Wellington put them first; they bowed and scraped right and left so oddly, and so actively, that he followed with a face much nearer a grin than a smile.

THE ADVANCE ON BORDEAUX

Before describing Hill's movements during the first week of March, those of Beresford should be outlined. On the 7th, after a week at Mont-de-Marsan and despite the filthy weather, Beresford received orders to march north with the 7th Division (again commanded by Dalhousie, back from wintering in England), followed a day later by the 4th. Ahead of them, at Roquefort, rode Vivian's cavalry. They followed the *chaussée* skirting the east side of the Landes to Bazas and Langon on the Garonne. Vandeleur's cavalry had ridden north directly from Bayonne to converge with them near Bordeaux. Having been kept constantly informed by Lynch of the situation there, and having come across virtually no opposition *en route*, Beresford decided that it would be safe to leave the 4th Division at Langon, where it could re-join Wellington if needed urgently, and veered north-west through Podensac with the 7th only. The 18th Hussars had been left to watch the crossing points of the Garonne in the unlikely event of an attack from the far bank, for it was now known that most of the few enemy units in the area were garrisoning the forts along the wide Garonne estuary or had been withdrawn to Libourne.

At 8.00 on the morning of 12 March Vivian's 1st Hussars of the K.G.L. reached the outskirts of Bordeaux, followed by three brigades of Dalhousie's infantry. On halting at the city gate, the Hussars were handed laurel sprays and informed that Lynch would shortly appear to receive them and declare for Louis XVIII. Vivian rode back to confer with Beresford, who had been ordered by Wellington to make it clear that the occupation of the city—at that time with a population of about 90,000—was a military event not a political one (although in fact the main reason for the operation *was* political, and had widespread repercussions). While he wished the royalist cause well, if that were the spontaneous will of the citizens, the Allies should remain neutral. On greeting Beresford effusively, Lynch tore the decoration of the Legion of Honour from his coat and the tricolour scarf from his waist. He then attached a large white cockade to his hat, at which gesture a high proportion of the crowd did likewise with that royalist badge distributed to them beforehand, and their flag was run up on the cathedral tower.

Beresford complimented Lynch on the enthusiasm of the citizens, expressed the hope that peace was at hand, and confirmed that until then he was taking possession in the name of Wellington but at the same time promised that his troops would respect the fact they were among friends: 'we have made war not on Frenchmen but only on the French Government.' Beresford was not expecting the egregious Duc d'Angoulême, who, un-known to Wellington, had ridden up from St-Sever—collecting other Bourbonists *en route*—to proclaim that he and Lynch had taken over the administration of Bordeaux in the name of the king and with the full approval of the Allies, which was precisely what Wellington was not authorised to state. Naturally, Beresford had to warn Lynch that while he did not wish to discourage the royalist, he had not received orders to hand over the government of regions being occupied to any civil authorities. Wellington, furious at Angoulême's tactless behaviour, wrote to inform him that he was carrying out military operations and had no orders from Whitehall either to restore the former régime or to put his troops at the disposition of claimants to the throne. He would be placed in a invidious position had the Congress of Châtillon ended with peace being concluded with Napo-leon! He had no objection to the proclamation of Louis XVIII, if that were the people's desire, but if Angoulême wanted to raise royalist troops to further that cause he would have to do so at his own expense. This, in the event, did not happen, for although numerous officers presented themselves, there were hardly any recruits for the rank and file. The populous in general had had enough of conscription and fighting. Even when Beresford sent a squadron of cavalry to summon a coastal fort to surrender, while the commandant mounted the white cockade, most of the garrison merely dispersed, only 200 National Guards agreeing to join the royalists. Most of the 400 other recruits were to be found drinking in the wine shops of Bordeaux.

On 15 March Beresford received orders to return to the main army, leaving only 5,000 men on the Gironde—three brigades under Dalhousie, two squadrons of cavalry under Vandeleur, one squadron of Vivian's cavalry and a single battery of artillery—and marched south-east, picking up the 4th Division *en route*. Dalhousie, who was to remain at Bordeaux until the cessation of hostilities, was later reinforced by Doyle's Portuguese brigade, while Inglis's was sent to Langon.

Wellington had problems of logistics to resolve, for he expected to be further extending his lines of communication and had a large army to feed, although he was now receiving, and paying for, substantial provisions from the local inhabitants. Captain Thomas Browne records that at about this time Wellington

> ... gave permission to every Town in his rear to form a City Guard ... which was to act under the orders of the Mayor ... They were empowered to arrest & send prisoners to the nearest Division ... all stragglers or Men committing irregularities in the rear of the Army, & to make any police regulations they pleased, transmitting them to Ld Wellington for his approval. These marks of confidence had wonderful effect on the inhabitants of the villages who were mostly in this part of France tired of the war, & glad to hope for any change. ... This disposition of the people ... contributed greatly to the success of Ld Wellington's operations, by leaving him under no anxiety for the rear of his Army & communications with his Flanks.

THE COMBAT AT AIRE

On 1 March Hill's corps had moved east along the left or south bank of the Adour from St-Sever, and the 3rd and 6th Divisions marched in two parallel columns along the far bank via Grenade (-sur-l'Adour) and Cazères. At the latter village they had to use some force to push back D'Erlon's two divisions (Foy's and Darmagnac's) towards Aire (-sur-l'Adour). Together with Reille's two (Taupin's and Rouget's), further east, they were withdrawn towards the village of Barcelonne (-du-Gers), for Soult, assuming that he had the whole of the Allied army facing him, wished to avoid a general engagement and was prepared to withdraw after fighting a cautious rearguard action. As the bridge at Aire had been carried away by flood several years earlier and never repaired, Soult ordered Reille to cross the river at Barcelonne while D'Erlon detained the Allies, and confirmed his intention to move south-east on Tarbes rather than due east, thus giving up communication with Bordeaux.

Clausel's divisions were aligned on a wooded ridge some 2,000 yards west of the Aire, rising steeply at right angles to the river.* Suddenly, at about 2.00 in the afternoon of 2

---

* And also west of the present N 143, leading south towards Pau.

March, Clausel's right wing, which was held by Villatte, found itself being assaulted by Barnes's brigade, closely followed by Byng's, with Hardinge's Portuguese coming up. About a mile further south Harispe was attacked likewise by Da Costa's brigade of Le Cor's division.

Barnes's men clambered to the summit of the ridge without difficulty, driving Villatte's troops down towards the town, but Da Costa's brigade, on reaching the brow of the hill, were charged by Dauture's brigade and forced back with considerable loss. William Stewart, seeing their precarious situation, detached the 50th and 92nd from Barnes's brigade to take Dauture in flank, while the rest of the brigade, facing Villatte, waited for Byng's units to reinforce them. Once Hardinge's Portuguese had come up behind Byng, Hill ordered the 71st to lead them against Villatte, while Byng's battalions followed in Barnes's wake along the saddle of the ridge, which enabled him to push Harispe back on his reserves, who retreated south-east. Thus Clausel's two divisions were separated. Villatte was forced to retire east, and might have been cut off when trying to cross a bridge over a stream partly encircling the lower town were it not that Reille, already over the Adour and hearing heavy firing in the town, had sent Rouget to cover their retreat and keep Hardinge's *Caçadores* at bay. Meanwhile the 71st and other units were clearing the streets of Aire. In general, Clausel's troops put up a feeble resistance, for British casualties were only 156 men. Regrettably, amongst those killed was Colonel Hood, 3rd Foot Guards, the Assistant Adjutant-General to the 2nd Division. Da Costa, having displayed his incapacity—he had lost over 100 men and had not even attempted to rally the rest—was replaced in command with Colonel João de Almeida and sent back to Lisbon in disgrace. French casualties may have been 250 men plus 100 prisoners, but as they straggled away as darkness fell, many conscripts took the opportunity to desert (Soult estimated that at least 3,000 were 'missing' after the combat).

D'Erlon's column retired as far south-east as Marciac, beyond Plaisance; Reille's was in cantonments at Maubourguet, on the Adour south of Plaisance, and Clausel's was near Vic-en-Bigorre, with Soult's headquarters at Rabastens, west of Vic. There they were able to regain their breath, for Wellington, still at St-Sever, only sent out cavalry reconnaissances during the next few days, during which the awful weather continued. The Commissariat needed more time now to keep the army provisioned, while the state of the roads left much to be desired.

It was Soult's intention to move south towards Tarbes, hoping to draw the Allies away from the *chaussée* leading east via Auch towards Toulouse to give time for that city's defences to be strengthened further as he had instructed they should be. Meanwhile he would continue to reorganise his forces. He had still approximately 36,600 of all arms to hand. Paris's brigade was disbanded and its units distributed among other divisions; Rouget handed back his division to Maransin, who had re-joined; and Fririon, interim commander of Foy's Division, was replaced by Daricau (also now present at Headquarters), whose former units were passed to Villatte.

William Napier states that, on the night of 7 March, Soult,

... thinking to find only some weak parties at Pau sent a strong detachment there to arrest the nobles who had assembled to welcome the duke of Angoulême, but general Fane getting there before him with a brigade of infantry and two regiments of cavalry the stroke failed ... [but] two days after, when Fane had quitted Pau, a French officer accompanied by only four hussars captured there thirty-four Portuguese with their commander and ten loaded mules.

Having temporarily deprived himself of the 4th and 7th Divisions, Wellington, while awaiting his heavy cavalry and Freire's divisions to reach the front, ordered Morillo to send forward half the units with which he was blockading Navarrenx. By 18 March he would have an additional 4,000 cavalrymen and 10,000 Spanish infantry to replace those which had been detached from Beresford's force. Meanwhile, Wellington had received a misleading report from the Catalan front to the effect that Suchet was sending several thousand of his veteran troops to aid Soult when in fact they were marching north towards Lyon as Napoleon had instructed. This was one reason why, on the 14th, Wellington had recalled the 4th Division, even if that left Dalhousie out on a limb.

During the second week of March Soult, becoming aware that at least two Allied divisions had been detached towards Bordeaux and stung by Napoleon's order to take the initiative, decided to make a ostentatious demonstration, and, on the 13th, his whole army advanced cautiously north-west over several ridges towards the little River Léez, there meeting Fane's cavalry screening Hill's line. This extended north from the village of Garlin to his headquarters in the hilltop village of St-Mont, overlooking a bridge spanning the Adour south-east of Aire.* Soult set up his own headquarters at the hamlet of Conchez-de-Béarn, east of Garlin. Wellington was surprised that Soult should be appearing to take the offensive, having been so recently mauled, and, assuming that in fact he had received reinforcements from Suchet, went on the defensive.

The 3rd and 6th Divisions near Barcelonne, together with their artillery and the headquarter's baggage were ordered to cross the Adour to join Hill, while Freire's troops, which had reached St-Sever that morning, were to do likewise, together with the two advance brigades (K.G.L. and Clifton's) of heavy dragoons which had just ridden in.† The main bridge over the Léez, by which they were to cross, had been destroyed by Soult except for the central pier; but this was soon replaced by cutting down some twenty-five elm trees, about 25 feet long, over which twelve-foot-long bundles of fascines were placed crosswise and then covered with dirt, which served splendidly.

Although Wellington's main force now faced Soult's line, his plan was to outflank Soult's right wing. Somerset's hussars and the Light Division, guarding his own left flank in front of Barcelonne, moved towards Plaisance on the 16th, where they were joined three days later by the 4th Division, making a forced march from Langon and Bazas, together with

---

* A private of the 15th Hussars, finding himself trapped in the church tower at St-Mont by a French patrol, escaped by throwing the bell rope over the side and rapidly descending by it to mount his horse.

† Regrettably, according to Captain Thomas Browne, the Spanish division commanded by O'Donnell, who had done his best to preserve discipline during the advance, had 'committed so many depredations' when in the rear 'that Ld Wellington found it necessary to make some severe examples, & several ... were hanged by his orders, which had a great effect on the rest, & assisted materially in restoring order.'

Vivian's cavalry and Beresford himself, who was to command this turning movement. It had been a difficult progress made in appalling weather, with mud reaching to the fetlocks of their baggage horses and mules.

On 16 March, hearing rumours that Wellington had received reinforcements, Soult withdrew south-east towards Lembeye and the next day ordered a general retreat on Tarbes. His explanation to Clarke at Paris was that this was to lure Wellington away from the direct road to Toulouse and allow him (Soult) to fall on his most advanced and isolated column. Little did Soult realise that Wellington was more interested in cornering him in a cul-de-sac of the Pyrenees south of Tarbes by cutting Soult's lines of retreat by that same road to Toulouse and two others leading north-east and south-east from Tarbes.

On the 17th, a Captain Daunia and 100 picked men of the 5th Chasseurs made a daring night raid by circling far south and, charging into Hagetmau at dawn, were able to captured two drafts of convalescents returning to the front, six medical officers and a small convoy—which Oman scathingly described as Soult's only effective move of the whole campaign. The incursion certainly did not effect Wellington's plans, for on the 18th a general advance of the Allied army took place. Hill, with 13,000 men, pushed ahead from Garlin; Wellington, with the central column of 25,000, pressed south-east from Aire, with headquarters at the village of Viella (south of St-Mont); and Beresford, with about 12,000, on entering Plaisance, swung round south, making for Maubourguet and Rabastans in the hope of turning Soult's right wing. Each of the three corps remained aligned and in close contact with each other: there would be no chance of Soult 'falling on an isolated column'; indeed, he had only a single regiment of *chasseurs* on his right wing, and seemed unaware of the danger he was in.

At dawn on the 19th there was cavalry skirmishing between these *chasseurs*, who were rapidly evicted from Rabastens by Somerset's hussars, while von Bülow's dragoons from Wellington's column approached Vic-en-Bigorre; but, after skirmishing with Berton's cavalry brigade, they drew back as Soult's main body entered the town from the west to reach the Tarbes road. Soult, thoroughly alarmed, ordered D'Erlon to hurry his two divisions to cover the line of retreat, while Clausel's and Reille's were instructed to cut across country directly towards Tarbes. D'Erlon arrived just in time to face Picton, at the head of Wellington's column, who attacked him with Power's Portuguese. When well engaged, D'Erlon noticed a second column—the Light Division—ascending the far bank of the Adour to turn his flank: he accordingly drew back and, when joined by Darmagnac's division, attempted to hold a line further south.*

Although D'Erlon carried out a fine delaying action against Picton's thrust, now supported by Clinton's division—each contender suffered between 250 and 300 casualties—he was in no position to stop Beresford's column from cutting Soult's first road of escape, that via Rabestans, Miélan, Mirande and Auch, while the second road, via Trie-sur-Baise, Castelnau-Magnoac, Boulogne-sur-Gesse and Lombez, was threatened.†

---

* It was at some point during this action that Colonel Henry Sturgeon of the Engineers was killed by a chance bullet.
† Soult's first road of escape was the present N 21, his second the present D 632.

THE COMBAT AT TARBES

Soult's army spent all day retreating across byways, each successive deployment being covered by an infantry rearguard that was hazardous for Hill's cavalry to attack without knowing its strength. Napier records the daring exploit of Captain William Light, who, after riding through the French skirmishing line, dropped his reins and leaned back, hanging half off his saddle, while his horse continued to canter along the front of the enemy's light troops, who, thinking him mortally wounded, took no further notice. He thus passed unobserved through the woods and, ascending to the open hilltop, put spurs to his horse and galloped along the French main line counting their regiments as he passed. He then turned back, breaking through the rear of the surprised skirmishers, to report to Wellington that there were only five battalions ahead.

By nightfall both Reille's and Clausel's divisions bivouacked near Ibos among other villages just west of Tarbes, with Hill's troops close behind them. The next morning, the 20th, Soult deployed Clausel's two divisions on the ridge where the windmill of Orléac stood, commanding the village of Orleix (north-east of Tarbes) to protect the road out to Trie, with Pierre Soult's cavalry on their right flank. Harispe's division lined the ridge to the north of the road and Villatte's was centred on the hilltop village of Boulin, through which the road ran. Taupin's division was left to defend the bridge over the Adour at Tarbes before withdrawing on to a lower ridge due east of the town, where he was to hold back Hill's column for as long as possible.

Soult's other three divisions were to march south-east along the Tournay–St-Gaudens road,* the longer (and, at first, steeper) route towards Toulouse. Soult had hoped to get at least a proportion of his force away by the shorter route (via Trie), while the main body would converge on Toulouse a day or two later. There was a long wooded ridge rising east of the Arret Darré (Larret) stream, a tributary of the Larros, further east, spanned by a single bridge at the village of Tournay, where a stand could also be made before retiring east. Some of his artillery and train were already *en route*.

In the morning of 20 March Hill's column, reinforced by the 3rd Division and von Bülow's dragoons, had no great difficulty evicting Taupin's troops from Tarbes, while Fane's cavalry were able to thread the narrow bridge over the Adour (unaccountably left undamaged) but were unable to pursue Taupin's rearguard across country, for the flats immediately east of the town were broken up by several impassable watercourses and they had to return to the main road. The cavalry were followed by Hill's ten infantry brigades, which traversed the bridge in succession, but, as it could only take four men abreast, it was not until late in the afternoon that the whole column was over.

More serious fighting took place when the Light Division veered east off the Rabastens road to attack the right of Harispe's division. The 6th had made a wider turn in an attempt to outflank it, while as soon as Pierre Soult's cavalry were discovered on the Trie road Somerset's Hussars rode further east to contain them. The ridge defended by Harispe's right-hand brigade was approached by a steep wooded slope, up which Alten sent all

* Now the N 117.

three battalions of the 95th. John Surtees described his battalion as forming the right, the 2nd Battalion the centre, and the 1st Battalion

> . . . the left of our line of skirmishers. We found them covered in front with a great number of light troops, which occupied us some time in driving in. . . . We had a considerably-sized brushwood to pass through before we could get at them. At length, after much smart skirmishing, we gained the height, but found the whole of their heavy infantry drawn up on a steep acclivity, near the windmill, which allowed them to have line behind line, all of which could fire at the same time over each other's heads, like the tiers of guns in a three-decker. We continued, however, to advance upon them, till we got within a hundred paces of this formidable body, the firing from which was the hottest I had ever been in, except perhaps Barossa. At this moment I received a shot through my right shoulder, which compelled me to retire; but meeting the main support of my battalion advancing with Colonel Ross at the head, and finding my wound had not disabled me, I again advanced with him . . .'

On reaching the brow they were charged, it being likely that the enemy mistook the dark-uniformed skirmishers as Portuguese, otherwise Harispe might have been more cautious. After some stiff fighting in the vicinity of the windmill of Oléac, the French gave way, for by now Clinton's troops were in evidence behind their right flank, separating them from Pierre Soult's cavalry placed to guard it. Both Harispe's and Villatte's troops, extending their line, were forced to retreat in some disorder south-east across parallel ridges towards Tournay, but, finding they were cut off from D'Erlon's divisions, they made their way due east towards Galan, as did Pierre Soult's cavalry.

The whole of Beresford's column had continued to press on south, with Manners' dragoons riding down the Rabastens road towards Tarbes. Taupin, realising the danger of remaining any longer in the position he had taken up east of the town, retired rapidly along the Tournay road. Hill's cavalry had by now spread out and reached the village of Barbazan, to the south-east, but it was not until after 4.00 in the afternoon that the vanguard of his infantry discovered Reille's and D'Erlon's divisions deployed on the wooded ridge beyond the Arret Darré stream.

John Cooke, with the 43rd, having followed the 95th up the ridge to support them, could, on reaching the summit, see Tarbes lying

> . . . in the valley to the right, close to the Adour. The dense red columns of our right wing were in the act of passing it with cavalry and artillery, while the glitter of the enemy's bayonets formed a brilliant spectacle. The tail of their winding columns covered the country, as they rapidly threaded the by-roads through small woods, villages, and over hill and dale. Threatened by the hussars and the horse artillery, they were running in a dense crowd on the high road towards Tournay, where a rapid interchange of cannon balls took place. We were in momentary expectation of overtaking them when broken ground and hedges suddenly intervened, and they eluded our grasp. A French captain, holding a commission in his hand, stood by the road side imploring his life. He called out in English, in evident fear of the Portuguese and Spaniards. Both his eyes were shot out of their sockets, and were hanging on his cheeks.

Many Allied officers expected a general attack to be made, although the ridge bristled with guns; for the enemy, when forced back, would find themselves jammed against the bridge at Tournay and, if the 6th Division had been able to turn their right flank also, Soult would have found himself in a very desperate situation. But it was getting dark, and the Allied troops had been marching or fighting for twelve hours already. Seeing his own line as yet unformed, Wellington chose to call it a day (to the annoyance of Pakenham among others, according to Surtees) and ordered his men to bivouac where they stood, facing the French. Total Allied casualties that day had been 125; those of the French were about 200.

Soult slipped away during the night, two-thirds of his army defiling across the one bridge at Tournay before toiling up the long ascent made by the St-Gaudens road towards Montréjeau, where they were joined by Clausel's troops and the cavalry. Soult had escaped with his army virtually intact.

George Simmons, wounded in the action at Orleix, wrote home to his parents while recuperating at Tarbes, confirming that 'in their towns the peaceable inhabitants have more faith in us, generally speaking, than in their own army', and recording the astonishment of the French at

> ... the liberality of the English ... for how many thousands of our brave fellows when wounded and left on the ground would not otherwise have been murdered by the injured peasants. Instead of that, they take the wounded to their houses, protect and feed them. The army that is now opposed to ours is Marshal Soult's. He is a persevering fellow. Though thrashed every time we come into contact with him, still he moves to another position, and waits till we move up and thrash him out of it. The French army fought very obstinately at the battle of Orthez, better than usual, but every cock ought to fight better upon its own dung-hill.

It was pointless to even attempt to catch up with Soult: Hill was directed only to follow cautiously, for he would be much outnumbered. Wellington and Beresford would lead the bulk of the Allied infantry along the shorter Trie–Castelnau road and strike directly at Toulouse, perhaps even reaching it before Soult.

Wellington spent the night of the 22nd at Galan, a village some eight miles south of Trie, where Larpent describes the eighty-two year old *maire* as having been

> ... an hour in the room with Lord Wellington before he found him out, talking by the fire in his quarter, until at last Lord Wellington, having let him go on some time, asked him to dinner. This staggered him, and led to an explanation. The *maire* said, that the night before he had had Generals Clausel and Harispe, and that they only ordered a dinner to be prepared, and did not ask him to eat part of his own, or thank him, or take the least notice of him. He could not, therefore, believe that Lord Wellington was the enemy's General, after being so treated, as he said, 'like a dog', by his friends.

Little did Wellington realise how execrable even the highways could be in that wet season, notably the long stretch traversing the waterlogged valley of the river Gesse between Boulogne and Lombez, where Augustus Frazer 'passed perhaps twenty horses and mules, which, in different parts of the road, had been suffocated in the mud'. Von Bülow's cavalry was ordered to advance parallel to it but to the south, keeping in daily contact with the flank guard of Hill's column. Somerset's and Vivian's hussars remained north of the road, sending out squadrons as far afield as Auch and Gimont, while Manners' dragoons rode in advance of the main body without finding any sign of hostile troops. The going was slow, for the pontoon train and 18-pounder siege guns had also to be dragged up and over several ridges fanning out from the distant Pyrenees, which the *chaussée* traversed. Headquarters were moved from Boulogne to L'Isle-en-Dordon, and then to Samatan and St-Lys, where, on 26 March, contact was regained with outposts of Soult's army near the River Touch, no great distance south-west of Toulouse. Although they had 50 miles more to cover, Soult had been able to concentrate his forces in and about Toulouse two days before the Allied vanguard entered the western outskirts. Meanwhile the Allies were largely 'fed on the country, and the rations paid for in bills or ready money', for, as Larpent admitted,

> Our transports, such as they were, are quite outrun by our continual marches and distance from the depots. We do not even resort to our grand prize-depot at Mont de Marsan. We are also boldly isolated in the country, with scarcely five hundred men the whole way between this [Samatan] and Bayonne; and between this and Tarbes I believe none at all.

In order to protect his communications, reluctantly, Wellington had ordered forward the Spanish '3rd Army', so-called, formerly commanded by General the Duque del Parque and now by the Príncipe de Anglona, which was ordered to occupy Pau and Orthez provisionally.

Such was the rapidity of Soult's retreat—his infantry made a forced march of 30 miles on the 21st—that Hill lost touch at an early stage in the pursuit. However, on the 22nd, the 13th Light Dragoons, led by Colonel Doherty, surprised Berton's *chasseurs*, Soult's rearguard, near St-Gaudens, routed it and took 100 prisoners.

Soult's army staggered into Toulouse on the 24th, 8,000 men of which—according to Soult—were shambling shoe-less in the mire, while his cavalry was busily occupied rounding up and shepherding forward 5,000 or so stragglers. Fortunately, they were approaching the main depot of military stores in southern France, its arsenal replete with artillery, ammunition, equipment and food: marauding was no longer necessary.

According to Larpent, a halt was made at St-Lys 'which most of the army is in very much need of . . . [and] to enable Lord Wellington to make arrangements and reconnoitre, &c.' From the church tower, Toulouse could be made out distinctly through Larpent's telescope, as it was a fine day. The weather had been wet, and the road—perhaps 'as bad as any we have ever passed with artillery'—quite churned up, with the troops 'splashed to their caps, and hundreds were walking barefoot in the clay up to the calves of their legs for about five miles . . .' Wellington's barouche, in which sat General Miguel de Alava with a badly bruised hip (he had been standing next to Wellington at Orthez) was stuck fast in the mud for three hours.*

---

* Wellington regarded Alava, his chief Spanish liaison officer since La Romana's demise, and on whom he much relied, as a personal friend. He had served aboard a Spanish man-of-war at Trafalgar in 1805 and was also to be present at Waterloo. With hindsight, it was a pity Alava was not able to influence the Duke four years later when he accepted the position of Master of the Ordnance. Thomas Creevey had asked Alava what he thought of the idea, the reply being that 'he never was more sorry for any event in his life—that the Duke of Wellington ought never have had anything to do with politicks [*sic*]—that he ought to have remained, not only the soldier of England, but of Europe, to be ready to appear again at its command whenever his talents and services might be wanted.' Creevey went on to add that he had 'seen a good deal of Alava at different times, and a more upright human being, to all appearance, I never beheld.'

17

THE BATTLE OF TOULOUSE

O N 24 March, the day Soult entered Toulouse, Hill's vanguard was still 40 miles south-west, at St-Martory, and Beresford's force was at Lombez, 30 miles west of the city. The ancient, brick-built capital of Languedoc, with a population of just over 50,000, was a focus of royalist sentiment, and Wellington was assured that if he could eject Soult's army it would follow the lead given by Bordeaux, together with the whole region.

Toulouse stood on the right or eastern bank of the Garonne, spanned by the solidly built Pont Neuf, crossing from St-Cyprien. The inner fortifications of this transpontine suburb were aligned with the present Allée Charles de Fitte and west wall of the La Grave Hospital, beyond which lay a marshy riverside. A line of outer defensive works, only just commenced, extended north from the Place Patte d'Oie, and circled round to meet the Garonne to the south-east. The three *chaussées* from Auch, Lombez and St-Gaudens converged on the Patte d'Oie.

On the right bank, the medieval walls extended north from the present Place St Pierre to the Boulevard Lascrosses and circled round to the Place Wilson, and then followed the Boulevard Carnot to the Jardin Royal and back to the Garonne. An outer line of defence was formed by the 100-metre-wide Canal du Midi (also known as the Canal Royal or Canal des Deux Mers, built by Pierre-Paul Riquet and opened to traffic in 1681), which surrounded a large part of the city, entering the Garonne near the Petit Gragnague. It was crossed by a series of bridges, in succession from the Ponts Jumeaux (close to the Garonne) by the Pont des Minimes (named after the convent beyond its north bank) on the *chaussée* to Montauban; the Pont de Matabiau (north-east), the exit to the Albi road, traversing the hamlet of Croix d'Aurade (now usually referred to as Daurade but frequently misspelt d'Orade) to cross the River Hers (a tributary of the Garonne, entering that river some twelve miles north of the city) and also a by-road to the hamlet of Périole, likewise with a bridge spanning the Hers. Between these two roads rose the Mamelon de la Pujade or Pujade hill, an extension of a long ridge known as Mont Rave or the Calvinet, which dominated Toulouse from the east by some 250 feet, between the canal and the Hers. Each bridge over the northern sector of the canal had been strongly fortified, and guns had been mounted on the bastions overlooking them.

The Périole road cut through the descending slope of the ridge below the Great Redoubt, which defended its northern extremity. East of the city walls lay the suburb of

St-Etienne, where the canal was crossed by another two bridges, from which the road to Lavaur forked left over the ridge to the Pont de Balma on the Hers; the right-hand fork climbed towards the redoubt of La Sypière before descending to the bridge of Les Bordas and continuing east to the village of Caraman. From the southern entrance of the city two roads diverged. One ran due south-east, crossing the canal by the Pont des Demoiselles and skirting the less abrupt southern slope of the Calvinet ridge past the hamlet of Montaudran and its bridge spanning the Hers; and the other was the main *chaussée* leading south, later veering south-east to Villefranche-de-Lauragais for Carcassonne, keeping to the south bank of the canal as far as Baziège.

As the occupation of Mont Rave by enemy artillery would place the city entirely at their mercy, it was essential that Soult included it in his perimeter of defence. Both conscript and civilian labour had been busy fortifying the height, digging lines of earthworks between the five redoubts along its summit, including the Great Redoubt at its northern end and the Sypière at its southern. Only at the last minute were any fortifications thrown up between the Garonne and the canal south of the city, where the Carcassonne road entered.

Wellington planned to span the Garonne upstream with his pontoons, dragged so laboriously from the coast, and to attack Toulouse from the south. To do this he would have to place his bridge under cover of darkness and establish a strong foothold before Soult's troops swarmed out to resist him. There appeared to be a convenient site at the village of Portet, hardly five miles south-west of the city. To distract Soult's attention, on the afternoon of 27 March Wellington ordered the 4th, 6th and Light Divisions, together with cavalry, to advance towards the outer defences of St-Cyprien, then being held by D'Erlon's two divisions (Daricau's and Darmagnac's), and this was accomplished after minor skirmishing at the bridge of Tournefeuille, on the River Touch. Soult, assuming that this was merely a demonstration in force, was convinced that the Allies intended forcing the Garonne *downstream*, and sent four cavalry regiments to patrol its banks north of the city, leaving only one picquet to the south.

Hill's divisions, now at Muret, five miles south-west of Portet, were warned to be ready to cross the moment the bridge had been laid; but, when it was placed across the swollen river, it was found to be too short by five pontoons and that it was not possible to build out trestles from the near bank. Wellington, however exasperated he must have been, had to accept the situation, brought about by his refusal to believe Colonel Elphinstone's assurance, made before leaving St-Jean-de-Luz, that he had insufficient pontoons with which to span a really large river. However, when writing to Hope on the 26th, Wellington had admitted that 'the Garonne is too full and large for our bridge, if not we shall be in that town I hope immediately'—as though he did not expect Soult to make any determined resistance.

Although frustrated here—and Soult was not even aware of the attempted crossing, so casual was his watch on this stretch of the stream—Wellington, impatient to cross, was not to be thwarted: the bridge was taken up and relaid slightly further upstream at

Pinsaguel, beyond the confluence of the Garonne and the narrower Ariège, although this meant that both rivers would have to be spanned. This was done, with some difficulty, during the night of the 30th: by the following morning Hill, together with 13,000 men, was over the Garonne unopposed. Soult's nearest cavalry vedette was at Vieille Toulouse (some three miles further east, opposite Portet), and a day elapsed before he was alerted. It was found that the nearest bridge over the Ariège was at the village of Cintegabelle, some fifteen miles upstream, and that there were no pontoons remaining with which to span that river. Hill halted his infantry there and sent a party of dragoons across to explore. Another party had found a solitary boat at Venerque, but after having ridden as far east as Villefranche they had returned to report that no passable roads led north through the hilly or waterlogged country between the Ariège and the Canal du Midi.

On hearing this equally frustrating news, Wellington reluctantly ordered Hill to counter-march to Pinsaguel, where the Garonne was re-crossed during the night of 1 April, after which the pontoons were taken up, replaced on their travelling carriages and dragged north. Several days had been completely wasted, largely due—and unusually—to Wellington's having failed to acquire adequate information about local conditions in advance of this second, petulantly made crossing. If scouts had been sent ahead, they would have reported back that the terrain and lack of communication would make the operation here additionally hazardous: but then Soult might have been alerted by their presence, and Hill would have been attacked in strength when only half his men were across.

Soult, belatedly advised of these movements, had sent Clausel's divisions to counter any attempt on Hill's part to pass the Ariège, but Clausel likewise found the right bank as impassable because of the lack of any practicable road, and so Soult, riding to a viewpoint at Vieille Toulouse to survey the Allied troops, then at a standstill, came to the conclusion that this had been another feint and that Wellington intended making his main attack at St-Cyprien or from the north, as he had first assumed he would. He therefore concentrated on further strengthening the city's defences, together with those of St-Cyprien, by mounting additional 40 guns of position from the arsenal along the walls and in his redoubts. He would have twice the number of guns the Allies had brought with them, and half of them were of heavier calibre and with a longer range.

By 31 March Headquarters were at Seysses, a village east of St-Lys and north-west of Muret. That morning the English mail sent on the 16th arrived with the disconcerting news that the operations being conducted by General Graham at Bergen-op-Zoom had failed, and that reinforcements intended for Wellington might be sent to Holland in consequence.

On 3 April Headquarters moved to Colomiers, and two days later the civil departments settled into Cornbarrieu, further north on the Grenade road, approached by clayey by-roads deep in mud churned up by the quantity of animals passing. Larpent records that he and Dr McGrigor, among others, were lucky enough to find themselves in a local château, which provided a panoramic view towards Toulouse—'the great big town where the French are', as the Irishmen described it.

After spending the whole of 2 April surveying the banks of the Garonne downstream, Wellington's staff reported that the most convenient spot from which to cross would appear to be at a bend in the river some eleven miles north, between Merville and Grenade, where the west bank commanded the more wooded far bank, on which coppices would mask the accumulation of troops. The hamlet of La Capellette, referred to by Oman, does not appear on modern maps, but the crossing was probably made between the present hamlet of La Dupine and the Château de Valentine.

The following afternoon, the pontoon train, escorted by the 4th Division, was ordered to be transported north from Pinsaguel that night by any practicable by-roads. The main body of the army would follow, with Freire's Spaniards marching along parallel tracks further west. The Light Division was to remain facing St-Cyprien until relieved by Hill's units, and then move to a position half way between there and the crossing point chosen. Should Soult make a sally in force from the bridgehead, Hill was to draw back the Light Division and Friedrich von Arentchildt's K.G.L. dragoons and remain on the defensive behind the Touch, where, with 18,000 men at his disposal, he should be able to hold his own until reinforced by Beresford. If no sally were made, and Soult were seen to be marching against the bulk of the Allied army by then over the Garonne, he was to attack the outer *enceinte* of St-Cyprien, which would compel Soult to rush back a proportion of his men to reinforce D'Erlon.

The pontoon bridge was laid in four hours. By dusk on the 4th, 19,000 men were across, unopposed, including the bulk of the cavalry and three divisional field batteries. With a cavalry screen well ahead, and also across the Hers, the army bivouacked between the two rivers, here only two miles apart.

Unfortunately, it started to pour with rain during the afternoon: the Garonne swelled, and the last squadrons of cavalry were obliged to lead their mounts across the ominously swaying pontoons. The bridge mooring broke soon after dark, and it was only with difficulty that the pontoons were drawn back to the west bank, with the exception of one which drifted rapidly downstream, leaving the Light Division, the K.G.L. dragoons, Freire's men and the reserve artillery marooned on the west bank. Beresford's troops were now divided, and many were left without their tents and baggage; many more, according to Larpent, were barefooted and awaiting a distribution of shoes.*

Although the missing pontoon was retrieved uninjured on a sand bank several miles downstream near Verdun, it was impossible to re-lay the bridge until the morning of the 7th, although Wellington was rowed across the Garonne repeatedly to confer with Beresford. Meanwhile the 22 guns of the reserve artillery were placed on the higher west bank, from

---

* It might be emphasised that at this time boots were referred to as 'shoes' to distinguish them from cavalry riding boots. There was no difference between the left and right with these shoes, and they were supplied by the army contractors not only as cheaply as possible but also without lace-holes, which had to be punched by the men themselves, often by a jab with a bayonet. They were liable to disintegrate far more rapidly than those of the French, making shoes pulled from the feet of their dead all the more valuable as they were of much better quality.

where they could enfilade any advance Soult might make against the Allied positions opposite them. In the event, he preferred to remain within his fortress, being under the impression that a much higher proportion of the Allied were facing him there than was the case. He did little to molest them—although they had hoped he would attack—except to float trees and barges loaded with stones, dead horses and a large old boat ('which struck a pontoon, and went down itself'), hoping that with the strong swirling current of the Garonne they might break the bridge. They did not: most of this flotsam ran aground before reaching the position of the pontoons, which happened to be drawn back again to the west bank at the time. Meanwhile Allied light cavalry beyond the Hers had cut the Montauban–Toulouse road and captured a dispatch from Montauban complaining of the deterioration of morale there: it was unlikely that any raid on their rear would be made from that quarter.

With the flow of Garonne subsiding during the night of the 7th, the pontoon bridge was re-laid the next morning and the remainder of Beresford's force crossed to the east bank. The Light Division was instructed to wait further south at the hamlet of Seilh, for Wellington now ordered the bridge to be placed there, anxious as he was to shorten his communications with Hill's troops, still threatening St-Cyprien. Larpent recounts two anecdotes concerning the positioning of the bridge. An engineer wanting to measure the breadth of the Garonne had shouted across to a French cavalry vedette patrolling the far bank, intent on stopping any such attempt. After some minutes of dialogue, and trying unsuccessfully to distract the enemy's attention and get him to move away, the engineer 'pretended that the calls of nature were imperative. The Frenchman, out of decency, withdrew. The engineer popped out his sextant, took the angle, &c., and was off.' When a convenient place was suggested to Wellington, he went himself to the spot with two other officers to see for himself. 'Concealing his General's hat with an oil-skin, he got into conversation with a French vedette, dismounted, got down to the water-side, looked all about them, saw all he wished, and came away'. This was, in Larpent's opinion, risking too much, but on the other hand no French soldier could even imagine the commander of the Allied forces going about thus with only two aides.

The time it took to remove and relay the pontoon bridge at Seilh was longer than calculated, and it was not until 3.00 on the afternoon of the 9th that the Light Division could even start to cross: it was certainly too late to begin the offensive movement planned for that day. Larpent records that Wellington 'was more vexed, and in a greater state of anger, than he usually is when things go wrong, even without any good cause.'

By this time the Allied troops had started to proceed south towards the northern perimeter of Toulouse, with Soult's cavalry falling back before them. Those on either side of the Hers broke each bridge as they retired south, with the exception of that at Croix d'Aurade, where Pierre Soult, who, with Vial's Brigade at the time, was surprised by a charge by Vivian's cavalry before he was able to destroy it. Vivian himself was disabled by a shot in the arm, but Ross's brigade was able to occupy the bridge, where 120 prisoners were taken.

By 8.00 the next morning (10 April, Easter Sunday), once the Light Division was over, which was well before dawn, very precise orders had been issued from Headquarters in the village of St-Jory, seven miles north-west of Toulouse.

While both Wellington and Soult were perfectly aware that troops of the Northern Allies had entered Paris on 31 March, little further news of import had been received since then. Soult had no reason to think that it was other than his duty to continue to resist Wellington for as long as possible, while Wellington regarded the destruction of any part of Napoleon's military machine as essential. Even with Paris lost, Napoleon would find Soult's army a very useful force with which to carry on hostilities, and Wellington was not prepared to let that happen. If he could evict Soult from Toulouse, the city might well follow the example of Bordeaux and precipitate a more extensive rising on behalf of the Bourbons—not that he was particularly in favour of them.

Although the redoubts on Mont Rave had been further strengthened during the days Wellington had spent transferring his army across the Garonne, he realised that only from the north could he attack Toulouse with any hope of success, even if it was unlikely that he could force any of the fortified bridges spanning the canal—which itself formed a broad moat protecting two-thirds of the city's perimeter. For the first time during the war, the ensuing encounter would not be an offensive or defensive battle fought in open country by lines of troops facing each other, nor would it be it the storming of a walled fortress: it was an attack on a strongly entrenched position, and Wellington had to deploy his forces in the appropriate manner. Hill was to maintain his demonstration against St-Cyprien and to 'regulate his operations in accordance with what was going on east of the river': it was vital that he detained as many enemy troops as he could for as long as possible.

Abutting the east bank of the Garonne was Picton's 3rd Division, extended to the east as far as the Albi road by the Light Division. Brisbane's brigade faced the canal near the Ponts Jumeaux, with Power's Portuguese to his left followed by Keane's brigade near the Convent of Minimes; Frederic von Arentschildt's cavalry were in their rear and towards the hamlet of Croix d'Aurade. A 'considerable part' of each division was to remain in reserve; the forward units were not expected to force their way across the canal but, by demonstrations against the bridges and locks, threaten to do so, and thus keep the enemy fully occupied along this northern stretch of their defences.

Freire had specifically requested that his two Spanish divisions be given an important part in the attack, and they were allocated the Great Redoubt at the northern end of Mont Rave as their objective; but they would have to occupy the separate knoll of La Pujade first. Freire was ordered to advance in two columns behind a skirmishing line to take the hamlet of that name, keeping one to the west of the Albi road; the other would press along the *chaussée*. Once the Pujade hill was in their hands, a Portuguese battery would take possession and start firing towards the Great Redoubt. The Light Division would be keeping in touch with Freire's right, and Charles Manners' cavalry would protect his left and be ready to give it immediate support.

Further east stood Beresford's force, waiting to advance south along the low-lying and partly flooded ground below Mont Rave and flanking the River Hers. Made up of the 4th and 6th Divisions, with Somerset's Hussar battalion in advance to cover the left flank of the 4th, this force, once it reached or drew near enough to the far right of the enemy position, was to deploy into two lines and ascend north-west up the slope of the Calvinet and attack its defenders. It was left to Beresford to decide when and where to turn. Two hussar regiments—temporarily commanded by von Grüben, Vivian having been wounded—were to push along the east bank of the Hers and try to seize any unbroken bridges and keep the French cavalry at arm's length from the left flank of Beresford's advance along the west bank.

Soult had deployed his troops as follows. Maransin's Division faced Hill at St-Cyprien, with orders to fall back on his strong inner line of defence rather than try to hold the outer. He was left fifteen heavy guns from the arsenal; the divisional battery was moved to Mont Rave, as was Taupin's division also, once the defences were completed. The latter, as a general reserve, waited in column on the lower western slope of the ridge, just beyond the suburb of St-Etienne, east of the canal. Daricau's division faced Picton's along the canal front, with a second line of troops, together with part of Travot's conscripts, positioned behind the old city walls, although it was thought unlikely that the canal bridges could be forced. Some guns of position had been mounted along this stretch also. The sector east of the Minimes' bridge was held by Darmagnac's division, one brigade of which stood beyond the Matabiau bridge over the canal, which here swung south, and on the lower, north-western slope of Mont Rave; the other would be held in reserve to support Villatte if required. Villatte's division occupied the north end of the ridge, including the Great Redoubt, with the Pujade knoll, on which two guns were placed, as an advanced bastion defended by St Pol's brigade, although it had been accepted that, as it was slightly isolated, it should be withdrawn to join Lamorandière's brigade when seriously attacked. The remaining two-thirds of the ridge was occupied by Harispe's division of thirteen battalions. The Colombette redoubt, the Mas des Augustins and the adjacent entrenchments were occupied by Baurot's brigade, while Dauture's held positions further south, including the Sypière redoubt, facing south-east down the Caraman road.* Berton's cavalry, most of it still on the east bank of the Hers, if driven back, was to destroy each bridge as it passed. Two of his regiments were to remain on the west bank—where, in the

---

* The French redoubts were approximately in the following positions: the Great Redoubt stood on the Plateau de Jolimont, between the Rue de Périole and the Rue des Redoutes, off the north-east end of the Avenue de Pompidou (south of which a 32-metre-high commemorative obelisk was erected between 1835 and 1839). The Colombette redoubt stood where the Chemin de Caillebens (between the cemeteries of Terre Cabade and Salonique) meets the Avenue de la Gloire, with the Mas des Augustins a short distance further east. Another redoubt stood adjacent to the junction of the Boulevard des Crêtes and the Avenue de Castres; and the Sypière redoubt abutted the Avenue Raymond Naves at its junction with the Chemin de Duroux.

event, they retired before Somerset's advance—and, if pressed, would wheel to the south-west and take up a position defending Dauture's flank near the Courrège (or Corriège) farm, east of the Pont des Demoiselles (presumably near the *caserne* or barracks of that name). Vial's cavalry vedettes were posted below the ridge, with its main body near the southern end.

At 5.00 in the morning of 10 April, O'Callaghan's brigade stormed with ease the fortified Bourrassol mill, an outlying defence abutting the Garonne north-west of St-Cyprien, and turned south towards the Patte d'Oie to outflank the exterior earthworks, which, together with those circling back to the Garonne, were evacuated by Maransin. O'Callaghan was supported by Barnes's brigade. They kept up a bickering fire against the main line of French defences for several hours. A Portuguese battery was brought forward and, having found good cover, exchanged a sporadic cannonade with the enemy. To their left, Maxwell's battery was moved towards the Garonne bank to enfilade Daricau's entrenchments at Les Ponts Jumeaux. None of Hill's other units were brought into action on this west front. His total losses that day were 82.

At about midday, leaving only 2,000 men behind the St-Cyprien fortifications, Rouget's brigade was unobtrusively withdrawn and marched through the city to reinforce those heavily engaged on Mont Rave. Inexplicably, Wellington did not withdraw two or three Allied brigades from the St-Cyprien front also; even if it took time for them to cross the pontoons at Seilh and reach the area of serious fighting on Mont Rave, they might have taken the place of the Light Division, which could then have been deployed to more advantage.

On the right bank of the Garonne, Picton carried out his orders, driving back outlying picquets and shelling the fortifications guarding the canal crossings, but at about 7.00 he became impatient, instructing Brisbane to occupy the large farm of Petit Gragnague and its outbuildings, which was done at some loss. Then, having got some cover, Picton—contrary to orders, which were to demonstrate only—tried to storm the palisaded Ponts Jumeaux bridgehead and fortified buildings near it, where his men suffered severely to no effect. Alten's Light Division did little more than send some *Caçadores* to skirmish with Soult's picquets, as ordered, while Bean's battery kept up shelling the fortifications oppo-site it.

Further east, Freire's 7,300 Spaniards approached the Pujade knoll from Croix d'Aurade, which they occupied after slight resistance only, St Pol's brigade retiring as advised. Here they halted while Victor von Arentscheldt's six-gun battery, together with four 18-pound-ers, was dragged up into position from which the Great Redoubt facing them was soon under fire. The infantry deployed—three brigades in one line and two others behind them, with Marcilla's remaining in reserve on the lower slope of the knoll—ready to assault the redoubt the moment Freire, as instructed, saw Beresford's units turn to ascend the south-eastern slopes of Mont Rave and gave the order to advance. All seemed to be going to plan.

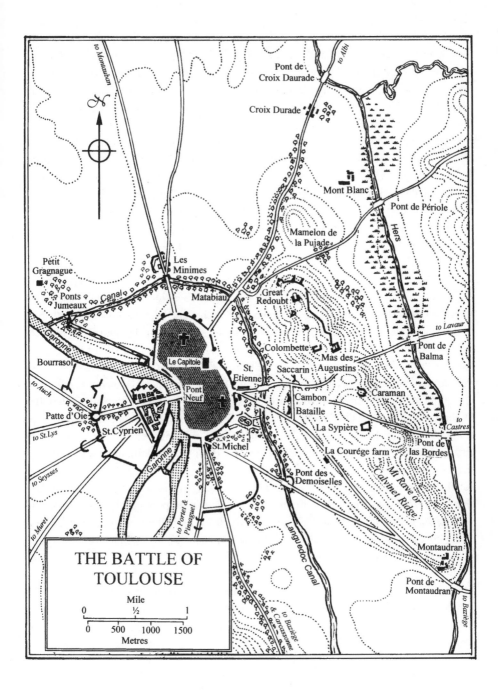

to Montauban

to Albi

Pont de
Croix Daurade

Croix Durade

Mont Blanc

Pont de Périole

Pétit
Gragnague

Les
Minimes

Mamelon de
la Pujade

Hers

Ponts
Jumeaux

Canal

Matabiau

Great
Redoubt

to Lavaur

Garonne

Colombette

Pont de
Balma

Bourrasol

Le Capitole

St.
Etienne

Saccarin

Mas des
Augustins

to Auch

Pont
Neuf

Cambon

Caraman

Patte d'Oie

to St.Lys

St.Cyprien

Bataille

La Sypière

to
Castres

St.Michel

La Courége farm

Pont de
las Bordes

to Seysses

Garonne

Mt Rave or
Calvinet Rudge

to Muret

to Portet &
Pinsaguel

Pont des
Demoiselles

Montaudran

THE BATTLE OF
TOULOUSE

Languedoc Canal

Pont de
Montaudran

to Baziège

Mile

0   ½   1

0   500   1000   1500
Metres

to Baziège & Carcassone

Beresford's columns had started their flank march in the meantime, but the speed of this advance had been slowed down by the rain-sodden, low-lying ploughed fields near the Hers. There was then no road parallel to the river, only cross-tracks descending to it from over the Mont Rave or at either end of the ridge.* The divisional batteries found it particularly heavy going, their wheels frequently up to the axles in mud, so much so that Beresford told them not even to attempt to keep up but to turn off on to slightly higher ground a mile or so south of the farm of Mont Blanc and fire uphill at the flank of the Great Redoubt. The going was slightly easier for Somerset's and von Grüben's cavalry, pushing south parallel to each other, but they were unable to get in direct touch as Berton's cavalry, retiring before them, blew up the bridges of Périole, Balma and Lasbordes before they had a chance to stop them. Cole's and Clinton's divisions were undisturbed for the first mile of their trudge, until Anson's and Lambert's brigade, on the right of their respective columns, came within range of the guns of Harispe's division near the Mas de Augustins redoubt. Luckily, as the fields flanking the Hers were sodden, little damage was done by the French artillery: their rounds of shot did not ricochet but sank directly into the earth.

At about 9.30, presumably on hearing Beresford's artillery opening fire, but certainly well before he could *see* his infantry commencing to wheel into line, Freire ordered his men forward. They advanced in good order, with their right-hand battalions slightly held back should they be counter-attacked from near the Matabiau bridge, and drove back the French skirmishing line. Even when under heavy fire from both artillery and the entrenched positions, they lost little momentum until reaching a deep cutting where the Périole road cut across the slope, barely 50 yards from the redoubt. Down into the cutting they plunged to take momentary breath, sheltering from both infantry and artillery fire. When their officers started to urge them up the far bank, they hung back and found themselves under fire from both the Matabiau guns enfilading the whole length of the cutting, on which they had been trained, but also from Villatte's infantry, which, springing forward from their trenches, rained down a hail of bullets into the struggling mass caught in the sunken road. Their right flank and rear were also attacked by Darmagnac's units from the Matabiau bridge. In great confusion, the survivors of the three battalions managed somehow to extricate themselves from the trap, their retreat to the Pujade knoll being covered by one of Marcilla's regiments (on their left wing) until called back on Wellington's orders.†

Meanwhile von Arentchildt's guns had been turned on Darmagnac's men, Manners' dragoons rode ahead to be level with the Pujade and the Light Division moved forward in case Soult should make a counter-attack. On observing Freire's repulse, Wellington sent an aide to Beresford advising him that it might be sensible to attack the ridge from where he

---

* This area is now traversed by the fast-flowing traffic of the eastern bypass of Toulouse, skirting playing-field, etc.
† The gallantry of both that regiment and their colonel, Leonardo de Sicilia, who was killed, was referred to in Wellington's next dispatch.

was, but Beresford preferred to keep to his original plan and pushed ahead to reach a point due east of the Sypière redoubt. Here both divisions were wheeled into three lines, with the 4th Division in advance—Anson's brigade in the first, Vasconcellos's behind it and Ross's in third place—while Lambert's, Douglas's and Pack's brigades of the 6th Division extended the deployment, advancing on their right, having also a rocket party with them.

When Soult saw Beresford's divisions continuing their line of march he ordered Taupin's units, held in reserve, to move south until level with those of Beresford's and then veer left over the skyline and charge downhill on to the flank of the long column. Although Taupin's artillery remained where it had been parked, Maransin's guns were ordered south, as was Darmagnac's reserve brigade from behind the Matabiau position. As an additional reinforcement, Rouget's brigade of Maransin's division at St-Cyprien was also sent for. Apparently Taupin found the terrain behind the crest of the ridge very slippery, and, although delayed by having to cross both the transverse sunken roads (to the Balma and Lasbordes bridges), arrived at his new position in good time, as had a regiment of Vial's *chasseurs* and six squadrons of Berton's horse, likewise brought forward.

Without waiting for Darmagnac's brigade to come up, and as Cole's brigades, with Clinton's slightly in echelon to their right, were already some way up the long slope towards the Sypière redoubt, Taupin led his two brigades, each massed in column of battalions, over the crest and hurtling downhill towards the Allied lines. As described by John Malcolm (42nd Foot), 'Darkening the whole hill, flanked by clouds of cavalry, and covered by the fire of their redoubts, the enemy came down upon us like a torrent, their generals and field-officers riding in front and waving their hats amidst the shouts of multitudes, resembling the roar of the sea.'

Although only Maransin's battery was able to play on Clinton's men, now also within musketry range from the Sypière redoubt and another work further north, the descent of Vial's cavalry looked dangerous enough to cause Pack to form square with the 79th on his right flank. Meanwhile Somerset's hussars had ridden up in time to keep Berton's cavalry at bay near the outer flank of Anson's brigade.

Taupin's massed infantry was given no time to deploy, and, after facing several volleys in which no ball could fail to find its mark, Rey's battalion started to lose confidence. It was while attempting to reanimate them that Taupin himself fell mortally wounded. The battalion then wavered, broke in the face of the implacable ascent of the Allied lines and poured back north past the Sypière redoubt, the garrison of which then evacuated it, panic-stricken. Gasquet's brigade, caught in cross-fire between Anson's and Lambert's units, after facing a shower of Congreve rockets likewise turned tail and sought safety down the west slope of the ridge, rallying at the so-called Saccarin–Cambon–Bataille entrenchments (named after the owners of houses in the suburb of St-Etienne which had been fortified to form a secondary line of defence close to the canal).

Soult, dismayed by the melting away of his right flank, sent in Darmagnac's men (Menne's brigade) and Rouget's, which had just reached Mont Rave, and repositioned

Maransin's battery, with which, together with that of Taupin's (brought forward on the initiative of its commander, Lapène), he hoped to resist the Allies' impending assault.

But Beresford was not ready, and a lull intervened while his own two batteries, left below the ridge, were dragged laboriously uphill. An aide was sent to Wellington to confirm that he would advance from his commanding position the moment the guns reached him. This should coincide with another attack by Freire from the north. The 4th Division was redeployed along the upper slope of the Calvinet below the Sypière redoubt, its left flank protected by Somerset's hussars as far down as the Courrège or Corriège farm, east of the Pont des Demoiselles, while the 6th was positioned at right angles to it, where a deep cutting formed by the Lavaur road sheltered its front from the French batteries placed near the Mas des Augustins redoubt. Douglas's Portuguese brigade was to the left of Pack's, with Lambert's men in reserve. Meanwhile, Beresford was reinforced by von Grüben's hussars, which, pressing south, had charged and scattered Berton's cavalry guarding the Montaudran bridge. This, like the rest, had been mined, but they succeeded in occupying it before the bridge guard had a chance to fire the mine. Crossing the Hers, the whole cavalry brigade galloped north-west up the *chaussée* towards the fortified Pont des Demoiselles spanning the canal, guarded by a detachment only of Travot's conscripts, and deployed between the farm and the canal.

Picton meanwhile, having seen the retreat of the Spaniards, had jumped to the conclusion, as the sound of firing further south had died down during the lull, that Beresford may have been repulsed also, and that it was up to him—regardless of orders to the contrary—to make another diversionary attack on the Ponts Jumeaux. At 2.00 he made three desperate attempts to force the crossing with successive regiments of Brisbane's brigade (except for a wing of the 88th), in which Brisbane was wounded, Colonel Thomas Forbes of the 45th was killed (and later buried in the vicinity) and his division sustained another 350 casualties. While enfilading fire from Maxwell's battery at St-Cyprien caused considerable damage and losses among any French units without cover, the whole exploit was deplorable and did nothing to relieve the pressure on troops elsewhere on the battlefield.

By about 2.30, after great difficulty had been experienced hauling them up the eastern slope of the Calvinet, Beresford's guns were positioned near the Sypière redoubt and started shelling the enemy emplacements near the canalside suburb of St-Etienne, partly to deter any flank attack from that direction. Augustus Frazer states that the whole face of the hill was 'exceedingly intersected with deep hollow roads; the soil is stiff heavy clay, in which with difficulty horses could move out of a walk. Aware of this, the enemy had judiciously made roads of planks, as communications for his artillery from one work to another.' Frazer also records that at about this time, when looking about, he noticed that the steeples and roofs of Toulouse were covered with spectators of the sanguinary scene.

Freire was desperate to re-gild his faded laurels, and, having eventually rallied his Spaniards, advanced again against the Great Redoubt, this time not frontally but from the side. Ordering even his personal escort to join him, Freire led them forward. Many of

his senior officers were killed or wounded in the ensuing action: they reached the outworks but could get no further, and after bickering for some time against the entrenched
enemy, they retired in confusion again towards the nearest brigade of the Light Division
and Manners' cavalry. According to Captain Arthur Kennedy, this had been placed by
Wellington 'in rear of them to cut down any that might again attempt to run'. Although
the Spaniards failed in their main objective, Villatte's attention had been fully occupied
keeping them at arms' length while Beresford was assaulting his defences further south.

Pack was waiting impassively for the order to continue the advance of the 6th Division
when a perfect storm of shot and shell commenced. One of his aides had his horse shot
under him, and soon afterwards Pack received a ball through his leg. He rode to the rear,
had his wound dressed and in a few minutes returned again to his brigade. The 6th now
emerged from the shelter of the Lavour road cutting and advanced towards Harispe's line,
now redeployed to oppose them, as was his artillery, until then facing east from the Mas
des Augustins.

The Mas des Augustins and Colombette redoubt were charged by two Highland
regiments (42nd and 79th), and they succeeded in breaking into both from the intercon-
necting trench. After making slight resistance only, their garrisons made off. John
Malcolm describes the event just before being disabled by a shot splintering a bone in
his arm, and taken prisoner:

> Amidst the clouds of smoke in which they were curtained, the whole line of redoubts would every
> now and again start into view amidst the wild and frightful blaze, and then vanish again into
> utter darkness. . . . Our men were mowed down in sections. I saw six of the company to which I
> belonged fall together, as if swept away by the discharge of one gun; and the whole ground over
> which we rushed, was covered with the dead. The redoubts were erected along the side of the
> road, and defended by broad ditches filled with water. Just before our troops reached the obstruc-
> tion, however, the enemy deserted them, and fled in all directions, leaving their last line of
> strongholds in our possession; but they still possessed two fortified houses close by, from which
> they kept up a galling and destructive fire.

Although now under artillery fire, the Highlanders—in some disorder—pushed on
until counter-attacked by Harispe's reserve of three regiments (probably reinforced by
some of Darmagnac's units), when they were forced back through the redoubts and suffered very heavy casualties (their total losses that day were 628 of the 1,228 present,
although only 73 were killed outright). They were not pursued further, the French preferring to reoccupy their redoubts, from which they were ejected briefly by the 91st and one
of Douglas's Portuguese battalions before counter-attacking yet again. It was not until
Beresford sent in Lambert's brigade, held in reserve, that Harispe's troops broke, fleeing
downhill towards the St-Etienne positions, although a few fell back on Villatte's rear.

Many years later, Cole stated that in his opinion the French had fought a hundred
times better at Orthez, and that he had never seen them fight so ill as at Toulouse, but it
had been an extremely bloody engagement. Frazer considered the action one of the
sharpest he had witnessed, and in none had he seen Wellington 'so animated; generally

quiet, and even apparently indifferent, the moment of danger arouses him, and shows at once the great man.' At about 3.30 Harispe had a foot shot off by a cannon ball, and Baurot, who took over from him, was also wounded: 64 of the 214 officers in Harispe's division were killed or disabled. Pack, although wounded, remained mounted until the battle was over. Douglas was also wounded, and some 1,500 of the 5,000 present in the 6th Division were casualties.

With skirmishers of the 6th edging forward in the rear of the Great Redoubt, Villatte's troops were in danger of being surrounded. Most of the horses of his artillery park were shot, as were a number of his gunners, and before long their trenches were being enfiladed by fire from an additional battery sent up by Wellington which had unlimbered near the Colombette redoubt. A brigade of the Light Division started to push ahead in support of a partial advance by the surviving men of Freire's divisions, who, at about 6.00, once Villatte's units had been ordered to evacuate their redoubt, moved in to replace them.

Arthur Kennedy was perhaps 'jumping the gun' in stating that 'About 2 o'clock it was evident that the day was ours, the heights had been carried except this one [the Great Redoubt] and the enemy's coaches caravans wagons etc. were all soon flying out of the town in full retreat.' Kennedy was sent down to cut them off, but although the canal prevented the 18th Dragoons from doing so, he was able to 'take six boats laden with arms, ammunition and provisions and about a hundred prisoners who were endeavouring to get off up the canal, several of them severely wounded.' Kennedy then rode back over the whole field of battle, 'one of the most horrid' he had seen.

Most of Villatte's guns had to be manhandled down to and across the canal, where his men redeployed in expectation of an attack developing in that sector, but no such movement occurred. Dusk was already falling, and the caissons of Beresford's divisional batteries were almost exhausted, as were those of the Portuguese guns on the Pujade knoll, which had been in action for seven hours. There were intermittent exchanges of infantry fire between the skirmishing line of the 4th Division and the enemy bridgehead close to the canal, but this died down soon after dark as the men of both armies settled to sleep, exhausted by the severe fighting in which many units had been engaged since dawn.

Malcolm described it as being 'a bright, beautiful evening', as he was dragged down from the ridge as a prisoner into the town, where, about 100 yards from the eastern entrance,

. . . sat Marshal Soult and his staff on horseback. He was looking earnestly towards the heights, from which he saw his troops beaten back in all directions. I passed close by the Marshal and his generals, who eyed me with a look of grave curiosity. At last I arrived in the town, which exhibited such a scene of confusion as I never witnessed. Almost the whole French army occupied the streets: the house-tops were covered with crowds, and the windows seemed bursting with the population. All was terror and excitement; for Soult was determined to make a stand even in the town, and Wellington commanded a position from which he could reduce it to ashes. I had no sooner entered the streets, than I became so faint and exhausted by fatigue and loss of blood, that I sunk down upon the ground. In a few minutes a French surgeon made his appearance and examined my wound, which he laid open with the knife at both orifices; but so much was my arm deadened by the ball, that I scarcely felt the operation. As soon as it was over, I was escorted by a file of *gens d'armes* to an [sic] hospital, prepared for the occupation of the wounded. As we passed along the streets, crowds of ladies rushed out from their houses, and presented me with wines and cordials; and being much exhausted and parched with thirst, I drank largely of every thing they offered me.

Many died of their wounds. James Anton records that Lieutenant Farquharson, who had befriended him, had fallen by his side on the road skirting the redoubts before they were entered, and that they were so closely engaged that he was unable at the time to render him any assistance. When the action closed he returned and found him:

> He had been for a few minutes in the power of the enemy, and had been stripped of his sash, sword, epaulettes, and money, but no other violence had been offered to him. I got him conveyed to a house which was enclosed in another redoubt, and now filled in every place with our wounded. From this he was removed on the morning of the 12th, to Toulouse, where he died of his wounds.

Little movement occurred on the 11th, although some had expected the fighting to recommence as firing had begun again at 4.00 in the morning and continued intermittently until 8.00, after which it lessened.

It was not until the afternoon that more ammunition for the Allied artillery was distributed, having been brought over the Garonne from a park behind Hill's position. Once the firing had ceased, the wounded were carried to the rear and the dead buried. Allied casualties had been high—a total of 4,558, of which 655 were killed. Freire's Spaniards alone had 1,922 casualties, of which 205 were killed, and it is not known how many of his wounded were mortally so or only slightly. French casualties, officially, were 3,236, including 322 killed.

John Cooke and another officer rode towards the cutting where Freire's men had been repulsed. He described it as having

> . . . steep banks . . . at least 25 feet in depth, with two or three narrow pathways by which the Spaniards had descended in hopes of obtaining a little shelter. This spot was strewn with heaps of slain, piled on top of each other in strange confusion. Many had tumbled over the precipitous banks and remained stuck on the twisted bayonets on whose points they had fallen. . . . Some were jammed in the crowd, and propped up in an erect posture against the bank; others were standing on their heads, or sprawling with legs and arms spread out. . . . Almost the whole of the cadaverous dead were without caps, which in the melee had been knocked off and were intermixed with knapsacks, breast-plates, broken arms, bayonets, and swords. . . . No voice broke on the stillness that reigned over the lacerated remains of the swarthy Spaniards. . . . The sight was too horrible to look upon, and we hastily remounted . . .

Wellington was now taking stock of the situation. Although he was in a dominating position, it was not his intention to bombard the city, nor was it likely that Soult would allow himself to be besieged. He might try to cut his way out, but the only practicable road remaining to him was the *chaussée* leading to Carcassonne, still on the far side of the broad canal. Before Wellington could even consider taking further action against Soult, it was vital that he replaced Beresford's battered units with Hill's or with the Light Division, both practically unscathed, as were a high proportion of Picton's units and most of his cavalry. Redeploying them, even if only to counter Soult's next move, would take time: any further action would have to be deferred for a day at least.

Soult, on his part, had already sent a dispatch to Suchet on the evening of the 10th, urgently requesting him to march his divisions towards Toulouse, where he was in grave danger and might be forced to cut his way out. Soult admitted that the fighting had been 'most bloody' and, although his adversary had suffered severely, the Allies now occupied a position commanding the city: although he would defend himself if attacked, it was unlikely that he could hold out for long, ending 'If communications are still open on the 11th, further news will be sent.' There is no suggestion here that he had beaten the Allies—rather the reverse. By next morning, having conferred with his corps commanders, Soult sent off another dispatch, this time to Clarke at Paris, stating that, whether attacked or not, the army had to escape that same night, otherwise it would be trapped. Even so, it was very possible that he would have to fight his way across the bridge at Baziège on the Carcassonne road should Wellington have detached any units to cut that line of retreat. However, while making the necessary preparations for the evacuation, he would continue to display a bold front. Augustus Frazer states that it was largely on the advice of General Darmagnac that Soult was persuaded not to remain obstinately in Toulouse, which would have caused great misery to the inhabitants and unavoidable damage to the city. As it was, although heavy guns were fired from their ramparts, 'the enemy consider our having forborne to fire in return on the town as generous'.

As soon as it was dark, and to the great relief of its citizens (of whom the majority were Royalists), Soult marched his depleted army out of the city by the Carcassonne road. Haversacks had been filled, as had his caissons, and these trundled off with as many guns as could be moved, although not all were transportable. Quantities of provisions were abandoned, and 1,600 of the more severely wounded, including three generals, were left behind. However, morale was bad. On the day of the battle a French officer had deserted, saying that he would 'serve no longer under a man who acts like a madman, as Soult now does, in defending a town like Toulouse in such a manner—It is madness.'

At 6.00 the next morning Wellington was already receiving invitations to enter Toulouse without delay. William Freer noted that, once the enemy had left the city,

> . . . different divisions were placed under arms and the pickets at the bridges over the canal hurried to clear away the obstacles which had been placed upon them. During this interval the alarmed inhabitants, in small numbers, ventured by degrees to leave their houses and see what the troops to whose mercy they were left were doing. The conduct of the pickets gave them courage. They rushed upon them, hailed them as their deliverers and covered them with laurels, as also a division of the 3rd, which was in column close to the road. The soldiers were not permitted to enter the town. At eight, an officer of the French National Guard came towards the bridge of the Paris road, dressed with the insignia of the Bourbons, and enquired for Lord Wellington. The Fleur-de-Lys explained the part he took.

Hill's troops, crossing the Garonne from St-Cyprien by the Pont Neuf, meanwhile marched through the city and followed in Soult's wake along the Carcassonne road. Some of Beresford's units later took a parallel road north of the canal, with orders not to engage except in conjunction with Hill; but no confrontation took place, although an isolated

THE BATTLE OF TOULOUSE

group or two of cavalry were taken prisoner. Soult was well ahead and, having blown up the canal bridge at Baziège behind him (which was soon repaired by Hill's engineers), continued to march east throughout the day and night of the 12th, still deluding himself that he might meet up with Suchet's army.

Some citizens had still reason to be alarmed. Larpent had been quartered overnight in a suburban hamlet, which had just been 'quitted by plundering Spaniards', some of whom were disarmed and seized. No wonder the people 'were screaming in every direction' on returning to their homes, for everything had been ransacked. One can well understand why Wellington issued orders that the Spanish wounded, who Larpent describes as 'moaning and crying most desperately' as they passed by in a procession of carts, were to be sent as far as possible from the centre of Toulouse, where their continuing depredations would not have been welcome.

Early on the 12th Larpent was told by his servant Henry that the French were off and that they could enter Toulouse forthwith. By 11.00 he found himself at the fortified entrance, where

> . . . the *maire* of the town [in fact his deputy, Lanneluc, the prefect and mayor having fled with Soult], almost all the officers of the *garde urbaine*, a considerable number of national guard deserters, &c., and about two hundred smart but awkward men of the city guard, and a band of music, all with the white cockade, and a great crowd of citizens besides, [were] all waiting with anxiety to receive Lord Wellington, and carry him in form to the mayoralty. Unluckily, from some mismanagement and mistake, he went in at another entrance . . .

Before long both parties had met up and introductions had taken place. Commissary Daniel relates that Wellington was 'rendered very conspicuous by the restiveness of his horse, which on entering the square reared on its hind legs and literally danced over the ground', that he had carried his hat in his hand the whole of the time and that he bowed to the people until the procession had entered the courtyard of the *Capitole*. Here he was offered the keys of the city as a representative of Louis XVIII, and showed himself at the window amid general applause, while within minutes a statue of Napoleon was flung from the roof and shattered, and the 'Ns' and 'Bs' which had embellished many public buildings were being hacked off. Wellington, hardly expecting to be received with such enthusiasm, announced that a ball would be held that evening, and retired.

John Cooke, among many others joining in the celebrations, was

> . . . not a little shocked to see moving through the crowd a car load of their countrymen, hussars and *chasseurs*, with their heads and faced wrapped in the folds of blood-stained bandages, their arms in slings or splints, and their jackets nearly glued to their backs from sabre cuts. The poor patient inanimate creatures looked as if life were on the ebb, and that they were quite unconscious of the fiddling, and the noisy mirth in the streets, which resembled a sort of unmasked carnival.

Augustus Frazer was only one of many who had found the day 'full of adventure': 'to whom should I be introduced on the bridge just now, but to a Monsieur de Medalle,* son-in-law to Sterne?', who spoke English perfectly well.

---

* Although Lydia, Laurence Sterne's daughter, who with her mother had settled in the area, had married Alexander Anne

At 5.00 that evening Colonel The Hon. Frederick Ponsonby rode in from Montauban, sent on by Dalhousie at Bordeaux, with the news that Napoleon had abdicated on the 6th and that they could expect to hear the news officially within a few hours. A celebratory dinner was rapidly organised, at which some forty were present, including most of the senior officers at hand, including Freire, while the principal French dignitaries and Royalist supporters were invited also.

As they were about to take their seats, Colonel Henry Cooke and Colonel St Simon (who had formerly served under Suchet and had been an aide-de-camp to Clarke, now ex-Minister of War) entered the city carrying authenticated copies of the Senate's decrees deposing Napoleon. They had left Paris late on the 7th, been detained by General Chasseloup at Orléans and reached Blois on the 8th. Here they were taken to Clarke, who had arrived from Paris together with the Empress a few days earlier. After some delay he permitted them to continue their journey towards Bordeaux, entered on the 11th, but even with all other authorities *en route* having recognised their credentials, it was virtually impossible to make up for the hours lost—however rapidly they travelled—and to have reached Toulouse in time to prevent the battle.

Naturally, their arrival brought the excitement of the day to a climax. Champagne went round. Wellington drank the health of Louis XVIII and General Alava gave the toast 'Wellington—liberator of Spain—of France—of Europe', at which he bowed, a little confused, and immediately called for coffee, although the cheering continued for some time. The party, wearing white cockades, went on to the theatre, where the new constitution was read aloud, followed by 'God save the King', which was received with great applause. The evening ended with the ball, adjourning to which the victorious entourage passed more wounded being conveyed to hospitals—a distressing sight momentarily dampening the animated scene.*

Wellington wasted no time in sending on the two emissaries to Soult. They caught up with him the next morning between Villefranche and Castelnaudary but were met with a rebuff. Soult professed to disbelieve their account of recent events in Paris, nor was he convinced of the authenticity of their credentials, demanding a warrant from Berthier, the Chief of the General Staff, before he would acknowledge the provisional government. Cooke returned to Toulouse to confirm that Soult would be prepared to sign an armistice, but only after receiving incontrovertible evidence that Napoleon had abdicated. St Simon was detained, although he managed to slip away to Suchet, now at Perpignan. Whether Soult was merely playing for time, still hoping that, together with Suchet's troops, he could carry on the struggle, is debatable. Suchet, who had no love for his senior, accepted St Simon's evidence without hesitation and wrote to Wellington requesting an armistice for his army.

Wellington had determined not to grant one to Soult until he had made his submission; and, to bring pressure on him, Beresford's and Hill's troops, who had halted on the

---

Medalle at Albi in 1772, the *Dictionary of National Biography* states that he died not long afterwards, while their only known child, a son, died in 1783. Perhaps the M. de Medalle mentioned was merely related to Lydia's husband, or another son?
* The main British hospital had been established in the dependencies of the Convent of Minimes.

14th, were instructed two days later to continue their advance east. However, on the 17th Soult received a formal notice of the cessation of hostilities from Berthier, dated the 9th. Reluctantly accepting the new order, he sent Gazan to Toulouse to conclude an armistice, which defined also the frontier between the armies, based on which areas were under occupation by them at that moment.*

Many years later, in November 1840, Stanhope recorded an anecdote told by the Duke over dinner, which occurred during his ambassadorship at Paris, when the battle of Toulouse was 'much praised'—for by then nobody disputed its being a British victory, although some referred to it as a didactic battle. Marshal Suchet had proposed to Wellington that he should be sent a plan of the battleground, drawn out by British engineers, on to which French engineers should then mark more exactly the positions which the Allied regiments had held. When the Duke came to peruse it, he found, written in one place,

> *Ici douze bataillons des Anglais furent culbutés*; in another place, *Ici le Général marcha sur le corps d'un régiment anglais*; and so on. So what I did was this: I merely said *Quel beau plan—c'est parfaitement dessiné, c'est fait à merveille!* and rolling it up again, I delivered it back to the Officer who had brought it, with a profound bow, telling him to give my Compliments to Marshal Suchet. And I heard no more of it afterwards.†

* Unfortunately, almost the entire area fought over during the battle of Toulouse is now part of an urban sprawl: the Calvinet ridge had already been built over when visited by Oman some eighty years ago. The theatre in the Capitole has been much restored, and the interior of the building, several time redecorated in the nineteenth century and since, is otherwise of slight interest. More so is the church of the Jacobins, a few minutes' walk to the west, which must be imagined, as it was at the time, together with other dependencies, being used by the French as a convenient cavalry barrack stable and forage store, their mounts being replaced by those of the Allies after the battle.

† 'Here twelve battalions of English took a tumble ... Here the General walked over the corps of an English regiment ... [I merely said] What a beautiful plan—it is perfectly drawn, wonderfully done! ...'

18

THE SORTIE FROM BAYONNE

R EGRETTABLY, the Battle of Toulouse was not the last sanguinary engagement of the war. A totally unnecessary action took place four days later, at Bayonne, where Thouvenot's garrison had been closely confined by Hope ever since the Adour had been spanned by a bridge of boats and the investment completed on 27 February.

Hope's force consisted of the 1st and 5th Divisions, Aylmer's, Archibald Campbell's and Bradford's brigades, and two Spanish divisions under Carlos de España.

Hope was of the opinion that formally laying siege to the place was unnecessary and that Bayonne was as likely to fall by being blockaded and starved into submission, as had happened at Pamplona. Although Wellington had assured Hope that he was quite wrong, and on 6 March had sent him a detailed 'Memorandum' concerning the moving forward of artillery and ammunition, etc., Hope displayed little enthusiasm, reporting to Wellington as late as 10 April (the day of the battle at Toulouse) that he did not intend to 'break ground' until the 27th—despite of the fact that, as John Jones has stated, 'Never before had the army possessed similar means for a siege', even if belatedly, for by 13 April Hope had 670 gunners at his disposal and an immense supply of shot and shell. The battering train had been landed at the mouth of the Adour, conveyed there from Pasajes in *chasse-marées* after their arrival from England, although—according to Captain Robert Batty— not a single siege gun had so far been disembarked! Engineers had assembled quanti- ties of fascines, gabions, platforms, splinter-proof timber, etc., nearly 400 well-trained sappers and miners, with an ample supply of tools and stores, were ready and scaling ladders had been constructed in the woods north of Bayonne (none of which, in the event, was used).

During the night of 13 April the investment line—circling from east to west above the right bank of the Adour—consisted of Bradford's Portuguese beyond the riverside suburb of St-Esprit, then the 1st Division and the K.G.L. brigade, with Stopford's brigade of the Guards in the centre. Maitland's extended the line towards the riverside hamlet of St-Bernard, with its *verrerie* or glassworks in the former convent (of which a chapel survives), which had been barricaded and fortified.

Although Oman suggests that both sides had refrained from sniping at each other, whether when strengthening the outworks of the Citadel or when picquets were relieved, their officers having come to a tacit agreement as to where their respective line of sentries might be placed, this contradicts entirely Batty's account of the situation there, where

> The duty of the soldiers . . . especially those on the right bank . . . investing the citadel, now became extremely harassing. They were constantly employed on some fatigue service, either in cutting and carrying wood for fascines, which were afterwards made up under the direction of engineer officers; or in digging entrenchments for the defence of the line of countervallation, during the most inclement weather, and which could only be done with any degree of security during the night: in addition to which, the necessity of their being almost continually on the alert to avoid surprise, rendered their present situation one of the most arduous of the whole campaign. In fact, the troops, during the whole period . . . from its first investment to the cessation of hostilities, were never suffered to sleep undressed. . . .Whenever the troops were discovered by the enemy from the citadel, they were immediately fired upon; and it was found expedient to place even the sentinels in such situations that they might be able to guard their posts without exposing their persons. It frequently occurred that they were shot while imprudently, or inadvertently, stepping forward from behind the walls and hedges which had concealed them. Strict orders were given not to return the fire of the enemy, as partial engagements of such a sort would be always much more disadvantageous to the blockading force, prior to the arrival of their battering train, than to the French, securely posted as they were in so strong a work as the citadel. Occasional instances occurred which showed the extreme accuracy of the French artillerymen in pointing their cannon . . .

Young George Gleig, serving in the 85th Regiment (part of Aylmer's brigade) and stationed with a mortar battery at St-Etienne within view of the Citadel, described his position as being the target of

> . . . an incessant fire of round shot, shells, grape, and occasionally of musketry . . . the enemy had upon their walls a number of long swivel guns, which they could elevate or depress, or turn in any direction, at will. . . . These threw, with great force, iron balls of about a quarter of a pound weight. . . . [Every so often] a nine-inch shell would tumble through the roof, and burst sometimes before we had time to escape into another apartment—Then the crashing of cannon-balls as they rushed through the partitions—the . . . rattle of grape and canister, which came pouring in by the windows . . . produced a species of feeling, of which no words can convey an adequate notion to him who has not experienced it.

On 10 April Edmund Wheatley, an ensign in the K.G.L., jotted down in his *Journal* that he had

> . . . now been piquetting for two months before this infernal fortress endeavouring to starve them out, while we are in want of food ourselves, For nothing but herrings and brandy are come-atable. . . . The duty is harrassing: On Monday on piquet in the Church of St Etienne, on Tuesday on the support near the Church, on Wednesday all night digging in the entrenchments near the Windmill, on Friday in the Church again, and so on. When sitting round the fire [in the church] one night a ball entered the door, passed through the aisle over the men's heads, and split the altar into a thousand pieces, without injuring a single person . . .

All being very still on the afternoon of that Easter Sunday, Wheatley, peeping out, noticed that the French batteries were 'lined with ladies and gentlemen', when suddenly

> . . . the whole Citadel began a tremendous cannonading on the unfortunate steeple of St Etienne and after four hundred or more balls [?] had passed through it, it fell with a horrible crash. The

fools in the fortress gave loud huzzas and the ladies retired delighted with the afternoon's enter-
tainment. Then all became quiet as the grave again.

On that same day Hope had received news from Bordeaux of the momentous events
taking place in Paris, and although he did not pass on to Thouvenot a copy of the Senate's
'Decree' deposing Napoleon, this was soon made known to the garrison by Hope's officers,
after which the trickle of deserters passing through to the Allied lines notably increased.

According to Gleig, it was at about midnight (11/12 April) that a messenger reached
Hope's headquarters stating that in fact Napoleon had abdicated. Under a flag of truce,
an aide was sent into the Citadel to pass on the news to Thouvenot, who refused to believe
it until receiving confirmation from Soult. The aide returned to Hope with the message
that he would be hearing from Thouvenot on the subject before long.

However, Hope, in expectation that Thouvenot at least would cease hostilities meanwhile, did not further the work in hand of bringing forward and mounting guns; but for
form's sake the blockade would be continued. Picquets took up their stations as usual, the
garrison remained isolated and none of the inhabitants would be allowed to pass out
through the lines.

It chanced that, during the 14th, Hope had sent Hay's brigade across to Boucau to
strengthen the line protecting the bridge of boats, so vital to his communications, should
Thouvenot take it into his head to order out a detachment to destroy it. His garrison,
reduced by sickness and desertion, still amounted to 12,000 men, including Abbé's division, although it was suspected that only half that number could be said to be in fighting
condition.

Hay, 'general officer of the day', had placed himself in a central position with a
picquet near the hilltop church of St-Etienne, with Edward Stopford's Guards on his right
and Heinrich von Hinüber's K.G.L. to his left.

Early in the moonless night of the 14th, a deserter—Batty states that there were two—
crossed the lines and was taken to General Hay, who, not being a French speaker, either
misunderstood or disbelieved it when told that the garrison was under arms and was
expected to make a sortie. Von Hinüber, taking the warning more seriously, got his men
under arms; Hope, when informed, ordered up some 500 men in the rear to proceed to the
front.

Whatever may have been Thouvenot's reasons for making the sortie—most likely sheer
desperation and frustration at hearing of Napoleon's fall, but perhaps provoked additionally by the hubris of his more fanatical officers, hoping to take advantage of the relaxed
state of the troops investing them—at between 2.00 and 3.00 on the morning of the 15th,
almost 6,000 men swarmed out in three columns from the pitch dark shadow of the Citadel
and bayoneted several Allied sentries before they could give the alarm. The sudden sally
coincided with a feint attack against outposts in the direction of Anglet.

The more easterly column overran the picquets of the 5th Division, taking many
prisoners, and stormed and occupied most of the fortified houses in the vicinity of the

church of St-Etienne, through a loophole in which General Hay was shot early in the action.* Close to the church was a party of the 38th commanded by Captain Forster, which continued to hold out obstinately against the enemy now swarming around it, while the walled Jewish cemetery immediately to the north-west provided a another convenient position from which a vigorous resistance was maintained while awaiting reinforcements, for here, as elsewhere, its defenders were heavily outnumbered.

Meanwhile the other two columns had overrun the outworks extending west of St-Etienne,† capturing no fewer than 84 men of the Coldstream Guards and also a number of the 3rd Guards. Pressing on in confused fighting, the French converged on their more easterly column. From the Citadel, their artillery fired into the dark somewhat at random, while their surviving gunboats sailed downstream to shell the St-Bernard position, although none of this barrage proved very effective, however much the sound added to the uninterrupted roar of musketry.

Providentially, the advance was checked before it had reached any of the Allied magazines, although—as Gleig admits—they took 'the blue house', a small château overlooking the Citadel, which he had previously occupied as an outwork. Their fireballs and shells ignited piles of fascines, the flames from which cast a lurid light on the scene, and the air, 'filled with stars and shells' reminded Wheatley of a Vauxhall exhibition, 'for every bush and hedge was spangled with flashing stars from the musketry, and the fields covered with blue lights shot from Bayonne to shew the men on the ramparts . . . where to direct their guns', some of which—according to Wheatley—in order to save shells, were firing their shot almost perpendicularly so that they might drop on those sheltering behind stone walls! It was in this vicinity, according to Gleig, that the fighting was most ferocious, with bayonets, sabres and butts of muskets in full play, although the confused combat in the dark was carried on in the earthworks, over barricades and in dips and hollows of the surrounding fields.

Hope himself, on the first alarm, galloped up the partly sunken road from St-Bernard ascending towards St-Etienne and ran full tilt into a party of French filling in his trenches there. His mount was shot dead, bringing Hope, also wounded, to the ground and entangling his foot under its side. Two of his aides, Lieutenant William Moore (a nephew of Sir John Moore of Corunna) and Captain William Herries (in the Q.M.G.'s Department), were wounded when coming to his assistance. All three were taken prisoner, and Herries later had to have his leg amputated.

By now General Kenneth Howard had ordered Maitland's brigade forward from the dependencies of the St-Bernard convent to resist any enemy thrust towards the bridge of boats at Boucau; but, as they now appeared to be concentrating on the centre of the Allied line, Maitland's units, together with survivors from Stopford's brigade—Stopford himself

---

* His loss was not universally regretted. General Robinson had referred to him as fool, an arrant coward and 'a paltry, plundering old wretch', no officer and someone who 'ought not to be a General'. Hay's inept reaction to the deserter's warning would seem to justify this opinion.
† Approximately along the present Chemin de Laharie.

was wounded shortly after this, and command devolved on John Guise—were directed to fall on the disordered mass engaged near the church of St-Etienne and the Jewish cemetery. This they did, both brigades charging the enemy flank simultaneously.

Von Hinüber, on his own responsibility, had already sent his K.G.L. brigade of five battalions, together with Bradford's units, to converge on the enemy from the south-east. Finding themselves counter-attacked from two directions, and with their line of retreat threatened, Thouvenot's troops began to give way. Forster's remaining men, still holding out at St-Etienne, were rescued, and von Hinüber was able to bring a field piece to bear on the enemy, stumbling back in the dark: no fewer than thirteen rounds of grape and canister ploughed into the solid mass of fugitives before they reached the shelter of the Citadel, while when retreating over its glacis they suffered as severely from the destructive musketry of the Guards.

Firing petered out, and after half an hour—it was now about 7.30 in the morning—a flag of truce was run up on the Citadel. It was left to General Charles Colville, on whom command devolved—Hope was *hors de combat*—once his scattered units had been rallied and redeployed, to supervise the burying of the dead and the collection of the wounded for, as dawn broke, a dreadful scene of carnage presented itself.

Wheatley described the French pouring out, unarmed,

> ... they picking up their dead, and we ours. I went under the French batteries and had a long chat with some French officers who gave me some snuff. And as the French soldiers passed us with their dead comrades, we reflected on the miserable trade of war. Suddenly a blank shot was fired from the Citadel. We hastily shook hands and in five minutes I was as eager to shoot them as they had been to present their *rapé* to me.

Other Allied officers, when conversing with the French, must have felt the same. Batty had commented that

> On our expressing the deep regret we felt at the useless sacrifice that had been made of so many brave men, it was quite disgusting to observe the *nonchalance* affected by these gentlemen, and the light manner in which they pretended to treat it, remarking that, after all, it was nothing more than a *petit promenade militaire* [a little route march]. But it would be difficult to convey an idea of their astonishment, when we informed them of the events which had occurred in Paris, and they would not believe it possible that their idol Napoleon had abdicated the throne.

This suggests that Thouvenot very deliberately withheld the news from all but a few of his senior officers.

Casualties on both sides had been particularly heavy: the Allies, in addition to those taken prisoner, temporarily, suffered 150 killed and over 450 wounded and missing, including 42 officers; the French had 111 killed and almost 780 wounded, among them 42 officers also, but how many of the wounded were mortally injured is unknown.* Without

---

* Most of the British officers were buried in two cemeteries not far from the main field of action near the restored church at St-Etienne. That of the Coldstream Guards is approached by following the Chemin de Laharie and turning to the west off the N 10 (the Bordeaux road). To the right-hand side of a right-hand fork (Chemin de Laborde)—no great distance above the St-Bernard position—a path signposted 'Cimetière des Anglais' skirts a field and descends to its railed enclosure, which stands near the position of the Coldstream's camp. That of the 3rd Foot or Scots Guards is reached by continuing north

computing how many other wounded in earlier actions remained within the Citadel, Thouvenot still commanded a garrison of 11,800 men, even if several thousand of them were sick and disabled.

The 15th was spent in burying the remaining dead and removing the wounded to field hospitals. Gleig states that 'not a few perished from loss of blood ere assistance arrived', while the medical assistants had remarked that 'a greater proportion of incurable wounds were inflicted this night than they remembered to have seen. Many had received bayonet-thrusts in vital parts.'

Meanwhile, in view of the apparent reluctance of the part of the enemy to face the reality of the situation, Colville ordered that unremitting vigilance be observed on the part of the outposts until hostilities ceased. Even when provided with copies of the *Moniteur* and other Paris newspapers by Colville, the intransigent governor, having not been authorised to do so by his superiors, refused to conclude a suspension of arms until the 26th—and then only after receiving a copy of the armistice of 17 April, authenticated by Soult and sent on to him by Gazan, as 'la place de Bayonne' was also included in that document.

The sortie had no military justification. Wellington later referred to Thouvenot as a blackguard for making it when perfectly aware that, in the circumstances, he could gain nothing. Since Soult's sortie at St-Pierre, Thouvenot had remained passive. Personal rancour and vindictiveness did not apparently form a part of his character. Colville, after meeting him, had written to Wellington describing Thouvenot as appearing to be 'a most gentleman-like, well-intentioned man, having a difficult post with a garrison, the great part of which cannot be supposed to be in a moment reconciled to a revolution so extraordinary'. Later, when Robert Batty, taking advantage of permission having been granted to British officers to enter the town, was hauled before Thouvenot by an officious French officer for having sketched the cathedral tower, among other views of positions from which they had been driven, the governor had 'with great politeness, restored the [sketch-]book, and offered to send one of his own aide-de-camps to accompany the author, whenever he wished to exercise his pencil within the limits of the entrenched camp'—hardly the reaction of a man governed by malice (although, perhaps by then reconciled to the situation, he had determined to ingratiate himself with his former enemies). Nevertheless, giving the order to make the sortie, even if against his better judgement, made him responsible for the deaths of between 250 and 350 men (including the mortally wounded), apart from disabling several hundred more, and this must have weighed heavily on his conscience.

along the N 10 at the Jewish cemetery, turning left into the Rue du Barat and then right. After a few yards, a path to the left shortly descends to the tree-shaded enclosure.

James Vigors Harvey, formerly a captain in the Coldstreams, was slightly wounded in the sortie. Consul at Bayonne for many years until his death in 1842, he made himself responsible for the upkeep of the cemeteries (which, since 1988, has been taken on by the municipality of Bayonne). They were first described in any detail in Philip A. Hurt's *The Guards' Cemeteries, St Etienne, Bayonne*... (ND [1877]; 2nd edn, 1887); and they were visited by Queen Victoria on 20 March 1889 when she was on holiday at Biarritz. The churchyard of Arcangues, and those of St-Martin and St-Andrews at Biarritz, contain more graves, and several memorial plaques may be seen in the latter church.

19

WITHDRAWAL

L ARPENT records that, on the morning after the Battle of Toulouse, the whole conversation of the officers turned upon 'half-pay and starvation. With some, want of prefer-
ment; with others, promotion; and with those who have promotion, a determination to
enjoy themselves now that it is all over, and their dangers and sufferings past'. Toulouse
remained *en fête* for several weeks.

On 27 April Wellington, together with some 300 of the more senior officers of the
Allied armies, wearing their least-worn uniforms and displaying white cockades, rode out
to welcome the arrival of the Duc d'Angoulême and his entourage. The animated scene, as
they returned across the bridge towards the cathedral of St-Etienne, along streets congested by cheering crowds held back by a double line of English troops, reminded
Larpent of London at Nelson's funeral. From every window hung 'Sheets, table-cloths,
towels, etc., covered with green paper fleurs-de-lys. . . . The women, and some of the old
men, were quite mad with joy, and screamed *Vive le Roi et vivent les Anglois!* till they were
stopped by absolute exhaustion, or some by tears of joy.' After a grand dinner, the evening
ended with a play at the theatre in the Capitole. The next day Angoulême attended mass
and gave a reception, and in the evening the Capitole was again the scene of music and
dancing, although the crush so great that it was almost impossible to move. Both Clausel
and Villatte were in attendance, while on the following day Marshal Suchet put in an
appearance, together with several of his officers.*

According to Larpent, on his arrival at Toulouse Suchet presented 'a strange figure.
His head and cheeks and chin all overgrown with hair, like a wild man of the woods: and
his dress more splendid than the drum-major of one of our Guards' bands on a birth-day'.
Larpent noticed 'much conversation' taking place between Angoulême and Suchet, who,
after Soult's dismissal, was put in command of their combined armies. It was strange that,
while the populace extended a warm welcome to the British, Larpent never once heard a

---

* Augustus Frazer mentions that he had met a certain Monsieur de Kerboux, just arrived from Paris that evening with
dispatches from General Pierre Dupont, provisionally replacing Clarke. He was on his way to Suchet, with orders for him
to assume the chief command of Soult's army as well as his own. Soult was to report to Paris, giving an account of his conduct,
for it was still assumed by some that Soult was aware of the momentous events which had taken place in Paris prior to the
action on the 10th. De Kerboux was assured that it was impossible for either of the contestants to have known that
Napoleon's tentative abdication had been signed on the night of 4 April, and final renunciation on the 6th. De Kerboux
'had waited on the Duc d'Angouleme', but not on Wellington in person, although anxious that 'his lordship to be apprised
of so important a piece of intelligence'.

viva for either the Spaniards or Portuguese: in consequence, they were 'very angry and sulky, and I think a little jealous of us. This you may well imagine, when you learn that they all along consider that *they* have accomplished all that has happened, and that we have assisted a little certainly, but that they could have done without us.'

The enthusiasm and the euphoria of victory gradually evaporated and, although few disturbances took place during ensuing weeks, life soon resumed its natural course. British officers seemed 'all to have behaved with considerable propriety', but it was evident to Larpent that 'the inhabitants dread our departure, and the return of their own people. They say that all order ceases, and all security, the moment our side of the line of demarcation is passed.'

For the time being, Headquarters, together with the 2nd Division, remained in Toulouse itself: other divisions were dispersed some distance north and west of the city, the Light Division being quartered between Grisolles and Castelsarrazin. There Jonathan Leach was to spend 'five or six weeks very pleasantly, and received the greatest kindness and hospitality from the inhabitants. Dances, fêtes champêtres on the banks of the Garonne, horse-races, and various gaieties, filled up our time . . .' Edward Costello procured 'delightful quarters' with 'excellent beds', but so unused was he and his fellow riflemen to such luxury that they preferred to wrap a blanket round themselves and sleep on the floor! British troops had been strictly forbidden to enter any place within the French lines in order to avoid confrontations between the former adversaries, but some officers unobtrusively did so. At Montauban, where General Nicolas Loverdo commanded, although the local people were 'kind an obliging'—the return of peace was very welcome—William Surtees noticed that the officers of the French garrison quartered there, finding it hard to accept that they had been defeated, 'took every opportunity of quarrelling with ours'. Leach had also watched Angoulême's review of the combined French armies stationed in the vicinity of Montauban, recording that while the general appearance of the troops was fine and soldier-like,

> The Spanish sun had left its mark on their countenances, which were for the most part lively and animated, without the smallest appearance of despondency or disappointment at the late change. Marshal Soult alone appeared sullen and dejected. But this possibly was his natural manner. Marshal Suchet, who sat on horseback on the duke's left hand, laughed and joked, and had every appearance of being perfectly satisfied.

Larpent missed the occasion, but had this confirmed by others who had attended: they had reported also that, while the men were well equipped, the officers 'looked very shabby and unlike gentlemen', and 'Soult was only to be distinguished by a most enormous hat, and by a surly look, which is described as unpleasantly penetrating, and more bespeaking talent than amiability.'

It was rumoured as very likely that Wellington would be nominated the English commissioner at any forthcoming peace conference. Larpent, who from personal experience knew his ways, wryly suggested that were he to go, other diplomats 'would be surprised at his methods of getting through business', but at least we 'should have a general peace many weeks sooner, if not months, than we are likely to have otherwise.'

On 30 April Wellington started off for Paris—via Cahors, where he considerately dropped in briefly on General Foy, who was recuperating from the wound received at Orthez.* After consulting with Castlereagh, Wellington was back in Toulouse on 14 May, preceded by the Paris papers of the 8th (received there on the 13th), confirming that he was now a duke and had been appointed ambassador to France.†

Within three days Wellington set out again, this time for Madrid, having been urged by Castlereagh to try—without positively interfering—whether he could at least 'prevail upon all parties to be more moderate, and to adopt a constitution most likely to be practicable and to contribute to the peace and happiness of nations.' Fernando VII's reappearance had opened the Iberian Pandora's box; and with the return of so many troops from France, there was a distinct possibility of a military *coup* and civil war breaking out between the *Liberales* and *Serviles*, as the former contemptuously referred to the Conservative party.‡

Traversing Orthez, Bayonne and St-Jean-de-Luz, Wellington's carriage made the steep climb through the Basque mountains to cross the battlefield of Vitoria and the bleak Castilian *meseta*, clattering into Madrid on 24 May. Inevitably, the fleeting diplomatic visit to Fernando VII—who by then had been back in Spain for exactly two months—was fruitless: there was not the slightest chance of persuading him to temper his inveterate hostility to the Liberals. Long confined at Valençay, the king can have had little idea of the sufferings of his subjects under the protracted French occupation, should he have given them a thought, and wilfully neglected the opportunity of exploiting their misplaced goodwill. Repressive absolutism was reinstated, with deplorable results throughout ensuing decades. Seventeen years later, when dining with Stanhope, Wellington, on remarking that Fernando had not impressed him as being a bad character—had the gift to him of the royal paintings captured at Vitoria influenced his judgement?—had submitted that it was virtually impossible for anyone to have done any better in governing Spain than he was during that troubled period.§

Arrangements for the dispersal of the Allied troops were being put in hand. Already, on 26 April, a 'General Order' directed that all Portuguese and Spanish women not married to British soldiers 'should be separated from those with whom they lived', with the

---

* Wellington had always regarded Foy as 'a very distinguished officer'.

† It was on this occasion, as reported by Stanhope, that Soult, when travellng in the opposite direction, first saw Wellington at close quarters. 'The postillons have a habit there [in France] of changing horses on the road, and so did ours [with six horses]. I was half asleep at the time but I was told afterwards that Soult, hearing whose carriage is was, had got out and walked round and round several times with his spying glass to reconnoitre what was inside. [Here the Duke laughed when telling the story.]' He also described Soult, whom he met later in Paris, as 'a very large man—very tall and large, like Marshal Beresford—a harsh voice, and not a very pleasant countenance or manner.'

‡ The complex situation is explained in Charles Esdaile's *The Duke if Wellington and the Command of the Spanish Army, 1812-14.*

§ The present author will be forgiven for interposing an anecdote in the words of Richard Ford (author of the *Hand-Book for Spain* of 1845), when describing the late Duke's collection of paintings in Apsley House in the *Quarterly Review* of March 1853 and referring to the return of plundered paintings to their rightful owners. It provides a nice example of Wellington's

exception of those few who 'had proved themselves useful and regular', who would be allowed to marry those to whom they were attached, and with whom they had had children. The 'unsettled habits of the majority' prevented them from being entitled to this privilege: in due course they would be escorted home by troops of their own nationality.

Allied units were progressively evacuated from their cantonments and camps in the vicinity of Toulouse throughout May, most of them proceeding towards the Garonne estuary. On the 31st the Light Division received orders to march next day for Bordeaux, reached on 15 June via Lectour, Condom, Bazas, Langon and Barsac. They camped at Blanquefort, north of the city, to await transports home from Pauillac, some distance downstream and the main port of embarkation. George Simmons, passing through Bazas on the 11th, describes the men of the 52nd and 1/9th Regiments 'drawn up on each side of the market-place', who 'presented arms and gave three cheers to the regiments as they filed through us, which mark of our attention highly flattered the Portuguese'. These were the Portuguese units of the division (1st and 3rd *Caçadores* and 17th Line), which now diverged towards Bayonne, forming a brigade, in whose charge were placed the unfortunate Spanish and Portuguese women being returned to their homes, together with a number of goat-boys and their goats. Their departure caused many heavy hearts, both among themselves and among those with whom they had lived as 'soldier's wives', although it was insinuated that 'several on both sides were not oppressed with too fine feelings'.

An officer in the Portuguese service later described to Surtees how the women had

> ... formed a column of 800 or 900 strong; that they were told off in regular companies; and that the commanding-officer, a major, and all the captains, were married men, who had families with them—all excellent arrangements; but that they were the most unmanageable set of animals that ever marched across a country. The officers had to draw rations for them all the way; but many of them . . . left the column and went wherever they pleased. Few reached Portugal in the order in which they started.

Commissary Schaumann, at that time recuperating from illness at Mont-de-Marsan, saw Portuguese troops passing through the place 'with innumerable brigades of mules that had been released, and a vast gang of contractors, servants, head drivers, sporting dogs, mistresses, canteen men and women—in fact the whole body composing the camp followers . . .' In the town itself—where the 'general feeling of the inhabitants was altogether against the Bourbons, who were openly cursed in the streets, while Bonaparte was extolled'—the local girls 'were eager to marry', and many of them eloped with English officers. At an earlier date, several Spanish regiments had passed him on their way home, making 'a dreadful tumult as they marched along'. Apparently there was considerable antipathy between the British and Spanish, as confirmed by Schaumann:

---

laconic sense of humour: 'While the Louvre was being stripped of borrowed plumes, Wellington fell into great disfavour, and was coldly received by some French marshals on one occasion, as he passed through their Salle in the Tuileries on a visit to Louis XVIII; when the king subsequently expressed his surprise and vexation in hearing that they had "turned their backs" on him, "It is of no consequence, Sire," was the reply: "c'est leur habitude [it's their way]." '

Their hatred of the English, and particularly Lord Wellington, who had them hanged whenever they robbed or were guilty of disobedience, manifested itself even towards me as I turned aside and halted to let them march by. They used insolent language, made threatening gestures with their bayonets, insulting my men; and seemed disposed to plunder my baggage. This behaviour, which, with my pistols clasped in my hands, I could only encounter with the most contemptuous of looks, was allowed to continue without the smallest reproof from the Spanish officers, who did not dare to open their mouths, but, looking a little shamefast, slunk by in a state of complete apathy.

Although some Portuguese units had sailed home from Bordeaux, their remaining troops stayed with the British until the commissaries could manage without mule trans-port. They then separated, 'taking all the mules and muleteers with them attached to different regiments for rations, etc., and set out through Spain for Portugal, a good three months' trip.' General D'Urban had the invidious task of commanding them on their long march, which he accomplished 'without leaving anything behind, without any instance of disorder or irregularity', reaching Lisbon on 30 August.

The main body of the British infantry was transported home from Bordeaux, although a battalion each from several regiments was unlucky enough to be sent to North America, where the Anglo-American war was to continue for several months. Among Peninsular generals 'sniped' by American riflemen in the ensuing campaign were Robert Ross (known as 'Ross of Bladensburg' after his victory there in August), mortally wounded at Baltimore that September, and Edward Pakenham, Wellington's brother-in-law, killed at New Orleans the following January, a fortnight after the official end of hostilities.

Doubtless, many of the rank and file sincerely regretted having to leave France, where they were generally accepted as deliverers rather than conquerors, for food and wine were good and cheap. John Timewell, a private in the 43rd, having spent seven weeks near Toulouse, wrote in his diary:

> Never was [sic] men better used than the inhabitants done to the English soldiers; the friend-liest people I met with in all my travels; never were soldiers used half so well in England . . . There we had puncheons of wine in every house, as good as you pay in England five shillings a bottle. If you had but seen the soldiers in glory there, with fifty glasses on their table all full from morning to night, and even washed potatoes in it, it was so plenty.'

It was not always easy to disengage after such a long war, although one commissary whose duty it was to pay off public and private debts and claims promptly, found it 'a thankless and disgusting task', due to 'the various attempts at fraud and imposition' made by some of the French, for 'Enormous demands were made (but very properly rejected) even for marks left by encampments, whereas in almost every instance, and always when possible, the troops encamped on heaths and uncultivated ground', and so many 'were enriched in every direction we moved'.

Larpent left for Bordeaux on 4 June, the day before the last infantry units marched from Toulouse. He felt that, in general, the troops were welcome, certainly so by the tradesmen, who had

... made a famous time of it these last three months, for the army has in that time received six months' pay, and most of it had found its way into the pockets of the ... restauranteurs [sic], the hotels, etc. Bordeaux has had its full share of the spoils of the *milords*. Nor have the inhabitants suffered ... except the little inconvenience of giving up a room or two ... as quarters for the officers.

Ensign Wheatley, writing on 8 July while still awaiting orders to march to a place of embarkation, had to provide himself with shelter on Blanquefort heath by placing two blankets thrown over a stick: tents having been sent to store already, the troops had to shift as they could. However, he states that they had received not six but only three months' pay out of the nine due to them. As far as Wheatley was concerned, he would spend it in dissipation and amusement:

The Theatre [in Bordeaux, 'the external ... magnificent in the extreme'] I attended regularly and discovered the Gascon ladies not inferior to the Parisians in vivacité. Respectable girls sometimes dress themselves as men, and three or four, arm in arm, would lounge in the evening along the Promenade with all the airs of our Bond Street petit maîtres, then, giggling when they met anyone, run as if to entice a pursuit. This is gaieté!!!

According to Quartermaster Surtees, several desertions took place, with men—most of them bad characters—running off into the interior after having helped themselves to their officer's property before absconding; and he could speak from experience, because he had been robbed also. Most of the depredations made by the troops involved stealing from local allotments, although this had been exaggerated: much of it was done

... by the French peasantry and country servants, who, if a soldier takes six cabbages, immediately take a dozen more themselves, sell them in the camp, and swear to the owners that the soldiers are the culprits ... [while those with vineyards have] their full revenge in the price of their wines, which are immediately doubled, by the arrival of the troops ... it is fortunate for the inhabitants that we shall be off before the grapes begin to ripen; and for our own soldiers likewise ... [for otherwise] the temptations would be irresistible ...

On 1 June the first cavalry units, together with some of the horse artillery and horses of the waggon train, set off from near Toulouse on their long, dusty ride home. As the weather was exceedingly sultry, they usually left at 4.00 each morning, according to Woodberry. The whole had been divided into two columns, following two separate routes, and each column was subdivided into four groups, their departures being staggered. One column rode due north towards Montauban on its leisurely way across France to Calais; the other followed the main *chaussée* further west, traversing Bordeaux, Angoulême, Poitiers and Tours *en route*. At Tours, Wellington had passed them and, as he was apparently satisfied with their conduct (which had given no cause for complaint), had told Vandeleur that those officers who wished to, might visit Paris. The columns had not always been hospitably received, depending on whether or not the town through which they rode favoured the new regime, and occasional disputes had been reported. Captain Kennedy (18th Dragoons), trotting back in no haste, found the highways covered with French troops and conscripts making their way home and also passed 'immense numbers' of prisoners of war just landed from England, where they had been confined in camps or hulks—some for years. He confessed to a presentiment, having noticed an inclination 'to cry *Vive Napoleon*' among the soldiers, for some, 'indeed almost all of them, seem fond of the rascal and go so far as to say they think he will come back among them. I think if great care is not taken of him there will be a disturbance in this country before long . . .' It was not until the first two weeks of July that the van of each column reined up in either Boulogne or Calais, where some units had to wait impatiently for several days before transports were able to put into port.

During the second week of June, Wellington drove north from Madrid back to Bayonne, and then Bordeaux. He may not have even paused to survey the melancholy scenes of former actions. While, in later years, celebratory anniversary dinners were held at Apsley House for his former comrades-in-arms, the Duke was not one to take any pleasure in revisiting battlefields; and on the occasion he did so, dutifully escorting George IV over that of Waterloo, he was disillusioned because the erection of the *Butte de Lion* by his former aide, the Prince of Orange (by then William II of the Netherlands) had 'spoiled' it and he never returned there.

On the 14th Wellington paid his formal farewell to his forces. Although it has been recorded that some officers and men displayed their disappointment, sensing a lack of gratitude and having expected the Duke to be more emphatically complimentary to his remaining troops—which would have been totally out of character—Jonathan Leach, for one, witnessed him riding off 'amidst loud cheers of men and officers, many of whom had followed him through seven successive campaigns in the Peninsula and the south of France.' Nine days later, after an absence from the shores of Britain of five years and two months, the 45-year-old Duke of Wellington disembarked at Dover to a hero's welcome.

Dalhousie, left in charge of the remaining troops in and around Bordeaux, wrote to Charles Colville, still in command at Bayonne, and complained: 'We are hanging on here in the utmost ignorance of any arrangements to remove us, without a transport here of any description; a state of idleness and suspense most tedious and unpleasant'. Colville was requested to

> Direct everything with Admiral Penrose with the view of bringing away your part of the Army in a military style, embarking first your sick and lumber, and then marching your troops clean on board when a sufficiency of transports is arrived for you. I mean that sufficiency of force that will command the respect and quiet behaviour of our affectionate Allies in your neighbourhood.
>
> Here they are very tired of us and we of them, but I have little hope of getting away before the end of July.

For several weeks now the wounded had been transported home as soon as sufficiently recuperated to endure the passage. Those still convalescing had not been ignored by itinerant merchants, who found it worth their while sailing out from England: one, mentioned by Lieutenant Keep, had arrived with a cargo of 'shoes and boots, stockings and shirts and eatable, to dispose of.' Keep was amused to see a group of young Basques— 'chiefly mariners and fishermen, very fair and good looking young fellows'—gathered on the beach at Fuenterrabia one morning 'in possession of what seemed to them great curiosities . . . and laughing over some cotton hand kerchiefs from Manchester . . . for caricatures had been printed on them of Bonaparte's reverses of fortune, and defeats in Russia, etc, with other comic subjects.'

Private William Wheeler was discharged from a 'General hospital' at Fuenterrabia at the beginning of July, where he had been since he was wounded at the Nivelle in November. He convalesced in a nearby convent and by mid-August had been moved nearer to Pasajes, but it was not until 9 September that he embarked for England. Few of those waiting impatiently to clamber aboard the transports sent belatedly to pick them up, whether here or at Pauillac, can have imagined that they would be called upon to fight the French yet again—and so soon—at Waterloo.

And so the Peninsular War petered out.

*   *   *

In *The Subaltern Officer*, written a decade later, Captain George Wood expressed his disillusionment in print, for Peninsular veterans received neither the two years' service bonus nor any commemorative medal awarded automatically to survivors of the Waterloo campaign, unless they had been on those battlefields as well.* At the same time he thus excused himself: 'God forbid that I should be thought to mention the glorious field of Waterloo with envy! I am too well aware of the laurels gained by the heroes who fought there, to deprecate their merit in the least'. Nevertheless, he maintained that those officers who had seen service in Spain would confirm that they had behaved there with as much bravery; nor would they dispute that the battles of the Pyrenees were

> . . . certainly the most arduous and enterprising duty that British troops ever performed: I do not by any means except the last campaign in Flanders; for that, with the exception of the three days' conflict, I regard as a mere party of pleasure in comparison with the affairs of the Pyrenees and the disastrous retreats of the Peninsula. The troops in Flanders were never without their Commissariat at hand, plenty of all kinds of necessaries, a general run of good weather, with the exception of two or three days, and a fine country to pass through . . .

Ensign Eccles, writing from Dublin, may be taken as a example of the situation in which many were to find themselves. He had been wounded at Toulouse in both his feet and his back. Fifteen years later he was requesting a pension, being unable to walk 'any distance without considerable pain'. He had been

> . . . afflicted for these 3 years past with a weakness in my back which still continues to cause me excruciating agony at times, (which the surgeon who attends me can certify) [which he did].

---

* Many among those disillusioned during their struggle for survival during subsequent months and years would have subscribed as readily to the 'terminated, and with it all remembrance of the veterans' services'—William Napier's scathing words of condemnation in the last volume of his *History*, issued in 1840, and an assertion hard to contradict. It was not for another eight years that the distribution was authorised of the silver General Service Medal, with a clasp added for each battle between 1793 and 1814 at which the recipient had been present; but by then many of those entitled to them were dead. As John Hall remarked in his Introduction to the supplementary volume VIII of Oman's *History*, such 'national amnesia is not new': it is a complex and painful subject deserving further scholarly research.

Under the circumstances I feel totally unfit for active service, which I would choose were I able, as the increase of pay would be a great object to me in supporting a Wife & five children, having no situation whatever Civil or Military under Government or any private employment, my half pay being my chief support, which if diminished by any means, will reduce me to great distress. I receive nor never did receive any pension for my wounds although for 2 years I was lame. Notwithstanding I place myself at the disposal of the Government.

*   *   *

The 'Great War' of the time was over at last, although many British units would be engaging another adversary, the Americans. Few of the officers and men who had landed at Mondego Bay with Sir Arthur Wellesley in August 1808 could have imagined that the bitter struggle in the Peninsula would drag on interminably, or so it seemed. There, after their rebuff at Baylen, French armies were soon to find themselves in a hornet's nest. They were also to suffer a series of reverses whenever engaged with the Anglo-Portuguese forces which would erode their prestige and any residual reputation of invincibility. The British presence galvanised the Spanish guerrillas into continuing their ubiquitous resistance, in turn preventing the French from concentrating against the main Allied army.

Napoleon had 300,000 men dispersed throughout Spain in 1810–11 but could only collect together 70,000 for Masséna's invasion of Portugal, after which no further reinforcements of any consequence were poured across the Pyrenees. The Emperor then made the fatal mistake of marching against Russia before—and under the illusion that—the Peninsula had been 'pacified', as he too confidently anticipated it would be; thus he was obliged to leave half his veteran French regiments there to repress the populace.

The outcome of the Dresden/Leipzig campaign of 1813 might have been very different had Napoleon been able march a higher proportion of the French troops still dispersed in Old Castile and Catalonia to the Elbe. Those remaining in Spain were insufficient to restrain Wellington, determined on taking the offensive again, and were soundly thrashed in his brilliant Vitoria campaign.

As described in the foregoing pages, Soult was able to put up a courageous resistance with his already depleted forces for several months until succumbing to relentless Allied pressure. At bay as Wellington inexorably advanced on Toulouse, Soult was unable to supply any additional veterans to Napoleon's army—largely composed of raw conscripts—without putting his own in jeopardy. Thus Napoleon, facing Schwarzenberg's forces in north-eastern France, after conducting an impressive last-ditch campaign, was obliged to abdicate.

At Waterloo, Napoleon not only disparaged Wellington (that *'mauvais général'*), but also disdained to listen to the advice of those of his generals with personal experience of the hazards of making a frontal attack on his new adversary when on the defensive—many would have remembered their discomfiture at Vimeiro, Busaco, Fuentes de Oñoro, Sorauren, and elsewhere: he had hurled his columns against British infantry in line and had been defeated.

While the comparative importance of the several campaigns and naval engagements taking place during the Revolutionary and Napoleonic wars, and the determining factors in the eventual overthrow of Napoleonic France, will long continue to be the subject of debate, few who have studied the war in the Peninsula in any depth can doubt that the successful outcome of that terrible conflict, taking place in the Pyrenees and terminating in Wellington's invasion of France, was a principal component.

APPENDICES

A. CHRONOLOGY

1813

May	2		Allies defeated at Lützen
	20–21		Battle of Bautzen
	22	Wellington commences spring offensive	
June	4		Armistice of Pläswitz/Pleiswitz between Northern Allies and Napoleon, extending truce until 20 July
	3–12	Tarragona besieged by Murray	
	21	French defeated at Vitoria	
	25	Pamplona blockaded	
	26	Action at Tolosa	
	27		Treaty of Reichenbach: Austria agrees to re-enter the war if Napoleon does not agree to minimum peace terms
	28	San Sebastián invested by Allies	
July	1		Napoleon, at Dresden, learns of defeat at Vitoria
	9–12	Conference at Trachenberg	
	11	Soult reaches Bayonne and plans counter-offensive in Pyrenees	
	16–17	O'Donnell's troops arrive to blockade Pamplona	
	16	Wellington learns that Clausel is back in France	
	25	Failure of first assault on San Sebastián: actions at Maya and Roncesvalles take place simultaneously	
	28–30	Soult defeated at Sorauren, and near Lizaso	
Aug	1	Soult retreats down Bidasoa valley: actions at Sumbilla and bridge of Yanci	
	2	Action at Etxalar	
	12		Austria declares war on France
	26		French, under Macdonald, defeated at Katzbach
	26–27		Napoleon defeats Allies at Dresden

	30		French, under Vandamme, defeated at Kulm, report of which reaches Wellington on 15 Sept.
	31	Spanish troops repulse Soult at San Marcial	
		San Sebastián successfully stormed	
Sept	3	Wellington hears of rupture of Armistice of Pläswitz (Pleiswitz) and that Austria has re-entered war	
	8	San Sebastián's citadel surrenders	
	15	Wellington receives detailed report on fords at mouth of Bidasoa	
	19	Wellington informs Bathurst of decision to invade France	
Oct	3		Anglo-Austrian treaty signed
	7	Passage of Bidasoa: Allied troops enter France	
	16–19		Napoleon defeated at Leipzig
	20		Battle of Hanau
	31	Pamplona surrenders	
Nov	10	Battle of the Nivelle	
Dec	8	Wellington receives confirmation of Napoleon's defeat at Leipzig	
	9–13	Battles of the Nive and St Pierre (13th)	
	10		Treaty of Valençay signed
	17		Graham's expeditionary force lands in Holland
1814			
Jan	7		Castlereagh reaches the Hague, and Basle on 18th
	16	Action at Molins de Rey, Catalonia	
	29		Battle of Brienne
Feb	1		Battle of La Rothière
	5		Peace Congress opens at Châtillon
	10–14		Battles of Champaubert, Montmirail, Vauchamps
	15	Combat at Garris	
	17	Jaca surrenders	
	18		Battle of Montereau
	26	Hope crosses bridge of boats at Bayonne	
	27	Soult defeated at Battle of Orthez	
Mar	2	Combat at Aire	
	8	Beresford detached towards Bordeaux	
	8–9		British failure at Bergen-op-Zoom
	9		Signing of Treaty of Chaumont or 'Quadruple Alliance' (dated 1st)
	9–10		Napoleon defeated at Laon
	12	Beresford's troops occupy Bordeaux	
	20	French rearguard actions near Tarbes	
	20–21		Napoleon defeated at Arcis-sur-Aube
	24	Soult's army enters Toulouse	
	25		Marmont and Mortier defeated at Fère-Champenoise
	31		Marmont signs Capitulation of Paris

Apr	6		Napoleon abdicates unconditionally
	7	Action at Etauliers (north-east of Bordeaux)	
	10	Soult defeated at Toulouse	
	12	Wellington receives news of Napoleon's abdication	
	14	Sortie from Bayonne	
	16		Treaty of Fontainebleau signed
	27	Bayonne formally surrenders	
	30	Wellington leaves Toulouse for Paris, returning on 14 May	
May	3	Wellington created Duke	
	17	Wellington leaves Toulouse for Madrid	
	24	Wellington in Madrid until 8 June	
	30		Treaty of Paris signed
June	13	Wellington resigns command of Spanish forces	
	14	Wellington's Farewell to his troops at Bordeaux	
	23		Wellington reaches Dover after continuous absence from Britain of 5 years 2 months
June/July		Allied troops near Bayonne dispersed	
Aug	8		Wellington leaves for Paris as ambassador
1815			
Jan	24		Wellington leaves Paris for Congress of Vienna
Feb	26		Napoleon escapes from Elba
Mar	7		News of escape reaches Wellington at Vienna
	20		Napoleon enters Paris
	29		Wellington leaves Vienna for Brussels, arriving 5 Apr
June	18		Napoleon defeated at Waterloo

B. ORDERS OF BATTLE
Marching strengths, 25 May 1813

ANGLO-PORTUGUESE FORCES
Commanded by Arthur, Viscount Wellington.
*Note: Several minor changes took place after the Battle of Vitoria (21 June)
and before the battles of the Pyrenees.*

INFANTRY

1st Division
(Kenneth Alexander Howard)

The Hon. Edward Stopford: 1st Coldstream Guards; 3rd Guards, 1st Scots Guards; one company 5/60th
Sir Colin Halkett: K.G.L.: 1st, 2nd, 5th Line Bns; 1st, 2nd Light Bns

*Note: The 1/1st and 3/1st Guards, having marched from Oporto, did not reach the front at San Sebastián until early August, having
covered a distance of 268 miles in 22 days, with three halt days.*

2nd Division
(Sir Rowland Hill)

The Hon. Henry Cadogan: 1/50th; 1/71st; 1/92nd; one company 5/60th (Cadogan, killed at Vitoria, was
   replaced by John Cameron)
John Byng: 1/3rd; 1/57th; 1st Provisional Bn (2/31st; 2/66th); one company 5/60th
Hon. Robert O'Callaghan: 1/28th; 2/34th; 1/39th: one company 5/60th (O'Callaghan was later replaced by
   William Pringle)
Sir Charles Ashworth's Portuguese Brigade: 6th; 18th; 6th Caçadores

3rd Division
(Sir Thomas Picton)

Sir Thomas Brisbane: 1/45th; 74th; 1/88th; three companies 5/60th
The Hon. Charles Colville: 1/5th; 2/83rd; 2/87th; 94th
Sir Manley Power's Portuguese Brigade: 9th; 21st; 11th Caçadores

4th Division
(Sir Galbraith Lowry Cole)

William Anson: 3/27th; 1/40th; 1/48th; 2nd Prov. Bn (2nd and 2/53rd); one company of 5/60th
John Skerrett: 1/7th; 20th; 1/23rd; one company Brunswick Oels
George Stubbs: 11th; 23rd; 7th Caçadores

5th Division
(John Oswald—for Sir James Leith)

Andrew Hay: 3/1st; 1/9th; 1/38th; one company Brunswick Oels
Sir Frederick Robinson: 1/4th; 2/27th; 2/59th; one company Brunswick Oels
William Spry's Portuguese Brigade: 3rd; 15th; 8th Caçadores

6th Division
(Sir Edward Pakenham—for Henry Clinton)

Stirling: 1/42nd; 1/79th; 1/91st; one company 5/60th
Hinde: 1/11th; 1/32nd; 1/36th; 1/61st (Hinde was later replaced by John Lambert)
George Madden's Portuguese Brigade: 8th; 12th; 9th Caçadores

7th Division
(George, Earl of Dalhousie)

Edward Barnes: 1/6th; 3rd Prov. Bn (2/24th; 2/58th); nine companies Brunswick Oels
William Grant: 51st; 68th; 1/82nd; Chasseurs Britanniques (Grant was later replaced by William Inglis)

Carlos Le Cor's Portuguese Brigade
7th; 19th; 2nd Caçadores

Light Division
(Sir Charles von Alten)

Sir James Kempt: 1/43rd; 1st and 3/95th
Sir John Ormsby Vandeleur: 1/52nd; 2/95th
Portuguese battalions: 17th; 1st and 3rd Caçadores

Portuguese Division
(Francisco Silveira)

Hippolito da Costa: 2nd; 14th
Archibald Campbell: 4th; 10th; 10th Caçadores

Sir Denis Pack's Portuguese Brigade
1st; 16th; 4th Caçadores

Henry Bradford's Portuguese Brigade
3th; 24th; 5th Caçadores

CAVALRY

Sir Robert Hill: 1st and 2nd Life Guards, Horse Guards
The Hon. William Ponsonby: 5th Dragoon Guards; 3rd and 4th Dragoons
George Anson: 11th?, 12th and 16th Dragoons
Robert Long: 13th Light Dragoons
Victor von Alten: 14th Light Dragoons; 1st Hussars K.G.L.
Eberhard von Bock 1st and 2nd Dragoons K.G.L.
Henry Fane: 3rd Dragoon Guards; 1st Dragoons
Colquhuon Grant: 10th, 15th, 18th Hussars
Benjamin D'Urban's Portuguese Brigade: 1st, 11th, 12th
Campbell's 6th Portuguese

ARTILLERY

R.H.A. and drivers
Field Artillery, train, ammunition, etc
K.G.L. Artillery
Portuguese Artillery

Engineers and Sappers
Staff Corps
Wagon train

SPANISH FORCES

INFANTRY

Pedro Augustín Girón's 4th Army
Pablo Morillo's Division
Francisco Xavier Losada's Galician Division (6 battalions)
Pedro Barcena's Galician Division (7 battalions)
Juan Diaz Porlier's Asturian Division (3 battalions)
Francisco Longa's Division (5 battalions)
Carlos de España's Division (5 battalions); joined on 28 July
Enrique O'Donnell's 'Army of Reserve of Andalusia'; joined on 16 July

CAVALRY

Conde de Penne Villemur's cavalry (7 regiments)
Julián Sánchez's cavalry (2 regiments)
Pedro Barcena's cavalry (2 regiments)

ARTILLERY

Pedro de Echevarri's Division (7 battalions)
Creagh's Division (7 battalions)

FRENCH FORCES
Commanded by Joseph Bonaparte and Jean-Baptiste Jourdan
Line regiments unless Léger specified

ARMY OF THE SOUTH
Honoré Gazan de la Peyrière

1st Division
(Jean-François Leval)

Mocquery: 9th Léger, 24th
Morgan: 88th, 96th
Divisional battery and train

2nd Division
On loan to the Army of the Centre—see below

3rd Division
(Eugène Villatte)

Rignoux: 27th
Etienne-Nicolas Lefol: 94th, 85th Léger, 63rd
Divisional battery and train

4th Division
(Nicolas Conroux)

Jean-Pierre Rey: 32nd, 43rd
Schwitter: 55th, 58th
Divisional battery and train

5th Division
(Jean-Pierre Maransin)

12th Léger, 45th

6th Division
(Augustin Daricau)

St Pol: 21st Léger, 100th
Rémond: 28th Léger, 103rd
Divisional battery and train

Pierre Soult's Cavalry Division
2nd Hussars, 5th, 10th, 21st Chasseurs; one battery H.A. and train
Jacques-Louis Tilly's Division: 2nd, 4th, 14th, 17th, 26th, 27th Dragoons
Alexandre Digeon's Division: 5th, 12th, 16th, 21st Dragoons; one battery H.A. and train

Artillery Reserve: two batteries and train
Artillery Park: two companies field artillery; one company pontoniers, artificers, and train
Engineers: two companies of sappers, two of miners and wagon train
Gendarmerie

ARMY OF THE CENTRE

1st Division
(Jean-Barthélemy Darmagnac)

Chassé: 28th, 75th
Neuenstein: 2nd Nassau (2)?, 4th Baden, Frankfort

2nd Division
(Cassagne)

Braun: 16th Léger, 8th
Blondeau 51st, 54th

Anne-François Treillard's Division
13th, 18th, 19th, 22nd Dragoons
Antoine-Sylvain Avy's Light Cavalry: 27th Chasseurs, Nassau Chasseurs
Artillery: 3 batteries and train
Engineers: 1 company sappers
Wagon train, etc.

The King's Spanish Army
Guy: Royal Guards: Grenadiers, tirailleurs, voltiguers of the Guard,Hussars and Lancers of the Guard
Casapalacio: Regiments of Castile, Toledo, Royal Étranger
Cavalry: 1st and 2nd Chasseurs, Hussars of Guadalajara
Artillery: one battery

ARMY OF PORTUGAL
(Honoré Reille)

4th Division
(Sarrut)

Joseph Fririon: 2nd Léger, 36th
Menne: 4th Léger, 65th
Divisional field battery and train

6th Division
(Thomas Lamartinière)

Gauthier: 118th, 119th
120th, 122nd
Divisional field battery and train

Julien Mermet's Cavalry Division
Jean-Baptiste Curto: 13th and 22nd Chasseurs
?: 3rd Hussars, 14th and 26th Chasseurs

Joseph Boyer's Division
6th, 11th, 15th, 25th Dragoons

Reserve Artillery
One H.A. four field batteries
One company pontoniers, artificers, train
Engineers: two companies sappers
Gendarmerie
Wagon train, mule train, etc.

Note: After Vitoria, the army was consolidated under Nicolas Soult, and the following changes took place:

1st Division
(Maximilien Foy)

Fririon: 6th Léger, 69th (2), 76th
Berlier: 36th (2), 39th, 65th (2)

2nd Division
(Jean-Barthélemy Darmagnac)

Chassé: 16th Léger, 8th, 28th (2)
Gruardet: 51st, 54th, 75th (2)

3rd Division
(Louis-Jean Abbé)

Rignoux (later replaced by Boivin): 27th Léger, 63rd, 64th (2)
Rémond (later replaced by Maucomble): 5th Léger (2), 32rd (2), 43rd (2)

4th Division
(Nicolas Conroux)

Jean-Pierre Rey: 12 Léger, 32nd (2), 43rd (2)
Schwitter (later replaced by Jean-Baptiste Baurot): 45th, 55th, 58th

5th Division
(Louis van der Maessen—later replaced by Jean-Pierre Maransin)

Barbot: 25th Léger, 1st, 27th
Rouget: 50th, 59th, 130th (2)

6th Division
(Jean-Pierre Maransin—later replaced by Augustin Daricau)

St Pol: 21st Léger, 24th, 96th
Mocquery: 28th Léger, 101st (2), 103rd

7th Division
(Antoine-Louis Maucune)

Pierre-Armand Pinoteau: 17th Léger, 15th (2), 66th
Montfort: 34th Léger, 82nd, 86th

8th Division
(Eloi Taupin)

Béchaud: 9th Léger (2), 26th, 47th (2)
Lecamus(later replaced by Dein): 31st Léger, 70th (2), 88th

9th Division
(Thomas Lamartinière—later replaced by Joseph Boyer)

Menne: 2nd Léger, 118th (2), 119th (2)
Gauthier: 120th (3), 122nd (2)

Reserve Division
(Eugène Villatte)

Pierre Thouvenot and Boivin: (? J.-B. Jamin) 1/4th Léger, 1 & 2/10th Léger, 3/31st Léger; 1/3rd, 2/34th,
    1 & 3/40th, 1/101st, 1 & 2/105th
From old Bayonne Reserve: 4/114th (detachment), 4 & 5/115th, 4/116th, 4/117th, 3/118th, 3/119th
From among foreign troops:
Neuenstein's German Brigade: 4th Baden, 2nd Nassau (2), Frankfort
St Pol's Italian Brigade: 2nd Léger, 4th, 6th
Casapalacio's Spanish Brigade: Castile, Toledo, Royal Étranger
Guy: King Joseph's Guard: three regiments.
Also
Gendarmes of the 4th and 5th Legions
National Guards

Acting as corps cavalry with field army: 13th, 15th, 22nd Chasseurs
Pierre Soult's Division: 5th and 12th Dragoons, 2nd Hussars, 5th, 10th, 21st Chasseurs, Nassau Chasseurs,
    and Spanish cavalry
Anne-François Treillard's Division: 4th, 14th, 16th, 17th, 21st, 26th Dragoons

At the battles of the Pyrenees the French infantry divisions were grouped under the following commands:
Reille: 1st, 7th, and 9th
Clausel: 4th, 5th, and 8th
D'Erlon: 2nd, 3rd, and 6th
Reserve under Villatte facing Graham on the coast

C. DISTRIBUTION OF TROOPS
DURING THE BATTLES OF THE PYRENEES

ANGLO-PORTUGUESE FORCES
*Note: There may have been other units near these battlegrounds
which neither went into action nor suffered casualties.*

At Maya

2nd Division
(Sir William Stewart)

John Cameron's Brigade: 1/50th; 1/71st; 1/92nd
William Pringle's Brigade: 1/28th; 2/34th; 1/39th
Two companies 5/60th attached to the above
Da Costa's Portuguese Brigade: 2nd; 14th

7th Division
Edward Barnes: 1/6th; 1/82nd; Brunswick Oels
Also some Artillery

At Roncesvalles

2nd Division
John Byng's Brigade: 1/3rd; 57th; 1st Provisional Battalion (2/31st; 2/66th)

4th Division
(Sir Galbraith Lowry Cole)

Robert Ross's Brigade: 1/7th; 20th. 1/23rd; one company Brunswick Oels
William Anson's Brigade: 3/27th; 1/40th; 1/48th; 2nd Provisional Battalion (2nd and 2/53rd)
Archibald Campbell's Portuguese Brigade: 4th; 10th; 10th *Caçadores*
George Stubbs's Portuguese Brigade: 11th; 23rd; 7th *Caçadores*

Pablo Morillo's Regiment of León

At Sorauren
28 July; additionally in action on 30 July

2nd Division
John Byng's Brigade: See above, plus 1/57th
Sir Charles Ashworth's Portuguese Brigade: 6th; 18th; 6th *Caçadores*

3rd Division
(Sir Thomas Picton)
Suffered no losses on the 28th

Sir Thomas Brisbane's Brigade: 1/45th; 74th; 1/88th; four companies 5/60th
Sir Manley Power's Portuguese Brigade: 9th; 21st; 11th *Caçadores*

4th Division
See above

6th Division
(Sir Denis Pack—wounded; replaced by Sir Edward Pakenham on 30 July)
Stirling's Brigade: 1/42nd; 1/79th; 1/91st; one company 5/60th
John Lambert's Brigade: 1/11th; 1/32nd; 1/36th; 1/61st
George Madden's Port. Brigade: 8th; 12th; 9th *Caçadores*

7th Division
(George, Earl of Dalhousie)
Saw no action on the 28th
Edward Barnes's Brigade: 1/6th; 3rd Prov. Batt. (2/24th and 2/58th); nine companies Brunswick Oels
William Inglis's Brigade: 51st; 68th;1/82nd; Chasseurs Britaniques
Carlos Le Cor's Portuguese. Brigade: 7th; 19th; 2nd *Caçadores*

At Beunza/ Lizaso

2nd Division
John Fitzgerald's Brigade (formerly John Cameron's): See above
William Pringle's Brigade: See above
Sir Charles Ashworth's Portuguese. Brigade: See above

Cavalry: 14th Light Dragoons; 1st Hussars K.G.L.

4th Division
Hippolito Da Costa's Portuguese Brigade: See above

7th Division
William Inglis's Brigade: See above

At Dona Maria

2nd Division
John Fitzgerald's Brigade: See above
William Pringle's Brigade: See above

4th Division
William Inglis's Brigade: See above

At Etxalar

7th Division
Edward Barnes's Brigade: See above

Light Division
Sir James Kempt's Brigade: 1/43rd; 1/95th; 3/95th

SPANISH FORCES
Status at 1 June

Girón's 4th Army
  Morillo's division
  Losada's Galician division (6 battalions)
  Pedro Barcena's Galician division (7 battalions)
  Porlier's Asturian division (3 battalions)
  Longa's division (5 battalions)
  Penne Villemur's cavalry (7 regiments)
  Julián Sánchez's cavalry (2 regiments)
  Artillery

Joined on 16 July

Echevarri's division (7 battalions)
Creagh's division (7 battalions)
C.G. Barcena's cavalry (2 regiments)
Artillery

Re-joined on 28 July

De España's division of 4th Army (5 battalions)

Some of Espoz y Mina's irregulars were also operating in the area

FRENCH INFANTRY

At Roncesvalles and Sorauren

Reille's command

1st Division (Foy)
7th Division (Maucune)
9th Division (Lamartinière)

Clausel's command

4th Division (Conroux)
5th Division (van der Maessen)
8th Division (Taupin)

At Maya and Beunza/Lizaso

D'Erlon's command

2nd Division (Darmagnac)
3rd Division (Abbé)
6th Division (Maransin)

D. ORDERS OF BATTLE
October/early November 1813

ANGLO-PORTUGUESE FORCES
Commanded by Arthur, Viscount Wellington

INFANTRY

Sir John Hope's Corps, consisting of the 1st and 5th Divisions, was engaged at the Passage of the Bidasoa, Nivelle/Nive, and then Bayonne, but it was not at Orthez nor at Toulouse; Sir Rowland Hill's Corps consisted of the 2nd, 6th, and Portuguese Divisions; and Sir William Carr Beresford's Corps consisted of the 3rd, 4th, 7th, and Light Divisions.

1st Division
(Kenneth Alexander Howard)

Sir Peregrine Maitland: 1st Guards, 1st and 3rd Battalions

The Hon. Edward Stopford: 1st Coldstream Guards; 1/3rd (Scots) Guards

Heinrich von Hinüber (replacing Sir Colin Halkett on 20 Oct.): K.G.L.: 1st, 2nd, 5th Line Battalions; 1st, 2nd Light Battalions

Sir Matthew Aylmer's Independent Brigade: 2/62nd; 76th; 77th; 2/84th; 85th

2nd Division
Sir William Stewart

George Walker (previously John Fitzgerald's, who had replaced John Cameron; Walker was replaced by Edward Barnes at St-Pierre): 1/50th; 1/71st; 1/92nd

John Byng: 1/3rd; 1/57th; 1st Provisional Battalion (four companies each 2/31st; 2/66th)

William Pringle: 1/28th; 2/34th; 1/39th

Sir Charles Ashworth's Portuguese Brigade: 6th; 18th; 6th *Caçadores*

3rd Division
(The Hon. Charles Colville; previously Sir Thomas Picton's)

Sir Thomas Brisbane: 1/45th; 74th; 1/88th; 5/60th (seven companies were distributed among other brigades at the Bidasoa)

Sir John Keane (previously The Hon. Charles Colville's): 1/5th; 2/83rd; 2/87th; 94th

Sir Manley Power's Portuguese Brigade: 9th; 21st; 11th *Caçadores*

4th Division
(Sir Galbraith Lowry Cole)

William Anson: 3/27th; 1/40th; 1/48th; 2nd Provisional Battalion (2nd and 2/53rd)

Robert Ross (previously John Skerrett's?): 1/7th; 20th; 1/23rd

José Vasconcellos's Portuguese Brigade (previously George Stubbs', then James Miller's): 11th; 23rd; 7th *Caçadores*

5th Division
(Andrew Hay, replacing John Oswald, and then Sir James Leith, wounded at San Sebastián)

Charles Greville (replacing Andrew Hay): 3/1st; 1/9th; 1/38th

Sir Frederick Robinson: 1/4th; 2/27th; 2/59th

Luiz de Regoa's Portuguese Brigade (William Spry): 3rd; 15th; 8th *Caçadores*

John Wilson's Independent Portuguese Brigade (previously Sir Denis Pack's; Wilson was replaced by Archibald Campbell at Nivelle): 1st; 16th; 4th *Caçadores*

Henry Bradford's Independent Portuguese Brigade: 13th; 24th; 5th *Caçadores*

6th Division
(Sir Henry Clinton, although Pack commanded at Sorauren,
and when wounded was temporarily replaced by Pakenham, and then by Colville)

Sir Denis Pack (previously Stirling): 1/42nd; 1/79th; 1/91st
John Lambert (previously Hinde): 1/11th; 1/32nd; 1/36th; 1/61st
Sir James Douglas's Portuguese Brigade (previously George Madden's): 8th; 12th; 9th *Caçadores*

7th Division
(Carlos Le Cor, replacing George, Earl of Dalhousie, and himself replaced by George Walker at Nive)

Edward Barnes: 1/6th; 3rd Provisional Battalion (2/24th; 2/58th); Brunswick Oels Chasseurs (which had
 been with 1st and 2nd Divisions at Bidasoa)
William Inglis (previously William Grant's): 51st; 68th; 1/82nd; Chasseurs Britanniques
Charles Doyle's Portuguese Brigade (previously Carlos Le Cor's): 7th; 19th; 2nd Caçadores

Light Division
(Sir Charles Alten)

Sir James Kempt: 1/43rd; 1/95th; 3/95th
Sir John Colborne (replacing John Skerrett): 1/52nd; 2/95th
Portuguese Battalions: 17th; 1st and 3rd Caçadores

Portuguese Division
(Sir John Hamilton; provisionally Francisco Silveira's; Hamilton replaced by Le Cor at Nive)

Hippolito da Costa: 4th; 10th; 10th *Caçadores*: (Archibald Campbell at Nivelle; later commanded by John Buchan)
John Buchan: 2nd; 14th: (with Da Costa at St Pierre; later Archibald Campbell's brigade)

CAVALRY
See following Orders of Battle:

Sir Stapleton Cotton, Bart.
Henry Fane, Hussey Vivian, Lord Edward Somerset, Lord Charles Manners (replacing The Hon William
 Ponsonby), Johann von Bülow, and Clifton
? Campbell
O'Loghlin
Sir John Vandeleur

ARTILLERY

Alexander Dickson
Victor von Arentchildt
H. A. Gardner

SPANISH FORCES

INFANTRY

Manuel Freire's 4th Army 'of Galicia'
1st Division: Pablo Morillo (half with Hill at St-Jean-Pied-de-Port, half remaining at Navarrenx later)
2nd Division: Carlos de España (blockaded Pamplona and later invested Bayonne)
3rd Division: Francisco Xavier Losada (wounded at San Marcial, replaced by Diego Del Barco; later half invested Bayonne and half served at Toulouse)
4th Division: Pedro Barcena (replaced by José Manuel Espeleta)

5th Division: Juan Diaz Porlier (later, half at Bayonne and half served at Toulouse; picked battalions from 4th amalgamated with the 5th, plus one battalion from 3rd Division under Antonio Garcés de Marcilla; served at Toulouse)

6th Division: Francisco Longa (sent back to Spain after Nivelle)

7th Division: Gabriel Mendizábal (sent back to Spain and to Santoña after San Marcial)

8th Division: Francisco Espoz y Mina (blockaded St-Jean-Pied-de-Port)

CAVALRY
Remained in the Ebro valley

ARTILLERY
And engineers

Pedro Augustin Girón's 'Army of Reserve of Andalusia' (sent back to Spain after Nivelle but recalled to Bayonne in late Feb. 1814)

1st Division: Virues

2nd Division: La Torre; Creagh

Pedro, Principe de Anglona's '3rd Army' (17,000 strong in Dec. 1813, crossed the Pyrenees and in Apr. 1814 occupied Pau and Orthez, when 21,000 strong)

Enrique O'Donnell's 'Andalusian Reserve' (about 5,000 strong, plus 700 cavalry and 300 artillery, were to blockade Pamplona, relieving De España's troops)

FRENCH FORCES
Commanded by Marshal Nicolas Soult, Duc de Dalmatie

The army was divided into three 'corps', at first with the 2nd, 3rd, and 6th Divisions under Jean-Baptiste Drouet, Comte D'Erlon; the 7th and 9th under Honoré Reille; and the 4th, 5th, and 8th under Bertrand Clausel. However, the divisions under their control varied during the period prior to the Battle of Toulouse.

INFANTRY
Note: Those at Nivelle are listed in the left-hand column and those at Toulouse in the right-hand column. Each regiment—Line unless Léger—had one battalion each unless a '2' or '3' is indicated in parentheses.

1st Division
(Foy; wounded at Orthez, replaced by Daricau at Toulouse)

Fririon: 6th Léger, 69th (2), 76th	No change
Berlier: 36th (2), 39th, 65th (2)	No change

2nd Division
(Darmagnac)

Chassé: 16th Léger, 8th, 28th (2)	Leseur: 31st Léger, 51st, 75th (2)
Gruardet: 51st, 54th, 75th (2)	Menne: 118th (3), 120th (3)

3rd Division
(Abbé; the division remained at Bayonne after the battle of St-Pierre)

Boivin: 27th Léger, 63rd, 64th (2). Boivin replaced by Baurot at Nive

Maucomble: 5th Léger, 94th (2), 95th

4th Division
(Conroux; killed at Nivelle, and replaced by Taupin)

Rey: 12th Léger (2), 32nd (2), 43rd (2)   Similar but only 1 batt. 12th
Jean-Baptiste Baurot: 45th, 55th, 58th   Gasquet: 47th (2), 55th, 58th

5th Division
(Maransin; replaced by Claude-Pierre Rouget at Orthez but again in command at Toulouse)

Barbot: 4th Léger, 34th, 40th (2), 50th   Similar, but no 34th
Rouget: 27th, 59th, 130th (2)   27th, 34th, 59th

6th Division
(Daricau; replaced by Villatte at Orthez)

St Pol: 21st Léger, 24th, 96th   21st Léger, 86th, 96th, 100th
Mocquery: 28th Léger, 100th, 103rd   Lamorandière: 28th Léger, 103rd, 119th (2)

7th Division
(Maucune; replaced by Leval at Nivelle, and the division ordered to the Rhine front)

Pinoteau: 17th Léger, 3rd, 15th Line
Montfort: 16th Léger (2), 101st, 105th (2)

8th Division
(Taupin; the division was dissolved after the Nivelle and replaced by Villatte's reserves and Paris's troops under Jean-Isadore Harispe)

Béchaud: 9th Léger (2), 26th, 47th (2)   Dauture: 9th Léger (2), 25th
                                                 Léger (2), 34th Léger (2)
Dein: 31st Léger (3), 70th, 88th   Baurot: 10th Léger (2), 45th,
                                                 81st, 115th, 116th, 117th

9th Division
(Boyer; ordered to the Rhine front after Nive)

Boyer: 2nd Léger (2), 32nd (2), 43rd (2)
Gauthier: 120th (3), 122nd (2)
Marie-Auguste Paris's Brigade   Absorbed by the 6th Division after the Nive

Reserve Division
(Villatte; replaced by Jean-Pierre Travot after Orthez)

Absorbed after Nive by 6th Division   Brigades under Pourailly and Wouillemont;
Jamin: 34th Léger (2), 66th, 82nd, 115th (2),   conscript battalions
Spanish Brigade (4), Italian Brigade (3) and
   German Brigade (4)

Garrisons at Bayonne under Thouvenot; at
   St-Jean-Pied-de-Port; and at Pamplona under
   Louis-Pierre Cassan.

                                                 Gendarmerie

ARTILLERY and train, pontoniers, etc.   Also at Toulouse
ENGINEERS, sappers, etc.   Also at Toulouse

CAVALRY, largely cantoned in the rear under Treilhard and, after the Nive, commanded by Pierre Soult

At Toulouse were two brigades, under Berton, with 2nd Hussars and 13th and 21st Chasseurs; and Vial, with 5th, 10th, 15th and ?22nd Chasseurs

FRENCH DIVISIONAL COMMANDERS

		Bidasoa	Nivelle/Nive	Orthez	Toulouse
1	Foy			Wounded 27 Feb. (Fririon, Paris)	Daricau
2	Darmagnac				
3	Abbé			(Left at Bayonne)	
4	Conroux		Killed 10 Nov.	Taupin	(Killed)
5	Van der Maessen	Killed 31 Aug.		Rouget	Maransin
6	Daricau			Villatte	
7	Maucune		Leval (7 Oct.), then went to join Napoleon		
8	Taupin		Harispe		
9	Lamartinière		Boyer (7 Oct.), then went to join Napoleon		
Res.	Villatte	Maransin] (from Res.) Paris's Brigade			Travot
Cavalry				Pierre Soult	

E. ORDERS OF BATTLE
January/February 1814

ANGLO-PORTUGUESE FORCES

INFANTRY

1st Division
(Kenneth Alexander Howard)

Sir Peregrine Maitland: 1 and 3/1st Guards; one company 5/60th

The Hon. Edward Stopford: 1st Coldstream; 1st Scots; one company 5/60th (Stopford, wounded at Bayonne, was replaced by John Wright Guise)

Heinrich von Hinüber: 1st, 2nd, 5th K.G.L.; 1st. 2nd Light Battalions K.G.L.

Sir Matthew Aylmer: 2/62nd; 76th; 77th; 85th. The 1/37th joined by 25 March

2nd Division
(Sir William Stewart)

Edward Barnes: 1/50th; 1/71st; 1/92nd; one company 5/60th

John Byng: 1/3rd; 1/57th; 1st. Provisional Battalion (2/31st and 2/66th); one company 5/60th

William Pringle: 1/28th; 2/34th; 1/39th; one company 5/60th (Pringle was wounded on 15 February and replaced by The Hon. Robert O'Callaghan at Orthez)

Sir Charles Ashworth's Portuguese (Ashworth was replaced by Henry Harding on 16 January)

3rd Division
(Sir Thomas Picton, who returned to replace The Hon. Charles Colville before Orthez)

Sir Thomas Brisbane: 1/45th; Headquarters 5/60th; 74th; 1/88th (Brisbane was slightly wounded at Toulouse)

Sir John Keane: 1/5th; 2/83rd; 2/87th; 94th

Sir Manley Power's Portuguese

4th Division
(Sir Galbraith Lowry Cole)

William Anson: 3/27th; 1/40th; 1/48th; 2nd Provisional Battalion (2nd and 2/53rd); one company Brunswick Oels

Robert Ross: 1/7th; 1/20th; 1/23rd; one company 5/60th (Ross was wounded at Orthez)

José Vasconcellos's Portuguese

5th Division
(The Hon. Charles Colville)

Andrew Hay: 3/1st; 1/9th; 1/38th; 2/47th; one company Brunswick Oels (Hay was killed at Bayonne on 14 April)

Sir Frederick Robinson: 1/4th; 2/59th; 2/84th; one company Brunswick Oels (Robinson was absent after 1 February)

Luiz de Regoa's Portuguese

6th Division
(Sir Henry Clinton)

Sir Denis Pack: 1/42nd; 1/79th; 1/91st; one company 5/60th (Pack was wounded at Toulouse)

John Lambert: 1/11th; 1/32nd (absent at Toulouse); 1/36th; 1/61st

Sir James Douglas's Portuguese (Douglas was wounded at Toulouse)

7th Division
(George Walker; Walker was wounded at Orthez
and went home, and the Earl of Dalhousie resumed command)

John Gardiner (replacing Edward Barnes): 1/6th; 3rd Provisional Battalion (2/24th and 2/58th); Headquarters Brunswick Oels
William Inglis: 51st; 68th; 1/82nd; Chasseurs Britanniques
Charles Doyle's Portuguese

Light Division
(Sir Charles von Alten)

Sir James Kempt: 1/43rd; 1/95th; 3/95th; 1st *Caçadores* (both the 1/43rd and the 1/95th were absent from Orthez)
Sir John Colborne: 1/52nd; 2/95th; 3rd *Caçadores*; 17th Portuguese

Portuguese Division
(Carlos Le Cor; replacing Sir John Hamilton)

Hippolito da Costa's and John Buchan's brigades (da Costa was ordered back to Portugal by 15 March and replaced by Almeida after the combat at Aire)
Archibald Campbell's and Henry Bradford's unattached brigades

CAVALRY
(Sir Stapleton Cotton, Bart.)

I. O'Loghlin: 1st and 2nd Life Guards; Royal Horse Guards
F. The Hon. William Ponsonby: 5th Dragoon Guards; 3rd (Lord Charles Manners) and 4th Dragoons (Ponsonby absent from 25 January and replaced by Manners)
C. Sir John Vandeleur: 12th and 16th Light Dragoons
D. Sir Richard Hussey Vivian: 13th (Doherty) and 14th Light Dragoons
E. Victor von Alten: 18th Hussars; 1st Hussars K.G.L. (von Alten replaced on 16 January by Vivian, who when wounded on 8 April was replaced by Frederic Augustus von Arentschildt; also H. von Grüben?)
G. Baron von Bock: 1st (F. A. von Arentschildt) and 2nd Dragoons K.G.L. (Bock, drowned *en route* to England in February, was replaced by F. A. von Arentschildt by 25 March, who was himself replaced by Johann von Bülow)
B. Henry Fane: 3rd Dragoon Guards; 1st (Royal) Dragoons (Clifton) (by 16 January Fane had replaced Vivian, under whom Clifton and Doherty commanded B and D Brigades, respectively)
H. Lord Edward Somerset: 7th, 10th, and 15th Hussars

For Orders of Battle for the French forces at Toulouse, see pp. 275–60.

F. Numbers of Troops Present at Actions

The figures in brackets in the left-hand column are those of Vitoria less casualties. These are provided only to give some very rough idea of the numbers available, although the figures may well have been higher, on the assumption that those only slightly wounded would have returned to the ranks. The 1st and 5th Divisions were to form Hope's Corps, the 2nd and 6th to form Hill's, and the 3rd, 4th, 7th and Light to form Beresford's

	Pyrenees	Nivelle	Nive/St-P.	Orthez	Toulouse	Bayonne
Anglo-Portuguese Infantry						
1st Division	Howard					
	Stopford					
	Halkett	v. Hinüber				
		Maitland				
	(4,800)	6,898				7,263 inc. 5th Div.
2nd Division	Hill	Stewart				
	Walker		Barnes			
	Byng					
	Pringle			O'Callaghan		
	Ashworth			Harding		
	(9,702)	8,480		7,780	6,940	
3rd Division	Picton	Colville		Picton		
	Brisbane					
	Colville	Keane				
	Power					
	(6,054)	7,334		6,626	4,566	
4th Division	Cole					
	W. Anson					
	Ross					
	Stubbs	Vasconcellos				
	(7,445)	6,585		5,952	5,363	
5th Division	Oswald	Hay				
	Hay	Greville				
	Robinson					
	Spry	De Regoa				
	Bradford	4,553				
		Aylmer				
		1,816				See 1st Div.
	(8,509)	6,369				
6th Division	H. Clinton					
	Pack/Paken-	Colville		Pack		
	ham					
	Lambert					
	Douglas					
	?Madden					
	(7,347)	6,456		5,571		

7th Division	Dalhousie	Le Cor	Walker			
	Barnes			Gardiner	–	
	W. Grant	Inglis			–	
	Le Cor	Doyle			–	
	?Miller					
	(7,047)	6,068		5,643	Then with Dalhousie at Bordeaux	
Light Division	C. Alten					
	Kempt					
	Vandeleur	Colborne				
	Portuguese					
	Skerrett					
	(5,319)	4,970		3,480	4,275	
Silveira's former Portuguese Div.	Hamilton	Le Cor				
	Da Costa	2,558				
	Wilson	2,185				
	Buchan	2,391				
	Bradford	1,614				
	(5,277)	8,748		4,465	3,952	
Pack's Portu- guese Brigade	(2,222)					

			Nivelle	Orthez	Toulouse
Infantry:	Brit.		38,264	22,323	18,136
	Port.		24,020	17,194	12,653
	Anglo- Port.	c.60,000	62,284	39,517	30,789
Artillery:	British		628	1,052	1,510
	Port.		220	110	440
	Anglo- Port.		848	1,162	1,950
Cavalry:	Anglo- Port.	(8,160) (see below)		3,373	6,490 (6,025 engaged)
Staff, Eng., Wagon, etc.				(350)	(500, less than)
Spanish:	Infantry (see below)		7,653 (Girón) 17,720 (Freire) 25,373		2,001 (Morillo) 7,916 (Freire) 9,917
Totals			88,505	44,052	49,149

Spanish Infantry

Brig.		Freire's Divisions				
6	1st	(Morillo)	5,129 then at Navarrenx		2,001	
7	3rd	(Losada/Barcena)	5,830			(2,500)
6	4th	(Barcena)	4,154	(Espeleta)	3,576	
3	5th	(Porlier) 4,544				(1,865)

5	6th	(Longa)	2,607			
5	2nd	(De España)	4,580 (3,200 July) blockading Pamplona, then 3,963			
9	8th	(Mina)	8,472 blockading St-Jean-Pied-de-Port			
	Amalg.	(Ant. Garcés de Marcilla)			3,959 + 381 sappers	
			17,720		9,917	
	(artillery, sappers		+856		381	765 at Bayonne)

	Girón's Divisions		
1st	(Virues)	4,123	(5,008)
2nd	(La Torre)	3,530	(4,286)
		7,653	(9,294)
		25,373	9,917

3 7th (Mendizábal)

O'Donnell's Reserve at Pamplona relieving De España c. 5,000, plus 700 cavalry and 300 artillery
Cavalry: 14 squadrons under Penne Villemur
Julián Sánchez?

Anglo-Portuguese Cavalry	Orthez	Toulouse
Stapleton Cotton:		engaged of
Fane	765	816
Vivian	986	895 (939)
Somerset	1,619	1,611 (1,717)
Manners		1,111 (1,426)
Von Bulow		701
Clifton		891
Totals	3,373	6,025 (6,490)

Soult's Army	Pyrenees	Bidasoa	Nivelle	Nive/St-P.	Orthez	Toulouse	Bayonne
Morning states	*1813*				*1814*		
	July	1 Oct	1 Nov	1 Dec	27 Feb	1 April	
1st Division	5,922	4,654	5,136	5,608	4,600	3,839	
2nd Division	6,961	4,447	4,705	5,914	5,500	5,022	
3rd Division	8,030	6,051	6,326	6,372	–	5,455	
4th Division	7,056	4,962	5,399	6,098	5,600	3,727	
5th Division	4,181	5,575	5,579	5,216	5,000	4,609	
6th Division	5,966	4,092	5,782	5,519	5,200	5,084	
7th Division	4,186	3,996	4,539	4,704	–	–	
8th Division	5,981	4,778	4,889	amalg.	6,600 *	–	
9th Division	7,127	6,515	6,569	6,423	–	–	
(10th)				3,881	–	–	
Reserve	9,102	8,018	8,319	5,397	–	7,267	
Plus foreign troops, etc.	8,152						
Total infantry	72,664 †	53,088	61,443	55,132	32,500	34,993	
Cavalry	7,147 (6,788 in rear)			3,200	2,700		
	79,811				35,700	37,693	

Garrisons at:

Bayonne			4,633		8,801	
St-Jean-Pied-de-Port	(1,600/2,400)					
Pamplona			3,800 combatants			
Artillery	4,000	2,000	4,200	1,300	3,603	?
Engin./Sap.			2,000			
			in forts		541	
Gendarmes					206	

	83,811 (see above)	55,088	70,276	65,935	37,000	42,043	14,294

Approximate comparative numbers:

Anglo-Port.   Inc. Spanish

	57,962?	88,505	44,052	49,149
French, inc. Arty	69,543 (but see †)	70,276 inc. Bayonne garrison	37,000	42,043

Casualties in main actions, but not including San Sebastián:

	Pyrenees	31 Aug.	Bidasoa	Nivelle/ Nive	Orthez	Toulouse	Bayonne sortie
British	4,524		573	2,116	1,645	2,103	809
Portuguese	1,732		242	408	529	533	29
	6,256	844	815	2,524 +4,662 ‡	2,174	2,636	838
Spanish	?	1,679 San Marcial	?	c.820	?	1,922	?

Wellington returned 5,047—say 4,900 in round figures, of which 1,900 or more were Portuguese.

French (approx.)	12,563	3,808	1,800	4,600	5,950	3,236	905

---

* Made up by the 10th and Reserve Divisions

† Oman states that Soult only gave himself credit for 69,543, including the Reserve, for his field army. It is possible that Soult was referring to his three infantry corps only, the cavalry, and Villatte's Gendarmes and National Guards together with his foreign troops *less* Casalpalacio's Spaniards, but *not* including the rest of the Reserves, for this comes to almost exactly this lower figure

‡ 294 crossing Nive; 336 Anglet/Bassussary; 1,497 Barrouillet, but including c.400 taken prisoner; 224 Arcangues; 328 on 11th; 207 on 12th; and 1,775 on 13th.

GLOSSARY

Abatis (abattis) A defensive work formed of trees with their branches facing outwards, usually placed a short distance in front of field works.

Afrancesados Either Spaniards sympathizing with the French and their Revolutionary tenets, among the more prominent of whom were many cultured persons; or merely collaborators.

Bastion A section of fortifications formed at the angle of two walls, and extending beyond the main defences.

Bivouac A temporary improvised shelter against the elements; camping in the open, without tents. See *Cantonments*.

Breach A gap made in a rampart or wall by gunfire or an exploded mine, to allow troops to break in: 'practicable' indicates that it is in a state to be entered without an undue amount of climbing.

Breastwork A 4–5-foot-high protective wall.

Bridgehead (*tête de pont*) Fortifications designed to defend the far end of a bridge or pontoon, sometimes on both banks.

Caçadores (hunters) Portuguese light infantry, armed with rifles.

Caisson A chest containing explosives or a wagon conveying ammunition.

Canister (case shot) A projectile formed by a thin metal tube filled with lead musket balls, fired from guns at short range and at a low trajectory over attacking troops, scattering over a wide area and often causing widespread casualties. It is frequently confused with grapeshot (q.v.)

Cantonments Lodgings assigned to troops, more permanent than a bivouac (q.v.).

Case shot See *Canister*.

Chasseurs Light infantry.

Chasseurs à cheval Cavalry.

Chaussée A paved highway or trunk road. During this period there were few: almost all others were furrowed, knee-deep in mud and well-nigh impassable during wet weather and throughout the winter.

Chevaux-de-frise Literally, 'horses of Friesland'. This form of barrier was invented by the Frisians, who had no cavalry. It was usually constructed by setting large nails, swords, bayonets and other sharp objects into a heavy beam, placed within a breach, and providing an additional hazard to assaulting troops.

Congreve rocket An erratic and inaccurate projectile, invented in 1805 by Colonel Sir William Congreve (1772–1828). Its loud hiss effectively frightened troops encountering them for the first time.

Counterscarp The abrupt nearer side to the glacis (q.v.) of an excavated ditch, often of brick or stone, constructed to make its descent more difficult.

Covered way An area between the glacis (q.v.) and ditch surrounding fortifications along which troops could pass from one position to another while being protected by a palisade (q.v.). Not actually 'covered'.

Curtain wall One joining two projecting bastions (q.v.).

Ditch A trench some 16 feet deep and usually at least five times as wide, encircling defensive works, its outer supporting wall being designated a counterscarp (q.v.).

Earthworks (or fieldworks) Any form of temporary fortification (or trench) providing shelter from enemy fire, direct or enfilading.

Embrasure An opening in the flank of fortifications through which guns might fire and enfilade (q.v.).

Enfilade Gunfire from a position directed against the flank of approaching troops or their earthworks (q.v.).

Escalade To assault fortifications by means of ladders rather than by making a breach in the walls.

Fascines Bundles of brushwood or small branches, roped together, to support the earthen walls of trenches, or when constructing a battery.

'Forlorn Hope' Volunteers advancing ahead of the main body to assault a breach.

Frise A line of sharpened stakes set into the lower slope of a rampart, partly to ensure that the outworks are not taken by surprise.

Gabion An open-ended basket, about 3 feet high, filled with earth and placed above ground to provide cover for men approaching siege works.

Gendarmes In the context of this book, constabulary.

Glacis The gentle exterior slope of defensive works, extending beyond a parapet and/or ditch, constructed to provide an uncluttered target area over which approaching troops had to cross.

Grapeshot Often confused with that of canister (q.v.), but a heavier shot (usually nine golf-ball-sized projectiles) tightly encased in a canvas cylinder and fired from cannon, designed to break spars and foul rigging in naval engagements, but infrequently used on land.

Horn-work An outwork of two demi-bastions connected to the main work by parallel wings.

Howitzer A short-barrelled gun projecting a common shell at low velocity but at a high angle; unlike a mortar, it was supported by trunnions and pivoted from the middle of its barrel.

Investment A preliminary action to isolate a town to be besieged from receiving any reinforcements or supplies.

K.G.L. King's German Legion. A formation of largely Hanoverian-officered troops serving with the British army after Napoleon's invasion of Hanover in 1803.

Lunette Works on either side of a ravelin, larger than a redan, and with two faces and two flanks.

Magazine A bomb-proof arsenal storing arms, powder and ammunition. Also a store for provisions.

Mine An aperture or tunnel excavated below fortifications in which gunpowder was placed to explode, weakening or destroying the walls.

Mortar A large-bore cannon mounted to fire combustible material at a high elevation.

Ordnance (piece of) Any gun, mortar or howitzer. Such weapons were classified by the weight of the solid shot they fired: thus a 24-pounder howitzer threw a shot weighing 24lb.

Palisade A fence of stakes some nine feet long, set into the ground, often close to the crest of a glacis (q.v.), and protecting the covered way between that point of the counterscarp (q.v.) of a defensive ditch.

Parallel(s) A deep and wide trench or trenches dug at the approaches to a besieged place, from which troops excavating a sap (q.v.) could be supported. They were usually zig-zag in plan, partly to evade enfilading fire, and two or three (or more) in number.

Parapet A thick protective wall of earth raised above the crest of a rampart, usually with a ledge behind it to prevent the earth—if hit by enemy fire—from falling into and filling the adjacent ditch.

Picquet (piquet, picket) A small outpost of troops—infantry or cavalry—placed to guard against surprise attack, by day or night, from which a vedette (q.v.) might be advanced.

Puerto A door: in this context, a mountain pass.

Ravelin (demi-lune) A work beyond a curtain wall, usually of two walls set at an angle, or triangular in construction, providing a position from which the approaching enemy would receive flanking fire.

Redoubt A defensive work detached from the main fortifications of a town.

Revetment A wall of brick or stone supporting the side of a rampart or ditch.

Ricochet fire Round shot fired at a low angle, the bounding trajectory of which on hard ground would cause great havoc among massed troops.

Rockets See *Congreve*.

Round shot A solid metal ball between 3 and 4¼ inches in diameter. Cannon were categorized by the weight of shot they fired, which in the Napoleonic period ranged from 6-, 8- or 9-pounders to 12-pounders, the heaviest used in the field.

Sap A trench, approached by parallels and usually covered to protect the sappers from the garrison's fire, excavated close to defensive walls, from which they could be undermined or mined. The insidious burrowing operations of sappers were usually directed by an engineer.

Semaphore See *Telegraph*.

Shrapnel A projectile composed of carbine balls, and later of musket-balls mixed with gunpowder, fired from cannon as well as from howitzers and timed to explode just short of a target, over which the shot would shower. This type of shell, invented by Henry Shrapnell (1761–1842) of the Royal Artillery, was improved and adopted by the Army about 1804.

Spherical case shot The official name for shrapnel.

Square A roughly square (or oblong) formation, having a frontage of approximately 100 feet, into which infantry would deploy when in expectation of a cavalry charge. Each side might be anything from four to six ranks in depth, of which those on the outer would be kneeling, holding their muskets, butts on the ground, at an angle, making a bristling hedge of sharp bayonets which attacking cavalry would steer clear of rather than collide with, usually swerving round the sides of the square. In the hollow centre of the tightly packed formation stood sergeants and officers, exhorting their men to hold their fire and keep steady. Squares were vulnerable to artillery fire, both round shot and canister.

Telegraph A system of visual communication from one area to another made by varying the position of flags or balls on the yardarms of masts placed on conspicuous heights.

Tirailleur The French name for a skirmisher or sharpshooter.

Vedette A mounted sentry placed on high ground beyond an outpost to observe and give notice of enemy movements. See *Picquet*.

BIBLIOGRAPHY

The formidable body of books devoted to the Peninsular War makes selectivity essential in compiling what may seem to be an idiosyncratic choice. Even in 1913 Sir Charles Oman recorded over one hundred Peninsular narratives in the third Appendix to his *Wellington's Army*, since then many more manuscript journals etc. have been discovered and edited—some perfunctorily so, others more generously and judiciously—most of which are listed in Paddy Griffith's 'Bibliography of Peninsular War Books since Oman' in the supplementary Volume IX (1999) to the reprint of Oman's *History*. A number of them contain an informative Introduction, but many such preambles are little less than 'platitudinous' (in Griffith's discriminating opinion). His updated Bibliography, although of great utility, would have been even more so had it been annotated and had its introductory paragraphs extended. The Bibliographical Essays in Rory Muir's *Britain and the Defeat of Napoleon* and *Tactics and the Experience of War* are admirable.

An asterix (*) following an entry indicates that the work has been reprinted within comparatively recent years; other titles of which the present author is unaware may well have been reissued; and, doubtless, there are other works which deserve inclusion. Some have been listed as being of general interest, although not necessarily describing the period covered in this book, while only a few which are largely concerned with the earlier years of the war have been included. First-hand narratives, and other titles of particular value are suffixed by a dagger (†). The numbers of the regiments concerned in a particular are indicated within square brackets.

Aitchison, (ed. Thompson, W. F. K.), *An Ensign in the Peninsular War: The Letters of John Aitchison* *† (1981). [3rd Foot Guards]

Anton, James, *Retrospect of a Military Life* † (1841). [42nd]

Aspinall-Oglander, Cecil, *Freshly Remembered: The Story of Thomas Graham, Lord Lyndoch* (1956).

Bacler d'Albe, Albert-Louis, *Campagne d'Espagne, Souvenirs Pittoresque*, Tome II (1824). For its lithographs.

Batty, Robert, *Campaign of the Left Wing of the Allied Army, in the Western Pyrenees and South of France* * †(1823). Well illustrated. [1st Foot Guards]

Beamish, North Ludlow, *History of The King's German Legion* *(1832,1837).

Beatson, F.C., *With Wellington in the Pyrenees, being an account of the Operations between ... July 25 to August 2 1813* * (1914).

———, *Wellington: Crossing the Gaves and Battle of Orthez* * (1925).

———, *Wellington: The Bidassoa and Nivelle* * (1931).

Bell, Sir George, *Soldier's Glory, Reminiscences of ...* (1867). Ed. Stuart, Brian, and retitled *Soldier's Glory, being 'Rough Notes of an Old Soldier'* * (1956). [34th]

Belmas, Jacques Vital, *Journaux des sieges faits ou soutenus par les français dans la péninsule, de 1807 à 1814* (1836–37).

Blackmore, Howard, *British Military Firearms, 1650–1850* * (1961).

Blakeney, (ed. Sturgis, Julian), *A Boy in the Peninsular War: the Services, Adventures, and Experiences of Robert Blakeney* * (1899). [28th]

Blakiston, John, *Twelve Years' Military Adventure* ... (1829). [17th Portuguese]

Boutflower, Charles, *The Journal of an Army Surgeon during the Peninsular War* ...* (1912). Reprint, with an Introduction by Christopher Ticehurst.

Bragge, (ed. Cassels, S. A. C.), *Peninsular Portrait, 1811–14: The Letters of Captain William Bragge* (1963). [3rd (King's Own) Dragoons]

Brett-James, Antony, *Life in Wellington's Army* *† (1972)

———, *General Graham, Lord Lynedoch* (1959). See Costello.

Brotherton, (ed. Perrett, Bryan), *A Hawk at War. The Peninsular Reminiscences of General Sir Thomas Brotherton* (1986). [14th Light Dragoons]

Broughton, Samuel Daniel, *Letters from Portugal, Spain, & France, written during the Campaigns of 1812, 1813, & 1814* ... (1815).

Brown, William, *The Autobiography, or Narrative of a Soldier* * (1829). [45th]

Browne, (ed. Buckley, Roger Norman), *The Napoleonic Journal of Captain Thomas Henry Browne* † (1987). [HQ staff]

[Buckham, E. W.], *Personal Narrative of Adventures ... during the War in 1812–1813* * (1827). [Cavalry staff corps]

Bunbury, Thomas, *Reminiscences of a Veteran* ... (1861). [20th Portuguese]

Cadell, Charles, *Narrative of the Campaigns of the Twenty-Eighth Regiment* ... (1835).

Campbell. See Shadwell.

Cantlie, Sir Neil, *A History of the Army Medical Department*, Vol. 1 (1974).

Colborne, (ed. Moore-Smith, G. C.), *The Life of Sir John Colborne* ... (1903). [52nd]

Cole, (ed. Cole, Maud Lowry, and Gwynn, Stephen), *Memoirs of Sir [Galbraith] Lowry Cole* (1934).

Colville, John, *Portrait of a General [Charles Colville]* (1980).

Cooke, *Memoirs of the Late War: Comprising the Personal Narrative of Captain J[ohn] H. Cooke, 43rd Regiment of Light Infantry* (1831).

———, *A Narrative of Events in the South of France ... [and America] in 1814–1815* (1835). The first volume of a new edition by Eileen Hathaway was retitled *A True Soldier Gentleman* (2000); the second, *Drums Beat Up Again,*† and the American volume are forthcoming. [43rd]

Cooper, John Spencer, *Rough Notes of Seven Campaigns ... 1809–1815* * (1869). Reprint (1996), with an Introduction by Ian Fletcher. [7th]

Cope, Sir William H., Bart., *The History of the Rifle Brigade* ... (1877).

Corrigan, Gordon, *Wellington: a Military Life* (2001).

Costello, Edward, *Adventures of a Soldier; written by himself* * (1841; 2nd edn 1852). Ed. Brett-James, Antony, as *The Peninsular and Waterloo Campaigns* (1967), but see Hathaway. [95th]

Cowell Stepney. See Stepney.

Dallas, Alexander, *Autobiography of, including his service in the Peninsula in the Commissariat Department* (1870).

[Daniel, John Edgecombe], *Journal of an Officer in the Commissariat* ... * (1820).

Delavoye. See Graham.

Dickson, Sir Alexander, (ed. Leslie, John H.), *The Dickson Manuscripts* ...* (2 vols, 1908–12; reprinted in 5 vols 1987–91). See John Leslie. [Artillery]

Donaldson, Joseph, *Recollections of an Eventful Life of a Soldier* * (1825; new edn 1856). [94th]

Douglas, Sir Howard, Bart., *An Essay on the Principles and Construction of Military Bridges, and the Passage of Rivers in Military Operations** (1816).

Duffy, Christopher, *Military Experience in the Age of Reason* (1987).

Duncan, Francis, *History of the Royal Regiment of Artillery* (1872).

D'Urban, (ed. Rousseau, I. J.), *Peninsular Journal of Major-General Sir Benjamin D'Urban, 1808–1817** (1930).

Dyneley, (ed. Whinyates, F. A.), *Letters Written by Lieut.-General Thomas Dyneley* ...* (1895; in book form in 1984) [R.A.].

Esdaile, Charles J., *The Spanish Army in the Peninsular War* (1988)

———, *The Duke of Wellington and the Command of the Spanish Army* (1990).

————, *The Peninsular War: A New History* (2002).

Fletcher, Ian, *Galloping at everything: British Cavalry in the Peninsular War* (1999)

Fletcher, Ian, and Poulter, Ron, *Gentlemen's Sons: The Foot Guards in the Peninsula and at Waterloo* (1992). See also Cooper, Keep, Kincaid, Mills, Rous and Surtees.

Fortescue, The Hon. Sir John William, *A History of the British Army*, vols 6–10 (1910–20).

Foy, Maximilien, *History of the War in the Peninsula...* (1827).

Frazer, (ed. Sabine, Edward), *Letters of Colonel Sir Augustus Simon Frazer...commanding the Royal Horse Artillery...*† (1859).

Freer, (ed. Scarfe, Norman), *Letters from the Peninsula: The Freer Family Correspondence*, 1807–1814 (1853). [43rd]

Gardyne, C. Greenhill, *The Life of a Regiment* (1901). [Gordon Highlanders; 91st]

Gash, Norman, (ed.), *Wellington: Studies in the Military and Political Career of the First Duke of Wellington* (1990).

Gipuzkoa, *Documentos Cartográficos Históricos de Gipuzkoa* (2 vols, San Sebastián, 1994–99). Contains reproductions of numerous early maps and plans of San Sebastián, Fuenterrabia and the region.

Girod de l'Ain, Maurice, *Vie Militaire du Général Foy* (1900). Contains numerous extracts from Foy's diaries.

Gleig, George Robert, *The Subaltern*† (1825). Edited and with an Introduction by Ian C. Robertson, 2001. See also Landsheit. [85th]

Glover, Richard, *Peninsular Preparation: The Reform of the British Army, 1795–1809*† (1963).

Gomm, (ed. Culling Carr-Gomm, Francis), *Letters and Journals of Field-Marshal Sir William Maynard Gomm...* (1881). [Staff]

Gordon, Sir Alexander, *At Wellington's Right Hand: The Letters of Lt-Col. Sir Alexander Gordon, 1808–1815*. Edited by Rory Muir, forthcoming.

Graham, Sir Thomas, (ed. Delavoye, Alex. M.), *Life of Thomas Graham Lord Lynedoch* (1880). See Aspinall-Oglander, Brett-James.

Graham, William, *Travels through Portugal and Spain during the Peninsular War* (1880).

Grattan, William, *Adventures with the Connaught Rangers, 1809–14* (1847; 1853). Edited by Sir Charles Oman, 1902. [88th]

Green, John, *The Vicissitudes of a Soldier's Life...from 1806 to 1815* (1827). [68th]

Green, William, *A Brief Outline of the Travels and Adventures of...* (1857). Edited by John and Dorothea Teague as *Where Duty Calls Me: The Experiences of William Green...in the Napoleonic Wars* (1975). [95th]

Griffith, Paddy, *Wellington—Commander: The Iron Duke's Generalship* (1985).

————, *The Art of War of Revolutionary France, 1789–1802* (1989).

Griffith, Paddy, (ed.), *Modern Studies of the War in Spain and Portugal, 1808–1814*† (1999). The complementary vol. IX to Oman's *History*, containing pertinent essays, a bibliography of narrative and analytical works published since 1930 and another, supplementing the list of memoirs in Oman's *Wellington's Army*, etc.

Hall, John A., *The Biographical Dictionary of British Officers Killed and Wounded, 1808–1814, Together with Non-Combat Casualties*† (1998). The complementary vol. VIII to Oman's *History*.

Hamilton, Thomas (revised and augmented by Hardman, Frederick), *Annals of the Peninsular Campaigns* (1849).

Hardman. See Hamilton.

Harris, Benjamin Randell, (ed. Curling, Henry), *Recollections of Rifleman Harris* (1848). Edited by Christopher Hibbert 1970, but see also Hathaway. [95th]

Hathaway, Eileen, (ed.), *A Dorset Soldier: The Autobiography of Sgt William Lawrence, 1790–1869* (1886; 1993). [40th]

————, *A Dorset Rifleman: The Recollections of Benjamin Harris* (1995). [95th]

————, *Costello: The True Story of a Peninsular War Rifleman*† (1997). See also Cooke. [95th]

Hay, Sir Andrew Leith, *A Narrative of the Peninsular War* (3rd edn, 1829). [Staff and 29th]

Hayman, Peter, *Soult: Napoleon's Maligned Marshal* (1990).

Haythornthwaite, Philip J., *Weapons and Equipment of the Napoleonic Wars* (1979).

———, *The Armies of Wellington* (1994). See Sherer, Smith.

Hennell, (ed. Glover, Michael), *A Gentleman Volunteer: The Letters of George Hennell from the Peninsula, 1812–13* (1979). [43rd]

Henry, Walter, *Events of a Military Life …** (1843). The 1970 reprint (ed. Hayward, Pat) is entitled *Surgeon Henry's Trifles…* [66th]

Hill. See Teffeteller.

Howard, Martin, *Wellington's Doctors* (2002).

[Howell, Thomas , (ed.?)], *Journal of T.S., a Soldier of the 71st Highland Light Infantry, from 1806 to 1815** (1819). Or as *Vicissitudes in the Life of a Scottish Soldier* (1828), also attributed to Thomas Pococke and edited by Christopher Hibbert (1975), and to James Todd.

Hughes, B. P., *Firepower. Weapons' Effectiveness on the Battlefield, 1630–1850** (1974).

Hunt, Eric E., *Charging Against Napoleon: Diaries & Letters of Three Hussars* [James Hughes, Arthur Kennedy and George Woodberry; but also Loftus Otway et al.] (2001). [18th Hussars]

James, William Hill, *Battles around Biarritz* (1899).

Jones, Sir John Thomas, *Journals of Sieges … in Spain, During the Years 1811 to 1814** (3rd edn, ed. Harry D. Jones, 1846). Includes the *Memoranda Relative to the Lines thrown up to cover Lisbon in 1810*.

Jones, Rice, (ed. Shore, The Hon. Henry), *An Engineer Officer under Wellington in the Peninsula*†* (1986).

Keep, (ed. Fletcher, Ian), *In the Service of the King: The Letters of William Thornton Keep… 1808–1814* (1997). [77th/28th]

Kincaid, Sir John, *Adventures in the Rifle Brigade …** (1830). Reprinted with his *Random Shots from a Rifleman* (1835) in 1998, with an Introduction by Ian Fletcher. [95th]

Landscheit, (ed. Gleig, George Robert), *The Hussar: The Story of Norbert Landscheit …** (1837). [20th Light Dragoons]

Larpent, (ed. Larpent, Sir George, Bart.), *The Private Journal of Judge-Advocate [Francis Seymour] Larpent . ..*†* (3rd edn, 1854). Reprinted 2000 with an Introduction by Ian C. Robertson. [Staff]

Lawrence, (ed. Banks, George Nugent), *The Autobiography of Sergeant William Lawrence …** (1886). See also Hathaway. [40th]

Leach, Jonathan, *Rough Sketches of the Life of an Old Soldier …*†* (1831). [95th]

———, *Rambles on the Banks of Styx* (1847).

Leslie, John H., *The Services of the Royal Regiment of Artillery in the Peninsular War, 1808–1814* (1912). See Dickson.

Leslie of Balquhain, Charles, *Military Journal of Colonel Leslie … in the Peninsula …* (1887). [29th]

Levinge, Sir Richard George Augustus, *Historical Records of the 43rd Regiment …* (1868).

Locker, Edward Hawke, *Views in Spain* (1824). For its lithographs.

Lowry Cole. See Cole.

MacGrigor, *The Autobiography and Services of Sir James MacGrigor, Bart, late Director-General of the Army Medical Department** (1861).

Malcolm, John, *Reminiscenses of the Campaign in the Pyrenees and the South of France in 1813–14*†* (1828). [42nd]

Malet, Harold, *The Historical Memoirs of the XVIIIth Hussars** (1907).

Mampel, Johann Christian, *The Adventures of a Young Rifleman in the French and English Armies, During the War in Spain and Portugal from 1806 to 1816* (1826).

Maxwell, William Hamilton, (ed.), *Peninsular Sketches, by Actors on the Scene** (1845).

Mills, (ed. Fletcher, Ian), *For King and Country: The Letters and Diaries of John Mills, Coldstream Guards, 1811–1814* (1995).

Mitchell. See Wyld.

Mollo, John, *The Prince's Dolls: Scandals, Skirmishes and Splendours of the first British Hussars, 1793–1815* (1997).

Moorsom, William Scarth, *Historical Record of the 52nd Regiment …** (1860).

Moyle Sherer. See Sherer.

Muir, Rory J. B., *Britain and the Defeat of Napoleon, 1807–1815*† (1996).

———, *Salamanca, 1812*† (2001).

———, *Tactics and the Experience of Battle in the Age of Napoleon*† (1998). See Gordon.

Murray, Sir George. See Wyld.

Myatt, Frederick, *British Sieges of the Peninsular War* (1987).

Napier, Sir William, *History of the War in the Peninsula and the South of France** (1828–40).

———, *English Battles and Sieges in the Peninsula** (1852).

Nosworthy, Brent, *Battle Tactics of Napoleon and his Enemies* (1995).

Oman, Sir Charles William Chadwick, *Wellington's Army, 1809–14**† (1913)

———, *History of the Peninsular War*,*† 7 vols (1902–30). Reprinted in 1995–97. See also Grattan, Griffith, Hall.

Ompteda, Baron Christian (tr. Hill, John), *A Hanovarian-English Officer a Hundred Years Ago...** (1892). Reissued as *In the King's German Legion: Memoirs of Baron Ompteda...* (1894).

Pakenham, Gen. Sir Edward, (ed. Longford, 5th Earl of), *The Pakenham Letters, 1800–1815* (1913–14).

Petre, Francis Loraine, *Napoleon at Bay** (1814).

Picton, (ed. Robinson, Heaton B.), *Memoirs of...Sir Thomas Picton* (1836). [Staff]

[Pococke]. See Howell.

Poulter, Ron. See Fletcher.

Quentin, *The Trial of Colonel [George Augustus] Quentin, of the Tenth, or Prince of Wales's Own Regiment of Hussars, by a General Court-Martial* (1814). Concerns incidents prior to the Battle of Toulouse.

Riley, Jonathan P., *Napoleon and the World War of 1813* (2001).

Robertson, Ian C., *Wellington at War in the Peninsula, 1808–1814: An Overview and Guide* (2000). See also Gleig, Larpent, Weller.

Ross-Lewin, Harry, *Life of a Soldier: A Narrative of 27 Years' Service...* (1834).

———, (ed. Wardell, John), *With the 32nd in the Peninsula* (1904).

Rothenberg, Gunther E., *The Art of Warfare in the Age of Napoleon* (1977).

Rous, John Edward Cornwallis, (ed. Fletcher, Ian), *A Guards Officer in the Peninsula: The...Letters of... Coldstream Guards, 1812–14* (1992).

Schaumann, August Ludolf Friedrich, (tr. and ed. Ludovici, Anthony M.), *On the Road with Wellington. The Diary of a War Commissary...**† (1924). With an Introduction by Bernard Cornwell (1999).

Shadwell, Laurence, *Life of Colin Campbell, Lord Clyde* (1881).

[Sherer, G. Moyle], *Recollections of the Peninsula** (1824). Reprinted and with an Introduction by Philip J. Haythornthwaite. [34th]

Sherwig, John M., *Guineas and Gunpowder: British Foreign Aid in the Wars with France, 1793–1815* (1969).

Simmons, (ed. Verner, Willoughby), *A British Rifle Man. The Journals and Correspondence of Major George Simmons...during the Peninsular War...**† (1899). [95th]

Smith, Charles Hamilton, *Wellington's Army: Uniforms of the British Soldier, 1812–1815* (2002). With explanatory text to the 60 illustrations by Philip J. Haythornthwaite.

Smith, Henry [Harry] George Wakelyn, (ed. Moore Smith, G. C.), *Autobiography of Sir Harry Smith, 1787–1819** (one-vol. edn, 1910). Reprinted and with an Introduction by Philip J. Haythornthwaite. [95th]

Stanhope, Philip Henry, 5th Earl, *Notes of Conversations with the Duke of Wellington, 1831–1851** (1888).

Stepney, John Cowell, *Leaves from the Diary of an Officer in the Guards** (1854). [2nd Foot Guards]

Surtees, William, *Twenty-Five Years in the Rifle Brigade**† (1833). Reprinted and with an Introduction by Ian Fletcher. [95th]

Swabey, William, (ed. Whinyates, F. A.), *Diary of Campaigns in the Peninsula for the Years 1811, 1812 and 1813** (1895). [Artillery]

[Tale, W., Sgt-Major], *Jottings from my Sabretache, by a Chelsea Pensioner* (1847). [15th Light Dragoons]

Teffeteller, Gordon L., *The Surpriser: The Life of Rowland, Lord Hill* (1983).

Todd. See Howell.

Tomkinson, William, (ed. Tomkinson, James), *The Diary of a Cavalry Officer ... 1809–1815** (1894).
  Reprinted and with an Introduction by the 7th Marquess of Anglesey. [16th Light Dragoons]

Verner, Willoughby, *History & Campaigns of the Rifle Brigade, 1800–1813** (1912; 1919). See Simmons.

Vivian, Richard Hussey, (ed. Vivian, The Hon. Claud), *Memoir and Letters* (1897). [7th Hussars]

Ward, Stephen George Peregrine, *Wellington's Headquarters: A Study of the Administrative Problems in the
  Peninsula, 1809–1814*† (1957).

Webster, C.K., *The Foreign Policy of Castlereagh, 1812–1815** (1931).

Weller, Jac [John Allen Claude], (ed. Robertson, Ian C.), *Wellington in the Peninsula, 1808–1814** (1962).

[Wellington], (ed. Gurwood, John), *General Orders of ... Wellington* (1839).

————, *Selections from the Dispatches and General Orders of ... Wellington* (1841).

Wheatley, Edmund, (ed. Hibbert, Christopher), *The Wheatley Diary ...*† (1964). [K.G.L.]

Wheeler, William, (ed. Liddell-Hart, Basil H.), *The Letters of Private Wheeler, 1809–1828** (1951). [51st]

Wood, George, *The Subaltern Officer ...** (1825). [82nd]

Woodberry, George, *Journal of Lieutenant Woodberry in the Campaigns of 1813–15* (Paris, 1896). See Hunt.
  [18th Hussars]

Wyld, James, (cartographer and publisher), *Atlas Showing the Principal Movements, Battles, and Sieges ...
  during the War from 1808 to 1814 ...* (1841). Largely compiled by Thomas Livingstone Mitchell,
  together with the *Memoir* annexed, by Sir George Murray.

INDEX

This index of a dense text lists all persons and places, and the more pertinent references only to those persons which are ubiquitous. The majority have been identified by the inclusion of their rank, dates and units. The identities of one or two persons with similar surnames remain problematic—and I stand to be corrected. For further details of British and K.G.L. officers, one may refer to John Hall's *Biographical Dictionary of British Officers Killed and Wounded, 1808–1814* (Oman, vol. VIII, Greenhill 1998), the *D.N.B.* and the forthcoming *New Oxford D.N.B.*

Villava, 32, 72
Villefranche-de-Lauragais, 227, 242
Villefranque (Nive), 158, 164–6, 174, 176, 177, 179
Vimeiro, 19
Viscarret, 68
Vitoria, 26, 84, 139
Vivian, Col. Richard Hussey (1775–1842) [7th Hussars], 164, 176, 191, 192, 194, 202, 203, 213, 216, 217, 220, 223, 229, 230

W
Walker, Col. George Townsend (1764–1842), 63, 202, 209
Waters, Maj. John (1774–1842), 80
Wellesley, Gen. The Hon. Sir Arthur, see Wellington

Wellesley, Henry, The Hon. (1773–1847), diplomat, 41, 138
Wellington, Viscount (later Duke of) (1769–1852), passim
Wheatley, Ensign Edmund (?1793–1841) [K.G.L.], 147, 182, 245, 247, 248, 255
Wheeler, Pte William (c. 1785–?) [51st], 118, 119, 257
Wildman, Capt. Thomas (1787–1859) [7th Hussars], 210
Wilson, Col. John (1780–1856), 107, 130, 131, 156
Wood, Capt. George [82nd], 81, 257
Woodberry, Lieut. George (1792–) [18th Hussars], 36, 205, 255

X
Xoldokogana, see Choldocogagna

Y
Yanci, 65, 91, 93
Yolimun farm, see Jolimont
York (and Albany), Frederick, Duke of (1763–1827), 141
Young, Arthur (1741–1820), agricultural writer, 197

Z
Zabaldica (Zabaldika), 72, 73, 87
Zadorra, valley, 26
Zamora, 25
Zaragoza, 33
Zubieta, 44, 74, 86, 92
Zubiri, 43, 71
Zugarramurdi, 96, 120, 130
Zurbieta, 44, 87